Being and Goodness

Being and Goodness

THE CONCEPT OF THE GOOD IN METAPHYSICS AND PHILOSOPHICAL THEOLOGY

EDITED BY

Scott MacDonald

Cornell University Press

ITHACA AND LONDON

First published 1991 by Cornell University Press.

International Standard Book Number 0–8014–2312–0
Library of Congress Catalog Card Number 90–55197
Printed in the United States of America
Librarians: Library of Congress cataloging information
appears on the last page of the book.

♾ The paper in this book meets the minimum requirements
of the American National Standard for Information Sciences—
Permanence of Paper for Printed Library Materials, ANSI Z39.48–1984.

Contents

Contributors

JAN A. AERTSEN is Professor of Medieval Philosophy and Modern Catholic Philosophy at the Free University, Amsterdam.

JORGE J. E. GRACIA is Professor of Philosophy at the State University of New York, Buffalo.

MARK D. JORDAN is Associate Professor in the Medieval Institute at the University of Notre Dame.

NORMAN KRETZMANN is Susan Linn Sage Professor of Philosophy at Cornell University.

SCOTT MACDONALD is Associate Professor of Philosophy at the University of Iowa.

RALPH MCINERNY is Michael P. Grace Professor of Medieval Studies at the University of Notre Dame.

WILLIAM E. MANN is Professor of Philosophy at the University of Vermont.

THOMAS V. MORRIS is Associate Professor of Philosophy at the University of Notre Dame.

ELEONORE STUMP is Professor of Philosophy at Virginia Polytechnic Institute and State University.

Abbreviations for
Frequently Cited Texts

CH	Bonaventure, *Collationes in Hexaemeron*
DH	Boethius, *De hebdomadibus*
Disp.	Francisco Suárez, *Disputationes metaphysicae*
DM	Thomas Aquinas, *De malo*
DN	Albert the Great, *Super Dionysium De divinis nominibus*
DP	Thomas Aquinas, *De potentia*
DV	Thomas Aquinas, *De veritate*
IMD	Bonaventure, *Itinerarium mentis in Deum*
InDH	Thomas Aquinas, *In Boetii De hebdomadibus expositio*
In Sent.	Bonaventure, *Commentarium in Sententias*
PL	*Patrologiae Latinae Cursus Completus*
SB	Albert the Great, *Summa de bono*
SCG	Thomas Aquinas, *Summa contra gentiles*
SENT	Albert the Great, *Commentarii in libros Sententiarum*
ST	Thomas Aquinas, *Summa theologiae*
Super Sent.	Thomas Aquinas, *Scriptum super Sententias*

Being and Goodness

The Relation between Being and Goodness

Scott MacDonald

Since the 1960s scholarship in medieval philosophy has begun to flourish, and the field now displays such vigor that it seems reasonable to hope that we will soon witness a recovery and appreciation of medieval philosophy equal to that already achieved in the neighboring fields of ancient and early modern philosophy. The attention now being given to philosophy in the Middle Ages is unprecedented, but the recovery and evaluation of the medieval philosophical achievement is only just beginning: most medieval philosophical texts have not yet received critical editions, let alone translation or the sort of philosophical commentary and analysis that would open them up to the contemporary philosophical community. Hence, we remain ignorant of many of the positions and arguments central to a tradition comprising a thousand years of our philosophical heritage. This collection of essays is intended as a first step toward removing that ignorance with respect to one important topic, the metaphysics of goodness.

A long and rich philosophical tradition, stemming from ancient Greek philosophy and running through the Middle Ages, has been guided by the intuition that there is some sort of interesting necessary connection between being and goodness. This intuition has come to the surface in the history of philosophy in various ways. Plato argued, for example, that the Form of the Good gives being to all the other Forms; Aristotle maintained that the good is spoken of in as many ways as being; Augustine's famous doctrine that evil is merely the privation of good is a corollary of his view that everything that exists is good insofar as it exists; and thirteenth-century philosophers such as Albert the

1

Great and Thomas Aquinas held that the terms 'being' and 'good' are interchangeable (or convertible) and that goodness, like being, transcends the categories. Taken by themselves, these claims appear extravagant and even paradoxical. But they are explained and justified within systematic, sophisticated, historically influential philosophical theories. This book explores part of the philosophical tradition comprised of these theories.

An exploration of this tradition is warranted, if for no other reason, by its prominence in the history of philosophy. Any philosophical tradition that can claim the support of philosophers of the stature of those just mentioned deserves careful attention. But exploration is warranted for purely philosophical reasons as well. As is evident in the essays collected herein, the philosophical positions representative of this tradition are interesting quite apart from historical considerations and have significant contributions to make to contemporary discussions in metaphysics, ethics, and philosophical theology.

Thus, two distinguishable, though in practice largely inseparable, central themes run through the book, one philosophical and the other historical. The main philosophical theme is the account of the nature of goodness that grows out of the attempt to explicate the necessary connection between being and goodness. Several of the essays in Part One deal primarily with the nature and merit of accounts of this sort, while some in Part One and all in Part Two focus on theses in metaphysics, ethics, or philosophical theology that are logically or historically associated with these central accounts. Since these accounts received their most elaborate development and careful defense at the hands of philosophers in the Middle Ages, the essays in this book also have a historical interest. Each essay has some connection with the history of medieval philosophy: some merely allude to developments in medieval philosophy, some develop arguments of medieval philosophers in order to apply them to contemporary philosophical issues, and some focus primarily on the explication of a particular medieval text or view. The book's main historical theme, then, is the fruitful tradition in medieval philosophy committed to defending and developing the implications of an account of the nature of goodness that elucidates a necessary connection between being and goodness.

But for two reasons this book cannot be an exhaustive exploration of either the historical or the philosophical theme. First, present knowledge of the tradition is inadequate to provide the basis for an exhaustive treatment: we simply do not know enough about the details of the tradition to be able to write the history of its development or to offer a full philosophical appraisal of it. The work undertaken by the contributors to this volume provides some foundation for more comprehensive histories and appraisals, but (as is the case for nearly every area of medieval philosophy) much basic research remains to be done. Second, these essays cannot provide a comprehensive account of this tradition in the metaphysics of goodness simply because it is too long and rich to be exhausted in a single volume. The essays included here range over a period extending from Augustine (d. 430) to Suárez (d. 1617)—with excursus to Descartes (d. 1650) and Leibniz (d. 1716)—and discuss such prominent figures as Boethius, Albert the Great, Thomas Aquinas, Bonaventure, and William Ockham; but the tradition includes important figures and issues not discussed here which would deserve careful attention in any discussion that aims to be complete.

When I asked philosophers to contribute to this collection, therefore, my aim was not the impossible one of producing a complete account of this tradition, but the pragmatic one of providing a selective introduction to it. By highlighting certain distinctive landmarks of this territory in the history of philosophy, the collection as a whole provides a rough historical and philosophical map. Moreover, by exploring just a few of its regions in detail, these essays provide tantalizing views of what is clearly an extensive and relatively little-known frontier. These initial forays seem to me to show—for these particular issues and for medieval philosophy generally—what is by now taken for granted for other historical periods, namely, that careful attention to philosophical texts and traditions of the past can advance our understanding not only of the thought of a historical period but also of the philosophical issues themselves and our contemporary discussions of them. The evidence in this volume suggests that the philosophical territory marked out here is rich enough to repay the effort of further investigation. It seemed to me, then, that a selective introduction of this sort is not only the best result we can hope for given present conditions but also the natural first step toward improving those conditions.

I have been talking about the philosophical tradition as if it were a clearly distinct and identifiable development in the history of philosophy, but of course that is an oversimplification. In the remainder of this Introduction I sketch a backdrop for the essays that follow and highlight some of the threads knitting together the wide variety of texts and positions they discuss. In Sections 1–3 I focus on the historical development of the issues discussed in these papers; in Sections 4 and 5 I set out some of the main systematic topics they address.

1. The Foundations of the Tradition

The tradition in the metaphysics of goodness explored in this volume has its roots in classical Greek philosophy, but it first comes into the mainstream of medieval philosophy not through Plato and Aristotle directly but through late ancient and early medieval thinkers educated in the classical tradition. Virtually none of Plato's writings was known in the Middle Ages until very late, and Aristotle's works had very little direct impact on medieval discussions of the metaphysics of goodness until early in the thirteenth century (when their influence was profound—see Section 3 below), but the varieties of neo-Platonism that find expression in the Church Fathers, especially Augustine, and influential philosophers of the early medieval period, such as Boethius and pseudo-Dionysius, provided medieval philosophers with the conceptual foundations for a metaphysics of goodness.

One prominent strand running through the book investigates the relation between two dominant elements in the foundation inherited from Greek philosophy. These elements seem to suggest two distinct ways of conceiving of the necessary connection between being and goodness, and so they are the basis for a tension in the later tradition that seems both fruitful and worrisome. The first element, essentially Platonist, maintains a necessary metaphysical and causal dependence of being on goodness. In the *Republic* Plato had asserted that all Forms, and hence all being, participate in the Good, and in the *Timaeus* he at least suggested that this account of the metaphysical priority of goodness could be developed into a cosmological theory explaining the origin of the universe. Later Platonists, especially the neo-Platonists, developed this strand of Plato's thought into a full-fledged cosmology involving the emanation of all things from the Good and their return to it.

Many early Christian thinkers found this cosmological view congenial. They found it quite natural to identify God with the Good, and, although the Christian doctrine of creation is incompatible with emanationism, they were able nevertheless to accommodate the Platonist notion of participation within the doctrine of creation. Christian Platonists such as Augustine and Boethius took the doctrine of creation as asserting the necessary dependence of created being on the Christian God, who is himself the Good, and explained the goodness of created things in terms of their participation in, their being derived from, that which is good in itself. Boethius comes very close to using the very language of emanationism: he argues that created things are good in virtue of their having 'flowed from' God, the First Good. (For more on

Augustine and Boethius, see Section 2 below.) Thus, in the early Middle Ages this essentially Platonist approach to understanding the relation between being and goodness (I call it the *participation* approach) characteristically leads in the direction of a theological and relational conception of goodness: God is the first and highest good, and created being is good in virtue of participating in the first and highest good.[1]

A second important element in the Greek foundation, less peculiarly Platonist than the participation approach, starts from the identification of the notion of the good with the notion of an end. This identification leads to an influential moral-psychological view: since desires are end-directed and an end is a good, desire necessarily aims at some good (a view I return to in Section 4 below), but as a foundation for a metaphysics of goodness, the identification of the notion of the good with the notion of an end is linked with a kind of metaphysical or natural teleology. According to this view a natural substance is constituted by a substantial form or nature by virtue of which the substance possesses a capacity for performing the activity characteristic of substances of the same species. The end, completion, or perfection of a natural substance is its having fully actualized its specifying capacity, its actually performing the activity for which its form or nature provides the capacity. Since the state or activity that constitutes a substance's full actuality is that substance's end and an end is a good, that state or activity constitutes the substance's good. On this account, then, the good for a substance of a given nature is the end determined by its nature, its being complete or fully actual as a thing of that nature. I will call this approach to understanding the relation between being and goodness the *nature* approach. Unlike the participation approach, the nature approach seems to lead to an account of goodness that is neither essentially theological nor relational: goodness consists in the completion or actualization of a nature, and the relevant state of completion or actualization is a state that, when achieved, is intrinsic to natural things.

The sort of metaphysical teleology that grounds the nature approach can be found in both Plato and Aristotle, and it also has an extremely influential proponent in Augustine.[2] When Augustine claims that ev-

1. For reasons having to do with its influence among Christian Platonists, I referred to this approach (in MacDonald 1988) as the *creation* approach. But because several of the essays in this book focus specifically on the approach's Platonist roots (e.g., Chapters 2, 3, 8, and 9), it seems to me more illuminating to characterize it here in more general terms, i.e., in terms of participation rather than creation.

2. Aristotle's development of this sort of metaphysical teleology into a metaphysics of goodness in Book I of the *Nicomachean Ethics* is paradigmatic of the nature approach. See MacDonald 1989a for an account of that development.

erything that has being is good insofar as it has being, he means that each natural substance is good to the extent to which it realizes its nature. As Augustine points out, everything that has being realizes its nature to some extent (otherwise it would not exist), and so it follows that everything is good to some extent. When philosophers in the twelfth and thirteenth centuries first began to get a clear picture of the Aristotelian metaphysics and ethics, what they saw was not entirely new to them: the main lines of the view are generically Greek and were familiar to them from Augustine and other early sources.

I have characterized the participation and nature approaches to the metaphysics of goodness in such a way as to highlight their differences, but the two approaches are closely linked in the medieval tradition and they develop together. Despite the apparent tension between them on fundamental issues, there are historical reasons for their developing together. First, medieval philosophers find them together in respected authorities: I have claimed, for instance, that Augustine's views on the nature of goodness can be seen as exemplifying both approaches. Second, medieval philosophers were committed, perhaps more than philosophers from any other period, to preserving and synthesizing their philosophical inheritance. As a result, later medieval philosophers, even when they recognized the differences between the participation and nature approaches, took them to be two parts of a single foundation and not two distinct foundations.

The linking of the two approaches in the medieval tradition is sometimes fruitful: for example, Jan Aertsen, Ralph McInerny, and Mark Jordan (Chapters 2, 3, and 5) each suggest that Aquinas's struggle to reconcile the two approaches plays an important role in the development of his highly original conception of the divine nature and of God's relation to creation. But sometimes the linking of the two approaches leads to confusion: I argue (Chapter 1) that on one occasion Albert the Great is led by his sympathies with each approach to endorse two incompatible accounts of goodness; and Norman Kretzmann argues (Chapter 8) that for similar reasons Aquinas's claim that God is free to choose whether or not to create is inconsistent with his views about the nature of goodness.

In Sections 2 and 3 below I trace the development of these two approaches in the Middle Ages, but first I want to draw attention to a counterintuitive corollary of both approaches, which displays a significant respect in which the approaches converge. It is a consequence of each approach—in fact, it would appear to be a consequence of *any* account that postulates a necessary connection between being and goodness—that everything that exists (or has being) is good. I will call this the *universality* thesis. The universality thesis follows from the participation approach since, on that approach, a thing is good either in virtue of being good in itself or in virtue of participating in that which is good in itself, and everything that exists (other than God, who is good in himself) participates in God. The thesis follows from the nature approach, too, since on that approach a thing is good in virtue of realizing its nature, and everything that exists realizes its nature to some extent. So even if the participation and nature approaches conflict in some respects, they both support an intriguing thesis about the universality of goodness. This may be one reason that medieval philosophers fail to distinguish the two approaches as clearly as they might: they are attracted by the universality thesis itself and tend to overlook the differences between the bases it has in the tradition.

Medieval philosophers were intrigued by the universality thesis not only because of the impressive support it had among respected philosophical authorities, including Augustine's and Boethius's explicit defenses of it, but also because it seemed to them to have impressive biblical support. They took passages such as Genesis 1:31, "And God saw everything that he had made, and behold, it was very good," and 1 Timothy 4:4, "For everything created by God is good," as endorsements of the thesis. In fact, the universality thesis becomes a focal point for the more general discussion of the nature of goodness, and medieval philosophers often present their systematic metaphysics of goodness by way of explicating and defending that thesis.

The doctrine of the transcendentals, another well-known medieval metaphysical doctrine, is closely related to the universality thesis. Beginning in the early thirteenth century, philosophers discussed the universality thesis as part of a larger doctrine that holds that unity and truth, in addition to goodness, are connected with being in such a way that they, like being, transcend the ten categories. Insofar as the thirteenth-century systematic developments of the doctrine of the transcendentals incorporate detailed reflection on the necessary connection between being and goodness, they are an important part of the philosophical tradition this book traces. Jan Aertsen, Mark Jordan, and I (Chapters 2, 5, and 1) explicitly take up the doctrine and discuss its role in the larger tradition.

2. Early Medieval Paradigms: Augustine and Boethius

In describing the participation and nature approaches as two basic approaches to the nature of goodness growing out of ancient Greek philosophy, I mentioned Boethius's view as an example of the former and Augustine's as an example of the latter. Boethius and Augustine do not merely provide particularly clear early medieval illustrations of the sorts of account I want to discuss; their views are in fact the soil in which later developments in the tradition take root. Their particular views on goodness remain influential throughout the Middle Ages.

In the third of his five theological treatises, known in the Middle Ages as *De hebdomadibus*, Boethius explicitly takes up a variant of the universality thesis. (See the Appendix for a translation of *De hebdomadibus*.) He intends to explain the thesis that all substances are good in virtue of the fact that they have being, although they are not substantial goods. As Boethius points out, the thesis appears to be paradoxical since any property possessed by a substance in virtue of the fact that it has being appears to be part of its nature, a substantial property, and no property that is merely accidental to a substance seems to belong to it in virtue of its having being. Boethius resolves the apparent paradox by distinguishing between two senses of 'in virtue of the fact that it has being': on the one hand, it can mean 'in virtue of the fact that it is the substance or nature it is,' and on the other, it can mean 'in virtue of the fact that it exists.' He claims that all substances are good in virtue of the fact that they exist, although they are not good in virtue of their substance or nature. Therefore, goodness does not constitute the substance of created substances (it constitutes the substance only of God, the first good), but it does characterize each created substance in virtue of its existing.

Boethius uses a thought experiment to establish that all created substances are good in virtue of the fact that they exist. He asks the reader to imagine that God exists and creates but is not good, and he claims that one will see that on this hypothesis it could not be the case that created things are good in virtue of the fact that they exist because they will not have flowed from the good. In the actual world, however, things have flowed from the First Good, and so they are secondary goods that are good in virtue of their flowing from the First Good. They exist in virtue of having been created by God, who is the First Good, and so they are necessarily dependent for their existence on the First Good and they are themselves good in virtue of this relation to the First Good.

The details of these arguments are puzzling and difficult to follow, but their Christian-Platonist inspiration is clear. God is the First Good and all other things have both being and goodness by being appropriately related to—by participating in—the First Good.[3] Jan Aertsen and

Ralph McInerny (Chapters 2 and 3) examine Boethius's views in their discussions of Aquinas's commentary on Boethius's treatise.

Whatever the philosophical merits of Boethius's little treatise, it occupies an important position in the development of the tradition. It is the subject of a commentary tradition extending from the ninth century to the Renaissance, and as such it presents medieval philosophers with a puzzling variant of the universality thesis and challenges them to reflect on deeper questions about the nature of goodness. Gilbert of Poitiers, Thierry of Chartres, Clarembald of Arras, and Thomas Aquinas are among those in the High Middle Ages who wrote commentaries on *De hebdomadibus*. But its influence is apparent not only in this commentary tradition but also in the frequency with which it is cited in other contexts, for example, in systematic thirteenth-century discussions devoted to the metaphysics of goodness or the doctrine of the transcendentals. To take just one example: in the first half of the thirteenth century philosophers such as William of Auxerre, Philip the Chancellor, and Albert the Great began treating issues concerning the nature of goodness systematically by discussing a relatively fixed set of questions. Two of those questions—"Is everything that exists good in virtue of the fact that it exists?" and "What is the relation between being and good?"—seem to have arisen in part out of reflection on the central issue of *De hebdomadibus*, and treatments of them regularly cite Boethius's text and rehearse certain of his main arguments. Boethius's thought experiment is particularly interesting to these philosophers, and in the thirteenth century it seems to acquire a life of its own apart from the rest of *De hebdomadibus*.[4]

Augustine's influence on the later medieval discussion of the nature of goodness is at least as great as Boethius's, but it is more difficult to identify clearly. There is no explicit commentary tradition like that devoted to *De hebdomadibus* for the relevant treatises of Augustine. His views are frequently cited in later discussions of goodness, but often there is no explicit reference to him even when his views seem to be just below the surface. At least part of the explanation, no doubt, is that medieval philosophers could take for granted their audience's familiarity with the Augustinian texts.

In Book VII of the *Confessions* Augustine describes his coming to see

3. For more detailed discussion of Boethius's views, see MacDonald 1988 and Chapters 2 and 3 below.
4. For an example of the independent use of Boethius's thought experiment, see Chapter 1, Section 5.

the truth of the universality thesis as the cornerstone of his intellectual reconciliation to Christianity. He had been plagued by the problem of evil and had turned to Manichaean dualism primarily because it offered a clear explanation of the existence of evil. According to Augustine, the Manichaeans were cosmological and theological dualists: they held that the cosmos is composed of two kinds of substances, good and evil, and that there are two ultimate principles, one good and one evil, that explain, respectively, the existence of the good and evil substances in the universe. As he reports it, he was convinced by reading the Platonists that evil is not a nature or substance but a corruption or privation, and hence that all substances are good to some extent. If all substances are good to some extent, then Manichaean cosmological dualism is false and there is no need for Manichaean theological dualism as an explanation of cosmological dualism. Augustine's passionate struggle to understand the nature and existence of evil, then, leads him to the universality thesis.[5]

In virtually all his polemical writings against the Manichaeans, Augustine adopts the strategy of arguing in favor of the universality thesis as a way of refuting the fundamental tenets of Manichaeanism.[6] But despite all the attention he gives to the universality thesis, he gives very little explicit attention to the metaphysics of goodness that underlies it. A passage from Book XII of *The City of God*, however, suggests the account of the nature of goodness he has in mind. Augustine tells us that the apostate angels are evil not by nature but by a corruption or perversion of their nature. The angels are by nature rational beings, and as such it is their nature to act rationally. It is rational to act so as to obtain happiness, and there is only one thing—adhering to the highest good, namely, God—in which happiness consists. Adhering to anything other than God is irrational in that it consists in choosing a lesser good in preference to a higher good and so is contrary to nature for a rational creature. When the apostate angels choose to adhere to something other than God, they act irrationally, and so their nature is corrupted. They are evil but only insofar as their nature is corrupted.[7]

Augustine is less clear about the account of goodness that corresponds to this account of evil, but it is possible to see how it might go.

---

5. For discussion of Augustine's defense of the universality thesis and his views on the nature of goodness in general, see MacDonald 1989b.

6. In addition to the well-known discussion in *Confessions* VII, see especially *De natura boni* and *De moribus Manichaeorum*.

7. *De civitate Dei* XII.1; see the parallel discussion in *De libero arbitrio* I.8.

Insofar as a rational creature acts rationally, it realizes or actualizes its rational nature, and since to realize one's nature is to achieve one's natural end, a rational creature is good to the extent to which it acts rationally. Of course, this account of goodness, generalized, is a version of the nature approach. It relies on the view central to that approach, that each substance, in virtue of having a nature, has an end that is the good for substances of that nature.

Augustine points out that the universality thesis follows from his view of what it is for a nature to be realized or corrupted. Everything that exists actualizes its nature to *some* extent, and so everything that exists is good to some extent. As long as there is nature, there is goodness; and if a being's nature is entirely corrupted, that being ceases to exist. These reflections on the nature of goodness and evil seemed to Augustine to resolve the problem of evil, but they also seem to raise worries of their own since there seem to be evils that are not mere privations. Jorge Gracia (Chapter 6) examines Suárez's attempt to resolve issues of this sort, issues that naturally arise within a tradition of reflection on the Augustinian position.

Thus, Boethius's *De hebdomadibus* and passages scattered throughout the Augustinian corpus provide later philosophers with clear statements and defenses of the universality thesis together with two supporting accounts of the nature of goodness. It is enough material to ensure that the thesis and the two accounts would be taken seriously in the later Middle Ages.

3. The Tradition in the Later Middle Ages

The single most important development affecting the discussion of issues in the metaphysics of goodness in the later Middle Ages is the influx into the Latin West in the late twelfth and early thirteenth centuries of the Aristotelian natural philosophy, metaphysics, and ethics along with certain treatises by Muslim philosophers, especially Avicenna.[8] The availability of these new texts and ideas partially explains the remarkable development in the first half of the thirteenth century of unprecedented, systematic, comprehensive treatises organized around the concept of the good (I have more to say about this development below); but there is a continuous stream running from Boethius and

---

8. For an account of this development, see Dod 1982 and Lohr 1982.

Augustine through the twelfth century into which the new Aristotelian ideas feed.

One particularly visible part of that stream is the tradition of commentaries on Boethius's *De hebdomadibus* that flourishes in the twelfth century. Three substantial twelfth-century commentaries exist, all associated in some way with the influential school at Chartres: one by Gilbert of Poitiers (written ca. 1140), one by Thierry of Chartres (written ca. 1150), and one by Clarembald of Arras (written 1157–58). Each develops in a different way the sort of participation account suggested by Boethius.[9]

We know that Boethius's views were discussed in the twelfth century in places other than these three commentaries. In his commentary, for instance, Clarembald refers to certain interpretations of *De hebdomadibus* that are neither his own nor those to be found in Gilbert's or Thierry's commentaries. But in addition to the sort of indirect evidence provided by Clarembald's allusions, there is direct evidence of twelfth-century interest in *De hebdomadibus*. In an early summa *Quoniam homines* (ca. 1160), Alan of Lille, in the course of arguing for the claim that even evil actions are good in virtue of the fact that they have being, refers to Boethius's treatise as a source for the universality thesis.[10] In the discussion Alan also cites Augustine's version of the universality thesis and clearly sees that Augustine's view that everything that has a nature is good insofar as it realizes that nature can be applied to human actions as well as to natural substances. Alan applies the same Augustinian version of the thesis to another question in *Quoniam homines*, namely, "Is the Devil good?" In each of these contexts Alan appeals to the universality thesis but does not elaborate the metaphysical view that lies behind it. It is clear, therefore, that Boethius's and Augustine's views on the nature of goodness were at least known and used in the twelfth century outside the extant commentary tradition.[11]

The movement, exemplified by Alan's *Quoniam homines*, toward organizing philosophical discussion around particular issues presented in the form of disputed questions is especially important for the discussion of issues associated with the metaphysics of goodness.[12] By about

9. For texts of these commentaries, see Clarembald 1965, Gilbert 1966, and Thierry 1971; I have translated them and discussed their significance in MacDonald 1986. See also Schrimpf 1966.

10. For the text, see Alan 1953.

11. Peter Lombard's *Sentences*, composed about the same time as *Quoniam homines*, seems to contain no references to *De hebdomadibus* and only passing references to Augustine's views on being and goodness (e.g., I.46 and II.15, 35, and 39).

12. For a discussion of this literary development, see Kenny and Pinborg 1982.

1228 Philip the Chancellor had composed a lengthy summa of meta-physical, moral, and theological doctrine called *Summa de bono*.[13] As its title suggests, the notion of the good is the *summa*'s organizing princi-ple, and its first section consists of a set of questions dealing with issues fundamental to the metaphysics of goodness.[14] These opening ques-tions take up topics such as the relation between good and being (Ques-tion 1) and whether being is the same as being good for every created thing (Question 8). Philip supplements these questions investigating the necessary connection between being and goodness with others rais-ing the issue of the relation between goodness and truth and between truth and being (Questions 2 and 3). His aim in this opening part of *Summa de bono* is clearly to provide a systematic account of the nature of goodness—in Question 1, for instance, he explains and evaluates three different candidates for such an account (derived from Aristotle, pseudo-Dionysius, and Avicenna)—and to place it within a broad meta-physical framework. The result seems to be the first extended, gen-uinely systematic treatment of both the nature of goodness and the doctrine of the transcendentals.[15]

Philip's *Summa de bono* is historically important not only because it is the first treatise of its kind but also because it serves as a model for subsequent thirteenth-century discussion.[16] Near the middle of the century (ca. 1245) Albert the Great modeled his own *Summa de bono* on Philip's.[17] Moreover, it appears that during the two decades between Philip's summa and Albert's a commonly recognized canon of questions concerning the metaphysics of goodness emerged, deriving from the base provided by the first section of Philip's *Summa de bono*.[18] These standard questions include, among others: "What is the good?" "Is good interchangeable with being?" "Is everything that has being good insofar as it has being?" "How is good related to being?" and "What does good add to being?" They appear together in systematic discus-sions of goodness—as in the introductory sections of the two *summae de bono*, in other *summae* such as the *Summa theologica* attributed to Alex-

13. For the text of *Summa de bono*, see Philip 1985.
14. I have translated this set of questions in MacDonald forthcoming(b).
15. See Pouillon 1939 and Wicki's introduction in Philip 1985. But Philip's treatise draws on William of Auxerre's discussion of goodness in *Summa aurea* III.10.4. For William's text, see William 1980–87; I have translated the relevant questions in Mac-Donald forthcoming(b).
16. See Wicki's introduction in Philip 1985, Lottin 1960b, and Brady 1953.
17. See Albert 1951.
18. The outline of this base can already be discerned in William of Auxerre. For discussion of this development, see MacDonald forthcoming(b).

ander of Hales (compiled before 1245),[19] Aquinas's *Summa theologiae* (Part I, 1266–68),[20] and Albert's *Summa theologiae* (1270s),[21] and in collections of disputed questions such as Aquinas's *De veritate* (1258–59)[22]—and also individually as some one of these issues arises within some other context—as in sentences-commentaries such as Aquinas's *Scriptum super libros Sententiarum* (1252–56),[23] and in commentaries on other texts, for example, Albert's question-commentary on *De divinis nominibus*.[24]

Of course, the commentary traditions continue. Aquinas wrote a commentary on *De hebdomadibus* (1256–59), discussed by Aertsen and McInerny in Chapters 2 and 3; Robert Grosseteste, Albert the Great, and Aquinas wrote commentaries on the *Nicomachean Ethics*; Albert and Aquinas wrote commentaries on *De divinis nominibus* (chapter 4 of which is sometimes referred to as Dionysius's treatise on the good). These commentaries constitute a valuable part of the thirteen-century discussion, but from a philosophical point of view the new and most interesting feature of this fruitful development is the move toward systematic treatment of the issues. The developing canon of disputed questions identifies the philosophical theses central to the tradition, gives logical structure to the discussion of them, and provides a framework within which the rapidly increasing number of authoritative texts and positions on these issues can be collated and adjudicated. Albert, for instance, begins his *Summa de bono* with the question "What is the good?" in which he introduces two sorts of accounts, one associated with Aristotle that analyzes goodness in terms of the notions of an end and desire, and one associated with Avicenna and Algazel that analyzes goodness in terms of a certain sort of actuality. Albert presents arguments for and against each account, explicitly citing Aristotle's *Physics*, *Metaphysics*, and *Ethics*, Boethius's *De hebdomadibus*, pseudo-Dionysius's *De divinis nominibus*, the neo-Platonist *Liber de causis*, and Avicenna's *Metaphysics*. Albert adjudicates the apparently rival accounts by developing what he takes to be the underlying metaphysical theory they share. He then claims that the apparent rivals are both defensible insofar as each draws attention to different features of one and the same underlying theory. Hence, Albert's first question requires him to lay the

19. *Summa theologica* Book I, Treatise 3, Part 3.
20. *ST* Ia.5–6. See Chapters 2 and 4 below.
21. *Summa theologiae* Book I, Treatise 6, Part I.
22. *DV* XXI. See Chapter 5.
23. For references, see Chapter 5.
24. For references, see Chapter 1.

foundation of a metaphysics of goodness that in turn provides the systematic foundation for the subsequent discussion. Having provided an account of the concept of the good, he next takes up questions that explore the relation between this concept and other concepts such as being (Questions 6 and 7) and truth (Questions 8 and 9).[25]

The assimilation of new philosophical material and the sort of systematization characteristic of this period in the thirteenth century result in substantive philosophical development. I have claimed that within the single tradition there are at least two basic elements that seem to diverge in important respects, the participation approach paradigmatically represented by Boethius's *De hebdomadibus* and the nature approach found in Augustine's views on good and evil, and I have suggested that before the early thirteenth century the prominent discussions of the metaphysics of goodness occur in commentaries on Boethius and hence focus attention on the participation approach. The wealth of new Aristotelian material available in the first half of the thirteenth century, however, begins attracting attention toward the nature approach. Aristotle's *Physics*, *Metaphysics*, *De anima*, and *Ethics* provide these medieval philosophers with metaphysical foundations for the nature approach unrivaled in breadth and sophistication.

The story of the tradition extending from Philip the Chancellor (d. 1236) to Thomas Aquinas (d. 1274) is largely the story of the development of the nature approach and the attempt to fit the results of both approaches into a single comprehensive theory. Four of the essays included here deal with parts of this story. In "The Metaphysics of Goodness and the Doctrine of the Transcendentals" (Chapter 1) I argue that the two approaches fundamental to the tradition are in tension, and that the tension collapses into incompatibility in at least one text of Albert the Great's. In his commentary on *De divinis nominibus* he takes Boethius's position, which he endorses, to be that goodness in created things is a purely extrinsic relation. For created things, being good consists solely in standing in a certain relation to God that is grounded in no monadic properties intrinsic to the created things themselves. But this account of the nature of goodness is incompatible with the account, which Albert seems to espouse elsewhere, deriving from the nature approach. The nature approach suggests that for a thing to be good is for it to have realized its nature to some extent, and the properties in virtue of which a thing can be said to have realized its nature will at least in part be properties intrinsic to the thing itself. If I am right about this

25. See MacDonald forthcoming(b).

text of Albert's, the two approaches do in fact lead to inconsistency on at least one occasion.

Jan Aertsen and Ralph McInerny (Chapters 2 and 3) follow out this theme in Aquinas. They discuss elements of Aquinas's development of the nature approach within the context of his explicit reflections on the participation approach. Aquinas agrees with the Christian-Platonist representatives of the participation approach in identifying God with the Good and viewing creation as the outpouring of goodness itself, but his sympathy for the nature approach (and Aristotelianism, as he understands it) leads him to assert (against the Platonists, as he sees it) that created goods are good in virtue of some intrinsic form's inhering in the created goods themselves and not solely in virtue of their relation to some extrinsic or separate form. Aertsen and McInerny examine Aquinas's commentary on Boethius's *De hebdomadibus*; it is not surprising to find in it an explicit attempt to interpret Boethius's account in a way that renders it consistent with Aquinas's own sympathies for the nature account. Moreover, in at least two places (*ST* Ia.6 and *DV* XXI) Aquinas discusses the question "Are all things good by the first goodness?" which had become associated with the sort of theological and relational account of goodness suggested by the Platonist strain in Augustine and by the account in *De hebdomadibus*.[26] Aertsen's and McInerny's analyses of these texts illuminate Aquinas's efforts to forge a coherent account of the nature of goodness that preserves what is true in each of the two divergent traditional approaches.

In "Good as Transcendental and the Transcendence of the Good" Aertsen argues that despite Aquinas's maintaining that God alone is essentially good and that creatures are good by participation, his development of the nature approach (as in *ST* Ia.5) commits him to rejecting the view, characteristic of the participation approach, that the goodness of created things consists solely in their relation to God, the First Good. According to Aertsen, Aquinas sides with the Platonist tradition in using the notion of participation to explain the universal predicability of the transcendentals, including goodness, but he rejects the Platonist explanation of predication in general in terms of participation. Aquinas's assimilation of the Platonism expressed in the participation approach, then, appears to be essentially connected with his understand-

---

26. This particular question is a well-established part of the tradition Aquinas inherits from William, Philip, and Albert: see, e.g., William's *Summa aurea* III.10.4.1 ("What is the good, what is goodness, and are all things called good by virtue of the first goodness?") and Albert's *Summa de bono* I.1.2 ("Is every good good by one simple goodness which is the highest good?").

ing of the transcendentality of goodness and a key to his understanding of the relation between the doctrine of the transcendentals, on the one hand, and the doctrine of the transcendence of the Good (that is, God), on the other.

In "Saint Thomas on *De hebdomadibus*" McInerny investigates Aquinas's use of his doctrine of analogical predication in his exposition of Boethius's solution to the central problem of *De hebdomadibus*. Boethius seems to say that created goods are good by virtue of standing in a certain relation to God, the First Good, and Aquinas explains the nature of this relation by appealing to the way in which certain things are called healthy or medical by virtue of their standing in a certain relation to health in an animal or to the art of medicine. McInerny argues that Aquinas's appeal to the doctrine of analogy allows him to interpret Boethius as asserting that the divine nature is goodness itself and that the divine goodness is ontologically prior to created goodness; hence, created goods are called good insofar as they are effects of and directed toward divine goodness. But according to McInerny, this claim of ontological priority for the divine goodness does not undermine Aquinas's understanding of the epistemological priority of created goodness. Created goods are good by virtue of an intrinsic form, and we come to know the divine goodness only by means of knowing created goodness.

In "Being and Goodness" (Chapter 4) Eleonore Stump and Norman Kretzmann provide a detailed explication and analysis of a fully developed account representative of the nature approach. They focus on *Summa theologiae* Ia.5, where Aquinas explains the relation between being and goodness in terms of the thesis that the terms 'being' and 'good' are the same in reference (*secundum rem*), differing only in sense (*secundum rationem*). On this account, 'good' essentially expresses the notion of an end or of desirability, whereas 'being' essentially expresses the notion of actuality; hence, the two terms differ in sense. But they are the same in reference because, with respect to any given thing, being and goodness both supervene on the same set of intrinsic, natural properties, viz., those properties in virtue of which that thing has actualized its specifying potentialities—that is to say, those potentialities that belong to it in virtue of its nature or substantial form.

Aquinas is heir to the flourishing early thirteenth-century discussion of the metaphysics of goodness, and his work provides us with a particularly clear explicit attempt to accommodate the apparently disparate elements in that discussion. Unfortunately, we do not know as much about other thirteenth- and fourteenth-century figures who contribute to the developing tradition; in fact, apart from conspicuous discussions in some of the major *summae* of the thirteenth century, we are not even certain of where those contributions are to be found. These essays suggest promising directions for further research. Aertsen, for instance, finds useful material in Aquinas's commentary on Book I of the *Nicomachean Ethics* and in his commentary on chapter 4 of *De divinis nominibus*, and my discussion of Albert the Great focuses on a question from Albert's question-commentary on *De divinis nominibus*. It is natural to suppose that exploration of the medieval commentary traditions associated with these authoritative texts, both before and after Aquinas, will turn up interesting contributions to the tradition of reflection on the nature of goodness. At present, however, these commentary traditions remain virtually unexplored.

Of course, discussion of the metaphysics of goodness continued after Aquinas's generation. One essay in the book, Jorge Gracia's "Evil and the Transcendentality of Goodness: Suárez's Solution to the Problem of Positive Evils" (Chapter 6), which focuses on a text representative of the late revival of scholasticism in the sixteenth and seventeenth centuries, shows that the tradition that flourishes in the thirteenth century is still flourishing three hundred years later.

Gracia explores an incompatibility in the work of Francisco Suárez similar to the one I find in Albert's commentary on *De divinis nominibus*. Gracia focuses on Suárez's exploration of the close relation (suggested by Augustine) between a metaphysical account of goodness, on the one hand, and evil, on the other. Suárez argues that the account of evil as a privation—a view common in the tradition stemming from Augustine—must be refined in order to account for the existence of 'positive' evils, that is, entities that are clearly evil but not plausibly taken to be mere privations, such as pains and vicious acts. He develops a distinction between what is evil in itself and what is evil in relation to something else and claims that the account of evil as privation applies only to what is evil in itself. Pain and vicious acts, for example, are not evils in themselves but only in relation to something else, and Suárez characterizes this relation as disagreeability (*disconvenientia*). So evil in itself is not a positive reality but a mere privation, though there are things, real entities, that are evil in relation to something else in virtue of being disagreeable to it. Corresponding to his account of evil, his account of goodness is based on a distinction between good in itself and what is good in relation to something else, and he defines goodness in terms of the notion of agreeability (*convenientia*). But he takes the relational notion of agreeability to define not just the notion of being good in relation to something else but also the notion of good in itself. This much seems to commit Suárez to an essentially relational account of goodness but one that is compatible with the nature approach since one might understand the properties in virtue of which a thing has realized its nature as being agreeable to it (insofar as it is a thing of that nature). But Gracia argues that Suárez requires the relata of the relation of agreeability to be distinct entities and that this requirement renders the account incompatible with the nature approach. Hence, Gracia attributes to Suárez a very strong relational account of goodness. Unlike Albert, Suárez seems not to have been attracted to this strong relational account because of the presence in the tradition of the participation approach but because of his failure to distinguish two different sorts of relations, the sort that holds between two distinct real things and the sort that holds between an existing thing and its nature.

4. Metaethics, Ethics, and Moral Psychology

The main lines of the tradition I have been sketching are concerned with providing an account of the nature of goodness, an account that is properly within the domain of metaphysics. But metaphysical views of this sort have natural application in other areas of philosophy.

Any metaphysics of goodness, for instance, at least suggests a metaphysical foundation for ethics, and in fact philosophers such as Aquinas present their moral philosophy as founded on their account of goodness in general. According to Aquinas's account of the nature of goodness (in *ST* Ia.5.1), a thing is good to the extent to which it has actualized the potentialities that belong to it in virtue of its being the specific kind of thing it is. This sort of metaphysics of goodness, applied to the particular case of human beings, yields an account of the human good: the human good is the state or activity in which the actualization of the potentialities specific to human beings consists. Following the ancient tradition, medieval philosophers call this state or activity 'happiness' or 'beatitude' and view ethics as the branch of philosophy devoted to specifying the precise nature of happiness and the means of attaining it.[27]

In "Being and Goodness" (Chapter 4) Stump and Kretzmann discuss the derivation of a metaethics and normative ethics from the metaphysical account of goodness they find in Aquinas. They argue that Aqui-

27. See MacDonald forthcoming(a).

nas's metaphysics provides a foundation for his virtue-centered ethical theory: the human good consists in acting in accordance with reason, since the potentialities that specify a human being's nature are those grouped together under the heading 'reason.' Hence, morally good actions are actions done in accordance with reason, and the moral virtues are those human dispositions, Aristotelian first actualities, that dispose a human being to actions of this sort, Aristotelian second actualities. Stump and Kretzmann defend the normative theory Aquinas derives from these considerations and claim that his conception of the particular moral virtue of justice provides a way of resolving the alleged paradox of agent-centered restrictions that has been said to infect certain kinds of ethical theory.

A characteristic sort of moral psychology, and specifically a view of the nature of the will, grows out of the same metaphysical views that give rise to the eudaimonistic ethical theory I have just sketched. The view of natural teleology underlying the nature approach to the relation between being and goodness maintains that each natural substance has its own end or completed state that consists in its having actualized the potentialities that belong to it by nature. To have a nature, then, is to have a set of specifying potentialities, and on this view, to have a set of potentialities of this sort is to be inclined or directed toward their actualization. Hence, natural substances are naturally inclined toward their complete actualization, that is to say, toward their end or good. This natural inclination is typically called natural 'appetite.' A natural inclination or appetite belongs to human beings in virtue of their nature, and since human nature is rational nature, this natural inclination in human beings is called 'rational appetite' or 'will.' The human will, then, is an inclination possessed by human beings in virtue of their having a rational soul. Because the will is a power belonging to a rational substance, the operation of the will is intimately bound up with another of the soul's powers, namely, intellect. Will is a *rational* appetite insofar as it is an inclination toward what intellect presents to it as an end or a good.[28]

I have said that the identification of the notion of the good with the notion of an end is an essential feature of the nature approach to understanding the nature of goodness, and the view of natural inclination in general and rational appetite in particular I have just sketched illuminates the connection medieval philosophers saw between the no-

28. See MacDonald 1990a.

tion of an end and the concept of appetite or desire. Medieval philosophers understood the aphorism that all things seek the good, which they frequently cite in their discussion of the nature of goodness, in terms of this teleological conception of appetite.[29] All things seek the good because all things, by virtue of their natures, are naturally inclined toward (have a natural appetite for) the complete state or full actuality that is their end or good. In virtue of possessing rational appetite, human beings seek the good in a particular way: they seek the good as it is conceived by intellect.

Mark Jordan and Eleonore Stump explore this conception of the will from different angles. In "The Transcendentality of Goodness and the Human Will" (Chapter 5) Jordan examines Aquinas's account of the relation between goodness and the will. He develops the theoretical connections linking Aquinas's frequent characterization of the transcendental good in terms of the end of appetite (in *De veritate*, *De potentia*, and his commentary on the *Sentences*) with his systematic treatments of the nature of will and of the causal relations holding between intellect and will (in *Summa theologiae* and *De malo*). Aquinas conceives of the will as an appetite in rational creatures that naturally follows intellect's apprehension of the good, and so he is committed to holding that intellect causally influences the will; he also holds that the will can direct the activity of the intellect and so can causally influence its judgments. Jordan focuses on Aquinas's explanation of this interdependence of intellect and will and his attempt to explain human freedom and the nature of human action in terms of it. Jordan claims that Aquinas's views on the nature of the interdependence and his corresponding account of the origin of the will's activity develop in significant respects over the course of his career. He links the development with Aquinas's coming to appreciate, prior to his writing *Summa theologiae* IaIIae and *De malo*, a short passage from Aristotle's *Eudemian Ethics*. According to Jordan, in the earlier account (for instance, *DV* XXI) Aquinas's view of the interaction between will and intellect leads him to maintain that no explanation of the will's motion is required beyond its being a natural inclination and its having been presented

---

29. The aphorism is typically associated with Aristotle, who presents it in the opening lines of the *Nicomachean Ethics* as a traditional view of which he approves. But medieval philosophers were familiar with it from elsewhere and knew it before they read it in or came to associate it primarily with the *Ethics*. In Question 1 of his *Summa de bono*, for instance, Philip presents it as pseudo-Dionysius's view, and in his *Summa theologiae* Albert associates it with Boethius's *Consolation of Philosophy*.

with a good by intellect. But in the later account (in *ST* IaIIae), apparently because of the influence of the passage from the *Eudemian Ethics*, Aquinas maintains that the ultimate explanation of the will's motion must refer not to the will's status as a natural inclination but to the will's having been incited to activity by God. Jordan links this development in Aquinas's thought with his apparently puzzling assertion in *ST* IaIIae.9 that the will can refuse to exercise its act even with regard to willing its ultimate end, happiness.

In "Aquinas on Faith and Goodness" (Chapter 7) Stump links Aquinas's metaphysics of goodness with his conception of the will in order to explain his view of the nature of faith. Aquinas conceives of faith as firm assent to truths about God, caused by the will's being moved by the object of faith rather than intellect's being moved by the evidence of the truths themselves. This account seems open to obvious objections. First, it appears to be incoherent since it requires that the intellectual assent characteristic of faith be caused by will, but intellectual assent seems not to be subject to voluntary control. Second, even if it is not incoherent in this way, it seems to require irrationality on the part of one who has faith insofar as it requires one to will assent to a proposition without sufficient evidence for its truth. Stump argues that Aquinas's general account of the powers of the rational soul, which explains the causal interrelations of intellect and will, provides the basis for an account of how the will can influence belief and so constitutes the basis for a reply to the first objection. Aquinas holds that in some cases, including those relevant to faith, the evidence for a given proposition entertained by the intellect is insufficient to move the intellect to assent. In cases of this sort (though, as he acknowledges, not in cases in which there is sufficient evidence to move the intellect to assent) there is room for the will to move the intellect on the basis of its being drawn by the goodness of the object entertained. Moreover, she claims that Aquinas's view that goodness supervenes on being, and hence perfect goodness on perfect being (developed in detail in Chapter 4), provides a way of responding to the second objection. There is justification for one's assenting to propositions about the existence of God on the basis of the will's desire for the goodness they describe because they describe perfect goodness, and perfect goodness entails perfect being, which necessarily exists. Stump not only defends Aquinas's understanding of the role of the will in faith against common objections but also claims that his account has the advantage of explaining how faith can be conceived of as a virtue and why faith should be central to the Christian understanding of salvation.

5. Philosophical Theology

Philosophers such as Aquinas who were committed to the account of human will as a natural inclination toward the good saw that it could be developed into a general account of the will and extended, with some modifications, to provide an account of God's will. This extension of the doctrine had particularly fruitful results in philosophical theology.

But the account of will as a natural inclination toward the good as it is conceived by intellect raises special worries about freedom. As a natural power, must the will necessarily will the good presented to it by intellect? Is the will entirely dependent on the dictates of intellect, or is it self-determining in any significant respects? Can the will be independent and autonomous in such a way that its actions are intelligible and not purely random or arbitrary? Jordan (Chapter 5) examines Aquinas's responses to some of these worries for the particular case of human freedom. But the difficulties for this account of will are exacerbated when the account is applied to the divine will. God's omniscience seems to entail that God's intellect can present to God's will only what is in fact the best; and it seems that the will of a perfectly good being cannot do other than will the best. So it might seem to follow from commonly accepted views about God's nature and the account of will as a natural inclination toward the good as it is conceived by intellect that God's will is constrained in every case to willing what is in fact the best. Moreover, if one believes, as most medieval philosophers did, that God is himself the personification of perfect goodness, it might seem that God could have no reason to will anything other than himself. Medieval philosophers were acutely aware of these worries, and they addressed them most directly within their discussions of the paradigm instance of divine willing: creation.

Three essays in Part Two address the problem of divine freedom in creation. In the first of his two papers on the problem of creation, "A General Problem of Creation: Why Would God Create Anything at All?" (Chapter 8), Norman Kretzmann traces two distinct lines of explanation of God's choosing to create that run through the medieval period. One line—the necessitarian line—grows out of the Platonist view of the dependence of being on goodness. Kretzmann finds its roots in Plato's 'creation' story in the *Timaeus* (one of the few texts of Plato known to medieval philosophers) and its most influential expression in the principle (attributed by medieval philosophers to the neo-Platonist pseudo-Dionysius) that goodness is essentially diffusive of itself. If God's nature includes essential goodness and goodness is essentially diffusive, then it seems that God is constrained by natural necessity to create. The other line—the libertarian line—maintains that God's choice of whether or not to create is entirely free and not necessitated, and that God's perfection would not have been impugned had he chosen not to create. The libertarian but not the necessitarian line of explanation seems to medieval Christian philosophers to be compatible with Scripture, and so most, including Aquinas, endorse it despite their sympathies with the Dionysian principle. But Kretzmann argues that, at least in Aquinas's case, the tension between the two lines collapses into inconsistency. He argues that Aquinas is inconsistent in endorsing the Dionysian principle and at the same time maintaining that God is free to choose whether to create. According to Kretzmann, Bonaventure is unlike Aquinas in accepting the implications of the Platonistic necessitarian line, and Bonaventure rejects the Aristotelian conception of God as entirely self-sufficient that attracts Aquinas.

In his second paper, "A Particular Problem of Creation: Why Would God Create This World?" (Chapter 9), Kretzmann raises the logically next question: given that God chooses to create (whether freely or of necessity), is he free to choose what to create? As Kretzmann points out, there are reasons, well known to modern philosophers from Leibniz's *Theodicy* and to medieval philosophers from Plato's *Timaeus*, for thinking that if God creates any world, he is constrained to create the best possible world. Kretzmann examines Aquinas's reasons for denying this consequence and thinking that God has free choice with respect to what to create. According to Kretzmann, Aquinas holds that there is no best possible world, that is, that for any world God might choose to create, there is some world better than it. Given that there is no best possible world, God cannot be constrained to create it. But this initial solution seems to raise problems of its own: if for any world God might choose to create there is always one better, what could account for God's actual choice of one world? Moreover, what could account for his actual choice of this world, a world containing created wills whose freedom threatens disruption, corruption, and evil? Kretzmann develops an answer out of Aquinas's suggestion that creation is the manifestation or representation of the divine goodness. Kretzmann argues that if the purpose of creation is representation, it follows that there must be created understanding *for which* creation is a representation; and if creation is a representation of perfect goodness understood as both productive and attractive goodness, it follows that creation must contain persons who can freely choose to love God. Hence, Kretzmann's development of Aquinas's account preserves the neo-

Platonist vision of a cosmic cycle: creation proceeds from God as the outpouring of divine goodness and returns to him in the form of freely chosen creaturely love attracted by the divine goodness.

In "The Best of All Possible Worlds" (Chapter 10) William Mann explores the problem of creation by focusing on the apparent tension between two of the divine attributes, freedom and perfect goodness. If God is maximally free, it seems he can create any possible world; but if he is perfectly good, it seems that there are some possible worlds he cannot create. Mann examines two extreme resolutions of this tension. One view—a sort of theological voluntarism, which Mann finds in Vital du Four, William Ockham, and Descartes—resolves the tension by emphasizing God's freedom or will. The divine freedom entails God's absolute sovereignty and independence; hence, possible worlds can possess no independent value that might constrain God's choice of which to create. God's freedom entails that he determines the realm of value by the free choice of his will so that things and worlds have value solely by virtue of God's decrees. The other resolution—a sort of rationalism paradigmatically represented by Leibniz—emphasizes God's nature or intellect. God has a reason for creating the actual world: he is a rational optimizer and in his omniscience knows the relative values of all possible worlds and that the actual world is uniquely best. God is constrained by his goodness and knowledge, but the constraint arises from his own nature and not from some source extrinsic to God. Mann argues that each of these resolutions exacts too high a price, and he offers an alternative. Against Leibniz, Mann argues that there is no uniquely best possible world because some possible worlds are incommensurable. His argument rests on an analogy with different lives within a single world: since it is plausible to suppose that two hypothetical future lives—for example, Teresa's possible future life as an accomplished operatic soprano and her possible future life devoted to caring for the dying poor—are incommensurable, it is plausible to suppose that two different worlds—for example, worlds exactly alike except that in one Teresa pursues her operatic career and in the other she devotes herself to the dying poor—can be incommensurable. So Mann's thesis about the incommensurability among possible worlds preserves God's freedom with respect to which world to create, even if it is only the freedom of arbitrary choice. But against the radical voluntarists, Mann's thesis supposes that possible worlds possess the values they do independently of God's will. Mann argues, however, that this supposition need not be taken as impugning God's sovereignty, as the voluntarists claim. He suggests, following Aquinas and other medieval philosophers, that God is absolutely simple, and hence that will and intellect are really identical in God. If willing and knowing are identical in God, God's knowing certain necessary truths—for instance, the truths expressing the value structure and incommensurability of possible worlds—cannot be prior to his willing those truths, and his knowing (and willing) those truths is just his knowing (and willing) his own nature. According to Mann, then, the doctrine of divine simplicity together with the value-incommensurability of possible worlds provides a way between the horns of voluntarism and rationalism.

The theological doctrine of divine simplicity that Mann uses to ground his solution to the problem of creation is actually integrally related to the metaphysical doctrine of the necessary connection between being and goodness. In "Being and Goodness" (Chapter 4) Stump and Kretzmann argue that an important part of the doctrine of simplicity follows from Aquinas's metaphysics of goodness and his conception of God as essentially and uniquely being itself, understood as perfect being or pure actuality. If God is pure actuality and goodness supervenes on actuality, then God is identical with goodness itself. Stump and Kretzmann suggest, along lines similar to those Mann sketches, that this conception of God as identical with goodness can provide a basis for an objective religious morality.

The problems of creation addressed by Kretzmann and Mann are closely related to and bring into focus some of the central elements of the traditional problem of evil, and that problem is an underlying theme of other essays in the book as well. In "Being and Goodness," for example, Stump and Kretzmann argue that Aquinas's conception of justice imposes rational, agent-centered restrictions against perpetrating (or permitting) actions that constitute an injustice, regardless of the good to be achieved by those actions, and that these restrictions undermine well-known attempts to resolve the problem of evil. In Chapter 6, Gracia examines Suárez's account of the metaphysical nature of evil and his attempts to deal with an apparent difficulty for the famous Augustinian account of evil that grounds Augustine's theodicy.

The problems of creation, religious morality, and evil are only some of the areas in philosophical theology to which the metaphysics of goodness developed in the tradition I have been tracing can be applied. Medieval philosophers in this tradition took their metaphysics of goodness to be an integral part of their doctrine of God. They conceived of God as a perfect being and worked out a detailed account of the divine nature and activity under the guidance of the concept of perfection. Aquinas's account of the connection between being and goodness, as set out by Stump and Kretzmann in "Being and Goodness," shows how the notion of perfection provides the conceptual link between being and goodness: for a thing of some kind, to be perfected (to some extent) is to be complete or fully actual, and hence to have being (to that extent); and it is also to be desirable, and hence good (to that extent). Thus, according to Aquinas, an absolutely perfect being must be pure actuality and the source of all being (or 'being itself,' as Aquinas puts it), on the one hand, and perfectly good (or 'goodness itself'), on the other. In "Aquinas on Faith and Goodness" (Chapter 7) Stump draws on this identification of perfect being with perfect goodness in defending Aquinas's understanding of the nature of faith.

In "Metaphysical Dependence, Independence, and Perfection" (Chapter 11) Thomas Morris argues that the conception of God as a perfect being incorporates two apparently rival views of the nature of divinity: one that emphasizes God's being, conceiving of God primarily as creator, and another that emphasizes God's goodness, conceiving of God as that than which nothing greater can be conceived. Morris argues that common assumptions about creation acceptable to most proponents of the former view entail the latter view, that is, that God is the greatest possible being. According to Morris, then, the conception of God as a perfect being unites intuitions about God's being and God's goodness and provides a fruitful starting point for exploring the nature of God.

One way of proceeding to a determinate doctrine of God from the starting point provided by perfect-being theology is by investigating the concept of perfection: for example, philosophical theologians have debated whether perfection entails specific attributes such as omnipotence or omniscience. Some philosophers committed to the doctrine that God is a perfect being have claimed that the doctrine of divine simplicity deployed here by Mann and Stump and Kretzmann is a central and essential part of perfect-being theology. In the second half of his paper Morris argues that divine simplicity does not follow from divine perfection, and hence that perfect-being theologians need not commit themselves to the doctrine of simplicity. Perfect-being theologians who accept the doctrine of simplicity sometimes support the doctrine by means of an argument from dependence: they claim that perfection entails ontological independence and that any being that is metaphysically complex is necessarily dependent on its metaphysical parts; hence, they conclude that a perfect being must be metaphysically simple. Morris examines this argument for the doctrine of simplicity and concludes that the dependence that God has on his metaphysical parts is not of the sort that would impugn the divine aseity. According to Morris, then, perfection does not entail simplicity, and perfect-being theology should not be rejected on the grounds that it entails that counterintuitive and perhaps incoherent doctrine.

6. Conclusion

The historical and conceptual strands I have traced are by no means the only ones that emerge in the essays that follow. But they are sufficient, I think, not only to identify some of the historical and philosophical themes of a recognizable tradition exploring the metaphysics of goodness but also to show some of the many variations on those themes to be found within the tradition. Some of the fundamental metaphysical positions developed within the tradition and applied to problems in ethics and philosophical theology deserve serious attention; I have been able merely to suggest their interest and significance. Whether my suggestions are correct depends ultimately on the evaluation of the detailed evidence presented in this book and the research still to be done.

PART ONE

THE CONCEPT
OF THE GOOD
IN METAPHYSICS

CHAPTER 1

The Metaphysics of Goodness and the Doctrine of the Transcendentals

Scott MacDonald

The medieval metaphysical doctrine of the transcendentals is well known but not well understood. The transcendentals are sometimes taken to be terms, in which case the most commonly recognized transcendentals are the terms 'being,' 'one,' 'true,' and 'good'; sometimes concepts, in which case they are the concepts of being, unity, truth, and goodness; and sometimes properties, in which case they are the corresponding properties.[1] Perhaps the best known succinct statement characteristic of the doctrine is the claim that 'being,' 'one,' 'true,' and 'good' are interchangeable (or convertible).[2] I call this the *Interchangeability Thesis* (IT).

In this chapter I provide an explanation of this peculiar-sounding thesis and see what justification can be offered for it. I focus for the most part on just one corollary of IT, the claim that 'being' and 'good' are interchangeable (*ens et bonum convertuntur*); I call this corollary the *Interchangeability Thesis for Being and Goodness* (ITBG).[3] I have two rea-

---

1. *Ens, unum, verum,* and *bonum*. For the history of the doctrine, see Knittermeyer 1920, Schulemann 1929, Pouillon 1939, and Kuehle 1930.

2. *Ens, unum, verum, et bonum convertuntur.* For a statement of this thesis, see, e.g., Philip the Chancellor, *Summa de bono* Q. 7 (Philip 1985), and Albert the Great, *Summa de bono* I.1.10 (Albert 1951) and *Summa theologiae* I.6.28 (Albert 1978). The Interchangeability Thesis was not often discussed as such by thirteenth-century philosophers; it was generally broken up for the purposes of discussion into parts: "Are being and good interchangeable?" "Are being and true interchangeable?" "What is the relation among true, good, and being?" See Philip, *Summa de bono* Qq. 1–11, and Albert, *Summa de bono* I.1.1–10.

3. Albert the Great discusses ITBG in Distinction 46, Q. 13, of his commentary on the first book of the *Sentences* (Albert 1893), *Summa de bono* I.1.6, and *Summa theologiae* I.6.28.

sons for focusing on ITBG. The first is pragmatic: much of what we discover about ITBG is generalizable to IT, and by taking just this one corollary, we are able to look at a particular set of arguments in greater detail (in Sections 2–6 below). My second reason is that it seems that the metaphysical underpinnings for this corollary of IT must contain a metaphysics of goodness. I'm convinced that at least one of the accounts of the nature of goodness underlying ITBG is philosophically interesting and deserves careful attention quite apart from ITBG or medieval metaphysics (I briefly sketch it in Section 6 below).

Moreover, I focus on Albert the Great's statement and defense of ITBG in works written between ca. 1245 and 1250.[4] I choose Albert because his views seem to me to be in the mainstream of the long and rich tradition discussing these matters,[5] but also because one feature unique (so far as I can tell) to Albert's account is interestingly and instructively confused. I argue that Albert's confusion is at least in part a result of the radically different views thirteenth-century philosophers gleaned from the philosophical tradition to support ITBG.

My second purpose is to see what role IT plays in the doctrine of the transcendentals. I think it is sometimes thought that IT states or is equivalent to the doctrine of the transcendentals, but I argue that this assumption is mistaken. The doctrine of the transcendentals entails IT, but the converse is not true: commitment to IT does not require commitment to the doctrine of the transcendentals. I argue that, in the thirteenth century, radically different metaphysical views were appealed to in support of IT and that only some of those views require the transcendentality of the properties or terms that IT claims to be interchangeable. The wide acceptance of IT among thirteenth-century philosophers in fact masks deep metaphysical diversity in their views. Albert the Great's treatment of IT manifests this diversity.

Philip the Chancellor takes up ITBG explicitly in *Summa de bono* Q. 8, Alexander of Hales in *Summa theologica* 3.1.1.1 (Alexander 1924), and Aquinas in *DV* XXI.2 and *ST* Ia.5.3. For discussion of it with special reference to Aquinas, see Hoenes 1968 and Aertsen 1985.

4. The passages I will focus on are from *Super Dionysium De divinis nominibus* Chapter IV (Albert 1972); *Summa de bono* Treatise I, Question 1, Articles 1, 6, and 7 (Albert 1951); and *Commentarii in libros Sententiarum* Book I, Distinction 1, Question 20 (Albert 1893). All of these works date from 1245–50. I do not consider in any detail Albert's latest work (after 1270) on the transcendentals, viz., *Summa theologiae* Book I, Treatise 6, Questions 26–29 (Albert 1978). For the dating of Albert's works, see Weisheipl 1980b.

5. For Albert's place in the history of the discussion, see the references in n. 1 above and the Introduction in this volume.

1. The Aristotelian Backdrop

Lying behind IT and the particular arguments I discuss are at least two fundamental doctrines of Aristotelian metaphysics. I am not able to explain them fully or evaluate them here, but I do need to point them out and show their relation to IT.

The first is part of the Aristotelian doctrine of being. For the philosophers who maintain IT, its importance is not just that it shows a certain set of predicates to be interchangeable but that it shows certain predicates to be interchangeable with '*being*.' IT is part of an explanation of these other predicates ('one,' 'true,' and 'good'); and it functions as part of such an explanation because 'being,' that which 'one,' 'true,' and 'good' are claimed to be interchangeable with, is already understood.

Being has a unique, commonly recognized place in the Aristotelian classificatory scheme: everything that falls into the scheme at all falls under being. Individual primary substances, their species, genera, differentiae, and accidents (and the genera of accidents) are all beings. In order to be classifiable at all, a thing must be a being, and to say of a thing that it is a being is not to classify it but only to say that it is classifiable. Hence, being is not a particular kind of thing; the ten categories are the most fundamental kinds of being, the most basic ways in which to be. This is the sense in which being is a transcendental: it is not a classificatory notion; it applies to things in some sense prior to their classification into kinds, and so in the standard classificatory scheme it 'transcends' even the most basic categories.

It is worth making explicit two of the corollaries of this view that are significant for IT. First, it follows from the fact that being transcends the most basic categories that it cannot be explained in terms of or analyzed into anything more general or fundamental. Being is indefinable or unanalyzable strictly speaking because defining a thing consists in providing its genus (the larger kind to which it belongs) and differentia (the specifying characteristic that distinguishes it from other sorts of things within the genus). There is no larger kind to which beings, as such, belong and no possible characteristic that would carve out all and only beings from some larger kind. Second, it follows from being's 'transcendent' position in the Aristotelian classificatory scheme that it is universally predicable. Anything that can be classified at all must fall under being.

Viewed against this metaphysical backdrop, the doctrine of the transcendentals is a doctrine about where the predicates 'one,' 'true,' and 'good' should be located in the standard classificatory scheme. It is the view that these predicates are transcendental in the way that being is. If this doctrine can be established, the results might be expected to be significant. Are goodness and truth (for instance) also in some sense indefinable, unanalyzable, and universally predicable?

The second piece of Aristotelian metaphysics we need is the view that the notion of the good is equivalent to the notion of an end.[6] Since on this view a good is an end, a subsidiary good is just a subsidiary end or, as Albert prefers to say, what is ordered toward the (ultimate) end. Hence, anything that has the status of an end, either ultimate or subsidiary, is a good.

2. The Notion of Interchangeability: ITBG

I want to start out by looking at Albert's discussion of ITBG, the thesis that being and good are interchangeable. In contexts in which he is explaining or defending ITBG, Albert denies that the thesis is true in the unqualified version I have given: "It must be said that 'good' and 'being' can be considered in two ways, namely, intensionally (*secundum intentiones*) and extensionally (*secundum supposita*). If they are considered intensionally, they are not interchangeable. . . . If 'good' and 'being' are considered extensionally, however, they are indeed interchangeable" (*SENT* I.1.20).[7] ITBG, then, holds for 'being' and 'good' considered extensionally but not intensionally.

Given Albert's distinction between the intension and extension of the terms, it is tempting to take his qualified statement of ITBG as the claim that 'being' and 'good' are extensionally though not intensionally *equivalent.* We are unlikely to find worrisome Albert's claim that 'being' and 'good' differ intensionally, but before I leave it to pursue the interesting hypothesis that they are extensionally equivalent, I need to say a little more about it.

Albert claims that the concept of being is the most basic concept—in the sense that it cannot be analyzed into any other concepts of which it can be said to be composed—whereas the concept of good, like every other concept, presupposes the concept of being. "For the concept of being is the concept of the simplest thing, which is not analyzable into

6. For a discussion of this view in Aristotle, who is one of the main sources for the view in the Middle Ages, see MacDonald 1989a.
7. See also *SB* I.1.6.

anything that is conceptually prior to it. But good is analyzable into 'being ordered toward an end' (*ens relatum ad finem*)" (*SB* I.1.6). Albert's point is that in characterizing or conceptualizing anything merely as a being, one is characterizing it in the most basic and therefore most general way possible. The thing may also be characterized as a living thing, an animal, or a human being, for example, but these characterizations presuppose that the thing characterized is a being.

If the concept of being is unanalyzable and absolutely general, then all other concepts, including the concept of good, determine or add detail in some way to the concept of being; they contain the concept of being specified in some way or other. Albert tells us that the concept of good is to be analyzed as 'being ordered toward an end.'[8] The analysis of 'good' as 'being ordered toward an end' involves and is more detailed than the concept of being alone. Thus, it is a feature of this particular view of Albert's that characterizing something as good implies that it is a being, but not vice versa.[9]

It's clear, then, that at least as far as ITBG is concerned, 'interchangeable' does not mean something like 'interchangeable *salva veritate* in all contexts.' There will be opaque contexts in which 'being' and 'good' will not be interchangeable in this way because of the intensional or conceptual difference between them. So ITBG quite sensibly denies that 'being' and 'good' are synonyms.

Now, does 'interchangeable' mean something like 'extensionally equivalent'? Aristotle's use of 'interchangeable' suggests that it does.[10] He suggests that two propositions are interchangeable if each is a consequence of the other; that is, P and Q are interchangeable if P implies Q and Q implies P. We might suppose, then, that when Albert claims that 'being' and 'good' are interchangeable, he means that 'X is a being' implies 'X is good,' and vice versa.[11]

---

8. Strictly speaking, this is the concept only of created good. The notion of good is the notion of an end, and God is the ultimate end to which created good is subordinate: hence, created good is subordinate good, i.e., good ordered toward an end (viz., God).

9. Notice that this conclusion shows that even if good occupies a place in the classificatory scheme analogous to that occupied by being, good will not be 'unanalyzable' in the way that being is. The concept of being is the most general concept, and hence is unanalyzable, whereas all other concepts can be analyzed into being plus something else.

10. *Sophistici elenchi* 5 (167b1 ff.).

11. This seems to be the sense of 'interchangeable' expressed in the first objection of *SB* I.1.6, for example, and at least suggested by Albert's statement of part of his own position in the same article: "But if one considers 'good' and 'being' . . . extensionally, that is, if one considers that which is a being and that which is good, then 'good' and 'being' are interchangeable because there is nothing which is not good either perfectly or imperfectly."

His argument for the interchangeability of 'being' and 'good,' however, establishes not just coextension but necessary coextension. He clearly thinks that there is a necessary connection between being and goodness.

If 'good' and 'being' are considered extensionally, however, they are indeed interchangeable because, although 'good' is associated with an agent insofar as [the agent] is good and 'being' is associated with an agent insofar as [the agent] is a being, nevertheless good always accompanies being itself and is not extensionally separated from it (although it is conceptually separate) because an agent acts only for an intended good. (*SENT* I.1.20)[12]

Albert's view is that the concept of agency essentially involves both being and goodness: an agent is what has being and so is able to cause something else to have being, but an agent acts (causes something else to have being) only for some intended good. Though the agent's exercise of efficient causality explains the existence of the effect, appeal to some final cause is necessary to explain the agent's action.[13] All products of agency, then, can be viewed as the products of an efficient cause, and so as having being, and as the products of good-directed action, and so as good.

This general account of agency raises at least two serious worries. First, it relies on a dubious assumption about universal teleology; and second, it clearly does not follow from the fact that an agent acts for the sake of some good that the effect of the agent's action can be viewed as good. But such worries can be left aside here since the only instance of agency Albert needs for his defense of ITBG is God's act of creation.[14] God can be supposed always to act for the sake of some perceived good, and since God can neither misperceive the goodness of an intended state of affairs nor fail to realize the good he intends, it follows that what God brings about is good. Hence, all products of God's agency, at least, can be viewed as good, that is, as ordered appropriately with respect to God's end in acting. And since Albert believes that necessarily everything that has being (other than God) is a product of God's

12. See also *SB* I.1.7, where Albert employs the same sort of argument and then concludes: "being good is not the same as being but is a *necessary consequent* of being, which is separable from it only conceptually."

13. Medieval philosophers often refer to the final cause as the cause of causes, meaning that the final cause has explanatory priority over the other three Aristotelian causes: the final cause explains the action of the efficient cause, which imparts form to matter.

14. Albert does seem to want to make the universal claim, however.

act of creation, it follows that everything is good. Necessarily, every-thing that can be considered a being, then, can also be considered good.

We are accustomed, of course, to explanations of the *existence* of things other than God that refer to God's causal activity—that is, to his efficient causality; Albert's point is that the fact that God acts as an efficient cause necessarily implies that there is an intended good or final cause, and so things other than God can be viewed in relation to final as well as efficient causality. Hence, 'good' refers to precisely the things to which 'being' refers and does so in virtue of the conceptual connection between being and goodness located in the concept of agency.

I call this account of the relation between being and goodness the *Agency Account*. The Agency Account, then, is Albert's argument for ITBG, and it shows that for Albert 'interchangeable' means 'necessarily coextensive.' When Albert asserts ITBG on the basis of the Agency Account, he is asserting the necessary coextension of 'being' and 'good,' and henceforth I understand ITBG as the thesis that 'being' and 'good' are necessarily coextensive.

I have been focusing on the way the Agency Account supports ITBG, but in fact three of the four transcendentals—truth as well as being and goodness—can be obtained by means of the Agency Account. God's act of creation is the relevant instance of agency, and, as in all cases of agency, one can distinguish the efficient, formal, and final causes involved.[15] Created things, then, can be considered as the products of efficient causality (and hence as beings), as the products of formal causality (and hence as appropriately related to the divine ideas, and so true), and as the products of final causality (and hence as appropriately related to the divine end, and so good).[16] Solely as a result of their being created, then, created things can correctly be considered as true and good.[17]

15. There is no material cause, of course, in the case of God's act of creation.
16. Transcendental truth is, at least primarily, a property of things rather than propositions (though propositions might be one kind of thing). We do sometimes use expressions like 'true friend,' 'true scholar,' 'true competitor' where 'true' is synonymous with 'genuine' or 'real.' The idea behind the part of the Agency Account having to do with truth is that any oak tree, for instance, that corresponds in the right way with the divine idea of an oak tree is true (a true oak tree).
17. The Agency Account is also at the center of Philip the Chancellor's theory of the transcendentals, and a version of it is used by Thierry of Chartres in the twelfth century to try to explain Boethius's claim that all substances are good in virtue of the fact that they have being. See Philip's *Summa de bono* Q. 7 (Philip 1985) and Thierry of Chartres's *Commentary on De hebdomadibus* (Thierry 1971, pp. 405–35).

3. The Agency Account and the Metaphysics of Goodness

ITBG asserts the necessary coextension of 'being' and 'good,' and so given the doctrine of being sketched in Section 1, it entails the universal predicability of 'good.' But there are two important issues about which ITBG is silent. First, it gives us no reason to suppose that good is a transcendental, if transcendentality involves not being subsumable under any of the Aristotelian categories. Transcendentality entails universal predicability, but the converse entailment does not hold since it is at least possible that some property in some particular category characterizes everything that exists.[18] So even if 'good' is necessarily coextensive with 'being,' it does not follow that good is transcendental in the way that being is. Second, ITBG doesn't seem to offer or require a particular account of the nature of goodness. The assertion that 'good' is necessarily coextensive with 'being' leaves open the question of the sort of property goodness is. One might suspect that settling this second matter is a necessary condition for settling the first: explaining the transcendentality of goodness involves, at least in part, an account of the nature of goodness.

That ITBG requires no particular account of the nature of goodness can be seen by noticing that two radically different sorts of account are compatible with it. On the one hand, the property of being good might consist in some monadic property (or set of properties) intrinsic to good things. Someone committed to this view of the nature of goodness can accept the Agency Account, according to which all things can be considered good by virtue of being objects of God's choice, by understanding God's choice of some object as indicative (though not constitutive) of that object's goodness. On an objectivist view of this sort, things are good in virtue of their monadic properties, and so independently of God's choosing to create them. Nevertheless, God, in his goodness, omnipotence, and omniscience, would choose to create only good things; and so it follows from the fact that some object has been created by God that it is good.

Albert, in fact, entertains and rejects an account of this sort.[19] The specific account he rejects maintains that goodness is a form inherent in good things. He rejects it not because he thinks it incompatible with the Agency Account, however, but because he takes it to be an inadequate

18. I discuss this possibility in MacDonald 1989a.
19. In *DN*—see Section 5 below.

independent account of goodness. I return to Albert's discussion of this rival account in Section 5.

On the other hand, one might take the property of being good to be not an intrinsic, monadic property of things but a purely relational property. A well-known version of this type of account is the view that the property of being good just is the property of being the object of some choice or some act of valuing. A medieval subjectivist who supposes that the relevant choice or act of valuing is God's might combine this sort of theological subjectivism with the Agency Account to get an account according to which all things can be considered good because all existing things are objects of God's choice. On this account, all created things are objects of God's choice, and being the object of God's choice is just what it is for created things to be good.

If accounts of the nature of goodness as different as these are compatible with ITBG, Albert's own metaphysics of goodness is virtually unrestrained by anything we have seen so far. I argue that Albert is in fact pulled in the directions of *both* of the radically different sorts of account I've just sketched; that is, I argue that he commits himself to *both* the view that goodness is a property (or set of properties) intrinsic to good things *and* the view that it is a relational property entirely extrinsic to good things. So Albert has *two* metaphysics of goodness. This is the interesting confusion in Albert's account I alluded to above. First, I show that Albert is confused in this way, and then I suggest how he might have fallen into such a confusion.

In his commentary on pseudo-Dionysius's *Divine Names* Albert raises the question "Does 'good' add any reality (*res*) to 'being'?" and in discussing it he sketches the main lines of an account of the nature of goodness. Here is his direct answer to the question: "We say, however, that 'good' adds no reality to 'being' (*ens*); thus, the goodness of a thing is its being (*essentia*)—truth and unity are of this sort too—but [goodness, truth, and unity] add only a mode of signifying. Thus, goodness is [merely] being (*ens*) signified under another concept" (*DN* IV, pp. 115–16). I call the view that 'good' adds no reality, but only a mode of signifying, to 'being' Albert's *No Reality Thesis*. What does he mean when he says that 'good' adds no *reality* to 'being' but adds only a *mode of signifying*?

Different modes of signifying seem to be different ways of characterizing or conceiving of one and the same thing. The descriptions 'living thing,' 'green tree,' 'tree on the riverbank,' and 'tree I'm now thinking of' are all ways of characterizing the tree outside my window and hence are all modes of signifying it. According to Albert, however, not all modes of signifying are on a par, and he offers the following taxonomy:

But there are two modes [of signifying]. [1] One of them is based on negation, and it does not introduce anything in reality but only conceptually (*in ratione*), for negation belongs to reason not to nature. 'One' (*unum*) adds this mode [of signifying] to 'being,' for 'one' is '[being] undivided in itself and divided from others.' . . . [2] But there is a mode [of signifying] based on affirmation, and there are two sorts [of this mode of signifying]. [2a] One is based on absolute affirmation, and this sort introduces something in reality, as 'white man' adds a mode [of signifying] *and* a certain reality to 'man.' [2b] But there is a mode based on affirmation relative to something extrinsic, and there are two sorts [of this mode of signifying]. [2b'] There is the sort of relation that comes to hold [of a thing] as a result of a change in that thing—for example, paternity and sonship—and relations of this sort are real, and the mode [of signifying] based on the affirmation of such relations adds something in reality. [2b''] But there are relations which do not come to hold [of a thing] as a result of a change in the thing but rather from a change in something else—for example, [the relation of] being-to-the-right is caused in an immobile column by the motion of a man—and such relations are conceptual rather than real. . . . 'True' and 'good' add to 'being' in the manner based on relations of this second sort [viz., 2b'']; for one calls [something] true in virtue of a relation to an idea, and one calls [something] good in virtue of a relation to an agent moved by its goodness as an end. (*DN* IV, pp. 115–16)

This classification seems not to be a classification of modes of signifying as such, but of the ways in which a more determinate or specific mode of signifying can be related to the less determinate or more general mode of signifying which it determines. Assuming that Albert intends the taxonomy to be exhaustive, the main claim seems to be this:

If x and y are two modes of signifying the same object O, and x (or the correct analysis of x) contains y (or the correct analysis of y) as a proper part, then x either:
(1) merely denies something of O conceived of as y,
(2a) affirms something F of O conceived of as y, where F is a real monadic property,
(2b') affirms that O conceived of as y stands in some relation R, where R is a real relation, or
(2b'') affirms that O conceived of as y stands in some relation R, where R is a merely conceptual relation.

Albert intends these distinctions to make the general point that not all modes of signifying that specify some more general mode of signifying are *ontologically* on a par. Types (2a) and (2b′) require a sort of ontological grounding that types (1) and (2b″) do not. Put more carefully, not every mode of signifying, *x*, that signifies some object *O* and is constructed on the basis of (specifies or determines) another mode of signifying, *y*, that signifies *O* requires some ontological basis additional to what is required by *y* in order to signify *O* successfully. Only when *x* is such that (2a) or (2b′) is the case does *x* require any ontological ground beyond that required by *y*. (1) and (2b″) do not require any such ontological ground. As Albert puts it, every mode of signifying, *x*, that determines or specifies another mode, *y*, "adds a mode of signifying"; only some, however, also "add a reality." A couple of examples will help to clarify the point.

Let *x* be 'white man,' as in Albert's own example, and let *y* be 'man.' Socrates, let's say, can be considered either as a man or, more specifically, as a white man. In this case 'white man,' if it succeeds in signifying Socrates, requires not only that Socrates be a man but also that the real property or nature whiteness inhere in Socrates. Of course, when we characterize Socrates merely as a man, we make no claims beyond the claim that the nature humanity is instantiated in Socrates. So 'white man' introduces a feature of reality that 'man' does not; it commits us to whiteness as well as humanity.

Now let *x* be 'nonwhite man' and *y* be 'man.' In this case *x* specifies *y* in some sense; *x* is more determinate than *y*. But 'nonwhite man' does not determine 'man' by introducing some feature of reality, as 'white man' does, because there is no such nature or real property as nonwhiteness. Characterizing Socrates as a nonwhite man does not tell us what natures are instantiated in Socrates other than humanity; it does not attribute any particular real property to Socrates beyond humanity.[20]

Thus, Albert's claim that 'good' adds only a mode of signifying but not any reality to 'being' is the claim that the mode of signifying 'good' determines or specifies the mode of signifying 'being' but does not do so by introducing a feature of reality or requiring an ontological ground beyond that involved in 'being.' Albert tells us that 'good' can be analyzed as 'being ordered toward an end,' and this latter mode of signifying is related to the mode of signifying 'being' in the manner described by (2b″) in the taxonomy; that is, 'good' is a more determi-

---

20. I take it that the surface structure of a mode of signifying might not represent its deep structure. For example, 'blind man' bears a surface resemblance to 'white man,' but blindness, unlike whiteness, is a privation, not a real nature. Thus, 'blind man' is a mode of signifying of type (1) rather than type (2a). No interesting questions about what predicates correspond to real natures are settled by this taxonomy.

nate mode of signifying some object than 'being' is, but only in virtue of affirming a merely conceptual relation of the object. Hence, 'good' adds no reality to 'being.'

Albert's view regarding the nature of goodness, then, is not simply that goodness is the relational property of being ordered toward an end. On Albert's account, that relational 'property' is merely conceptual, and so there isn't any such *nature* as being ordered toward an end. Albert seems to be claiming that anything *can be considered* or *can be signified* as ordered toward an end (in virtue of having been created by God) but there is no nature, no ontological foundation, in the things so considered or signified beyond that in virtue of which they are beings.[21]

For our purposes, the crucial part of the theory expressed by the No Reality Thesis is the distinction between real and merely conceptual relations, for Albert's claim that good adds no reality to being depends on his construing goodness as a merely conceptual rather than a real relation. Before going any further we need to see what that distinction comes to.

4. Real and Merely Conceptual Relations

The principle of the distinction between real and merely conceptual relations as it is introduced in the passage I quoted above is not something having to do with the relation as such but with the way in which the relation comes to hold of a given thing.[22] If a given relation comes to hold of a particular subject because of a change in that subject, the relation is real; if it comes to hold of a particular subject when there has been no change in that subject, the relation is merely conceptual.[23]

---

21. Both Philip the Chancellor and Aquinas adopt a strategy similar to Albert's; viz., they explain the transcendentals other than being as involving *merely conceptual* rather than real specifications of being—see Philip's *Summa de bono* Q. 7 and Aquinas's *DV* I.1 and XXI.1—though Aquinas understands merely conceptual relations differently (see nn. 22 and 23 below).

22. Henninger 1987 and 1989 provide some background to the medieval discussion of real relations and contain useful discussion of Aquinas's distinction between real and merely conceptual relations.

23. This condition of a relation's being a real relation distinguishes Albert's position from Aquinas's. Aquinas is willing to allow that some relations that come to hold of a subject even when the subject itself remains unchanged are real relations—see Henninger 1987, pp. 499–504, and Aquinas's texts cited in Henninger's notes.

Albert's example of the relation of being-to-the-right-of coming to hold of an immobile column in virtue of a man's walking up beside it is like Boethius's example of one man

It appears to follow from the distinction's being based on the way in which the relation comes to hold of a subject that, at least for some kinds of relations, it is particular instances of relations rather than universals that are being distinguished. Albert's example of the relation of being-to-the-right-of coming to hold of the immobile column illustrates this point. Being-to-the-right-of is a merely conceptual relation with respect to the column because it comes to hold of the column when a man walks up beside it without the column's having changed. But, though Albert does not make this claim explicitly, the same universal, being-to-the-right-of, would be a real relation with respect to the man, if he were to walk round to the other side of the column, because the relation comes to hold of him in virtue of a change in the man himself. So it must be particular instances of the relation of being-to-the-right-of which are real or merely conceptual depending on how they come to hold of a given subject. For certain other kinds of relations, such as the relation of being-thought-of, however, every instance seems to be merely conceptual with respect to the thing thought of. It is always because of a change in the thinker and not in the thing thought of that a thing comes to be thought of.

These same considerations show that a given relation's being real or merely conceptual is relative to the relatum to which the relation is being ascribed. In Albert's example, being-to-the-right-of is a merely conceptual relation with respect to the column, but presumably being-to-the-left-of is a real relation with respect to the man who walks up

walking up beside another: "Suppose that someone is stationary. Then if I were to go up to him on his right side, he will be to-the-left compared to me, not because he is himself to-the-left but because I have gone up to him on his right. And further, if I go up to him on his left, he will then be to-the-right, not because he is to-the-right in himself (as he is pale or tall) but he comes to be to-the-right by virtue of my going up to him, and what he is [viz., to-the-right] is from me and by virtue of me and not at all by virtue of himself" (*De Trinitate* 5). But Albert's point is slightly different from Boethius's. Boethius intends to be drawing a distinction between predicates in the first three categories (substance, quantity, and quality) and the remaining seven (including the category of relation). Predicates in the former group characterize their subject intrinsically whereas predicates in the latter group (including relations) characterize their subject(s) only extrinsically. For discussion of Boethius's use of this distinction, see Stump 1983 and MacDonald 1988. Albert is drawing a distinction between two kinds of relations, both of which would fall into Boethius's second group.

Albert's distinction is closer to one of the distinctions Aristotle draws (e.g., in *Metaphysics* V.15) among kinds of relations (or relatives). Aristotle distinguishes between relatives such as measure and what-is-measurable and thought and what-is-thinkable and other kinds of relatives. In the case of the other kinds of relatives, each relative can be said to depend on the other for its being a relative; in the case of the relatives such as thought and what-is-thinkable, the latter relative depends on the former for its being a relative, though not vice versa.

beside the column. Similarly, being-thought-of is a merely conceptual relation with respect to the thing thought of by me though thinking-of is a real relation with respect to me. These relations, then, are asymmetrical with respect to their reality.

With these points in mind, we can make a first attempt at a partial analysis of Albert's conception of a merely conceptual relation:[24]

I. R is a *merely conceptual* relation with respect to subject s if for some y
   (a) sRy; and
   (b) s came to stand in R to y solely in virtue of y's changing.

The corresponding conception of a real relation would be:

I*. R is a *real* relation with respect to subject s if for some y
   (a) sRy; and
   (b) s came to stand in R to y in virtue of s's changing.

Of course, this analysis will not do because the notion of change used in condition (b) is ambiguous in this context. If there are real and merely conceptual relations, then presumably there are corresponding real and merely conceptual changes. In Albert's example the immobile column *does* come to be to the right of the man in virtue of a change in the column: the column changes from not being to the right of the man to being to the right of the man. But presumably Albert would want to call this a merely conceptual change in the column for the same reasons he wants to call the relation in which the column comes to stand a merely conceptual relation.

The general idea behind Albert's distinction seems to be that the ontological ground for some relations is located in only one of the relata.[25] A relation of this sort is real with respect to the relatum in which the relation is grounded but merely conceptual with respect to the other relatum. It seems to be properties *other* than the relation itself that constitute the relation's ground in the relevant relatum: thus, the man's spatial location grounds his spatial relations to the column, and my mental states ground certain intentional relations holding between me and other things.[26] A relation is merely conceptual with respect to

24. I take these analyses to offer only sufficient conditions for a relation's being merely conceptual or real, respectively.
25. See Albert's *Metaphysica* Bk. 5, t. 3, ch. 8 (Albert 1960, p. 270, ll. 28ff.).
26. Actually, the case of the man's being to the right of the column is more complicated than Albert indicates because x's being to the *right* of y in a given case depends on either x's or y's having right and left sides (for example, a man, who has a right and left hand) or

some subject, then, if the relation comes to hold of the subject solely in virtue of a change in the *other* properties of the other relatum. But in order to capture this idea in our analysis, we have to find a way to characterize these other properties.

Suppose we start with the distinction between a thing's intrinsic and extrinsic properties. Medieval philosophers, following Boethius, took this to be a distinction between properties falling in the first three Aristotelian categories (substance, quantity, and quality) and properties falling in the remaining seven.[27] For example, properties such as being a human being (the category of substance), being six feet tall (quantity), and being pale (quality) characterize their subjects intrinsically, whereas properties such as being in the marketplace (the category of place) characterize their subjects only extrinsically. A distinction along these lines seems intuitively clear though it is notoriously difficult to state precisely. We might say roughly that a thing's intrinsic properties are those properties of the thing we can discover by inspecting only the thing itself, and that a thing's extrinsic properties are those properties of it that are not intrinsic.

Given this distinction between types of properties, we might suppose that relations of the relevant sort are grounded in the *intrinsic* properties of only one of the relata. We could then say that a relation is merely conceptual with respect to some subject if the ontological ground for the relation is not in the subject itself but in the other relatum. We might put it as follows:

II. R is a *merely conceptual* relation with respect to subject s if for some y
  (a) sRy; and
  (b) s came to stand in R to y solely in virtue of y's acquiring some intrinsic property or properties.

Similarly, we might say that a relation is real with respect to some subject if (at least part of) the ontological ground for the relation's coming to hold is in the subject itself. Thus:

---

the case's being described from a particular point of view, in which case the relation becomes triadic rather than diadic. So the ground for the relation of being-to-the-right-of in the case described is not just the man's spatial location but also the man's having a right and left hand. The case of a tree growing up beside the column illustrates the point: an attribution to the column of the relation of being to the right of the tree would presuppose a particular point of view since neither the tree nor the column has a right and left side intrinsically. Aquinas notices this—see *Super Sent.* I, d. 1, q. 26, a. 2.

27. See n. 23 above.

II*. R is a *real* relation with respect to subject *s* if for some *y*
   (*a*) *sRy*; and
   (*b*) *s* came to stand in *R* to *y* (at least partly) in virtue of *s*'s acquiring some intrinsic property or properties.

The problem with (II) and (II*) is that condition (*b*) in each is now too restrictive. According to (II), being-to the-right-of will fail to be a merely conceptual relation with respect to the column because it comes to hold of the column solely in virtue of a change in the man's spatial location, which is an *extrinsic* property of the man.[28] Being-the-father-of, Albert's example of a real relation, will fail to satisfy (II*) for a similar reason. It doesn't seem to be the case that being-the-father-of comes to hold of someone in virtue of some particular change in the intrinsic properties of that person. What's crucial is the causing, and it's plausible to suppose that the causing just is the coming to be a father.

What seems to be important in the types of changes Albert seems to have in mind is that one of the relata *does* something or has something *done* to it, that is, exercises some active or passive capacity.[29] The man who walks up beside the column exercises his natural capacity for local motion, and his change in spatial location is a direct result of that exercise. The man who becomes a father exercises his natural capacity to procreate.[30] If we allow a distinction between a thing's intrinsic and extrinsic *capacities* analogous to the distinction between a thing's intrinsic and extrinsic properties, then I think the following analyses will work.

III. R is a *merely conceptual* relation with respect to subject *s* if for some *y*
   (*a*) *sRy*; and
   (*b*) *s* came to stand in *R* to *y* solely in virtue of (i) *y*'s acquiring some intrinsic property or properties, or (ii) *y*'s exercising some intrinsic capacity or capacities.

---

28. Though the man's having a right and left hand is intrinsic to him—see n. 26 above.

29. Aristotle says that relatives such as father and son, what heats and what is heatable (relatives with respect to capacity) are related in virtue of the actual functioning of the capacity on the part of the one and the actual being affected as a result of that functioning on the part of the other. The relative that is active (the father, what heats) has an intrinsic active capacity; the relative that is the recipient of the action (the son, what is heatable) has an intrinsic passive capacity. See *Metaphysics* V.15 (1021a14 ff.). When I speak generally of a thing's exercising a capacity, I intend 'exercising a capacity' to cover the exercise of either an active or a passive capacity.

30. The *son* does not exercise a capacity in becoming a son. Nevertheless, there is a natural potentiality intrinsic to the matter that develops into the son.

III*. R is a *real* relation with respect to subject s if for some y
  (*a*) sRy; and
  (*b*) s came to stand in R to y (at least partly) in virtue of (i) s's acquiring some intrinsic property or properties, or (ii) s's exercising some intrinsic capacity or capacities.

(III) seems to account for cases such as being-to-the-right-of holding of an immobile column and being-thought-of holding of the tree outside my window while ruling out paradigm real relations such as being-to-the-left-of holding of the man who walks up beside the column and being-the-father-of holding of some person. (III*) allows these paradigm real relations.

(III) and (III*) highlight the intuitions behind the distinction between real and merely conceptual relations central to Albert's No Reality Thesis and clarify the sort of claim Albert is making when he maintains that goodness is a merely conceptual relation. A thing is good in virtue of being ordered toward an end, and this is a merely conceptual relation—understood in terms of (III)—with respect to that thing. So Albert must think that there is no ontological ground for the relation in the thing itself; the thing stands in the relation solely in virtue of some property or activity of the other relatum. According to the Agency Account, each thing is ordered (by God) toward God's end in creating that thing, so the other relatum in this case is God's end. Each thing can be considered as ordered toward an end (and so as good) solely in virtue of some property of God, viz., God's having it as an end, and not in virtue of any of its own properties.[31] The ground of the relation of being ordered toward an end is to be located in the agent who has the end, not in the thing viewed as ordered toward the end.

5. Albert's Rejection of an Alternative Account

The evidence I've adduced so far seems to me to show that in the text we've looked at Albert takes the property of being good to be a special

31. Application of III* to cases in which God is the subject (e.g., being-the-creator-of) might seem to have the result that many relations are real with respect to God—a result Albert, like Aquinas, would find unacceptable. But if God is eternal and purely actual (as Albert supposes) and if conditions (bi) and (bii) of III* are taken as implying *change* in s (as Albert's original statement of the criterion that (bi) and (bii) are intended to explicate suggests they should), then a case in which God is subject of the relation will never satisfy III*. If God is eternal and purely actual, he will be active but immutable, and so it is impossible that some relation come to hold of God in virtue of a change in God himself.

sort of relational property that holds of good things independently of whatever intrinsic properties they may have. Albert's reply to a rival account of goodness confirms this conclusion.

The rival view maintains that "'good' adds something to 'being,' i.e., a kind of form participated from the goodness of the first cause," and that "one does not call [some subject] good in virtue of a relation to something extrinsic [to it] but in virtue of some form inhering in the subject" (*DN* IV, pp. 115–16). This rival view denies the No Reality Thesis because it maintains that 'good' adds a reality—a kind of form—to 'being' but is compatible with ITBG as long as it holds that every being has this form. Albert replies to it as follows:

That [Albert's own theory] is true is clear from Boethius's *De hebdomadibus*, for [Boethius] says that if one imagines for a little while that the first cause is not good and yet exists, the existing effects [of the first cause] will certainly exist and be white, etc., but none of them can be conceived of as being good.[32] But if goodness were some absolute form inhering in the effect, good *could* be conceived of in it. For example, heat [can be conceived of] in the air even when [the air] is separated in thought from the fire [which heats it]. It is because one [of two] relatives cannot be conceived of apart from the other that good cannot be conceived of in the effects without [conceiving of] good in the cause. (*DN* IV, pp. 115–16)

The argument contained in this passage seems to be this:

(1) If goodness were an intrinsic (monadic) property in a created thing, the conceptual removal of the goodness of the creator would not affect the goodness of the created thing.

(2) But an otherwise good created thing would *not* be good if the goodness of the creator were conceptually removed.

∴(3) Goodness cannot be an intrinsic (monadic) property of a created thing.

Premise (2) is supposed to be the result of Boethius's thought experiment.[33] Albert explains this result by pointing out that, given the conditions stipulated by the experiment, created things cannot be good because goodness is a relational property one relatum of which is God's goodness, the final cause of God's creative activity; if one relatum of the relation is removed, the relational property no longer holds of the other relatum.

32. For Boethius's text, see the Appendix to this volume, lines 80–111.
33. Albert has actually misrepresented Boethius's thought experiment and got Boethius's point wrong. I will not discuss this historical confusion here. For a discussion of Boethius's thought experiment and its context, see MacDonald 1988.

Notice that this use of the thought experiment does not depend on understanding goodness as a *merely conceptual* relation (as Albert does) but only as a relational property of some sort or other. Albert makes the general claim that one cannot conceive of one relatum as characterized by a relation without conceiving of the other relatum, and this claim, if true, appears to be true for all relations, real and merely conceptual. So one will agree with Albert about the results of the thought experiment even if one holds (contra Albert) that goodness is a real relational property.[34]

Now, whatever we think of this argument, it at least makes quite clear that Albert is maintaining that goodness is a relational property and one that a created thing may gain or lose without undergoing any change in its intrinsic properties. So the argument based on Boethius's thought experiment has the same result as Albert's account of 'good' as expressing a merely conceptual relation.

But the argument seems to me to be entirely unpersuasive; we are not likely to accept Albert's claims about the results of the thought experiment unless we are already convinced that goodness is a relational property. I think, along with many recent philosophers who have maintained that goodness is a property that supervenes on natural properties, that the thought experiment returns a different result than the one Albert claims. Given two worlds w_1 and w_2 and a created thing S that exists in both w_1 and w_2, if no intrinsic features differentiate S in w_2 from S in w_1, then S must be good in both worlds if good in either. This is an intuition, not an argument, but it is an intuition Albert's argument does nothing to dislodge.

6. A Moderate View: The Same Reality Thesis

The view that goodness is a merely conceptual relational property is an extreme version of the No Reality Thesis entailing what I take to be counterintuitive judgments of the sort Albert makes in the proposed thought experiment. But Albert sometimes seems to maintain a more moderate and, in my view, more interesting position that can accommodate the intuition that a thing's goodness is dependent in some way on the thing's intrinsic properties. Albert suggests the view while introduc-

---

34. In MacDonald 1988 I argue that Boethius himself accepts a relational account of goodness (he does not distinguish real and merely conceptual relations). Cf. Chapters 2 and 3 below.

ing the No Reality Thesis in the passage I've already quoted: "We say, however, that 'good' adds no reality to 'being' (*ens*); thus, the goodness of a thing is its being (*essentia*)—truth and unity are of this sort too—but [goodness, truth, and unity] add only a mode of signifying. Thus, goodness is [merely] being (*ens*) signified under another concept" (*DN* IV, pp. 115–16). After stating the first half of the thesis—that 'good' adds no reality to 'being'—Albert draws an interesting inference: "thus, the goodness of a thing is its being." As Albert goes on to develop the thesis in the passages we've already looked at, he seems entirely to neglect this identity claim and to develop instead the sort of merely conceptual relational account of goodness I laid out in Section 4 above. The identity claim, however, entails a different account.

The identity claim is that the nature of goodness is to be identified with certain other natures, viz., the natures in virtue of which a thing has being (whatever those are). I state it as follows and call it the *Same Reality Thesis*: The very natures in virtue of which a given thing is a being are the same as the natures in virtue of which it is good. The Same Reality Thesis entails the first half of the No Reality Thesis: that good adds no reality to being. Good *adds* no reality to being because the natures in virtue of which a thing is good are the same natures or realities as those in virtue of which it is a being; no realities or natures beyond those in virtue of which the thing is a being are required to account for its being good.

One gets a different explanation of the No Reality Thesis on the view that goodness is a merely conceptual relational property. According to that view, good adds no *reality* to being because goodness is a purely extrinsic relational property. So the No Reality Thesis is open to two different interpretations, along the lines of these two different accounts of the nature of goodness.

Furthermore, if we make the plausible supposition that at least some of the natures in virtue of which a thing is a being are intrinsic to the thing, then it is clear that the Same Reality Thesis is incompatible with the view that goodness is a merely conceptual relational property. On the latter view, the ontological ground of a thing's goodness is entirely extrinsic to the thing itself; on the Same Reality Thesis, a thing's goodness consists at least in part in properties intrinsic to the thing itself. Given Boethius's thought experiment, the two views will return contradictory results. Albert cannot *consistently* maintain both.

I have suggested that Albert has reason to be attracted by the merely conceptual relational account of goodness because of his views that the concept of good is the concept of being ordered toward an end and that being ordered toward an end is a merely conceptual relation. But why should he be attracted to the Same Reality Thesis? Why should he introduce his No Reality Thesis with the provocative parenthetical assertion of the Same Reality Thesis and then go on to develop an account of goodness incompatible with that thesis?

In another context, Albert develops an argument that would explain his commitment to the Same Reality Thesis. That other context is not a discussion of the relation between being and goodness but of goodness itself. The question being discussed is "What is the Good?" (*SB* I.1.1). Albert offers an argument that can be formulated as follows:

(1) A thing's being perfected is its being completed with respect to its end.
(2) A thing's being good is its having the essential character of its end.
∴(3) A thing's being good is its being perfected.
(4) A thing's being perfected is its having actuality conjoined with potentiality.
∴(5) A thing's being good is its having actuality conjoined with potentiality.[35]

A complete explanation of the premises of this tersely stated argument would require a story much longer that I can tell here;[36] I want only to suggest a couple of its more important features that show its relation to the Same Reality Thesis.

First, the notion of an end at work in this argument—premises (1) and (2)—is the notion of a thing's completed state. What constitutes a thing's completed state is determined by the thing's nature since its completed state is the state in virtue of which it is capable of performing the activity characteristic of things of that nature. A thing's nature gives the thing a set of potentialities that, when actualized, enable the thing to perform the activity characteristic of things with that nature.

Second, when Albert says that a thing is perfected in virtue of having actuality conjoined with potentiality—premise (4), he is claiming that a thing is perfected as a thing of its kind in virtue of having actualized the potentialities that specify things of that kind. Supposing that a thing's having actualized these potentialities can be a matter of degree, it fol-

---

35. "Every perfected thing, considered as such, has been completed with respect to an end; every good is good in virtue of [having] the character (*ratio*) of an end; therefore every good, considered as such, has been perfected. . . . Every perfected thing has perfection in virtue of [having] actuality conjoined with potentiality; and [so] good, in virtue of the fact that it is good, is a conjunction of actuality with potentiality" (*SB* I.1.1).

36. In MacDonald forthcoming(b) I discuss this argument in greater detail. For a detailed discussion of an argument in Aquinas (*ST* Ia.5.1) very much like this, see Chapters 2 and 4 below.

lows that a thing is perfected (and so good) as a thing of its kind to the extent to which it has actualized these potentialities.

Now, Albert thinks that a thing is a being (has being in actuality) in virtue of having actualized the potentialities that specify it.[37] So the state in virtue of which a thing is a being is precisely the same state as that in virtue of which the thing is perfected or good. It follows, then, that one and the same set of properties, the properties in virtue of which a thing is in a state of having actualized its specifying potentialities to some extent, constitutes both its being and its goodness.

This sort of theory, if true, would justify the identity claim we have seen Albert making: the goodness of a thing *is* its being. It would also justify our intuition that a thing's goodness is dependent on its intrinsic properties and so yield a different response to Boethius's thought experiment than Albert in fact makes. The properties in virtue of which a thing is good are the same as those in virtue of which the thing has being, and so a created thing will be good as long as the thing itself exists (has being), regardless of whether we are simultaneously conceiving of the goodness of the creator.[38]

So Albert endorses, on one occasion within the space of a few paragraphs, two radically different metaphysical accounts of goodness, the merely conceptual relational account and the account represented by the Same Reality Thesis.

7. ITBG and Albert's Two Accounts of Goodness

Now, our discussion of these accounts started from ITBG and the Agency Account, so I want to make explicit the relations among them that have emerged. The merely conceptual relational account of goodness is compatible with the Agency Account and together with it entails ITBG. It does not entail ITBG by itself. On the merely conceptual

37. "Being in actuality is in virtue of having actuality undivided from potentiality" (*SB* I.1.1).

38. This sort of theory would also constitute one way of specifying what philosophers could mean by calling goodness a supervenient property. On this theory the property of being good, for a given kind of thing, is identical with the set of properties that constitutes that kind of thing's being. But since this set will be different for different kinds of things, the property of being good is not identical with any single property or set of properties. Hence, goodness is dependent on the intrinsic properties of good things but is not identical with any single property or set of properties of those things. For a useful discussion of the supervenience of goodness, see Campbell and Pargetter 1986 and Chapter 4 below.

relational account (supplemented with the Agency Account), goodness is an absolutely universal characteristic of things, but it's not clear that it's a transcendental in the strict sense. Being is a transcendental in the strict sense because it transcends all the categories (and it is absolutely universal for *that* reason). But merely conceptual relations might be thought to fall under one of the categories—the category of relation—and so fail to be transcendental.[39] Some merely conceptual relations, such as goodness, happen to be universally predicable for the reasons specified by the Agency Account, but these reasons are extrinsic to the account of goodness itself.

The Same Reality Thesis, like the merely conceptual relational account, is compatible with the Agency Account, and so Albert could retain the Agency Account even if he were to reject his apparently preferred explanation of it in terms of the view that goodness is a merely conceptual relational property. But, unlike the view that goodness is a merely conceptual relational property, the Same Reality Thesis by itself entails ITBG: if the natures in virtue of which a thing is good are the same as those in virtue of which it is a being, 'good' and 'being' are necessarily coextensive. Because the Same Reality Thesis entails ITBG, Albert doesn't need the Agency Account as support for ITBG; he can have ITBG with or without the Agency Account. And since the Same Reality Thesis can be divorced from the Agency Account, it has the virtue of offering an account of goodness which is atheological (in the sense that it doesn't require reference to God). Furthermore, that thesis clearly makes goodness a transcendental. Being is a transcendental, for the reasons given, and the properties in virtue of which a thing is good are the same as those in virtue of which that thing has being.

I conclude, then, that Albert is confused. The accounts of goodness represented by the Same Reality Thesis and the merely conceptual relational account are different, incompatible accounts.

I think there are two separate *philosophical* explanations of his confusion. First, the notion of an end is central to Albert's arguments, but in different contexts 'end' has different referents. In the context of the Agency Account 'end' refers to God's intended end in creating, the end moving God to create. Thus, when Albert says that for created things 'good' is to be analyzed as 'being ordered toward an end' and that all created things are ordered toward an end, he means that all created

---

39. One might also suppose that only real relations fall under the category of relation. This seems to be Aquinas's view: he claims that nonreal relations can run through all being, though it's not clear that this is the same as claiming that they are transcendental—see *DV* XXI.1.ad3.

things are appropriately related to God's end in creating. This sort of end is clearly extrinsic to the created thing. But in the argument that I claim (in Section 6) lies behind the Same Reality Thesis, Albert is talking about the end that is the completed state of a thing with a particular nature. Hence, a thing has attained its end to the extent to which it has conjoined actuality with potentiality, that is, to the extent to which it has actualized its specifying potentialities. This sort of end is intrinsic to the thing whose end it is. Since Albert is committed to explicating the notion of goodness in terms of the notion of an end, focusing in different contexts on these two quite different sorts of end leads him to two quite different accounts of goodness.

Second, I think Albert fails to see the difference in the two accounts because his No Reality Thesis is ambiguous and can be read in such a way that it is compatible with either of them. There are two ways in which goodness might be said to add no reality to being. (A) Goodness might be said to add no reality to being if it is a *purely extrinsic*, that is, merely conceptual, relation. In that case no intrinsic feature of a thing is necessary for the relation to hold of it. But (B) goodness might also be said to add no reality to being if (i) a thing is good in virtue of possessing certain intrinsic properties and (ii) those intrinsic properties are identical to those in virtue of which the thing can be said to be a being. In case (B), good adds no reality in the sense that the properties in virtue of which it holds are not properties *additional* to those in virtue of which the thing is a being. So Albert is able to maintain the No Reality Thesis consistently with both accounts of goodness, but only in virtue of an ambiguity in the thesis.

I think there is also a closely related *historical* explanation of Albert's confusion. Albert is heir to a tradition of discussion of these issues that by the early thirteenth century had associated certain historical arguments with particular philosophical questions. In particular, the Agency Account and Boethius's thought experiment had both become associated with the question of the truth of ITBG. So when ITBG is at issue, the Agency Account and the thought experiment together focus attention on God's act of creation and God's end in creating and so pull Albert toward the merely conceptual relational account of goodness. But when Albert discusses the metaphysics of goodness apart from ITBG, he makes no appeal to the Agency Account or the thought experiment and relies instead on considerations having to do with the actualization of specifying potentialities, considerations that lead him to the Same Reality Thesis. In one context, viz., the discussion of the ambiguous No Reality Thesis, Albert (apparently unknowingly) wavers between the two incompatible accounts of the nature of goodness.

8. ITBG and the Doctrine of the Transcendentals

Now, the Agency Account, the merely conceptual relational account of goodness, and the account of goodness in terms of the actualization of specifying potentialities are more or less common property in the thirteenth century, and so Albert is not the only one tempted in the two directions I have indicated (though he may be the only one who succumbs to the temptation).[40] Philosophers who want to defend ITBG have significant philosophical decisions to make, and two defenders of ITBG might offer very different metaphysical foundations for it. Moreover, only some of those metaphysical foundations entail that goodness is a transcendental, and so commitment to ITBG does not by itself entail commitment to the doctrine of the transcendentals.[41]

40. See Philip the Chancellor *Summa de bono* Qq. 1 and 7, and Aquinas *DV* I and XXI and *ST* Ia.5. There are elements of the Agency Account in Aquinas's discussion in the former work, though he focuses exclusively on an account involving the actualization of potentialities in the latter. I do not mean to suggest that Aquinas is inconsistent (even over time) in the way I have argued Albert is. But there is an interesting passage in *De veritate* that shows at least that Aquinas felt the need to accommodate Boethius's thought experiment: "One finds still another difference between the divine goodness and [the goodness] of a creature. Goodness has the character of a final cause, and God has the character of a final cause since he is the ultimate end of all things (just as he is also the primary principle [of all things]). Because of this it must be the case that no other end has the disposition or character of an end except as a secondary [end] ordered toward the primary [final] cause. . . . Thus good, which has the character of an end, can be said of a creature only if one presupposes an ordering of the creator with respect to the creature. *Therefore, [even if] it were granted that the creature is its own being (ipsum suum esse) just as God is, still the being of the creature would not have the character of good unless one presupposes [its] being ordered toward the creator.* . . . This seems to be Boethius's intention in *De hebdomadibus*" (*DV* XXI.5).

41. Versions of this paper were read to the Iowa Philosophical Society and the Department of Philosophy at the University of Chicago. I'm grateful to members of the audiences on those occasions for their comments. I especially profited from discussions of this material with Eleonore Stump and Norman Kretzmann and from their detailed comments on an earlier draft.

CHAPTER 2

Good as Transcendental and the Transcendence of the Good

Jan A. Aertsen

1. Introduction

The thesis that there is an intrinsic connection between being and goodness has a long tradition in philosophy. In the thirteenth century, however, this thesis received a new systematic elaboration because it was placed within a new theoretical framework, the doctrine of transcendentals (*transcendentia*). The term 'transcendental' suggests a kind of surpassing or going beyond. What is transcended is the special modes of being which Aristotle called the "categories." Categories are determinations or contractions of that which is: not every being is a substance, or a quantity, or a quality, or a relation, etc. By contrast, the transcendentals are properties that belong to every being. So they transcend the categories, not because they refer to a reality beyond the categories but because they are not limited to one determinate category. Transcendentals are interchangeable or convertible with being that is itself a transcendental.[1]

The formation of the medieval doctrine of transcendentals is closely connected with the reception of Aristotle's *Metaphysics* in the thirteenth century. The term 'reception' is really somewhat too narrow. The assimilation of the Philosopher's work led to independent reflection on the nature of metaphysics and on the question of the proper subject of this science. Not without reason, someone has recently spoken of this development as "the second beginning of metaphysics." It is noteworthy that

---

1. On the medieval doctrine of transcendentals, see Aertsen 1988b.

the Middle Ages did not adopt the theological conception of meta-physics that prevailed among the Greek commentators on Aristotle. To the Greek commentators, metaphysics was concerned primarily with the first and principal being, but in the great medieval commentators, such as Thomas Aquinas and Duns Scotus, we find a decidedly on-tological view.[2] The proper subject of metaphysics is "being and the properties belonging to being as such." Against this background, the interest in and the importance of the transcendentals become under-standable. For they are precisely the universal properties of being.

What, then, are the properties belonging to every being? Medieval thinkers found scattered through the works of Aristotle a number of statements on the subject, which they used as basic elements in their elaboration of the doctrine of transcendentals. Important with respect to the transcendental property good is a passage in *Ethics* I.6 where Aristotle criticizes Plato's Form of the Good. Plato's account of the Form of the Good suggests that 'good' is said in one way of all the things that are good. But good is spoken of in as many ways as being is spoken of. The good is found in all categories, and the diversity of the categorial modes of being rules out a univocal predication of 'good.' There is no single Idea of the Good, the Good itself; "for if there were, it would be spoken of in only one of the categories, not in them all" (1096a27–9). This critique was seen by the medievals as an indication of the transcen-dental character of the good. 'Good' does not refer, as Plato supposed, to a separate, subsisting reality; it is something common. Characteristic of transcendentals, of which the most important besides 'good' are 'being,' 'one,' and 'true,' is that they are *communia*; to use a formulation of Thomas Aquinas's, they go through all the categories (*circumeunt*).

The transcendentals are, however, not only common names. They have another aspect, which comes out already in what is generally re-garded as the first treatise on transcendentals, the *Summa de bono* of Philip the Chancellor, written about 1230. In the prologue Philip estab-lishes not only that transcendentals are that which is most common but also that these are sometimes "appropriated," that is, treated as "prop-er" to something, namely, to God. For 'being,' 'one,' 'good,' and 'true' are predicates that in Scripture are attributed to God.[3]

The authoritative model for philosophical reflection on the divine names was the writing *De divinis nominibus* by pseudo-Dionysius the Areopagite. It was commented upon in the thirteenth century by

2. Cf. Honnefelder 1987.
3. Philip the Chancellor 1985, pp. 4–5. Cf. Pouillon 1939.

Thomas Aquinas, among others. The first name of God Dionysius handles is 'Good' (chapter 4), that is, the name which in neo-Platonism was attributed to the first principle. 'Good' is for Dionysius the primary name of God. In Holy Scripture this name, so he says, is ascribed preeminently to the highest godhead, which is distinguished from all other things in respect of goodness, as appears from Matthew 9: "No one is good save God."[4] The transcendence of the divine goodness could not be expressed more clearly than it is in this text, for the passage appears to prescribe exclusive predication of 'good.' The (neo-)Platonic way of thought is eminently suited to this transcendence, and Dionysius's treatment of the name 'good' is accordingly strongly inspired by it. His way of speaking of God is, as Thomas observes, Platonic: the divine good is "beyond" all that exists, is "the good itself," "the per se good," "the super good," the goodness of all good things.[5]

Reflection on the divine names plays a prominent role in the development of the medieval doctrine of transcendentals, for such reflection evokes a fundamental metaphysical problem. If transcendentals are, on the one hand, common names and, on the other, divine names, that is, names that are proper to God, then the question arises of how these two kinds of naming are related to each other. How is the transcendental character of the good that goes through all the categories related to the transcendence of the Good who surpasses all categories? Or, to put it in a more historical manner, is the approach inspired by Aristotle compatible with the neo-Platonic approach? There appears to be a conflict between the universal predicability of 'good' and the special attribution of 'good' to God. Transcendentality and transcendence seem to form two mutually repellant poles, as it were. If good is a property common to all things in virtue of their being, then how can justice be done to the uniqueness of the first Good? Conversely, affirmation of the transcendence of the Good appears to deny the transcendental character of the Good.

Medieval authors were alive to this polarity. It is not by chance that discussions of the transcendentals often take place within the framework of the doctrine of the divine attributes. This connection appears, for instance, in the construction of Thomas Aquinas's *Summa theologiae*. In *ST* Ia.5 the subject is "The good in general" (*De bono in communi*);

---

4. On 'goodness' as the primary name of God, see *De divinis nominibus* ch. 2, 1, 31; ch. 4, 1, 95; ch. 13, 3, 452.
5. Thomas Aquinas, in the prologue of his commentary to Dionysius's writing, points to this "Platonic mode of speaking."

Ia.6 deals with "The goodness of God" (*De bonitate Dei*). In my contribution to this book I analyze Thomas's reflections on the transcendentality and transcendence of the good and explain their philosophical importance.

2. The Question of the Good in Boethius's *De hebdomadibus*

The problem concerning the relation between the commonness of the good and the transcendence of the Good is posed in all its sharpness in a little book that was very influential in the Middle Ages, namely, Boethius's *De hebdomadibus*.[6] It is striking that Thomas wrote a commentary on this work. Boethius's treatise had been commented upon several times in the course of the centuries,[7] but a commentary on it was unusual in the thirteenth century. Thomas wrote his commentary during his first Parisian regency (1256–59). It does not seem too bold to surmise a connection between it and another of his works from the same period, *De veritate*.[8] Question XXI deals with the good (*De bono*) and refers to *De hebdomadibus* twelve times in the argumentation. In dealing with the transcendental 'good,' Thomas clearly felt the need to consider Boethius's problem explicitly and to comment on it.

The treatise *De hebdomadibus* is a response to a question propounded to Boethius by a friend: "How can substances be good in virtue of the fact that they have being when they are not substantial goods?" In the first lectio of his commentary Thomas calls this question "difficult." He also indicates directly the nature of the difficulty. If created substances are good insofar as they are, then they are substantial goods. But to be a substantial good is proper only to God (*proprium solius Dei*).[9] Thomas therefore takes the central theme of *De hebdomadibus* to be the polarity between the transcendentality and the transcendence of the good. If good is a common property because of an intrinsic relation between being and goodness, the distinction between created goodness and the divine goodness seems to disappear.

For my purposes it will not be necessary to present a complete pic-

---

6. The text can be found in Boethius 1978a, pp. 38–51 (a translation is provided in the Appendix to this volume). For a good analysis of Boethius's treatise, see MacDonald 1988.

7. See Schrimpf 1966.

8. For the dating of these works, see Weisheipl 1983, pp. 362, 382.

9. Thomas's commentary can be found in Thomas Aquinas 1954b. Here: lectio 1, n. 7.

ture of *De hebdomadibus*, which is a rather complicated text. I am interested in this treatise to the extent that it illuminates the background of Thomas's reflections on the good. For this reason I follow Boethius's account on the basis of Thomas's commentary, which, as it happens, keeps close to the text and presents a careful exposition.

Boethius's approach to the question addressed to him is, according to Thomas, first to make explicit what is presupposed in the question.[10] At issue in *De hebdomadibus* is the question *how* all things are good. This question is meaningful only if it is assumed *that* all things are good. The argument adduced for this presupposition is substantially as follows. (A) Everything tends toward its like—a premise based on one of the axioms Boethius had formulated earlier in *De hebdomadibus*. (B) Everything that is tends toward the good—a premise advanced as the commonly held view among the learned. Reference is made to Aristotle's statement at the beginning of his *Ethics* that the sages define the good as "that which all things desire." From (A) and (B) it follows that everything that is is good, for that which tends toward the good must be itself good. This conclusion, which expresses the commonness of the good, we may call from the thirteenth-century viewpoint the "transcendentality claim." This claim underlies the question "how all things are good." The distinction between the two—the claim and the how question—is essential for understanding Boethius's exposition.

The inquiry into the way in which things are good is presented by Boethius in a form that Thomas in his commentary calls a *dubium*.[11] This term does not mean 'something doubtful' but has a technical sense. It recalls the definition of 'question' given elsewhere by Boethius himself: a "question" is a *propositio dubitabilis*.[12] A *dubium* is a question in which two (Latin: *duo*) possibilities are posed in opposition to each other. The twofold question formulated in *De hebdomadibus* is: "Are things good by substance or by participation?"

This formulation suggests that "to be something by substance" and "to be something by participation" are mutually exclusive. But is this really so? Do the two possibilities in question necessarily form a contradictory pair? Thomas examines this assumption extensively. The result of his consideration is that the alternatives identified in the question are in opposition to each other only when 'participation' has reference to an accidental property of a substance. What is predicated of some-

10. *InDH* lectio 3, n. 40.
11. *InDH* lectio 3, n. 42.
12. Commentary on Cicero's *Topica* I (Boethius 1860, 1048D).

thing "substantially" belongs to it "per se," because the predicate is implied in the essence of the subject (for example, 'rational' said of a human being). What is predicated of something "by participation" is an accidental property that falls outside the substantial being of the subject (for example, 'white' said of a human being). Boethius clearly takes 'participation' in this sense.[13] Accordingly, the dilemma in *De hebdomadibus* actually comes down to the question whether things are substantially or accidentally good.

The strategy adopted by Boethius is to argue against both parts of the dilemma. First (I): Are things good by participation? If they are, then they are not good "per se." But if things are not good "per se," then they do not tend toward the good, for everything tends toward its like. But this consequence contradicts the premise of the argument for the transcendentality claim that all things tend toward the good. Therefore, it is not the case that beings are good by participation. (II): Are they good then by substance? If they are, then things are good in virtue of their being. This means that being and being good are identical in them. Then, however, they are like the first good, which is marked by the identity of being and being good. Therefore, all things are the first good. But the first good is God. Thus all things are God. But this assertion is absurd, and the premise upon which the argument is based, namely, that things are good by substance, is accordingly false. From (I)—things are not good by participation—and from (II)—things are not good by substance—follows the conclusion, on the assumption that being good by participation or by substance exhaust the possibilities, that things are in no way good. Yet this is in conflict with the transcendentality claim, which is the presupposition of the question.

Boethius's strategy is intended to sharpen the problem of *De hebdomadibus*. The question *how* all things are good seems unanswerable in a way that is compatible with the thesis *that* all things are good. For two possibilities present themselves as replies to the "how" question: the categories of the accidents and that of substance. The former account is untenable because it fails to do justice to the transcendental character of the good, whereas the latter account is untenable because it clashes with the transcendence of the first good. Yet the division of the categories into substance and accident is exhaustive. Is there a way out of this dilemma?

Boethius's own solution to the question begins with a kind of thought

13. *InDH* lectio 3, n. 45: "Boethius is here speaking according to that mode of participation in which a subject participates in an accident."

experiment. Let us, he says, remove from our mind the presence of the first good. What does this experiment entail for the goodness of things? The consequence of it is that in things there would be a non-identity between being and being good.[14] Things are certainly good, yet their goodness is not the same as their substance, but a property in addition to their substance, just like roundness and whiteness (the comparison is Boethius's own). Their substantial being itself is not good. Why is it necessary to accept this nonidentity? Suppose that substances were nothing else except good; then they would be the first principle of things of which the essence is goodness. There is, however, only one thing that is only good and nothing else. Therefore all good things, if they were nothing else except good, would be identical with this one thing. Yet this is false, and consequently the assertion that substances are nothing else except good is also false.

Boethius seems to follow the same strategy here as in his earlier argument suggesting the impossibility of the *dubium*. For there, too, it was argued that things are not substantially good, since in that case they would be like God. Yet there is a difference. There the sole remaining alternative was that things are only accidentally good. Here, however, Boethius does not employ this disjunction. Now he arrives at the conclusion of a nonidentity of being and being good in things. Being good is accidental, yet the possibility is left open that even substantial being itself, in some sense that remains to be qualified, is good. It is precisely this point that Boethius takes up in the second part of his solution.

Boethius seeks to account for the goodness of the being itself of things by establishing a connection with what thought had just removed from mind in the preceding argument, namely, the presence of the first good. Things would not be if they were not willed by God whose being is essentially goodness. The being of things is created. Because the being of things has flowed from the first good, the being itself of created things is good. Things are good insofar as they are, because they are by the good.

Boethius's solution to the question of how all things are good comes down to this (as Thomas summarizes the argument in De hebdomadibus), that the being of the first good is good in virtue of its own essence, that is, is good absolutely (*absolute*), because its nature is nothing else except goodness. The being of a second (created) good is good, too, to be sure, though not in virtue of its own essence (for its essence is not goodness itself), but in virtue of the relation to the first good as its cause (*ex*

14. *InDH* lectio 4, n. 60: "*Aliud esset in eis esse, et aliud bonum esse.*"

habitudine ad primum bonum).[15] The transcendentality claim is combined in this way with the transcendence of the first good. How is this solution of Boethius's to be assessed and evaluated?

In a recent paper Scott MacDonald has presented a valuable and incisive analysis of *De hebdomadibus*.[16] His interpretation of Boethius's account is summed up in his designation of it as "The Good-as-Relational-Property Interpretation." The relational property of depending for existence on the first good is just what being good consists in for created things. The importance of the relational account of the nature of goodness is, according to MacDonald, that it allows Boethius to occupy a middle ground between saying that good is an ordinary substantial property and saying that it is an accidental property. By maintaining that goodness is a relational property, Boethius can accommodate the observation that goodness cannot be an ordinary substantial or intrinsic accidental property of things.

The interesting thing about this interpretation is that it is an attempt to transcend the limits of the system of the categories. The problem, however, is whether the categories do indeed allow a middle between substance and accident. Relation, too, is a category, namely, an accident that comes to a substance. Now, if the nature of goodness should consist in one determinate category, this would be irreconcilable with what we earlier called "the transcendentality claim" of the good. MacDonald is aware of this difficulty. He accordingly stresses that what is at issue here is a relational property of a special type. "The property of depending for existence on the first good is metaphysically unique." In other words, what MacDonald has in mind is really a *transcendental* relation that is coextensive with being. As a matter of fact, the text in *De hebdomadibus* affords no support for the assumption that there is in Boethius the idea of breaking through the system of categories at a decisive point. Yet there is an even more fundamental objection to be raised against the "Goodness-as-Relational-Property Interpretation."

One of MacDonald's own criticisms of *De hebdomadibus* is that Boethius's account of the nature of goodness is not sufficiently general. There is not one place in the metaphysical framework for the property of goodness, but two. The property of being good that belongs to created substances is a relational property; the property of being good that belongs to the first good is not a property of that sort, however, but

15. *InDH* lectio 4, n. 62–63.
16. MacDonald 1988. See also his unpublished dissertation, 1986.

is an ordinary essential property. Thus there are two different types of property, both of which are called 'goodness.'

This criticism would be justified if Boethius's intention were indeed to provide an account of the nature of goodness in general and to show what property the property of being good consists in. But is that his intention? The question Boethius wants to answer is *how* all things are good, presupposing *that* all are good. His reply to this question is necessarily twofold, for divine goodness differs from created goodness. The first good is good in an absolute way, whereas created goodness is good through the relation to the first good. The "Goodness-as-Relational-Property Interpretation" suggests incorrectly that Boethius's claim is that the property of being good is a relation. This interpretation generalizes a part of Boethius's answer to the question how all things are good into an account of the nature of goodness as such.

The point in *De hebdomadibus* that deserves criticism is in my opinion first of all the way in which Boethius establishes the being good of created things. He posits a nonidentity between their being and their being good. Substantial being itself is not good but is good because it is derived from the first good. Substantial being is denominated good, not from any goodness inherent in it, but from the relation to an extrinsic good, that is, through an *extrinsic* denomination. This is also the sense in which Thomas Aquinas understood Boethius's solution.[17]

The unsatisfactory character of Boethius's solution stems, I think, from an essential lacuna in its development. Its permanent presupposition is *that* all things are good. This claim is argued for—everything tends toward its like, and everything tends toward the good—but not in such a way as to make clear the real nature of the intrinsic tie between being and goodness. Yet this insight is indispensable for an adequate answer to the question *how* all things are good. The first task to which *De hebdomadibus* gives rise is, therefore, to establish the transcendental character of the good metaphysically. In his independent works Thomas Aquinas thought this problem through.

3. The Transcendental Character of the Good

In *DV* XXI.2 and in *ST* Ia.5.1 (and 3) Thomas argues that "being and good are convertible." In the first text he adduces Boethius's transcen-

---

17. Thomas compares this way of being good with the way in which something is called 'healthy' (*InDH* lectio 4, n. 62). Cf. the account of Boethius's treatise in Geiger 1942, pp. 36ff.

dentality claim in *De hebdomadibus* as one of the arguments in favor of the thesis that every being is good.[18] But Thomas's own argumentation goes deeper. (I will follow his exposition in *ST* Ia.5.1, where the connection between being and good is developed in four steps.)[19]

The starting point is the concept of good (*ratio boni*). "The *ratio boni* consists in this, that the good is something desirable (*appetibile*)." For this determination Thomas refers to Aristotle's definition of the good in the *Ethics*, which was also one of the premises of Boethius's transcendentality claim: "the good is what all desire." The special character of this definition needs to be noticed: it is a definition "a posteriori," that is, through the proper effect of what is to be defined. Its meaning is not that something is good because and insofar as it is desired, but rather the opposite: something is desired because it is good. Through the effect the cause is manifested, that is, the nature of the good itself (*natura boni*).[20] Unlike Boethius, Thomas clarifies this nature in the continuation of his argument.

The second step in his exposition is that 'desirable' is identified with 'perfect' (*perfectum*). "Now it is clear that a thing is desirable only insofar as it is perfect, for all desire their own perfection." The notion of 'perfect' expresses completeness. It is defined by Aristotle in the *Physics* as "that which has nothing outside itself" (*cuius nihil est extra ipsum*).[21] Perfect is what has attained its end. What is this completion?

That is indicated by the third step in Thomas's argument: he identifies 'perfect' with 'act.' "But everything is perfect insofar as it is actual (*in actu*)." A thing is not perfect when its potentialities are not realized. It is not completed until it has its proper act. Therefore, every act is a perfection and a good.

By means of the notion of 'act' Thomas is now able to establish the connection between the *ratio boni* and the *ratio entis*. The final step in his argument is: "Now it is clear that a thing is good insofar as it is a being (*ens*); for to be (*esse*) is the actuality (*actualitas*) of every thing." With this step the analysis has arrived at the metaphysical foundation of the convertibility of being and good. For 'being' refers to the act of being;

---

18. *DV* XXI.2.s.c.(1): "Everything tends towards its like. Now, 'every being tends towards the good,' as Boethius says in *De hebdomadibus*. Therefore every being is good, and something cannot be good unless it is in some way. Therefore good and being are convertible."

19. This connection is dealt with more extensively in Aertsen 1985. (See also Chapter 4 in this volume.)

20. This distinction between the *ratio boni* and the *natura boni* is made by Thomas in *SCG* I.37 (n. 307).

21. *Physics* III.6 (207a9); Thomas's commentary, lectio 11, n. 385.

to be in act is to be perfect, and to be perfect is to be good. The terms 'being' and 'good' refer to the same reality but differ only in concept. 'Good' adds something that the term 'being' itself does not express, namely, the aspect of desirableness (*ratio appetibilis*).

The philosophical significance of Thomas's argument is that it establishes an intrinsic connection between being and goodness. The good does not come to a thing from the outside, but it pertains to what is most intimate in it, to its being. Every being, as being, is good.

Yet can the thesis that being and good are convertible be maintained? Surely something is not good simply on the basis of the fact that it is? To be a human being and to be a good human being are obviously quite different things. This experience of a nonidentity forms the core of the first objection in *ST* Ia.5.1. "It seems that 'good' differs really from 'being.'" For this view Thomas refers to Boethius's solution of the question of the good in *De hebdomadibus*, for in his exposition the nonidentity between a thing's being and its being good plays an essential role, as we saw. The objection states: "For Boethius says: 'I perceive that in nature the fact that things are good is one thing, that they are is another.'"

Thomas's reply to this objection is extremely enlightening, both for the sense of the convertibility thesis and for the divergence from Boethius. Although being and good are the same in reality, yet, so Thomas argues, there is a difference between 'being absolutely' (*ens simpliciter*) and 'good absolutely' (*bonum simpliciter*). 'Being' properly signifies that something is in act; something is therefore said to have 'being absolutely' insofar as it is primarily distinguished from that which is only in potency. This act is the substantial being of each thing. Hence, it is by its substantial being that something is said to have 'being absolutely'; but by acts added to the substance, a thing is said to have 'being in a certain respect' (*ens secundum quid*). Thus 'to be white' signifies 'being in a certain respect,' since this act is added to something that is already in act.

With regard to good the reverse applies. 'Good' expresses perfection and has therefore the character of being final (*rationem ultimi*). Hence, a thing is said to be 'good absolutely' when it has its ultimate perfection through acts added to the first, substantial being. In this way a thing that has substantial being is 'being absolutely' but is not 'good absolutely'; it is good only 'in a certain respect,' for insofar as it is actual, it has some perfection. Viewed in its *complete* actuality, that is, in having the ultimate perfection and act it ought to have, a thing is being 'in a certain respect' and 'good absolutely.' This completion concerns the actualization of the faculties and virtues of a thing; it consists in its activity or operation. Thus an unvirtuous person is good 'in a certain respect,' insofar as one is a human being; yet one is not 'good absolutely,' but rather evil because one lacks the perfection one ought to have. The statement of Boethius, Thomas concludes, is to be explained on the basis of this distinction between being good absolutely and being absolutely.

Without saying so expressly, Thomas clearly presents here a rein-terpretation of Boethius's view. For Boethius, the nonidentity of being and being good has to do with the distinction between substance and accident. The substantial being itself of things is not good, for this is proper to divine goodness. Yet Boethius, too, must ascribe a certain goodness to substantial being, since otherwise the transcendentality claim cannot be maintained. His solution is that substantial being is good in virtue of its relation to the first goodness. For Thomas, too, the nonidentity of being and being good has to do with the categorial division of being into substance and accident. However, he, unlike Boethius, takes even substantial being itself to be good, albeit not abso-lutely. There is no opposition but rather continuity between the being good of substance and the being good of accidents. In accidental acts each thing completes its own, initial goodness of its substantial being. The good is *both* in the category of substantial being *and* in the catego-ries of accidental being. That is precisely the mark of a transcendental: a transcendental is common, for it goes through all the categories. Thomas escapes Boethius's difficulty by understanding the good in a really transcendental way.

Being and good are convertible, although there is a real nonidentity between 'being absolutely' and 'good absolutely.' For Thomas this non-identity marks at the same time a difference between divine and crea-turely goodness. "In every creature to be and to be good are not the same absolutely, although each one is good insofar as it is."[22] No finite being attains to the perfection of its goodness through its (substantial) being alone, but through a multiplicity of acts. Only God has his entire goodness in a manner that is one and simple, namely, "in the fullness of his being."[23] The transcendental character of the good is found to be not incompatible with the transcendence of the Good.

With this conclusion, the transition has been made to the central question of *De hebdomadibus*: How are things good? We must now inves-

22. *SCG* III.20.
23. *ST* IaIIae.18.1.

tigate how Thomas, having established the intrinsic connection between being and being good, understands the relation between divine and created goodness.

4. Are Things Good by the Divine Goodness?

The substantial being of things is good, according to Boethius, because they have come forth from what is essentially good. Created things are good by relation to an extrinsic good; they are good by the divine goodness. Thomas takes up this theme of *De hebdomadibus* in *DV* XXI.4 ("Whether all things are good by the first goodness?") and in *ST* Ia.6.4 ("Whether all things are good by the divine goodness?"). The interesting thing about Thomas's discussion of this question is that it is not restricted to Boethius's position but has a much broader scope. Thomas realizes that the explanation in *De hebdomadibus* is strongly influenced by the Platonic way of thought, and he enters into discussion with this philosophy.

In *DV* XXI.4 Platonism is presented as a reaction against pantheistic forms of thought. The formulation that things are good by the divine goodness could suggest that the divine is an immanent principle of things. Now, "the Platonists said that all things are formally good by the first goodness, not as by a connected form but by a separate form (*forma separata*)." It is characteristic of Platonism that it endeavors to account for concrete things from a transcendent reality that is separate from these things.

Next Thomas works out the basic Platonic idea with respect to natural things and with respect to the good. Platonism posits separate, subsistent forms of natural things. Thus there is, for example, quite apart from the concrete individuals John and Peter, a "separate" man that Plato called 'Man per se' or 'the Idea of Man.' Through participation in the latter, John and Peter are called 'man.' Similarly, he posited a good that is separate from all particular goods. Through participation in the Idea of the Good, all things are called 'good.' Yet there is a difference between the Idea of the Good and the Idea of Man. The latter does not extend to everything, whereas the Idea of the Good has a universal extension. The Platonic view implies that the 'per se' Good is the universal principle of all things, that is, God. The consequence of this position is that all things are called good by the first goodness, which is God.

Thomas's criticism of the Platonic way of thought is concise and is based entirely on the fundamental conceptions of Aristotle.[24] With respect to the forms of natural things, Aristotle has shown, Thomas says, that things are what they are, not through an exemplar that is separated from them but through an intrinsic form or "whatness." In Aristotle's work we do indeed find an incisive critique of the Platonic model of predication, according to which a predicate is attributed to a subject in virtue of participation in an extrinsic form. "Human being" belongs however to the essence of John and Peter, it belongs to them per se. In the Aristotelian scheme of predication two types of predication are distinguished: 'per se' and 'per accidens.'[25] In predication per se a predicate is attributed to a subject in virtue of the essential form of the subject: between subject and predicate there is a necessary relation. Such a relation is absent in predication per accidens. With respect to the Idea of the Good, Thomas contents himself with repeating Aristotle's critique in the *Ethics*. 'Good' is not said in a univocal way of everything that is good. For good is found in all categories, and the categorial modes of being, substance and accident, are not equivalent. In what is not said univocally there is, however, according to the Platonic view itself, no need for an Idea.

Yet with this critique, inspired by Aristotle, the final word has not been spoken. Thomas criticizes two aspects of Platonic philosophy— the separated forms of natural things, and the Form of the Good—but striking in his discussion is the fact that the criticisms are different in character. With respect to the forms of natural things, he denies Platonic "extrinsicism": the essential forms are inherent in things. With respect to the Good, the emphasis of the critique is not so much on the separateness of the Form but on the univocity Plato subscribed to. We find this point confirmed in Thomas's commentary on the *Ethics*. There he states explicitly that Aristotle's critique of the Form of the Good is not intended to refute Plato's view that there is a separate good upon which all good things depend.[26] Thomas clearly feels the need for refining the Aristotelian critique of Platonism.

At the close of *DV* XXI.4 Thomas makes the surprising statement that in a certain sense "Plato's opinion can be sustained" (*opinio Platonis sustineri potest*). In order to understand this statement, we must put it

24. *DV* XXI.4: "*Haec opinio a Philosopho improbatur multipliciter.*"
25. See, e.g., *Posterior Analytics* I.4.
26. *In I Ethicorum* lectio 6.

into a broader context and draw other texts from Thomas's work into our analysis.

Particularly instructive is the prologue of Thomas's commentary on Dionysius's *De divinis nominibus*, where Thomas wants to justify Dionysius's Platonic way of speaking of God as 'the Good itself' and 'the per se Good.' He describes the Platonists as wanting to reduce all that is composed to simple and abstract (*abstracta*) principles. Thus they posit the existence of separate Forms of things. They apply this "abstract" approach not only to the species of natural things but also to that which is most common (*maxime communia*), namely, 'good,' 'one,' and 'being.' They hold that there is a first, which is the essence of goodness, of unity, and of being, a principle that we, Thomas says, call 'God.' The other things are called 'good,' 'one,' and 'being' because of their derivation from the first, because of their participation in that which is essentially.

In the continuation of the prologue Thomas rejects the first application of the Platonic method, again subscribing to Aristotle's denial: there are no separate, subsisting Forms of natural things. But with regard to what is most common, Thomas recognizes the legitimacy of the Platonic reduction.[27] Explicit arguments for this application are not given. Its validity, however, cannot lie in anything else than the "commonness" of the forms in question, that is, in their transcendental character. Already in *DV* XXI.4 it was noted that the Idea of the Good differs from that of Man: the former extends to all things. A transcendental is distinct in this respect from a universal such as 'man.' Connected with this commonness of the good is another characteristic that is also mentioned in *DV* XXI.4, namely, that 'good' is not said univocally. For this reason the good does not really fit into the Aristotelian scheme of predication per se or per accidens. For what is said per se of something is predicated in the same way of the subjects. Yet every being is good not per accidens but just as being. The necessity of another model of predication imposes itself. Thomas presents another mode of predicating in *Quodlibetum* II.2.1: "It must be said that something is predicated of something in two ways—essentially or by participation. Thus 'light' is predicated of an illumined body in the manner of participation, but if there were some separated light then it would be predicated of it essentially." The terminology and the (hypothetical) example Thomas uses to elucidate this mode of predication allow no room for doubt that he is here introducing the Platonic model of predi-

27. Similarly in *ST* Ia.6.4.

cation. From the continuation of this text it appears that Thomas adopts this model: "Therefore we must say that being (*ens*) is predicated essentially of God alone, inasmuch as divine being (*esse*) is subsistent and absolute being. It is, however, predicated of any creature by participation, for no creature is its being but is what has being."

Predication essentially or by participation is valid for Thomas insofar as what is predicated has a transcendental character. What is said in this way is 'being,' which "transcends" the categories. This interpretation is confirmed by the continuation of *Quodlibetum* II.2.1, where this mode of predication is also applied to the transcendental 'good.' "So also God is called 'good' essentially because He is goodness itself, but creatures are called 'good' by participation because they have goodness." The notion of participation that Thomas employs here is consequently different from the one Boethius uses in his *dubium* about the good. In the latter, participation bears upon a categorial—that is, accidental—determination, whereas in Thomas the notion concerns a transcendental property.

From the text cited it also becomes clear what function predication "essentially" and "by participation" has in Thomas. It is meant to indicate both the distinction and the relationship between God and creature. Here Thomas makes use in an original way of the transcendentals' property of not being predicated univocally. They are said according to a "prior" and a "posterior." 'Being' is said of the creature because its being refers to the divine, subsistent being, of which being is predicated primarily. The "commonness" of being (and good) must be reduced to a first to which this perfection is "proper" because it is this perfection essentially. Only God is being and good by his essence; he is being and goodness itself. All other things must then be thought of as participating in that perfection. That which is essentially is the origin of all that is. The other things have received being good; they are created. Creation is, one might say, a causality of a transcendental character: it pertains not just to the being this or being that of things but to their being as such.[28] The idea of creation is interpreted philosophically by Thomas in terms of "participation." This doctrine makes it possible to conceive transcendence and transcendentality together. God is "good" by virtue of his essence; to him the creature owes its being "good." In that sense things are good by the divine goodness. In that sense the Platonic view can be "sustained."

28. *ST* Ia.45.5: "To produce being (*esse*) absolutely, and not merely as this or that being, pertains to the essence of creation."

5. Conclusion

In *ST* Ia.6.4 ("Whether all things are good by the divine goodness?")
Thomas concludes that the Platonic view appears to be unreasonable in
affirming that there are separate forms of natural things subsisting of
themselves; still, it is absolutely true that there is something first that is
essentially being and essentially good which we call God. Hence, everything can be called 'good' and 'being,' insofar as it participates in the
first being, which is essentially good. To this conclusion Thomas still
adds, however, an important remark. That every being is good through
an external cause by no means excludes each thing's being called good
through a goodness that is formally its own goodness. "And so of all
things," Thomas ends, "there is one goodness, and yet many
goodnesses."

This text can serve as a summary of our analysis, which is focused on
the relation between the good as transcendental and the transcendence
of the Good. I want to emphasize four points of philosophical importance in Thomas's reflection on the good.

First, Thomas really understands the good transcendentally by establishing an intrinsic connection between being and goodness. To be is
the actuality of everything and thereby a good proper to each thing.
Things are called good in virtue of an inner goodness. It is characteristic of finite things that although being and good are convertible, there
is in them nonetheless a nonidentity between being absolutely and good
absolutely.

Second, because the good is transcendental, Thomas applies to it the
predication essentially or by participation. This predication expresses
the transcendence of the divine goodness and the creaturely character
of the goodness of other things. That which is in any way good must be
reduced to what is good by its essence as to its origin. That things are
good through an intrinsic goodness is not incompatible with their dependence on that which is the good itself.

Third, from a historical point of view, Thomas effects a kind of
synthesis between the Aristotelian way of thought and Aristotle's conception of the good, on the one hand—the good is something common
and the essential forms of things are inherent in them—and the Platonic way of thought and Plato's conception of the good, on the other
hand—the Form of the Good is "separate" from particular goods.

Fourth, Thomas effects a synthesis in still another respect. Characteristic of Boethius's position, according to MacDonald,[29] is the creation

29. MacDonald 1988. (See also the Introduction in this volume.)

approach to explaining the relation between being and goodness. Aristotle's view, in contrast, exemplifies what might be called the nature approach. This approach explains what it is for a thing to be good by referring to the nature of the thing. "The historical significance of *DH*," MacDonald says, "consists largely in its offering an interesting account of the nature of goodness which is possibly incompatible . . . with the sort of account medieval philosophers found in Aristotle." Thomas's reflection on the claim *that* all things are good and on the question *how* they are good can be regarded as a philosophically original synthesis of the nature approach and the creation approach.[30] The nature approach explains the intrinsic goodness of things, for 'nature' says what beings are *in themselves*; it always refers to an intrinsic principle. Now, it is Thomas's transcendentality claim that everything is good, insofar as it is. Things are good (in a certain respect) in virtue of their own being. So all things owe their being good to their nature. The creation approach explains that everything is called 'good' through an external cause, for 'creature' says *being-related* to the Origin of things. Creation expresses that things received their being and goodness from another. Their goodness consists in their relation to the transcendent good, that is, in their participation in what is goodness itself.[31]

30. The relation between nature and creature in Thomas is the central theme of Aertsen 1988a.

31. I am grateful to Norman Kretzmann and Scott MacDonald for their very valuable comments on an earlier draft.

CHAPTER 3

Saint Thomas on
De hebdomadibus

Ralph McInerny

Saint Thomas's exposition of the theological tractate that he and other medievals called *De hebdomadibus* is the only complete Thomistic commentary on Boethius that we have. He began one on *De trinitate*, but it breaks off in the middle of chapter 2. These two works are not of the same literary genre, however. That on *De trinitate* incorporates an exposition and a commentary, exhibiting the same form we find in Thomas's commentary on the *Sentences* of Peter Lombard, whereas what we have on *De hebdomadibus* could be called a truncated form of the work on *De trinitate*, incomplete though the latter be. Of late there has been much emphasis on the form of commentary popular among the Masters of the Faculty of Arts at Paris, but since Thomas never wrote such a commentary, it would be odd to invoke that form as if it were somehow regulative for him. It is unfortunate that most students of Thomas's *De trinitate* commentary ignore his *expositiones* of the text and concentrate exclusively on his independent questions. In the case of *De hebdomadibus* we have only an exposition and no independent questions raised on the basis of the text.

Although no one would hesitate to attribute to Thomas as his own thought what is found in the *quaestiones* of the *De trinitate* commentary, hesitation has been shown concerning the exposition of *De hebdomadibus*. Since Duhem,[1] students of Thomas have been almost unanimous in saying that the doctrine of the exposition is peculiarly Thomas's own and cannot be found in the text of Boethius. The parade

---

1. Duhem 1917, pp. 285–316.

of Thomists that formed behind Duhem seemed to march to some such reasoning as this: The recognition of the diversity of *esse* and *essentia* is unique to Saint Thomas; therefore, that distinction cannot be the meaning of the Boethian axiom *diversum est esse et id quod est*. But Thomas so interprets the Boethian dictum. Ergo, Thomas is telling us what he thinks, not what Boethius thinks.

The exposition might more fittingly have been taken as a basis for doubting the Thomistic uniqueness of the distinction involved, particularly since Thomas himself never suggests either that it is original with him or known only to a few. How could he, when he accepts the Boethian suggestion that *diversum est esse et id quod est* is one of the commonplaces to which anyone assents upon hearing it uttered? That is, it is *per se nota quoad omnes*.[2]

Boethius's announced method in the *De hebdomadibus*, we remember, was to proceed *more geometrico*—first set down the axioms, then use them to prove the theorem that whatever is is good just insofar as it is.[3] One of the oddities of the tradition of interpretation just alluded to, that which sees a chasm between the text and the commentary, is that interest is exhausted by the axioms, especially *diversum est esse et id quod est*, and almost no one goes on to study how the axioms function in the argument of the treatise.[4]

What I have to say in this essay is meant to reopen discussion of the standard Thomistic position—it is by no means confined to Thomists— as to the radical difference between the doctrine of the Boethian text and of Thomas's exposition. After a quick sketch of Thomas's reading of the tractate as a whole, I shall consider a methodological difficulty of

2. "*Communis animi conceptio est enuntiatio quam quisque probat auditam.*" See Boethius 1978a, p. 40, ll. 18–19 (I shall henceforth refer only to the line numbers of this edition [a translation is provided in the Appendix to this volume]). In his exposition, Thomas states the equivalence, "*communis animi conceptio, vel principium per se nota,*" lectio 1, n. 18. I shall be citing the text in Thomas Aquinas 1954b. I shall refer to the lectio and paragraph number of this edition. Calcaterra gives a continuous numbering of paragraphs, paying no attention to the division into lessons, and so I will often give the paragraph number alone. The English translations are my own except where otherwise noted.

3. *DH*, ll. 14–17. Saint Thomas, lectio 1, nn. 12–13.

4. See, e.g., Roland-Gosselin 1948, pp. 142–45. On p. 186, Roland-Gosselin, in a footnote, develops what he conceives to be differences between Boethius and Saint Thomas. Roland-Gosselin takes Duhem's claims as givens for his own discussion. See, too, Fabro 1963, pp. 24–35. In Fabro 1960, pp. 204–13, and in several other places, Fabro returns to *De hebdomadibus* and Thomas's exposition on it. Fabro is the most eminent of living Thomists, a champion of the Platonic elements in the Thomistic synthesis, and at odds with Gilsonian-style existential Thomists. In McInerny 1990 I discuss at length twentieth-century theories on the relation between Boethius and Saint Thomas. Schrimpf 1966 is still useful.

some moment—whether created goodness has any meaning apart from reference to God—that is suggested by n. 62, of lectio 4.[5] It would seem that Boethius has swept the rug out from under an analogical extension of 'good' from creatures to God. I will then consider a rule of analogy to be found in the treatment of 'true' as analogously common to God and creatures, a rule that raised the specter of extrinsic denomination as the only way of understanding 'true' as predicated of creatures. That is, creatures are denominated true from the truth God is, not from any truth within them. But isn't this what Boethius leaves us with in *De hebdomadibus* in the case of 'good'? What does Thomas think Boethius means in *De hebdomadibus*? We will seek the answer to that question in the exposition and in other writings of Saint Thomas.

1. A Thomistic Overview of the Tractate

The Axioms

It is not perhaps surprising that almost exclusive attention has been paid to what Thomas has to say about the axioms, so pellucid is it. His reading pulls the text together wonderfully. Having noted that common conceptions gain universal consent because they are self-evident, *per se notae*, that is, are propositions such that the predicate enters into the understanding of the subject, Thomas interprets Boethius's division of such conceptions into those made up of terms all know and those made up of terms requiring special knowledge to mean that the axioms are common conceptions of the first kind. No one could fail to know their terms. The reason for this is that the terms are 'being' and terms convertible with it. Indeed, Thomas divides the axioms into those having to do with being, those having to do with one, and those having to do with good. Moreover, there are four basic axioms, the others being corollaries of them.[6]

---

5. It is in lectio 4, n. 63, that Thomas, having discussed the Boethian solution, speaks of a twofold created goodness, suggesting that Boethius has considered only one of them.
6. The nine Roman numerals in the Stewart-Rand-Tester edition are of scant help. By making the meta-axiom I, the editors get off to a bad start. Thomas's four fundamental axioms relate to that text as follows: 1 = the first phrase of II; 2 = V up to the semicolon; 3 = VII and VIII; 4 = IX. It will be noticed that the Latin text on which Thomas comments gives the components of his Axiom 3 in reverse order from that of the Stewart-Rand-Tester text.

A. Axioms having to do with Being

1. *Diversum est esse et id quod est.*	1. To be and that which is are diverse.
2. *Diversum est tantum esse aliquid et esse aliquid in eo quod est.*	2. To be such-and-such and to be in the sense of that which is are diverse.

B. The Axiom having to do with One

3. *Omni composito aliud est esse, aliud ipsum est; omne simplex esse suum et id quod est unum habet.*	3. In every composite, to be is one thing, that which is, another; in every simple, its existence and what it is are one.

C. The Axiom having to do with the Good

4. *Omnis diversitas discors; similitudo vero appetenda est.*	4. All diversity [causes] discord, but likeness is to be desired.

Thomas is not of course wishing on Boethius a doctrine of transcendentals unknown to him. *De hebdomadibus* addresses a difficulty arising from the assumption that whatever is is good, and in *De duabus naturis*, as Thomas called *Contra Euthychen*, we read, "*esse enim atque unum convertitur et quodcumque unum est est*: to be and one convert, and whatever is one is" (ll. 37–39).

It will be noticed that neither the term *participare* nor its chief synonyms, *accipere* and *suscipere*, occur in the major axioms. In the three subaxioms illustrating Axiom 1 we find "*accepta forma essendi*: having taken on a form of being," "*fit enim participatio cum aliquid iam est*: participation comes about when something already is," and "*est autem aliquid cum esse susceperit*: something is when it receives existence." What is meant by 'participation'?

Thomas begins on the assumption that it can be understood in terms of predication and gives three meanings of the term, guided by its etymology, "*partem capere*: to take part," that is, partake.[7] What is the

---

7. Cf. lectio 2, n. 24. The threefold division of participation is as follows: (1) When something receives in a particular or determinate fashion what belongs to another universally. This is illustrated by the relation of species to genus and of individual to species. The participating subject does not receive the predicate in all its amplitude and extension. (2) When subject participates in accident and matter in form. What is participated in is determined by the subject. Here what is participated is not said of the subject *in quid* or essentially. (3) An effect is said to participate in its cause, particularly when the effect cannot manifest adequately the cause. This is exemplified by air illumined by the sun but unable to exhibit the full brightness of its cause.

meaning of the claim that to be and that which is are diverse? The infinitive 'to be' (*esse*) is made finite in two ways, either on the side of the subject or on the side of the predicate. We see that Thomas is taking *ipsum esse* to be the abstract expression of the copula. The subject is that which "has being: *esse habet*" in a first sense, and then can be said to have being of a sort thanks to other predicates that do not express what it is. Axiom 1 deals with the comparison of *esse* and *id quod est*; Axiom 2, with the comparison of being in the primary sense and being in a certain way.

Because terms having the predicable range of 'being,' 'one,' and 'good' are not confined to creatures, we are warned that the diversity of *esse* and *id quod est* is not to be understood as necessarily picking out complexity in the thing spoken of or referred to. With simple things, the complexity is due to our mode of understanding and the fact that the things we first and easily understand are really complex.

Dicit ergo primo quod diversum est esse, et id quod est. Quae quidem diversitas non est hic referenda ad res, de quibus adhuc non loquitur, sed ad ipsas rationes seu intentiones.	First he says that to be and that which is are diverse, a diversity which ought not here be referred to things, of which he has yet to speak, but to the notions and intentions themselves. (n. 22)

All we need have in mind to understand the axiom is the diversity between the meanings of abstract and concrete expressions, for example, between what is meant by 'a white thing' and 'whiteness,' 'the runner' and 'running.' Being (*ens*) expresses concretely what to be (*esse*) expresses abstractly.[8] The three axioms that explain Axiom 1 presuppose this. Only the concrete expression is referred to a subsistent thing; the abstract expression does not have a mode of signifying appropriate to the subsistent. What is expressed concretely can participate in, that is, have predicated of it, other things; the abstract cannot. A thing is concrete by virtue of receiving a form of existence, which is a necessary condition of its being a subject of predication or participation.[9] Insofar

8. As Pierre Hadot has pointed out, the diversity is explained by denying of *ipsum esse* three things that pertain to *id quod est*. (*a*) "*Ipsum enim esse nondum est, at vero quod est accepta essendi forma est atque consistit.*" (*b*) "*Quod est participare aliquod potest, sed ipsum esse nullo modo aliquo participat. (Fit enim participatio cum aliquid iam est; est autem aliquid, cum esse susceperit.)*" (*c*) "*Id quod est habere aliquid praeterquam quod ipsum est potest; ipsum vero esse nihil aliud praeter se habet admixtum*" (Hadot 1970, pp. 143–56. See, too, Hadot 1973, pp. 147–53).

9. The three explanatory subaxioms express the three features of *quod est* denied of *ipsum esse*: see n. 8 above.

as the abstract can be the subject of predication (for example, 'whiteness is a color'), what is predicated of it must be predicated per se; the concrete is not so restricted. But if this must be allowed of less universal terms, it does not affect the behavior of *ipsum esse*. There is nothing more universal, concrete or abstract, in which *ipsum esse* might participate.

What does Thomas mean when he says that Boethius is not yet talking of things? That he is not yet talking of the difference between simple and complex things? Of course, what is expressed in the first axiom is true of whatever is. But that includes God, with whom the tractate deals, in whom there is no real complexity. Were we to understand Axiom 1 as pointing to real as opposed to conceptual diversity, it would be at odds with Axiom 3, which denies a diversity of *esse* and *id quod est* in the simple. Hence, the diversity is real only in complex things (n. 31).

Est ergo primo considerandum, quod sicut esse et quod est differunt in simplicibus secundum intentiones, ita in compositis differunt realiter: quod quidem manifestum est ex praemissis; dictum est enim supra quod ipsum esse neque participat aliquid, ut eius ratio constituatur ex multis; neque habet aliquid extraneum admixtum, ut sit in eo compositio accidentis; et ideo ipsum esse non est compositum. Res ergo compositum non est suum esse.	The first thing to notice is that just as to be and what is differ conceptually in simple things, so in composite things they differ really. This is clear from the foregoing, since it was said earlier that to be itself neither participates in anything, so that its account would be made up of many, nor has anything extraneous mixed with it, as if it had an accident: so to be itself is not composite and that is why the composite thing is not identical with its being. (n. 32)

It might be thought that it is because of its glittering generality that to-be participates in nothing, that is, has nothing predicated of it, since there is nothing more general than it. (No need to deal here with such apparent counterexamples as "'to be' is an infinitive" and "'to be' is the opening of a soliloquy of Hamlet's.") This is just what Thomas wants us to think. Indeed, he allows the thought to generate a difficulty. Isn't being (*ens*) every bit as universal as to be (*esse*)?

Sed id quod est, sive ens, quamvis sit communissimum, tamen concretive dicitur; et ideo participat ipsum esse,	But that which is, or being, although it is most general, is concretely expressed, and thus it

non per modum quo magis commune participatur a minus communi, sed participat ipsum esse per modum quo concretum participat abstractum.

participates in existence itself, not in the way the less common participates in the more common, but rather in the way the concrete participates in the abstract. (n. 24)

In the case of the simple thing, the different modes of signifying it, concrete and abstract, do not pick out any diversity in the thing. The simple not only has being, it is being; the simple not only has goodness, it is goodness. In this tractate, unlike in *De trinitate*, Boethius makes no mention of simple or noncomposed substances other than God. In *De hebdomadibus* God alone is simple. In him there is no distinction of *esse* and *id quod est*. He is not a kind of being but being itself. Complex things, of course, are kinds of being. They receive or participate in existence because of or by way of their form (*accepta forma essendi*). As Axiom 2 points out, there are two fundamental modes of being, substantial and accidental, and each is read from a kind of form.

Quia enim forma est principium essendi, necesse est quod secundum quamlibet formam habitam, habens aliqualiter esse dicatur.

Since indeed form is a principle of being, necessarily a thing will be said to be in this way or that according to whatever form it has. (n. 27)

It is often said that Boethius could not have had anything like this in mind. We are told that Boethius meant by *diversum est esse et id quod est* only that there is a distinction of nature and individual, essence and supposit, but that he had no idea of existence.[10] This is of course nonsense. In complex things, actual existence (Boethius attributes to God's causality the fact that things *actu exsistere* [l. 143]) is the actual inherence of the form in the matter. That actual inherence cannot be equated with either form or matter or their composition. Nor of course can it be understood apart from form. It is this analysis that guides Thomas when he introduces simple things as intermediates between substances composed of matter and form and the utterly simple thing God is. Subsistent forms of the kind mentioned in *De trinitate* will not exhaust the possibilities of being, but are beings of a certain kind. Their

10. This was Duhem's interpretation. Noting that Themistius had distinguished between water (*hydor*) and the specific nature of water (*to hydati einai*), Duhem writes, "Pour Boèce, cette eau concrète, c'est le *id quod est*; la nature spécifique de l'eau, l'essence aqueuse, c'est l'*esse* que les Grecs nomment *ousia* et Saint Augustin *essentia*. Sans peine, nous allons reconnaître cette entière similitude entre la pensée de Boèce et celle de Themistius" (Duhem 1917, p. 288).

'kindness' is read from their form, which measures or restricts existence but is not identical with it. The reason for this is parasitic on (*a*) the basis of the real diversity of *esse* and *quod est* in complex things and (*b*) the denial of this diversity in God. Angels or separated substances are described within the constraints of these extremes. Only of one can it be said that He is identical with *ipsum esse* in all its amplitude: God has no form that limits existence.[11]

Our Aristotelian sensibilities are offended by this suggestion that the predicably most common has somehow become the ontologically richest. An indication of how this can be understood is found in Thomas's observation that subject and predicate terms restrict and make finite the perfection signified by the infinitive 'to be.' Taken as such, as *ipsum esse*, 'to be' suggests unlimited perfection. Elsewhere, Thomas will warn that this is not the equation of the predicably most universal and the ontologically most perfect.[12]

The axiom dealing with the good has it that like attracts like and unlikeness repels.

My contention, which I argue at length elsewhere,[13] is that what Thomas finds in the tractate is what Boethius put there, and this is particularly true of the axioms. An expositor should do just what Thomas has done here: spell out the underpinning of the text and clarify its implications. One need only look at the other medieval commentaries on Boethius to realize how remarkable Thomas's is.[14] The modern tradition of taking *diversum est esse et id quod est* to be equivalent to a distinction between essence and individual stems from Pierre Duhem, the incoherence of whose interpretation was overlooked by all those influenced by him.[15] Confronted by a presumed authoritative

11. Cf. Saint Thomas, n. 34: "*Si ergo inveniantur aliquae formae non in materia, unaquaeque earum est quidem simplex quantum ad hoc quod caret materia, et per consequens quantitate, quae est dispositio materiae; quia tamen quaelibet forma est determinativa ipsius esse, nulla earum est ipsum esse, sed est habens esse.*"

12. "*Nec oportet, si dicimus quod Deus est esse tantum, ut in illorum errorem incidamus qui Deum dixerunt esse illud esse universale quo quelibet res formaliter est. Hoc enim esse quod Deus est huiusmodi condicionis est ut nulla sibi additio fieri possit, unde per ipsam suam puritatem est esse distinctum ab omni esse; propter quod in commento none propositionis libri De causis dicitur quod indiuiduatio prime cause, que est esse tantum, est per puram bonitatem eius. Esse autem commune sicut in intellectu suo non includit aliquam additionem, ita non includit in intellecu suo precisionem additionis; quia, si hoc esset, nichil posset intelligi esse in quo super esse aliquid adderetur*" (*De ente et essentia* cap. v; Thomas Aquinas 1948, ll. 15–29). This little work, like the commentaries on Boethius, was written while Thomas was quite young, and it is particularly interesting to compare it with them.

13. McInerny 1990, particularly Part Three.

14. Cf. Shrimpf 1966 and Hadot 1970 and 1973.

15. Duhem interprets *De hebdomadibus* in terms of *De trinitate*, and vice versa. In the axioms of *De hebdomadibus*, *esse = forma = essentia*. What then does *omne namque esse ex*

and thus unexamined claim that Boethius meant something quite different from what Thomas attributed to him, Thomists turned the criticism into a claim of profundity and began to revel in the Master's alleged inability to read the text before him. All too soon this gave rise to those dithyrambic assertions about *esse* that have brought Thomism to its present crisis.

The Argument of the Tractate

Given the axioms, the question of the tractate, "How are substances good insofar as they are without for all that being substantial goods?" can be easily answered. Or so Boethius tells his correspondent. Nonetheless, he deigns to spell out the answer. He first establishes that whatever is is good and then asks whether good is predicated per se or per accidens of whatever is. An alternative form of the question is: Is good essentially, that is, substantially, predicated of whatever is or only by way of participation?

That 'by participation' and 'accidentally' are synonymous in the setting up of the problem may surprise, but there seems to be little doubt that this is the case.[16] The reader's interest is quickened by the claim that neither way of understanding how good might be predicated of being is acceptable. That is, 'every being is good' can be understood neither as 'every being is good substantially' nor as 'every being is good by participation' since each of these is reduced to an absurdity. If the division is exhaustive, we are left with the alarming result that a proposition validly derived from self-evident premises is incoherent.

Thomas, observing that all depends on *substantialiter* and *per participationem* being opposites, draws on the threefold division of participation he gives in lectio 2, n. 24, to show that 'by participation' has to mean 'accidentally' here (n. 44–45). In discussing the other horn, Thomas cautions us to understand 'per se' in the first mode of per se predication, the mode that was in play in discussing the nature of the axioms, not the second. Perseity in the second mode is had when the

---

forma mean? The whole context of *De trinitate*, cap. 2, cries out against the identification of *esse* and *forma*, yet Duhem blithely, or as he might say, *sans peine*, takes *omne namque esse ex forma est* to mean the identity of *esse* and *forma*. He never really confronts the at least apparent difficulty of the text. That an interpretation as slipshod as Duhem's should have been uncritically accepted for so long may not be one of the major scandals of the age, but it does surprise.

16. This restriction is not observed in the axioms themselves, where we read, "*Omne quod est participat eo quod est esse ut sit; alio vero participat ut aliquid sit*" (VI, ll. 41–42).

subject enters into the definition of its property, but the subject none-theless can be said to participate in that property (nn. 47).[17]

Boethius's dichotomy, then, is to be understood as a contrast between the way a subject participates in an accident and the way a predicate enters into the definition of a subject. (Or, as it could be put, in terms of Thomas's division, a contrast between the first and second modes of participation.) On this understanding, if a thing is said to be good by way of participation, and not essentially good, it will not seek the good. But it is a commonplace (*communis sententia doctorum*) that whatever is, seeks the good. This construal, then, runs afoul of the presuppositions of the inquiry. On the other hand, if things are understood to be essentially good, it is good for them to be, their existence is good, and then they are their existence and indistinguishable from the First Good.[18]

How resolve the dilemma? Imagine things without God, Boethius suggests, reminding us that in mathematics we think forms apart from sensible matter without committing ourselves to their separate exis-tence. The echoes of *De trinitate*, chapter 2, and his second discussion of the problem of universals are audible. We are asked to forget the First Good in this way, by separation, however difficult this will be both for the learned and unlearned, the civilized and the savage, for all of whom God's existence is all but self-evident. In the conceptually atheistic flat-land that results, things are good in the way they are round and heavy and red.[19] These characteristics are not of the essence of the subject. If

---

17. The modes of perseity are set forth in *Posterior Analytics* I.4 (Saint Thomas's com-mentary, lectio 14) and *Metaphysics* V.18 (Saint Thomas's commentary, lectio 18).

18. Thomas's way to this conclusion proceeds in stages. "[1] *Illa quorum substantia bona sint secundum id quod sunt, necesse est quod bona sint secundum id ipsum quod sunt.* [2] *Hoc enim ad substantiam cuiuscumque rei pertinet quod concurrit ad suum esse.* [3] *Sed quod aliqua sint, hoc habent ex eo quod est esse: dictum est enim supra quod est aliquid, cum esse susceperit.* [4] *Sequitur igitur ut eorum quae sunt bona secundum subjectum, ipsum esse sit bonum.* [5] *Si igitur omnia sunt bona secundum suam substantiam, sequitur quod omnium rerum ipsum esse sit bonum.*" And, since the premises from which he argues are convertible, he converts them. "[6] *Sequitur enim e converso quod si esse omnium rerum sit bonum, quod ea quae sunt, inquantum sunt, bona sint; ita scilicet quod idem sit unicuique rei esse, et bonum esse.*" From which follows the unacceptable: "[7] *Si ipsum esse rerum omnium sit bonum; cum ex hoc sequatur quod sint substantialia bona, consequens est etiam quod sint primo bono similia, quod est substantiale bonum, et cui idem est esse et bonum esse*" (nn. 48–51).

19. "*Intelligitur enim bonitas uniuscuiusque rei virtus ipsius, per quam perficit operationem bonam. Nam virtus est quae bonum facit habentem, et opus eius bonum redit*" (lectio 4, n. 60). In terms of *ST* Ia.5.1.ad1, Thomas is assuming that things are called good *simpliciter* and not *secundum quid*. But it is in virtue of what is, ontologically, an accident, e.g., virtues, that a person is said to be good *simpliciter*. Only on this assumption, as Thomas makes clear, will a thing's being and its being good differ. Thus, Thomas does not take Boethius to be saying that because a person's being fat and round and good differ from one another,

they were identical with the subject, they would be identical with one another, according to a version of the *communis conceptio* Boethius gives in ll. 21–22. But heavy and red and good differ. In order to avoid this consequence, we might suppose that goodness is the only attribute of things. But that won't do. "But if they were nothing else at all except good, neither heavy nor colored nor extended in spatial dimension nor were there any quality in them excepting only that they were good, then it would seem that they are not [merely] things but the source of things. Nor would 'they' seem [so], but rather 'it' would seem [so], for there is one and only one thing of this sort which is only good and nothing else."[20]

God, who has been imagined out of the picture, reenters as the result of this effort to imagine a thing with only the quality good, which is identical with what it is, for that is a description of God. There can be only one such, and he is the principle of other things. Things cannot be identical with God. What is the conclusion? Thomas states it thus: "*res creatae, amoto primo bono, nihil aliud essent quam hoc quod est esse bonum*: take away the First Good and then for created things, to be would be identical with being good" (n. 62). The price of this identification is the plurality of things and their otherness from God. So this is no way to explain how things are said to be good.

Boethius's solution to the dilemma involves a trickle-down theory. The only way things other than the First Good can be is if he wills them to exist. The existence of creatures flows from the will of him who is essentially good. Thus, there are secondary goods as well as the First Good.

'*Primum enim bonum,' scilicet Deus, 'in eo quod est, bonum est,' quia est essentialiter ipsa bonitas; sed secundum bonum, quod est creatum, est bonum secundum quod fluxit a primo bono, quod est per essentiam bonum. Cum igitur esse omnium rerum fluxerit a primo bono, consequens est quod ipsum esse rerum creatarum sit bonum, et quod unaquaeque res creata, inquantum est, sit bonum. Sed sic solum res creatae non*	The First Good, that is, God, is good just insofar as He is because he is goodness itself essentially; but a second good, which is created, is good because it flows from the First Good who is good in essence. Since then the existence of all things flows from the First Good, it follows that the existence of created things is good and that each created thing is good insofar as it is. The only

---

what a person is cannot be equated with all of these, since one could then ask, "But why not with one of them?" That all these properties are accidental properties is assumed from the beginning. See MacDonald 1988, pp. 257–58.

20. MacDonald's translation; see Appendix, ll. 106–11.

essent bonae in eo quod sunt, si esse
earum non procederet a summo bono.

way created things would not be
good insofar as they are is if they
did not proceed from the Highest
Good. (n. 62)

Since creatures receive existence from the First Good who is one with
its existence, their existence is as such good and they are essentially
good. Let us now look closely at Thomas's assessment of the Boethian
resolution, both within the exposition and elsewhere in his writings.

2. Are Creatures Good by Extrinsic Denomination?

If one searched the Boethian tractate for a *ratio boni*, some expression
or account that could be substituted for 'good,' one would come back
with empty hands. Well, not entirely. The Aristotelian account is implicit in the argument developed in the course of stating the problem.
Bonum est quod omnia appetunt. We might perhaps find intimations of
bonum est diffusivum sui as well in the tractate. But what are we to understand by "Whatever is is good" let alone "Guinness is good for you?"
    Boethius warned us at the outset that he was going to be oblique and
elusive. But it leaves one gasping that such a key word is given so little
conceptual content. When we are asked to imagine creatures without
God and think of something as fat and red and good, 'good' was no
more explained than fat and red. Is this nitpicking?
    Well, we are in effect being told how the term 'good' is common to
God and creatures. He is the First Good; creatures are secondary
goods. Consider this comment of Aquinas.

Redit ergo eius solutio ad hoc quod esse
primi boni est secundum propriam
rationem bonum, quia natura et essentia
primi boni nihil aliud est quam bonitas;
esse autem secundi boni est quidem
bonum, non secundum rationem
propriae essentiae, quia essentia eius non
est ipsa bonitas, sed vel humanitas, vel
aliquid aliud huiusmodi; sed eius esse
habet quod sit bonum ex habitudine ad
primum bonum, quod est eius causa: ad
quod quidem comparatur sicut ad
primum principium et ad ultimum

His solution comes to this that the
existence of the First Good is good
by its very definition, because the
nature and essence of the First
Good are nothing other than
goodness; the existence of the
second good is good but not in the
account of its very essence, since
goodness itself is not its essence, but
rather humanity or the like; but its
existence is good by relation to the
First Good, who is its cause, to
whom it is related as to a first

finem; per modum quo aliquid dicitur sanum, quo aliquid ordinatur ad finem sanitatis; ut dicitur medicinale secundum quod est a principio effectivo artis medicinae.

principle and an ultimate end, in the way something called healthy is referred to the end health or called medical from the effective principle of the art of medicine. (n. 62)

Thomas seems to be spelling out here our worst fears about Boethius's solution. It looks as though the creature is known to be good only with reference to God and thus is denominated good from the goodness of God. But a term is used analogically when it is used to speak of a group of things, some or one of which saves its usual meaning, the others being referred to by a secondary meaning dependent on the first or familiar one. To understand what is meant by saying 'aspirin is healthy,' I have to know what is meant by saying 'Joe is healthy.' Thus Thomas, in introducing Boethius's thought experiment whereby God is conceptually set aside, says this: *"remoto per intellectum primo bono, ponamus quod cetera sint bona: quia ex bonitate effectuum devenimus in cognitionem boni primi*: conceptually setting aside the First Good, we posit the other things as good; after all it is from the goodness of its effects that we come to knowledge of the First Good" (n. 60). The Boethian solution, in startling contrast to the account Thomas gives of names common to God and creature, seems to make the divine goodness more knowable to us than created goodness. The introduction of the standard examples of what Thomas calls analogous names,[21] namely, 'healthy' and 'medical,' suggests that God functions as do the quality health and the art of medicine in those examples.

It is just this Thomas seems to guard against when he introduces the notion of two kinds of goodness in creatures, one consisting of their relation to God, the other absolute, with the latter subdivided into whether the creature is regarded as *perfectum in esse* or *perfectum in operari*. That subdivision recalls the famous contrast of *ST* Ia.5.1.ad1 between *ens simpliciter/bonum secundum quid* and *ens secundum quid/bonum simpliciter*.

Thus arises a question that becomes part of Thomas's standard repertoire, *ut ita dicam*, namely: *"Utrum omnia sint bona bonitate prima*: Are all things good by the first goodness?"[22] This question is very much like

---

21. In contrast to Aristotle, who seems never to have used the Greek *kat'analogian* or *analogia* to speak of the relation between meanings of the same term. Rather, Aristotle speaks of equivocation *pros hen* or *pollakōs legomena*. Contrast Aristotelian and Thomistic usage in *Metaphysics* IV.1 and lectio 1.

22. Cf. *DV* XXI.4; *SCG* I.40; *ST* Ia.6.4.

another that was fateful for the history of interpreting what Thomas meant by analogous names: *"Utrum sit una sola veritas secundum quam omnia sunt vera:* Whether there is only one truth whereby all things are true?" If there is numerically one goodness and numerically one truth whereby all creatures are called good and true, this is what is meant by extrinsic denomination. When the question about truth is asked in *Summa theologiae,* Thomas expresses a universal rule about names analogously common.

In order to see this it should be noted that when something is univocally predicated of many it is found in each of them according to its proper notion, as 'animal' in every species of animal. But when something is said analogically of many things, it is found according to its proper notion in only one of them; the others are denominated from it. As 'healthy' is said of animal, urine, and medicine, though health is found only in the animal and medicine is denominated healthy from the animal's health, as effective of, and urine, as a sign of, that health. And though health is not in the medicine or urine there is in each something through which the former causes and the latter signifies health. (Ia.16.6)[23]

Now, if it were the case that every analogous name involves extrinsic denomination from what is first, and if creatures are denominated good and true analogically from God, it looks as if extrinsic denomination is all we have.

We are not surprised, accordingly, to find Cardinal Cajetan in his commentary on this text deny as universally true of analogous names the rule Thomas gives. Indeed, it is exemplified only in the case of what Cajetan says are misleadingly (*abusive*) called analogous names. Nor are we surprised when Cajetan refers us to his own book on the subject.[24]

23. "Ad cuius evidentiam, sciendum est quod, quando aliquid praedicatur univoce de multis, illud in quolibet eorum secundum propriam rationem invenitur, sicut 'animal' in qualibet specie animalis. Sed quando aliquid dicitur analogice de multis, illud invenitur secundum propriam rationem in uno eorum tantum, a quo alia denominantur. Sicut 'sanum' dicitur de animali et urina et medicina, non quod sanitas sit nisi in animali tantum, sed a sanitate animalis denominatur medicina sana, inquantum est effectiva, et urina, inquantum est illius sanitatis significativa. Et quamvis sanitas non sit in medicina neque in urina, tamen in utroque est aliquid per quod hoc quidem facit, illud autem significat sanitatem."

24. "Ad secundum vero dubitationem dicitur, quod illa regula de analogo tradita in littera, non est universalis de omni analogiae modo: imo, proprie loquendo, ut patet I Ethic., nulli analogo convenit, sed convenit nominibus 'ad unum' vel 'in uno' aut 'ab uno,' quae nos abusive vocamus analoga. Veritas autem, si comparetur ad res et intellectus, est nomen 'ab uno': quoniam in intellectu solo est veritas, a qua res dicuntur verae. Si vero comparetur ad intellectus inter se, sic est nomen analogum: nam proportionaliter salvatur, formaliter tamen, in quolibet intellectu cognoscente ver-

Cajetan's *De Nominum Analogia*[25] is easily the most influential interpretation of what Saint Thomas means by analogous names, and it is a work based on a misunderstanding of a text parallel to that in *ST* Ia.16.6. The text is *Super Sent.* I, d.19, q.5, a.2, ad 1. Cajetan took Thomas to be giving a threefold division of analogous names, and that supposed division forms the structure of his opusculum and has haunted discussions of analogy since its appearance in the last decade of the fifteenth century.[26]

The text on which Cajetan based his opusculum is a reply to an objection and can be understood only with reference to the problem it sets out to solve. Is there only one truth whereby all things are true? It seems that all things are true by one truth that is uncreated truth.

For as was said in the solution of the preceding article, true is said analogously of things in which there is truth, as health of all healthy things. But there is numerically one health from which the animal is denominated healthy (as its subject) and medicine healthy (as its cause), and urine healthy (as its sign). It seems therefore that there is one truth whereby all are called true. (*Super Sent.* I, d.19, q.5, a.2, obj.1)[27]

The argument is clear enough. An animal, medicine, and urine are called healthy analogously, and we can see that they are so denominated from the health that is in the animal; there is no need to look for a plurality of healths, one the quality of the animal, another the quality of the medicine, the other the quality of urine. These three are gathered under and share one name because medicine causes and urine shows the quality health in the animal. If this is the case with the

---

um. Esse ergo nomen aliquod secundum propriam rationem in uno tantum, est conditio nominum quae sunt 'ad unum' aut 'ab uno,' etc.: et non nominum proportionaliter dictorum. Veritas autem, respectu intellectus divini et aliorum, proportionale nomen est. Et ideo non sequitur quod in solo Deo sit. Iam enim dictum est in solutione primi dubii, quod omni praedicato formaliter de pluribus, convenit plurificari ad plurificationem subiectorum sive illud sit univocum, ut 'animal,' sive proportionale, ut 'ens,' etc.—De huiusmodi autem differentia nominum plene scriptum invenies in tractatu 'De Analogia Nominum.'" (In Iam, q. 16, a. 6, n. VI; Thomas Aquinas 1888–1906, vol. 4).

25. Cajetan 1952. The first edition by Zammit alone appeared in 1934.

26. In both McInerny 1961 and 1968, as well as in various articles written since the latter appeared, I have contested the Cajetanian interpretation. Nonetheless, it flourishes as if profound difficulties with it have not been pointed out. See, e.g., the otherwise excellent book of Avital Wohlman, Wohlman 1988. I am currently engaged in rewriting *The Logic of Analogy*, which has been out of print for some years.

27. *"Videtur quod omnia sint vera una veritate quae est veritas increata. Sicut enim dictum est in solutione praecedentis articuli, verum dicitur analogice de illis in quibus est veritas, sicut sanitas de omnibus sanis. Sed una est sanitas numero a qua denominatur animal sanum, sicut subjectum ejus, et medicina sana, sicut causa ejus, et urina sana, sicut signum ejus. Ergo videtur quod una sit veritas qua omnia dicuntur vera."*

analogous term 'healthy' and if 'true' is said to be analogously common to God and creature, then, so goes the objection, there must be numerically one truth in virtue of which this is so. The assumption is that a feature of the things called healthy is a necessary condition of their being named analogously, such that wherever there is an analogous name, that feature will be present. How does Thomas handle this objection?

In reply to the first objection it should be noted that something is said according to analogy in three ways: [1] *According to intention alone and not according to being*, as when one intention is referred to many according to prior and posterior, but exists in only one of them, as the intention of health is referred to animal, urine, and diet in different ways, according to prior and posterior, but not according to being, because health exists in the animal alone; [2] *According to being and not according to intention*, and this happens when many things are made equal in a common intention which does not exist as such in all, as all bodies are made equal in the intention of corporeity. Hence the dialectician who considers intentions alone says that the word 'body' is predicated univocally of all bodies, but this nature does not exist according to the same notion in corruptible and incorruptible bodies. For the metaphysician and the natural philosopher, therefore, who look on things as they exist, neither the term 'body' nor any other is said univocally of the corruptible and incorruptible, as Aristotle and Averroes make clear in *Metaphysics* X. [3] *According to intention and being*, as when there is equality neither of common intention nor of being, as 'being' is said of substance and accident. In such it is necessary that the common nature enjoy some existence in each of the things of which it is said, but differing according to greater and less perfection. So too I say that truth and goodness and the like are said analogically of God and creature. All these must exist in God and creature according to a notion of greater and less perfection, from which it follows that, since it cannot exist numerically the same in all, there are diverse truths. (*Super Sent.* I, d.19, q.5, a.2, ad 1)[28]

28. "*Ad primum igitur dicendum, quod aliquid dicitur secundum analogiam tripliciter:* [1] VEL SECUNDUM INTENTIONEM TANTUM, ET NON SECUNDUM ESSE; *et hoc est quando una intentio refertur ad plura per prius et posterius, quae tamen non habet esse nisi in uno; sicut intentio sanitatis refertur ad animal, urinam et diaetam diversimode, secundum prius et posterius; non tamen secundum diversum esse, quia esse sanitatis non est nisi in animali.* [2] VEL SECUNDUM ESSE ET NON SECUNDUM INTENTIONEM; *et hoc contingit quando plura parificantur in intentione alicujus communis, sed illud commune non habet esse unius rationis in omnibus, sicut omnia corpora parificantur in intentione corporeitatis. Unde Logicus, qui considerat intentiones tantum, dicit, hoc nomen, corpus, de omnibus corporibus univoce praedicari: sed esse hujus naturae non est ejusdem rationis in corporibus corruptibilibus et incorruptibilibus, ut patet X Meta., text. 5, ex Philosopho et Commentatore.* [3] VEL SECUNDUM INTENTIONEM ET SECUNDUM ESSE; *et hoc est quando neque parificatur in intentione communi, neque in esse; sicut ens dicitur de substantia et accidente; et de talibus oportet quod natura communis habeat aliquod esse in unoquoque eorum de quibus dicitur, sed differens secundum rationem majoris vel minoris perfectionis. Et similiter dico quod veritas et bonitas et omnia*

On the face of it, it does not seem surprising that Cajetan should have read this response as saying that there are three kinds of analogous name, although this assumption almost immediately gets him into difficulties. The second kind of analogous name is a univocal term! A generic term covers an inequality among its species, expressed by their differences, but does not thereby cease to be a univocal term. The inequality (*non parificantur*) of the species is said to be *secundum esse*. It is not to be confused with the inequality, the order *per prius et posterius* of a plurality of meanings of a common term. Thomas's response comes down to this. The objector is confusing the per accidens and the per se. While in the example of 'healthy' the quality health from which denomination is made exists in only one of the analogates, this is per accidens to being an analogous term.

Why? Because sometimes in things named analogously the *res significata* of the common term exists in only one of the analogates, whereas sometimes it exists in all of the analogates, though of course *per prius et posterius*. From this one concludes, not that there are two kinds of analogous name, but that these variants are per accidens to analogous naming. To underscore this, Thomas points out that inequality *secundum esse*, an order thanks to which one of the things named is primary and another secondary, is compatible with the term's being univocally common to them.

In short, Cajetan embraces the fallacy Thomas is intent on dissolving, joins what Thomas is putting asunder, and defines the truly analogous name as one in which there is both an order among the meanings of a common term *and* possession of the denominating form by all the analogates. But what Cajetan calls true analogy is invariably illustrated, in the text of Thomas, by what Cajetan considers to be an analogous name only abusively.

What, then, is the meaning of the rule for analogous names in *ST* Ia.16.6: *quando aliquid dicitur analogice de multis, illud invenitur secundum propriam rationem in uno eorum tantum, a quo alia denominantur*: when something is said analogically of many things, it is found according to its proper notion in only one of them? It does not mean that the form from which denomination is made exists in only one of the analogates. The rule is not a rule for 'healthy' alone but is meant to illuminate what is being discussed in the text where it is formulated, namely, 'true' as

---

hujusmodi dicuntur analogice de Deo et creaturis. Unde oportet quod secundum suum esse omnia haec in Deo sint, et in creaturis secundum rationem majoris perfectionis et minoris; ex quo sequitur, cum non possint esse secundum unum esse utrobique quod sint diversae veritates."

analogically common to God and creature and, to underscore the relevance of this for our purposes, for 'good' as common to God and creature. In names said analogously of God and creature, as in all analogous names, the *ratio propria* of the name is found in one of them alone.

The *ratio propria* is the way of signifying the denominating form that is controlling in understanding other, extended ways of signifying that form.[29] Whether the example be 'law' or 'virtue' or 'healthy' or 'being,' the rule will always obtain. This is not the place to discourse on analogous names as such, but this much is enough to prevent us from thinking that the divine names involve some special kind of analogy invented for the purpose. If they did, Thomas would not illustrate by 'healthy' what he means by saying that God and creature share a name analogously. Needless to say, our talk about God will, like the knowledge it reflects, reveal that we are at the very limits of our creaturely powers.

When we say of God that he is good or one or true or being, we are extending terms whose controlling meanings make them appropriate to creatures—their *rationes propriae* are rooted in creatures, not in God—and we use them to speak of the causative, creative source of these created perfections. The only way we can know God is via his effects; naming follows the path of knowing; the only way we can talk of God is to use of him words whose proper meanings were formed in knowing creatures.[30]

The problem with which this section begins will now be clearer. Unless we have a meaning or meanings for 'good' appropriate to our ordinary commerce with creatures, the term cannot be extended to God with appropriate alteration of meaning. Is it fair to say that Boethius does not provide us with any such controlling meaning? Is it fair to suggest that for him the controlling meaning is the divine goodness and that only derivatively are creatures good, known to be good and called good? A text as oblique and deliberately difficult as *De hebdomadibus* obviously should not be queried as if it were one of McGuffey's Readers. Indeed, one reaction to this problem could be to say that, if it is one for Boethius, it is also one for Thomas.

After all, it is Thomas in his commentary who says that the "*esse primi boni est secundum rationem propriam bonum*: the existence of the First Good is good according to its proper notion" and that "*esse autem secundi boni est quidem bonum, non secundum rationem propriae essentiae*: for a sec-

---

29. In short, a *ratio nominis* is a compound of the *res significata* and a *modus significandi*.
30. These are of course commonplaces, but cf. *ST* Ia.12 and 13.

ond good, to be is indeed good, but not because of the account of its very essence" (n. 62). Is Thomas saying that God saves the *ratio propria* of the analogously common term 'good' and that creatures do not, and that thus creatures are named good with reference to God's goodness, not the reverse?

The answer to the exegetical question is simple, but a wider question is raised. In the text, '*ratio propria*' means the essence or nature of the thing, what would be expressed in its definition, and the point is that goodness is identical with what God is, but this is not the claim made of the creature, "*quia essentia eius non est ipsa bonitas, sed vel humanitas, vel aliquid huiusmodi*: because goodness as such is not its essence, but rather humanity, or the like" (n. 62). In short, *ratio propria* is not to be understood here as it must be in the rule for things named analogously given in *ST* Ia.16.6. That being said, are we not told on considerable authority that it is from God that all fatherhood is named both in heaven and on earth?

Of course, of the things named 'good,' God is ontologically first; if he were not good, nothing else would be. He is the source of all goodness, both in heaven and on earth. Even as we, or Saint Paul, say such things, we are employing a human language whose first meanings and referents are the things of our experience, the things we see and touch and weigh and alter with our arts. The suppleness of language within even the most restricted range of so to speak terrestial usage reveals the scale and order and unifying that characterize our efforts to know that world. Thomas was struck in reading Aristotle's *Physics* how a term like *morphe*, whose obvious meaning is the external shape or contour of an object, is used in graded ways to mean any property of a thing, then its constituting essential element. All this in the first book of the *Physics*. And language so developed is the only one we have for speaking of God when knowledge of the things of this world enables us to come to knowledge of the invisible things of God. To speak of God's will and mind and ideas involves stretching our language to the breaking point. We come to do it with ease, as we learn easily to say the Lord's Prayer, but the Gospels knew we needed images and pictures of human fathers to catch this new meaning.

What is first in our knowledge and language may be last on the ontological scale, and vice versa. Aristotle had already suggested this. It is what characterizes names analogously common to God and creatures. The language as used of creatures controls its extension to speak of the divine. But that which is indicated in God, however imperfectly, is the source of the created perfections. This is captured by the distinction made between the order *secundum impositionem nominis* and the order *secundum rem nominis*.[31]

It seems clear enough that in *De hebdomadibus* Boethius adopts a sapiential viewpoint, the viewpoint of the theologian who would see everything with reference to God. In Thomas's words, the opusculum is concerned with the procession of good creatures from the good God: *de processione bonarum creaturarum a Deo bono*.[32] Nonetheless, like Thomas in *Summa theologiae*, Boethius has to rely on our knowledge of the contrast between good things and the First Good. It could be said that, to a great degree, though not exclusively, the axioms state that contrast.

In *De veritate* Thomas confronts the problematic of our discussion when he asks if all things are good because of the first goodness. The Boethian tractate is referred to again and again, and becomes the source of the objection that creatures are extrinsically denominated good from the divine goodness. Isn't that what *De hebdomadibus* establishes by showing the incoherences that result from trying to understand created goodness without reference to the First Good? Having recalled this in *DV* XXI.4.obj.1, Thomas continues in the next objection: "But notice that there is no goodness in creatures when the goodness in God is ignored because the goodness of the creature is caused by God's goodness, not because the thing is formally denominated good from God's goodness" (*DV* XXI.4.obj.2).[33]

Now this, as it happens, is Thomas's own view. The objector, however, continues by rejecting what I have just quoted and adding that when something is denominated solely with reference to another, it is extrinsically denominated, that is, not denominated from a form intrinsically possessed. And the old stand-by 'healthy' is invoked. Urine and exercise are denominated from the health in the animal, not from some intrinsic form of health in themselves. And isn't that the way creatures are denominated good from the divine goodness?

Thomas replies by distinguishing two ways in which a thing can be denominated something with reference to another. Sometimes it is the reference or relation itself that is the reason for the denomination, and that is the case with calling urine and exercise healthy with reference to the health of the animal.

---

31. See Thomas *In V Metaphysicorum* lectio 5, nn. 824–26.
32. *In Boethii de trinitate*, prologus, n. 7; Thomas Aquinas 1954b.
33. "*Sed dicendum quod ideo hoc contingit quod non intellecta bonitate in Deo non est bonitas in aliis creaturis, quia bonitas creaturae causatur a bonitate Dei, non quia denominetur res bona bonitate Dei formaliter.*"

Something is denominated with respect to another in a second way when the cause and not the respect is the reason for the denomination; just as air is said to be illumined by the sun, not because air's being related to the sun is for it to be lit, but because the direct opposition of air to sun is the cause that it is lit; and this is the way the creature is called good with respect to Good. (*DV* XXI.4.ad2)[34]

God is the cause of the goodness of the creature, but that is not the meaning of the term when the creature is *called* good, as if for the creature to be called good meant 'is dependent on God.' The creature would neither be nor be good if God did not cause it, but when we say that a thing is or is good, the meaning of these terms is not 'is caused by God.'[35]

A disputed question is always far more complicated and nuanced than a parallel discussion in *Summa theologiae*, but in neither case is what Thomas says of the goodness of creatures, while owing much to Boethius, confined to the crabbed, coded Boethian doctrine. The *sed contra est* of Ia.6.4 (which asks the by now familiar question: *Utrum omnia sint bona bonitate divina*) provides a crisp summary of Thomas's view. "On the contrary, all things are good just insofar as they are. But all things are not called being from the divine existence, but from their own existence. Not all things are good by the divine goodness, therefore, but by their own goodness" (*ST* Ia.6.4).[36] It is not God's goodness that is the goodness of creatures any more than his existence is theirs: there is created goodness and created existence thanks to which creatures are and are good. Thomas, in the body of the article, reminds us that Plato posited a realm of transcendental entities to which appeal had to be made to explain the fleeting things of this world. Odd as that sounds in the case of 'man' and 'white' and the like, Thomas says it makes a good deal of sense, even Aristotelian sense, to speak of something that is being as such and goodness as such. And how do created good things relate to God who is goodness itself?

---

34. "*Alio modo denominatur aliquid per respectum ad alterum, quando respectus non est ratio denominationis, sed causa; sicut si aer dicatur lucens a sole; non quod ipsum referri aerem ad solem sit lucere aeris, sed quia directa oppositio aeris ad solem est causa quod luceat; et hoc modo creatura dicitur bona per respectum ad bonum.*"

35. At the end of *DV* XXI.5, Thomas gives this interpretation of Boethius's exercise in mentally separating creatures from God. "*Dato igitur quod creatura esset ipsum suum esse, sicut et Deus; adhuc tamen esse creaturae non haberet rationem boni, nisi praesupposito ordine ad creatorem; et pro tanto adhuc diceretur bona per participationem, et non absolute in eo quod est. Sed esse divinum, quod habet rationem boni non praesupposito aliquo, habet rationem boni per seipsum; et haec videtur esse intentio Boethii in lib. de Hebd.*"

36. "*Sed contra est quod omnia sunt bona inquantum sunt. Sed non dicuntur omnia entia per esse divinum, sed per esse proprium. Ergo non omnia sunt bona bonitate divina, sed bonitate propria.*"

Anything can be called good and a being by way of some assimilation, however remote and defective, insofar as it participates in that which is goodness and being in its essence, as the foregoing has made clear. In this way something is called good from the divine goodness as from the first exemplar, efficient, and final cause of all goodness. Nonetheless, each thing is called good from a likeness of the divine goodness inherent in it which is the goodness formally denominating it. So it is that there is one goodness of all and many goodnesses. (*ST* Ia.6.4)[37]

We have here an account that incorporates the Boethian account into a more comprehensive one, the final pay-off on the quasi-demur registered in the exposition when, after analyzing Boethius's solution, Thomas notes that there is a *duplex bonitas*, a twofold goodness, in creatures. They are and are good thanks to the causality of the First Good, but as effects of the First Good they have their own existence and goodness thanks to which they are remotively and defectively like their cause. We of course are first aware of creatures, and our notions of existence and goodness reflect this epistemological priority that grounds a priority of nomenclature. Only when creatures are seen to require a cause very different from themselves does the possibility arise of speaking of being itself and goodness itself as referring to a unique entity. Then it can be said that because he is, we are; because he is good, other things are good. In *De hebdomadibus*, Boethius favors this sapiential approach, the *via descensus*; it is thoroughly characteristic of Thomas that he should constantly remind us of the complementary *via ascensus*.[38]

If the problem of *De hebdomadibus* arises from the seeming impossibility of saying of a creature either that it is good substantially or that it is good accidentally, it generates a further problem as to the relation between divine and created goodness. The tractate concludes by referring created goodness to the First Good as if what it means to say of a creature that it is good is that its existence is caused by God in whom existence and goodness are identical. On the other hand, it seems clear that we can know the divine goodness only on an analogy with created goodness. The question then becomes precisely the one Thomas asked

---

37. "*A primo igitur per suam essentiam ente et bono, unumquodque potest dici bonum et ens, inquantum participat ipsum per modum cuiusdam assimilationis, licet remote et deficienter, ut ex superioribus patet. Sic ergo unumquodque dicitur bonum bonitate divina, sicut primo principio exemplari, effectivo et finali totius bonitatis. Nihilominus tamen unumquodque dicitur bonum similitudine divinae bonitatis sibi inhaerente, quae est formaliter sua bonitas denominans ipsum. Et sic est bonitas una omnium; et etiam multae bonitates.*"

38. See *In Boethii de trinitate*, lectio 2, q. 2, a. 1; Thomas Aquinas 1954b (=Thomas Aquinas 1955, q. 6, a. 1, ad tertiam questionem), p. 382a–b.

in *ST* Ia.13.6: Are names analogically common to God and creature said first of God or of creature?

If a term is used metaphorically of God, Thomas notes, it is clear that the creature would be the point of reference for understanding its use in speaking of God. Furthermore, if all divine names were negative or relative, the same would be true—the reference to the creature would be primary. But what of affirmative divine names, names like 'wise' and 'good'? When we say that God is wise or that God is good, we do not only mean that he is the cause of created wisdom or goodness. What do we mean? "For when God is called good or wise this means not only that He is the cause of wisdom or goodness but that these preexist eminently in Him. On that account it should be said that with respect to the perfection meant by the name they are said first of God rather than of creatures, because these perfections emanate from God to creatures" (*ST* Ia.13.6).[39] But with respect to the imposition of the name, these are first imposed on creatures since we first know them.[40]

This does not mean that, contrary to the rule we discussed earlier, two of the analogates save the *ratio propria* of the common term, or that there are two *rationes propriae* of 'good' according to one of which it is first said of creatures and according to the other first said of God. In order to say that God's goodness is a perfection that he would have even if he had never created, we must mention created goodness. The relation of divine goodness to created goodness is not a real relation, but only one of reason. But it cannot be considered an epistemological prop we can dispense with so as to consider the divine goodness in itself. We have no such direct access.

When then it is said that God is good, the meaning is not that God is the cause of goodness, or that He is not evil, but rather this: *that which we call goodness in creatures preexists in God*, and indeed in a higher way. From this it does not follow that to be good pertains to God insofar as He causes goodness, but rather the reverse: because He is good, He diffuses goodness to things. (*ST* Ia.13.2)[41]

---

39. "*Cum enim dicitur* DEUS EST BONUS *vel* SAPIENS, *non solum significatur quod ipse est causa sapientis vel bonitatis, sed quod haec in eo eminentius praeexistunt. Unde, secundum hoc, dicendum est quod secundum rem signficatam per nomen, per prius dicuntur de Deo quam de creaturis: quia a Deo huiusmodi perfectiones in creaturas manant. Sed quantum ad impositionem nominis, per prius imponuntur creaturis, quas prius cognoscimus.*" My emphases.

40. *ST* Ia.13.6.

41. "*Cum igitur dicitur* DEUS EST BONUS, *non est sensus* DEUS EST CAUSA BONITATIS, *vel* DEUS NON EST MALUS: *sed est sensus,* ID QUOD BONITATEM DICIMUS IN CREATURIS, PRAEEXISTIT IN DEO, *et hoc quidem secundum modum altiorem. Unde ex hoc non sequitur quod Deo competat esse bonum inquantum causat bonitatem: sed potius e converso, quia est bonus, bonitatem rebus diffundit.*" Thomas adds a quotation from Augustine's *De doctrina christiana* I.32: "*inquantum bonus est, sumus*" (because He is good, we are). My emphases.

Thus the *ratio boni* as said of God includes the *ratio propria* of created goodness even while expressing the fact that God's goodness is prior to created goodness.

But what then of the fact that created goodness is an effect of God's causality? Must this not be the meaning of 'good' as said of creatures? The text we quoted earlier (*ST* Ia.6.4) provides the answer. God is the good of the creature as its first exemplar, efficient, and final cause. That is the final word on created goodness. But it cannot be the first. The creature is called good by a similitude of the divine goodness inherent in the creature, which is its own goodness whereby it is formally denominated good. Only when this formal goodness is grasped, and understood in terms of what is intrinsic to the creature, can there be an ascent to the divine goodness. But that ascent can never let go of its springboard, as Thomas makes clear in his account of 'God is good.'

Thus it is that Thomas's account of divine and created goodness incorporates but is not exhausted by the account he found in Boethius's *De hebdomadibus*.

CHAPTER 4

Being and Goodness

Eleonore Stump and Norman Kretzmann

1. Introduction

Parts of Aquinas's moral philosophy, particularly his treatment of the virtues and of natural law, are sometimes taken into account in contemporary discussions, but the unusual ethical naturalism that underlies all of his moral philosophy has been neglected. Consequently, the unity of his ethical theory and its basis in his metaphysics are not so well known as they should be, and even familiar parts of the theory are sometimes misunderstood.

We think Aquinas's naturalism is a kind of moral realism that deserves serious reconsideration. It supplies for his virtue-centered morality the sort of metaethical foundation that recent virtue-centered morality has been criticized for lacking.[1] Moreover, it complements Aquinas's Aristotelian emphasis on rationality as a moral standard by supplying a method of determining degrees of rationality.[2] And when Aquinas's naturalism is combined with his account of God as absolutely simple, it effects a connection between morality and theology that offers an attractive alternative to divine-command morality, construing morality not merely as a dictate of God's will, but as an expression of his nature.[3] Finally, Aquinas's brand of naturalism illuminates a side of the problem of evil that has been overlooked, raising the question whether

Reprinted from Eleonore Stump and Norman Kretzmann, "Being and Goodness," in *Divine and Human Action: Essays in the Metaphysics of Theism*, edited by Thomas V. Morris. Copyright © 1988 by Cornell University. Used by permission of the publisher, Cornell University Press.
1. See, e.g., Louden 1984; Pence 1984.
2. See Section 6 below.
3. See Stump and Kretzmann 1985, esp. pp. 375–76.

recent defenses against the problem are compatible with the doctrine of God's goodness.

Aquinas's ethics is embedded in his metaphysics, only the absolutely indispensable features of which can be summarized here. Consequently, we cannot undertake to argue fully for his ethical theory in this essay. For our purposes it will be enough to expound the theory, to consider some of the objections it gives rise to, and to point out some of the advantages it offers for dealing with recognized issues in ethics and philosophy of religion.

2. The Central Thesis of Aquinas's Metaethics

The central thesis of Aquinas's metaethics is that the terms *'being'* and *'goodness'* *are the same in reference, differing only in sense.*[4] What does Aquinas mean by this claim, and what are his grounds for it?

It will be helpful to begin with an observation about terminology. Contemporary metaphysics uses cognates of some Latin words crucial to Aquinas's presentation of his theory, but the terms 'essence,' 'actual,' and 'exists,' for example, have acquired meanings different from the meanings Aquinas understood the corresponding Latin terms to have. For instance, he does not identify essential characteristics with necessary characteristics; as he uses those terms, all essential characteristics are necessary, but not all necessary characteristics are essential. Furthermore, in Aquinas's usage what is actual is opposed to what is potential rather than to what is merely possible, as in standard contemporary usage. As he understands it, what is actual is, fundamentally, what is in being; and what is in being is, ordinarily, what exists. But, as we'll see, his conception of being is broader than the ordinary conception of actual existence.

Goodness is what all desire, says Aquinas, quoting Aristotle,[5] and what is desired is (or is at least perceived as) desirable. Desirability is an essential aspect of goodness. Now, if a thing is desirable as a thing of a certain kind (and anything at all *can* be desirable in that way, as a means, if not as an end), it is desirable to the extent to which it is perfect

---

4. *ST* Ia.5, esp. a. 1. We are interpreting Aquinas's *'sunt idem secundum rem'* as 'are the same in reference' and *'differunt secundum rationem'* as 'differ in sense.' Aquinas's treatment of this thesis about being and goodness is a particularly important development in a long and complicated tradition, on which see MacDonald 1986. See also Hoenes 1968.

5. See, e.g., *SCG* I.37.4 (n. 306); III.3.3 (n. 1880); Aristotle, *Nicomachean Ethics* I.1 (1094a1–3).

of that kind—that is to say, a whole, complete specimen, free from relevant defect.[6] But, then, a thing is perfect of its kind to the extent to which it is fully realized or developed, to the extent to which the potentialities definitive of its kind—its specifying potentialities—have been actualized. And so, Aquinas says, a thing is perfect and hence desirable (good of its kind) to the extent to which it is in being.[7] That's one way of seeing how it is true to say that a thing's goodness is its being.

Offering the same line of explanation from the standpoint of the thing rather than a desirer of the thing, Aquinas says that everything resists its own corruption in accordance with its nature, a tendency he interprets as its aiming (naturally) at being fully actual, not merely partially or defectively in being. Thus, since goodness is what all things aim at or desire, each thing's goodness is its full actuality.[8]

In another gloss on Aristotle's dictum Aquinas takes the sense of 'goodness' to be brought out in the notion of that in which desire culminates.[9] Now, what is desired is desired either for the sake of something else, for the sake of something else and for its own sake, or solely for its own sake. What is desired solely for its own sake is what the desirer perceives as the desirer's final good, that for the sake of which it desires all the other things it desires, that in which the hierarchy of its desires culminates. But what each desirer desires in that way is the fulfillment of its own nature, or at least that which the desirer perceives as the very best for the desirer to have or be.[10] Each thing aims above all at being as complete, whole, and free from defect as it can be.[11] But the state of its being complete and whole just is that thing's being fully actual, whether or not the desirer recognizes it as such. Therefore, full

---

6. Kinds must be broadly conceived of in this connection. For an exhibit at a plant pathology conference a stunted, diseased specimen of wheat may be perfect of its kind, just what's wanted. But the kind at issue in that case is not wheat, but wheat-afflicted-by-wheat-mildew. Alternatively, it might be said that the goodness of an exhibit, like that of other artifacts, is related to the rational purposes of its users, in which case the kind at issue is not wheat, but exhibit-specimen-of-mildewed-wheat.

7. *ST* Ia.5.1.

8. See, e.g., *SCG* I.37.4 (n. 306); *ST* IaIIae.94.2. Rational agents have goals over and above their natural aims, and so the objects of their conscious desires are sometimes only perceived by them as good and not also actually good for them.

9. *SCG* III.3, passim.

10. See, e.g., *ST* IaIIae.1.5.

11. As we have already suggested (n. 8 above), when the thing described is a rational being, the object of its aim will include its *conception* of the fulfillment of its nature, which can be more or less mistaken. Objectively, evil objects of desire are desired because they are perceived as good for the desirer to have.

actualization is equivalent to final goodness, aimed at or desired by every thing.[12]

Finally, Aquinas argues that every action is ordered toward being, toward preserving or enhancing being in some respect either in the individual or in its species: in acting, all things aim at being. Therefore, again, being is what all desire; and so being is goodness.[13]

On Aquinas's view, these various arguments show that when the terms 'being' and 'goodness' are associated with any particular sort of thing, both terms refer to the actualization of the potentialities that specify that thing's nature. Generally, then, 'being' and 'goodness' have the same referent: the actualization of specifying potentialities. The actualization of a thing's specifying potentialities to at least some extent is, on the one hand, its existence as such a thing; it is in this sense that the thing is said to have *being*. But, on the other hand, the actualization of a thing's specifying potentialities is, to the extent of the actualization, that thing's being whole, complete, free from defect—the state all things naturally aim at; it is in this sense that the thing is said to have *goodness*. Like the designations 'morning star' and 'evening star,' then, 'being' and 'goodness' refer to the same thing under two descriptions and so have different senses but the same referent.

This claim of Aquinas's about being and goodness, his central meta-ethical thesis, is bound to give rise to several objections. But since effective replies to such objections depend on certain elements of Aquinas's metaphysics, we postpone considering them until we've presented those elements.

3. Full Actuality and Substantial Form

On Aquinas's view, every thing has a substantial form.[14] The substantial form of any thing is the set of characteristics that place that thing in its species and that are thus essential to it in Aquinas's sense of 'essential.'[15] Some of these essential characteristics determine the genus within

12. What is meant by 'equivalent' here is spelled out in our discussion of supervenience in Section 5.

13. *SCG* III.3.4 (n. 1881).

14. Irwin 1980 is particularly useful for our purposes here because of Aquinas's dependence on Aristotle. On the relevant role of substantial form in particular, see esp. pp. 37–39 of Irwin's article.

15. See Section 2 above.

which the thing's species belongs; the others differentiate the thing's species from other species of that genus. The thing's genus-determining characteristics (or simply its genus) and differentiating characteristics (or simply its differentia) together constitute its substantial form or specific essence, what is essential to it as a member of its species. All the characteristics making up the thing's substantial form are essential to it as an individual, but if there are individual essences as well, they will include characteristics over and above those constituting the substantial form.[16]

The substantial form as a set of essential characteristics invariably includes at least one power, capacity, or potentiality, because every form (any set of real rather than merely conceptual characteristics) is a source of some activity or operation.[17] Among the essential characteristics, the thing's differentia is a characteristic peculiar to and constitutive of the thing's species, the characteristic that can be identified as the thing's specifying potentiality (or potentialities). The differentia is thus the source of an activity or operation (or set of them) peculiar to that species and essential to every member of the species. As Aquinas puts it, the thing's specific nature includes the power to engage in a specific operation determining of and essential to that thing as a member of that species.[18]

It follows that a thing's form is perfected when and to the extent to which the thing performs an instance of its specific operation, actualizing its specifying potentiality.[19] A thing's operation in accord with its specific power brings into actuality what was not actual but merely potential in that thing's form. So in Aquinas's basic, metaphysical sense of 'perfect,' a thing is perfect of its kind to the extent to which it actualizes the specifying potentiality in its form.[20] The derivative, evaluative sense of 'perfect' is explained by the connection between actuality and goodness: for something to be actual is for it to be in being, and 'being' and 'goodness' are the same in reference. Therefore, a thing is good of its kind to the extent to which it is actual.[21] Or, putting

16. See, e.g., ST Ia.5.5; IaIIae.85.4; DV XXI.6.
17. See, e.g., SCG III.7.7 (n. 1916); ST IaIIae.55.2. A contemporary counterpart of this view of forms might be seen in Shoemaker 1980.
18. See, e.g., SCG I.42.10 (n. 343): "The differentia that specifies a genus does not complete the nature (rationem) of the genus; instead, it is through the differentia that the genus acquires its being in actuality."
19. See, e.g., ST IaIIae.49.4, esp. ad1.
20. ST IaIIae.3.2: "Anything whatever is perfect to the extent to which it is in actuality, since potentiality without actuality is imperfect."
21. See, e.g., SCG III.16.3, 4 (nn. 1987 and 1988).

it another way, a thing is good of its kind (or perfect) to the extent to which its specifying potentiality is actualized, and bad of its kind (or imperfect) to the extent to which its specifying potentiality remains unactualized.[22]

4. From Metaethics to Normative Ethics

The specifying potentialities of a human being are in the cognitive and appetitive rational powers, intellect and will, that constitute its differentia, reason.[23] Although endowed with the freedom of choice, a human will in association with its intellect is inclined toward goodness not just naturally (like the appetitive aspect of every other being) but also "along with an awareness of the nature of the good—a condition that is a distinguishing characteristic of intellect."[24] Rational beings are "inclined toward goodness itself considered universally" rather than naturally directed toward one particular sort of goodness.[25] The operation deriving directly from the human essence, then, is acting in accordance with rationality, and actions of that sort actualize the specifying potentiality of human beings. A human being acting in accordance with rationality makes actual what would otherwise have been merely potential in his or her substantial form. By converting humanly specific potentiality into actuality, an agent's actions in accordance with rationality increase the extent to which the agent has being as a human being; and so, given the connection between being and goodness, such actions increase the extent to which the agent has goodness as a human being. Human goodness, like any other goodness appropriate to one species, is acquired in performing instances of the operation specific to that species, which in the case of humanity is the rational employment of the rational powers. The actions that contribute to a human agent's moral goodness will be acts of will in accordance with rationality.[26]

A thing's substantial form, the set of essential characteristics determining the thing's species, constitutes the nature of the thing. And so whatever actualizes a thing's specifying potentiality thereby also per-

22. See, e.g., *ST* IaIIae.18.1.
23. See, e.g., *ST* IaIIae.55.1, 2; 63.1.
24. *ST* Ia.59.1. As we've pointed out (nn. 8 and 11), the awareness concomitant with a rational appetite can be distorted.
25. *ST* Ia.59.1; cf. *SCG* II.47 and *DV* XXIII.1. See also our discussion in Stump and Kretzmann 1985, Section 5, pp. 359–62.
26. See, e.g., *SCG* III.9.1 (n. 1928); *ST* IaIIae.18.5.

fects the nature of the thing. Given what else we have seen of Aquinas's theory, it follows that in his view what is good for a thing is what is natural to it, and what is unnatural to a thing is bad for it. So, he says, the good is what is according to nature, and evil is what is against nature;[27] in fact, what is evil cannot be natural to anything.[28] As for human nature, since it is characterized essentially by a capacity for rationality, what is irrational is contrary to nature where human beings are concerned.[29]

Habits that dispose a person to act in accordance with nature—that is, rationally—are good habits, or virtues.[30] Vices, on the other hand, are habits disposing a person to irrationality and are therefore discordant with human nature.[31] Aquinas quotes with approval Augustine's appraisal of a vice as bad or evil to the extent to which it diminishes the integrity or wholeness of the agent's nature.[32]

It is an important consequence of this account of goodness and badness that no thing that exists or can exist is completely without goodness. This consequence can be inferred directly from the central thesis about being and goodness,[33] but some of its moral and theological

27. *ST* IaIIae.18.5.ad1.

28. *SCG* III.7.6 (n. 1915): "Therefore, since badness or evil is a privation of that which is natural, it cannot be natural to anything."

29. See, e.g., *ST* IaIIae.71.1.

30. See, e.g., *ST* IaIIae.55.1–4. For human beings, acting in accordance with rationality is their second actuality (as Aquinas says, following Aristotle). A newborn human being is only potentially a reasoning being. A mature human being acting in accordance with rationality, such as Aquinas when he is writing on ethics, is rationally exercising his rational powers; and that actual exercise of the specifying potentiality for human beings is their second, or more fully complete, actuality. But there is a state intermediate between the newborn's and that of the fully active mature human being—e.g., the state of Aquinas when he is asleep or in some other way not then actualizing his specifying potentiality. The sleeping Aquinas, unlike the philosophizing Aquinas, lacks the second actuality appropriate to human nature; but even the sleeping Aquinas has something the newborn infant lacks—an acquired disposition or habit to exercise his rational powers in certain ways. That is, the sleeping Aquinas has the being appropriate to human beings, but incompletely, in the condition picked out as first actuality (see, e.g., *ST* IaIIae.49.3, 4). Virtues are instances of first actuality relative to certain actions in accordance with rationality. Perfection as a human being (in this life) must include first actualities in part because the freedom associated with rational powers ranges over more alternatives than can be sorted out rationally and expeditiously on an occasion of action unless some disposition to respond in one way rather than another is part of the agent's character. That's one reason virtues are essential ingredients in human goodness. (See, e.g., *ST* IaIIae.49.4; 55.1.)

31. *ST* IaIIae.54.3: "And in this way good and bad habits are specifically distinct. For a habit that disposes [the agent] toward an action that is suited to the agent's nature is called good, while a habit that disposes [him] toward an action that is not suited to his nature is called bad."

32. *ST* IaIIae.73.8.s.c.

33. See, e.g., *SCG* III.7, passim.

implications are worth pointing out. Evil is always and only a defect in some respect to some extent; evil can have no essence of its own. Nor can there be a highest evil, an ultimate source of all other evils, because a *summum malum*, an evil devoid of all good, would be nothing at all.[34] A human being is defective, bad, or evil not because of certain positive attributes but because of privations of various forms of being appropriate to his or her nature.[35] And, in general, the extent to which a thing is not good of its kind is the extent to which it has not actualized, or cultivated dispositions for actualizing, the potentialities associated with its nature.[36] Every form of privation is covered by that observation—from physical or mental subnormality, through ineptitude and inattention, to debauchery and depravity. In each case some form of being theoretically available to the thing because of its nature is lacking.

These considerations put us in a better position to assess Aquinas's understanding of the difference in sense between 'being' and 'goodness.' It should be clear by now that being is to be considered both absolutely and in a certain respect. Considered *absolutely*, being is the instantiation of a certain substantial form, the mere existence of a thing of some sort. But since each substantial form also includes a specifying potentiality, when that potentiality is actualized, the thing actualizing it is more fully a thing of that sort, a better specimen. When being is considered in this second way, it is correct to say that *in a certain respect* there is an increase of being for that thing. The ordinary sense of 'being' is being considered absolutely, that is, a thing's mere existence as the instantiation of some substantial form. But since to be is to be something or other, even being considered absolutely entails the actualization to *some* extent of *some* specifying potentiality, and in this way everything that is is good (in some respect and to some extent).

5. Supervenience

Aquinas, then, may be added to the lengthening list of those who think that goodness supervenes on some natural property.[37] As we've seen, Aquinas would say in general that an object *a* has goodness (to

34. *SCG* III.15, passim.
35. See, e.g., *ST* Ia.5.3.ad2: "No being can be called bad or evil insofar as it is a being, but insofar as it lacks some sort of being—as a human being is called evil insofar as it lacks the being of virtue and an eye is called bad insofar as it lacks clarity of sight."
36. See, e.g., *SCG* III.20, 22.
37. For a helpful survey, examples, and much else of relevance, see Kim 1984.

any extent) as an *A* if and only if *a* has the property of having actualized its specifying potentiality (to that extent). In particular, moral goodness supervenes on rationality in such a way that if any human being is morally good (to any extent), that person has the property of having actualized his or her capacity for rationality (to that extent); and if any human being has that property (to any extent), he or she is morally good (to that extent). Goodness supervenes on actualization of specifying potentialities; human moral goodness supervenes on actualization of rationality.

The relationship Aquinas sees between goodness and natural properties is complex and can be shown most easily by analogy. Fragility supervenes on certain natural properties without being reducible to any one of them, as Campbell and Pargetter have recently argued.[38] In line with their argument, we might say that *x* is fragile in virtue of chemical bonding *A*, *y* in virtue of *B*, and *z* in virtue of *C*. Fragility cannot be reduced to or identified with bonding *A*, or *B*, or *C*, but it supervenes on each of them. It may be that what is common to *x*, *y*, and *z* is that each has weak chemical bonds in crucial spots, but those weak bonds are chemically quite distinct in connection with *A*, *B*, and *C*. In that case it can be said that the characteristic of being fragile and the characteristic of having weak chemical bonds in crucial spots are coextensive, and that fragility supervenes on natural characteristics, and yet it must be denied that fragility can be identified with any one of those characteristics.

The relationship between fragility and other characteristics in that analysis is like the relationship between goodness and natural characteristics in Aquinas's ethical naturalism. A thing's goodness and the actualization of the thing's specifying potentiality are coextensive. Goodness in general is not to be identified with a particular natural characteristic, however, because the natural characteristic that is the actualization of a specifying potentiality will vary from one species of things to another. And the same observation holds regarding being; what is required to be a fully actualized member of species *X* is different from what is required to be a fully actualized member of species *Y*.

38. Campbell and Pargetter 1986. "The relationship between fragility, fragility phenomena and the basis of the fragility is given by two identities. (1) being fragile = having some property which is responsible for being such that <X is dropped, X breaks>, etc. and (2) The property which is responsible for object O's being such that <O is dropped, O breaks>, etc. = having chemical bonding B. This explicates the 'because' relation for fragility, i.e., it tells us what is meant when we say that O is fragile because it has bonding B. And when we say that object N is fragile because it has bonding A, clause (1) remains unchanged and clause (2) is changed in the obvious way" (p. 161).

The degree of actualization of the specifying potentialities for an X is the degree of being as an X, and this is also the degree of goodness as an X. But the specifying potentialities for an X differ from the specifying potentialities for a Y. So being and goodness are identical, but neither is to be identified with any one particular natural characteristic on which it supervenes.

But is moral goodness in particular identical with the natural characteristic of actualized rationality? Since human beings are essentially rational animals, human moral goodness is coextensive with actualized rationality. But moral goodness (or badness) is a characteristic of all beings whose nature involves freedom of choice, whether or not they are human. And so not even moral goodness is necessarily coextensive with the actualization of rationality, the specifying potentiality for human beings in the actual world. Goodness as an X will, for every X, be identical with the actualization of an X's specifying potentialities, but there is no natural characteristic such that goodness (or even moral goodness) is identical with it (where identity of properties is taken to require at least necessary coextension).

6. Objections to the Central Thesis

On the basis of this exposition of Aquinas's central thesis against its metaphysical background we can reply to objections the thesis is almost certain to generate. (The first two of those we consider are in fact considered and rebutted by Aquinas himself.)

Objection 1

A thing's being and its being good are clearly not the same—many things that are, aren't good—and so being and goodness are clearly not coextensive. But if the terms are identical in reference, as Aquinas claims they are, being and goodness would have to be coextensive.[39]

This first objection trades on the counterintuitive character of a corollary of the central thesis—viz., everything is good insofar as it is in being. Aquinas accepts that corollary, associating it particularly with Augustine.[40] But the corollary cannot be reduced to an absurdity simply by observing that there are things that aren't good. In accordance

---

39. *ST* Ia.5.1.obj.1.
40. *ST* Ia.5.1.s.c. (Augustine, *De doctrina christiana* I.32).

with the central thesis, a thing has goodness in a certain respect and to a certain extent simply by virtue of possessing a substantial form and thus existing as a thing of a certain sort. As we've seen, however, the sense of 'goodness' is not simply the possession of some substantial form but, in particular, the actualization of the specifying potentiality inherent in that form. Only to the extent to which a thing has actualized that potentiality is it true to say unqualifiedly that the thing is good. For instance, to call Hitler good (without identifying some special respect, such as demagoguery) is to imply that he is good as a human being, or as a moral agent, which is false in ways that Aquinas's practical morality could detail by indicating how this or that action or decree of Hitler's fails to actualize rationality.

Objection 2

Goodness admits of degrees, but being is all or nothing. No rock, desk, or dog is in being just a little; no dog is in being more than another dog. On the other hand, things clearly can increase or decrease in goodness, and one thing can be better or worse than another thing of the same kind. Therefore, 'goodness' and 'being' can't have the same referent.[41]

It may be right to say of existence, at least abstractly, that it's all or nothing. But since every instance of existence is existence as something or other, and since existence as something or other typically admits of degrees—being a more or less fully developed actualized specimen—it is by no means clear that being is all or nothing. Making the same observation from Aquinas's point of view, we might say that there's more to being than just existence. Where contingent beings are concerned, potentiality for existing in a certain respect is a state of being that is intermediate between actually existing in that respect and not existing at all in that respect, as we've seen.[42] Furthermore, the actualization of potentialities is often gradual, so that the being of the thing whose specifying potentiality is being actualized admits of degrees. Stages in the actualization of a thing's specifying potentiality certainly can be and often are described in terms of goodness rather than being. All the same, the degrees of goodness picked out in such ordinary descriptions are supervenient on degrees of being.

41. *ST* Ia.5.1.obj.3.
42. N. 30 above.

Objection 3

According to Aquinas's central thesis, the more being, the more goodness. In that case unrestrained procreation, for example, would be a clear instance of promoting goodness, since the increase of the human population is an increase of being and consequently of goodness. But that consequence is absurd.

Human beings who bring another human being into existence have not in virtue of that fact alone produced any goodness in any ordinary sense. If with Aquinas we take the basic sense of 'goodness' to be actualization of a thing's specifying potentiality, then a human being produces goodness to the extent to which it actualizes its own or something else's specifying potentiality. Considered in itself, bringing children into the world does nothing to actualize any human being's specifying potentiality.[43] On the contrary, a man who fathered very many children would probably contribute to a *decrease* of goodness. He would be unable to have parental influence on the lives of his children or to give them the care they needed just because there were so many of them, and so it is at least a probable consequence of his unrestrained procreation that there would be more people whose chances of actualizing their specifying potentialities were unnaturally low.

But objection 3 is more complicated than the preceding objections just because goodness does supervene on being (in the way described in Section 5 above). Consequently, whenever a thing has being in any respect, it also has goodness in some respect to some extent. If Ahasuerus, with his many wives and concubines, fathered, say, 150 children, he was partially responsible for the existence of 150 human beings and, consequently, for the goodness supervening on the being that constituted their existence. But neither we nor Aquinas would count Ahasuerus as a moral hero or even morally praiseworthy just because he fathered all those children.

Our rejoinder to objection 1 will help here. The small amount of goodness that must supervene on even the mere existence of a thing is not enough to call that thing good. In fact, if the thing falls too far short of the full actualization of its specifying potentiality, it is bad (or evil) considered as an instance of its kind, even though there is goodness in it. So insofar as Ahasuerus couldn't do what he ought to have done to help his children develop into good human beings, his unrestrained

43. The capacity for reproduction is a potentiality human beings share with all living things.

procreation couldn't count as the production of goodness; and to the extent to which his fathering so many children would be a factor in diminishing or preventing his care of them, it could count as producing badness.

Objection 4

According to Aquinas, loss of being is loss of goodness: badness (or evil) is the privation of goodness, which is a privation of being. In that case, taking penicillin to cure strep throat would be a bad thing to do, since it would result in the destruction of countless bacteria. But that consequence is absurd.

Objection 4 gains a special strength from the fact that it forces a defender of Aquinas's position to take on the task of ranking natural kinds. The task may seem not just uncongenial but impossible for anyone who understands goodness as supervenient on being itself. In Jack London's story "To Build a Fire" either a man will save his life by killing his dog or the dog will continue to live but the man will die. Since in either case one being is left, it may look as if Aquinas's theory must be neutral on the question of which of those beings should survive. But a moral intuition that is at least widely shared would consider the case in which the dog dies and the man survives to be preferable.

Far from offending that intuition, Aquinas's theory can explain and support it because his metaphysics provides a systematic basis on which to rank natural kinds: the Porphyrian Tree, a standard device of medieval metaphysics inherited from Hellenistic philosophy. A Porphyrian Tree begins with an Aristotelian category (*substance* is the standard medieval example) and moves via a series of dichotomies from that most general genus through at least some of its species. (In theory, all its possible species can be uncovered by this means.) The dichotomies produce progressively more specific species by the application of a pair of complementary properties (differentiae) to a less specific species (a genus) already in the tree. In this way, for example, *substance* yields *corporeal substance* and *incorporeal substance* to begin the tree. Corporeal substances can in turn be divided into those capable and those incapable of growth and reproduction and other life processes; and corporeal substances capable of life processes can be divided into those capable and those incapable of perception—animals and plants, roughly speaking. Finally, those capable of perception can be divided into those capable and those incapable of rationality—human beings and other animals. In this schema, then, human beings are corporeal substances capable of life processes, perception, and rationality. Since each dichotomy in the tree is generated by the application of complementary characteristics, and since (setting aside the complicated case of the first dichotomy) all the characteristics applied involve capacities, one of the species (or genera) encountered in any pair after the first is characterized by a capacity its counterpart lacks. But, given Aquinas's views on being and actuality, an increment in capacity (or potentiality) constitutes an increment in being; and, because of the supervenience of goodness on being, a species (or genus) with more capacities of the sort that show up in the differentiae will have potentially more goodness than one with fewer. So, other things being equal, the goodness of a human life is greater than that of a dog's just because of rationality, the incremental capacity.[44]

We don't have to accept the universal applicability of the Porphyrian Tree in order to see that in it Aquinas does have a method for ranking at least some natural kinds relative to one another, and that the method is entirely consistent with his central thesis. Moreover, the method yields results that elucidate and support the intuitive reaction to the Jack London story: other things being equal, we value a human being more than a dog (or a colony of bacteria) because there's more to a human being than there is to a dog (or a colony of bacteria).

Finally, although Aquinas subordinates all other species of animal to the human species, this feature of his theory cannot be interpreted as sanctioning wanton cruelty toward nonhuman animals or their gratuitous destruction. It is another corollary of his central thesis that any destruction of being is always prima facie bad in some respect and to some extent. Because some destruction may often be less bad than the only available alternative, it may often be rationally chosen. But unless there is some greater good (some enhancement of being) that can be achieved only by means of destruction, an agent who chooses to destroy will choose irrationally.

---

44. The ceteris paribus clause in this claim is important. Even though species *A* outranks species *B* in the way described, it is theoretically possible that a particular individual of species *B* might outrank an individual of species *A*. Suppose that there are angels, that angels constitute a species as human beings do, that the species *angel* outranks the species *human being*, and that Satan is a fallen angel. It is theoretically possible that Mother Teresa outranks Satan in the relevant sense even though the amount of being available to an angel is greater than that available to any human being. For if Mother Teresa has actualized virtually all of her specifying potentialities and Satan very few of his, it will be possible to ascribe more being and hence more goodness to Mother Teresa than to Satan.

In expounding and defending Aquinas's metaethics, we have been moving toward a consideration of his normative ethics, to which we now turn.

7. The Evaluation of Actions

Aquinas's normative ethics is constructed around a theory of virtues and vices, which are conceived of as habitual inclinations, or dispositions toward certain sorts of actions. It will be helpful, therefore, to begin this consideration by looking briefly at his analysis and evaluation of human actions.[45]

A human action, strictly speaking, is one in which a human agent exercises the specifically human rational faculties of intellect and will.[46] (Absentminded gestures, consequently, are not human actions even though they are "actions associated with a human being.")[47] Every human action has an object, an end, and certain circumstances in which it is done.

An action's object, as Aquinas conceives of it, is fundamentally the state of affairs the agent intends to bring about as a direct effect of the action.[48] We might characterize the object as the immediate aim or purpose of the action. When Esther goes uninvited into the court of King Ahasuerus's palace, for instance, the object of her action is an audience with the king.

But in Aquinas's analysis of action, an action's object is distinguished from the action's end.[49] We might provisionally think of an action's end as the agent's motive for performing the action. So the end of Esther's action of coming to the palace is to try to persuade Ahasuerus to rescind his decree mandating the death of all the Jews in his kingdom.

Seen in this way, the *object* of an action is what the agent intends to accomplish as a direct result of her action, while its *end* is *why* she intends to accomplish it. Both the object and the end of an action are taken into account in determining the action's species, in determining

45. For a clear, succinct presentation of some of this material in more detail, see Donagan 1982.
46. Aquinas's "Treatise on Action" is contained in ST IaIIae.6–17; 18–21 are concerned with the evaluation of actions.
47. For this distinction, see ST IaIIae.1.1.
48. On the object of an action, see, e.g., ST IaIIae.10.2; 18.2.
49. On the end of an action, see, e.g., ST IaIIae.1.1–3; 18.4–6. For our purposes here, we are omitting some of the details of Aquinas's complex distinction between the object and the end of an action; for some of the complications see, e.g., ST IaIIae.18.7.

what the action essentially *is*.[50] Given Aquinas's central thesis regarding being and goodness, then, it is not surprising to find him maintaining that the goodness or badness of any action is to be decided on the basis of an assessment of the action's object and end. If the contemplated states of affairs that the action aims at and that motivate the agent are good, the action is good; if either the object or the end is not good, the action is not good.

So far, this account of the goodness of actions seems to ignore the fact that certain types of actions are morally neutral. The object of pitching horseshoes is to get them to fall around a stake, a state of affairs that certainly seems to be neither morally good nor morally bad. Suppose the end of such an action on a particular occasion is to entertain a sick child, which we may suppose is morally good. Then it might seem that the action itself, pitching horseshoes to entertain a sick child, would have to be evaluated by Aquinas as not good, for although its end is good, its object is not.

This counterintuitive evaluation can be dispelled by taking into account Aquinas's concept of the *circumstances* of an action: When was the action done? Where? By whom? How? etc.[51] An action's circumstances are obviously not essential features of a type of action, but they are what might be called *particularizing* accidents, because any broadly conceived type of action is particularized or recognized as the particular action it is by attending to its circumstances. So, for example, part of what makes Esther's action the particular action it is, is its circumstances. She comes uninvited to the court of the king's palace at a time when Ahasuerus has decreed death for anyone who comes into the court of the palace without having been called by the king, unless the intruder "finds favor with the king." Furthermore, because it has been a month since the king last sent for her, Esther has reason to believe she is out of favor with the king. Finally, she comes there at a time when Ahasuerus has decreed the death of all the Jews in his kingdom, and Esther's intention is to speak for her people. It is on the basis of a consideration of these circumstances that the action of coming uninvited to the king, which seems morally neutral, is particularized as Esther's act of courage and altruism.[52]

The importance of a consideration of circumstances in Aquinas's evaluation of actions can be seen in the fact that he takes any and every

50. On specifying an action, see, e.g., *ST* IaIIae.1.3; 18.2, 5, 7.
51. On the circumstances of an action, see esp. *ST* IaIIae.7, passim.
52. On the role of circumstances in the evaluation of actions, see, e.g., *ST* IaIIae.18.3, 10, 11.

action particularized by its circumstances to be either good or bad, even though the type of the action broadly conceived of may be morally neutral (his paradigms are picking a straw off the ground or taking a walk).[53]

Not all of an action's accidents are included among its circumstances. So, for example, Esther's action has the accidents of contributing to the death of Haman and of being commemorated in a book of the Bible. But on Aquinas's theory neither of those accidents can or should make any difference to an evaluation of Esther's action. An action's circumstances, he says, are those accidents of it that are related per se to the action being evaluated; all its other accidents are related to it only per accidens.[54]

By this distinction he seems to mean that the circumstances of Esther's particular action, the action being evaluated in our example, are features accidental to the *type* of action she performs, but not accidental to her particular action on that particular occasion. On the contrary, even our understanding of the object and end of her particular action is heavily influenced by what we know of its circumstances. In light of that knowledge we might want to revise our original broad assessment and say, more precisely, that the object of her action is a *dangerous and difficult* audience with the king, and that its end is a *resolute and self-sacrificial* attempt to get the king to rescind his edict.

The action's circumstances may be called its *intrinsic* accidents, the others its *extrinsic* accidents. The intrinsic accidents of Esther's action clarify and redefine our understanding of *what she does*, what she is responsible for; its extrinsic accidents—such as its being commemorated in a book of the Bible—obviously contribute nothing to such an understanding. Even the extrinsically accidental fact that her action has some causal relationship with Haman's death is not in any way a feature of what *she* does, because the connection between her action and his death is an unforeseeable and partly fortuitous chain of events, something she could not be held responsible for.

So Aquinas's evaluation of actions is based entirely on a consideration of *what* those actions *are* and not at all on a consideration of their extrinsic accidents. In that way it is a natural outgrowth of his central metaethical thesis. The object and end of an action determine the being of the action; the action's circumstances determine the being of the particular action that is actually performed, and in doing so they clarify

53. *ST* IaIIae.18.8.
54. See, e.g., *ST* IaIIae.7.2.ad2.

and refine our understanding of the particular action's object and end. A particular (actually performed) action, then, is good only in case both its object and its end as informed by its circumstances are good; otherwise, the particular action is bad. The goodness of the action's object or end depends, in turn, on whether the contemplated state of affairs motivating or aimed at by the agent is good, as judged by the central thesis.

The end of Esther's action, for example, is to persuade the king to rescind his decree of death for all the kingdom's Jews. But the king's decree was irrational, on Aquinas's view, since it would have resulted in a great loss of being and hence of goodness without any greater good to justify the loss. Helping to bring about the rescinding of an irrational decree, however, is rational, other things being equal, and therefore morally good.[55] (Analogous things can be said about the object of Esther's action.)

8. Problems for a Simpleminded Application of the Thesis

In the story of Esther, her attempt to save her people involves her knowingly risking her life: "and if I perish, I perish." How, if at all, is the evaluation of her action in terms of its object and end affected by that circumstance of the action? Aquinas would, not surprisingly, find that aspect of her action praiseworthy. In discussing courage, he praises risking one's life in the defense of the common good as a prime example of that virtue.[56] But suppose that Esther succeeds in saving her people and dies in the attempt. Would Aquinas's theory still evaluate her action as good in that case?

The simpleminded reply to that question is an emphatic affirmative: Of course Esther's action is good even if it costs her her life; it saves thousands of lives at the expense of one. On balance there is a great surplus of being and consequently of goodness.

Although the affirmative reply seems right, the reason given for it is repugnant. If this simpleminded bookkeeping approach were what Aquinas's thesis about being and goodness required, the thesis would lead to results that are egregiously inconsistent with the rest of Aquinas's moral theory as well as repugnant to moral intuitions shared by most people in his time and ours. We can show this by considering

---

55. On Aquinas's treatment of issues of this sort regarding decrees or laws, see Kretzmann 1988.
56. See, e.g., *ST* IIaIIae.123, passim.

applications of the simpleminded approach to three cases more complicated than our revised version of Esther's story. The first of them is a version of one of Aquinas's own examples.

The Heaven Case

Johnson is a murderer, and Williams is his innocent victim. But when Johnson murders him, Williams (unbeknownst to Johnson) is in a state of grace and so goes to heaven. The ultimate end of human existence is union with God in heaven, and so by bringing it about that Williams achieves the ultimate end, Johnson brings about an increase of being (and consequently of goodness). In reality, then, Johnson's murder of Williams is morally justified.

Aquinas considers his version of the heaven case as an objection to his own claim that the deliberate killing of an innocent person is never morally justified.[57] His rejoinder to this objection is that the fact that Williams goes to heaven, the good that is supposed to justify Johnson's murder of Williams, is an accident that is related to Johnson's action only per accidens; Williams's going to heaven is an extrinsic accident of Johnson's action. Aquinas is apparently thinking along this line: Williams's spiritual condition and not Johnson's action is what causes Williams to go to heaven, and it is an extrinsic accident of Johnson's action that Williams was in that condition at the time of the murder. Since it is a feature of Aquinas's theory that an action is to be evaluated solely on the basis of what it *is* and not on the basis of any of its extrinsic accidents, his evaluation of Johnson's action would not take any account of the fact that Williams goes to heaven. What Johnson's action *is*, as far as the story goes, is simply the murder of an innocent person, which is of course not morally justifiable in Aquinas's theory.

Aquinas's treatment of the heaven case strikes us as satisfactory, but his conclusion that sending Williams to heaven is only an extrinsic accident of Johnson's action seems to depend on the fact that Johnson does not (presumably cannot) know that Williams is in a state of grace. If Johnson knew that killing Williams would result in Williams's going to heaven, it would at least be harder to deny that achieving that result was part of the end of Johnson's action and thus part of what Johnson's action *was*. We want to consider some cases in which there is no relevant ignorance on the part of the agent.

57. *ST* IIaIIae.64.6.obj.2 and ad2.

The Hostage Case

A madman takes five people hostage and threatens to kill them all unless Brown kills Robinson, an innocent bystander. Brown decides that killing Robinson is morally justified by the surplus of being (and consequently of goodness) that will result from using Robinson's death to save the lives of the five hostages.

In the hostage case the object of Brown's action is Robinson's death, and its end appears to be the saving of five lives. Aquinas's way of dismissing the counterintuitive moral assessment in the heaven case is clearly unavailable as a way of dealing with the hostage case. The good that appears to justify Brown's action is the action's *end*, which *must* be taken into account in evaluating the action. In considering how Aquinas would deal with the hostage case, it will be helpful to look more closely at his conception of the end of an action.

Since it is Aquinas's view that actions should be evaluated only on the basis of what they are and not on the basis of their extrinsic accidents, and since it is also his view that actions are to be evaluated on the basis of their ends, the state of affairs sought after as the end of the action must be intrinsic to the action itself. For that reason it seems clear that the notion of motive, although it is in some respects close to Aquinas's notion of end, is not interchangeable with it. A state of affairs counts as the end of an action if and only if the agent performs the action for the sake of establishing that state of affairs, *and* the agent *can* in fact establish that state of affairs *solely by* performing that action.

In the hostage case the good that is supposed to justify Brown's killing the innocent Robinson is the saving of five lives. But that good cannot be the end of Brown's action because it is not a state of affairs he can establish by killing Robinson. The survival of the hostages depends not on Brown's action but on the action of the madman, who can of course kill them all even if Brown meets his demand. Therefore, the survival of the hostages is not a state of affairs Brown can be said to establish solely by killing Robinson. And once this more precise notion of the end of an action has been introduced, the hostage case can be assimilated to the heaven case after all. In both cases, the good that is supposed to justify the killing of an innocent person turns out not to be an intrinsic part of the action being evaluated but rather only an extrinsic accident of it that is for that reason to be left out of account in the evaluation of the action. When Brown's action in the hostage case is evaluated in that way, it is evaluated simply as the deliberate killing of an innocent person; and since that state of affairs is unquestionably bad, the action itself is not morally justified.

But even if this attempt to defend Aquinas's evaluation of actions succeeds in the hostage case, it will apparently fail if we alter the form of the counterexample in one crucial respect.

The Hospital Case

Five patients in a hospital are waiting for donors to be found so that they can undergo transplant operations. One of them needs a heart; the second, a liver; the third, lungs; and the fourth and fifth each need a kidney. Every one of the five patients will be able to lead a normal life if, but only if, an organ donor can be found. Each of them will die very soon without a transplant operation. Jones, the skilled transplant specialist in charge of these patients, decides that killing Smith, a healthy, innocent person, is morally justified by the surplus of being (and consequently of goodness) that will result from using Smith's organs to save the five critically ill patients.[58]

The end of Jones's action, even on the more precise interpretation of 'end,' is the saving of five lives. In the hospital case, unlike the hostage case, no other agent's action is needed to establish the state of affairs Jones aims at establishing, because he is a relevantly skilled specialist in charge of the five patients. And if the saving of their lives can in this case count as the end of Jones's action, then it must be taken into account in evaluating the action. For that reason, the tactic that was effective in defending Aquinas's evaluation of actions against the hostage case won't work against the hospital case.

But Aquinas's evaluation of actions requires taking into account the action's object as well as its end. Since the object and the end together make the action what it *is*, and since the goodness of anything is a function of its being, both object and end must be good if the action is to be good. But the object of Jones's action in the hospital case is the death of the innocent Smith and the removal of his organs, which is unquestionably morally bad. Aquinas would, more specifically, condemn the object of Jones's action in the hospital case as *unjust* (as we explain in the next section).

But the sacrifice of one to save many in the hospital case is formally like our revised version of Esther's story. In order to understand Aquinas's evaluation of the hospital case and to see whether it applies also to

58. For a well-known form of the problem in the hospital case, see Foot 1978.

Esther's courageous act of altruism, we need to understand something of Aquinas's theory of the virtues in general and of justice in particular.

9. Justice and Its Place in the Scheme of the Virtues

Assuming for now the metaphysical underpinnings of Aquinas's theory of the virtues—his accounts of intellect and will, passion and operation, disposition and habit—we can begin this brief synopsis by saying that (human) moral goodness is a kind of goodness attainable only by rational beings and, as we've seen, a rational being is good to the extent to which it actualizes its capacity for rationality. Summarizing drastically, we can say that moral virtue is the will's habit of choosing rationally in controlling passions and directing actions.[59] Of the cardinal virtues, prudence is the habit of skillfully choosing means appropriate for the attaining of ends and so is concerned with directing actions; in this way prudence links intellectual and moral virtues.[60] As for the cardinal virtues concerned with controlling passions, if the passions are of a sort that need to be controlled in order to keep them from thwarting rationality, the relevant habit is temperance. And if the passions are the sort that need to be controlled in order to keep them from deterring the agent from an action to which reason prompts him or her, the relevant habit is courage.[61] Finally, if what is at stake is the exercise of rationality not in the agent's governance of herself but in her actions affecting other people, the relevant habit is justice.[62]

In Aquinas's view, a society has a being of its own. Some things contribute to the being of a society, and others to its dissolution. In accordance with Aquinas's metaethics, the things that contribute to a society's being are part of the society's good, and the virtue of justice generally in the members of the society is directed toward establishing and preserving that common good. Aquinas, who follows Aristotle closely here, distinguishes distributive from commutative justice in respect of the rational moral principles to which the virtue conforms. Distributive justice is the rational regulation of the distribution of the society's worldly goods, aiming at a rational relationship in that respect between the society as a whole and any individual member of it.[63] Commutative

---

59. See, e.g., *ST* IaIIae.60, passim. For a good discussion of the Aristotelian background, see Kosman 1980.
60. See, e.g., *ST* IaIIae.57.5; 58.4; IIaIIae.47–56.
61. See, e.g., *ST* IaIIae.60.4.
62. See, e.g., *ST* IaIIae.61.2; IIaIIae.57–71.
63. *ST* IIaIIae.61.1.

justice, on the other hand, is the rational regulation of relationships among individuals or subgroups within the society. The basis of commutative justice in Aquinas's treatment of it seems to be that human beings considered just as persons are equals, and that it is therefore rational for them, considered just as persons, to treat one another as equals, and irrational for them to treat one another unequally, considered just as persons.[64]

A used-car dealer and a customer, considered just as persons, are equals. If the dealer is deceptive about the defects of a car and so cheats the customer out of much of the purchase price, then in that particular exchange of worldly goods the dealer gets a greater share than the customer gets—which is contrary to reason because the dealer and the customer are equals in all relevant respects. The inequality of the trade is part of what makes it an instance of cheating, and cheating is morally bad because it contravenes the principles of commutative justice.[65]

So, whenever one person takes another's worldly goods, the action will be just only if it is rational. A necessary (though not also sufficient) condition of its being rational is its involving an even trade. A slanderer, for instance, takes away the victim's reputation, one of the more important worldly goods, and gives nothing in return; slander is thus a gross injustice.[66] Murder is perhaps the grossest injustice of all, since in depriving the victim of life, the greatest of worldly goods, the murderer is not only providing no worldly compensation but also rendering the victim incapable of receiving any such compensation.[67]

In the hospital case the object of Dr. Jones's action is characterized by exactly that sort of injustice. His taking of Smith's life and vital organs involves considerable benefit for his five patients, but there can be no compensatory worldly good for Smith. The injustice in the object of Jones's action is a sufficient condition for evaluating the action as morally bad, regardless of the beneficial aspects of its end.

We began our investigation of the simpleminded application of Aquinas's central thesis by considering a revised version of the story of Esther, in which she loses her life in saving her people. It should now be clear that the intuitive positive evaluation of such an act of self-sacrifice is not affected by our negative evaluation of Jones's sacrifice of Smith in

---

64. *ST* IIaIIae.61.2.
65. See, e.g., *ST* IIaIIae.77, passim.
66. See *ST* IIaIIae.73, passim; for comparisons of slander (or "backbiting") with theft or murder, see esp. 73.3.
67. On murder as a vice in opposition to commutative justice and the vice "by which a man does the greatest harm to his neighbor," see *ST* IIaIIae.64, passim.

the hospital case. Esther would not be guilty of any injustice if she gave up her own life for her people, although of course Ahasuerus would be guilty of injustice if he took her life in those circumstances. In fact, according to Aquinas's account of commutative justice, it is impossible for Esther to be unjust to herself, because a person cannot take *for* herself an unfair share of worldly goods *from* herself. The reasons for disapproving of Jones's action in the hospital case do not apply to Esther's hypothetical self-sacrifice, and approval of her self-sacrifice need not and should not be based on the simpleminded bookkeeping application of Aquinas's central thesis.

10. Agent-Centered Restrictions in Aquinas's Ethics

These considerations give us reason to think that Aquinas's ethics is a deontological theory of morality that can handle the problem of agent-centered restrictions. Samuel Scheffler has recently described these restrictions as rendering "typical deontological views . . . apparently paradoxical."

An agent-centred restriction is, roughly, a restriction which it is at least sometimes impermissible to violate in circumstances where a violation would serve to minimize total overall violations of the very same restriction, and would have no other morally relevant consequences. Thus, for example, a prohibition against killing one innocent person even in order to minimize the total number of innocent people killed would ordinarily count as an agent-centred restriction. The inclusion of agent-centred restrictions gives traditional deontological views considerable anti-consequentialist force, and also considerable intuitive appeal. Despite their congeniality to moral common sense, however, agent-centred restrictions are puzzling. For how can it be rational to forbid the performance of a morally objectionable action that would have the effect of minimizing the total number of comparably objectionable actions that were performed and would have no other morally relevant consequences? How can the minimization of morally objectionable conduct be morally unacceptable?[68]

Though Aquinas's theory certainly endorses the truism that the good is to be maximized, it also interprets the nature of goodness in general and of good actions in particular in such a way that no action whose object is characterized by injustice can be rationally performed no mat-

68. Scheffler 1985, 409–19; 409. In this article Scheffler is commenting on Foot 1983 (revised 1985). For Scheffler's own resolution of the puzzle of agent-centered restrictions, see Scheffler 1982.

ter how great a good is incorporated in the action's end. On this basis, a generalization of agent-centered restrictions can be endorsed and accommodated in Aquinas's teleological deontology.

The generalized version of Scheffler's example is a prohibition against perpetrating or permitting one injustice of uncompensatable suffering even in order to minimize the total number of injustices, and at this level of generality "the very same restriction" is the restriction against perpetrating or permitting injustice. Agent-centered restrictions that prohibit agents from perpetrating or permitting actions that constitute an injustice are rational for that very reason, regardless of the good to be achieved by performing those actions.

11. The Theological Interpretation of Aquinas's Central Thesis

Aquinas's central metaethical thesis has a theological interpretation more fundamental than any of its applications to morality. For since Aquinas takes God to be essentially and uniquely "being itself" (*ipsum esse*), it is God alone who is essentially goodness itself.[69] This theological interpretation of Aquinas's thesis regarding being and goodness entails a relationship between God and morality that avoids the embarrassments of both "theological subjectivism" and "theological objectivism"[70] and provides a basis for an account of religious morality preferable to any other we know of.[71]

The question "What has God to do with morality?" has typically been given either of two answers by those who think the answer isn't "Nothing."[72] God's will is sometimes taken to create morality in the sense that whatever God wills is good just because he wills it: consequently, right actions are right just because God approves of them and wrong actions are wrong just because God disapproves of them. This divine-command morality may be thought of as theological subjectiv-

---

69. See, e.g., *ST* Ia.2.3 ("*Quarta via*"); 3.4, 7; 6.3. Bonaventure, Aquinas's contemporary and colleague at the University of Paris, forthrightly identifies God as the single referent of 'being' and 'goodness' in his own version of the central thesis, interpreting the Old Testament as emphasizing being, the New Testament as emphasizing goodness (see, e.g., *Itinerarium mentis in Deum* V.2).

70. See Kretzmann 1983a.

71. See Stump and Kretzmann 1985, pp. 375–76.

72. This brief discussion of religious morality is adapted from Stump and Kretzmann 1985.

ism (TS).[73] The second of these two typical answers takes morality to be grounded on principles transmitted by God but independent of him, so that a perfectly good God frames his will in accordance with those independent standards of goodness: consequently, God approves of right actions just because they are right and disapproves of wrong actions just because they are wrong (theological objectivism, TO).

The trouble with TS is that by its lights apparently anything at all could be established as morally right or good by divine fiat. So, although TS makes a consideration of God's will essential to an evaluation of actions, it does so at the cost of depriving the evaluation of its moral character. Because it cannot rule out anything as absolutely immoral, TS seems to be a theory of religious morality that has dropped *morality* as commonly understood out of the theory. TO, on the other hand, obviously provides the basis for an objective morality, but it seems equally clearly not to be a theory of *religious* morality since it suggests no essential connection between God and the standards for evaluating actions. Furthermore, the status of the standards to which God looks for morality according to TO seems to impugn God's sovereignty.

So the familiar candidates for theories of religious morality seem either, like TS, to be repugnant to moral intuitions or, like TO, to presuppose moral standards apart from God, which God may promulgate but does not produce. For different reasons, then, both TS and TO seem inadequate as theories of religious morality; neither one provides both an objective moral standard and an essential connection between religion and morality.

On the conception of God as essentially goodness itself, however, there is an essential relationship between God and the standard by which he prescribes or judges. The goodness for the sake of which and in accordance with which he wills whatever he wills regarding human morality is identical with his nature. On the other hand, because it is God's very nature and not any arbitrary decision of his that thereby constitutes the standard for morality, only things consonant with God's nature could be morally good. The theological interpretation of the central thesis of Aquinas's ethical theory thus provides the basis for an objective religious morality.

---

73. For an interesting, sophisticated treatment of divine-command theories of morality, see, e.g., Quinn 1978.

12. Justice, Uncompensated Suffering, and the Problem of Evil

But a more pointed theological application of Aquinas's central thesis can be developed by combining the conception of God as perfect goodness itself with the impermissibility of certain actions as brought out in our generalized account of agent-centered restrictions. The rationality of agent-centered restrictions is a consequence of the irrationality of treating the victim of the initial action unjustly in such a way that even achieving that action's laudable end leaves the victim uncompensated, and it is the injustice of the uncompensated suffering that makes the action impermissible.[74] It follows that it is impossible that a perfectly good God would permit, much less perform, any action whose object involves a victim who is treated unjustly and left uncompensated, no matter how much other evil might be prevented thereby.

Nevertheless, many, perhaps most, attempts to solve the problem of evil portray God as permitting or even performing actions that appear to be impermissible in just that way. For instance, Richard Swinburne's "argument from the need for knowledge," which is certainly not idiosyncratic in its attempt to provide a morally sufficient reason for God's permitting natural evil, takes the initially attractive line that many natural evils "are necessary if agents are to have the *knowledge* of how to bring about evil or prevent its occurrence, knowledge which they must have if they are to have a genuine choice between bringing about evil and bringing about good."[75] But as this line is developed, it turns out, not surprisingly, that in very many cases God must be portrayed as allowing some innocent person or persons to suffer without compensation so that others may learn to avoid or to prevent or mitigate such suffering on other occasions. "If God normally helps those who cannot help themselves when others do not help, others will not take the trouble to help the helpless next time."[76] Even if we suppose, as Swinburne does, that the knowledge gained in such a way cannot be gained other-

---

74. Dostoevsky presents the classic case of this sort of acknowledgment near the conclusion of Ivan's harangue of Alyosha over the problem of evil: "'Imagine that you are creating a fabric of human destiny with the object of making men happy in the end, giving them peace and rest at last, but that it was essential and inevitable to torture to death only one tiny creature—that baby beating its breast with its fist, for instance—and to found that edifice on its unavenged tears, would you consent to be the architect on those conditions? Tell me, and tell the truth.' 'No, I wouldn't consent,' said Alyosha softly" (*The Brothers Karamazov*, Bk. V, ch. 4).

75. Swinburne 1979, pp. 202–3.

76. Swinburne 1979, p. 210.

wise, at least not efficaciously, God's role in this arrangement seems morally on a par with that of Dr. Jones in the hospital case—or worse, since the end of Jones's action is the prevention of death whereas the end of God's nonintervention is the alleviation of ignorance.

Swinburne deals with difficulties of this sort by stressing God's right to treat us as we have no right to treat one another.[77] But to say in this context that God has such a right is to imply that there would be no injustice on God's part if he exercised the right. Swinburne's claim, then, comes to this: if God were to do something that would be unjust by human standards, it would not count as unjust simply because God was its perpetrator. If this claim is not to convey the morally repulsive suggestion that anything whatever that God might do would count as good solely because God did it (including, for instance, breaking his promise to save those who put their trust in him), then there must be morally relevant features of God's nature and action for which there are no counterparts in human nature and action.

Swinburne sometimes suggests that God's being the creator of the world is just such a feature. This seems to be the most promising line to take in support of Swinburne's claim about God's rights, but we do not think it succeeds. A mother is also in a sense the creator of her child. Although that relationship gives her rights over the child that others do not have, it is not nearly enough to justify her if she inflicts uncompensated suffering on her unwilling child. If she were to deny her daughter any college education in order to have money enough to send her son to Harvard when her daughter also wants an education and receives no compensating benefits for failing to get one, the mother would be outrageously unfair. That she was in some sense the creator of the children would in no way lessen the unfairness. Of course, God is the creator of human beings in a much more radical sense than a mother is the creator of her children. But would the assessment of the mother's unfairness be at all softened if it turned out that she had built these children from scratch in a laboratory? We see no respect in which the degree of radicalness in the claim that one person created another could be a morally relevant consideration in evaluating the justice of the creator's treatment of his creatures.

Similarly, Plantinga has suggested that natural evils might be perpetrated by fallen angels, and that the good there is in the exercise of free will on their part might provide a morally sufficient reason for God to allow instances of natural evil, if, and only if, the world characterized by

77. Swinburne 1979, pp. 216–18.

such an arrangement is one in which there is more good than evil.[78] On this view, an omniscient, omnipotent, perfectly good God might permit the inhabitants of Mexico City to suffer in an earthquake so that the good of freedom might thereby be achieved in the earthquake-causing activity of fallen angels, as long as the general preponderance of good over evil was not thereby destroyed.[79] Plantinga's Free Will Defense (FWD) has sometimes been challenged because it has been thought to impugn God's omnipotence, but as far as we know, the literature on FWD has not so far addressed the challenge that arises from Aquinas's sort of ethical theory, which provides grounds for doubting whether FWD preserves God's perfect goodness. As our earthquake example suggests, FWD does not explicitly rule out attributing to God an action Aquinas would consider unjust and hence immoral. If it does not, then on Aquinas's view, the reason FWD assigns to God for permitting some instances of evil (especially natural, but also some kinds of moral evil) is not a *morally* sufficient reason.

But the issue should not be construed as tied particularly to Aquinas's ethics. If moral goodness includes agent-centered restrictions, both general and particular, then God's justice and individual human rights must be taken into account in any attempt to explain God's permitting moral or natural evil. And it may be more effective to raise the issue in terms of agent-centered restrictions, which have a "considerable intuitive appeal" and "congeniality to moral common sense" quite independently of their involvement in Aquinas's or any other ethical theory. Putting the matter in those terms, if a proposed solution to the problem of evil depends on implicitly rejecting generalized agent-centered restrictions as having no application to God, it will be important to ask what sort of ethical theory is presupposed by the proposal and to consider whether such a theory is consistent with whatever else is held to be true about God by the defender of theism against the argument from evil.

In correspondence with us, Plantinga has said of FWD that agent-centered restrictions and the requirements of justice

clearly are not excluded; they just aren't explicitly mentioned. If you are right (and I'm not convinced you aren't) in thinking that God couldn't permit an innocent to suffer without some compensating good (accruing to that very

78. See, e.g., Plantinga 1974, pp. 192–93.
79. Something similar can be said about cases in which the justification for God's allowing one human being to treat another in a flagrantly unjust way (as occurs in murder or rape, for instance) is basically the freedom of the perpetrator.

person), then a world in which innocents suffer without such compensation won't be a very good world. In fact, if such a state of affairs is so evil that no amount of good can outweigh it, then *no* good possible world would be one in which there is such uncompensated suffering of innocents. . . . But can't we mend matters simply enough, just by adding . . . that *a* [the possible world God actualizes in FWD] meets the agent-centered restrictions: that *a* contains no instances of uncompensated suffering of innocents . . . [?]

Plantinga is plainly right to insist that FWD doesn't explicitly rule out agent-centered restrictions, but adding them successfully requires saying more about the nature of the world in which innocents suffer but are compensated.

Worries raised by consideration of agent-centered restrictions are not allayed simply by stipulating compensation for the suffering of innocent victims, as can be seen by considering an adaptation of an episode from Dickens's *Tale of Two Cities*. An enormously rich French aristocrat habitually has his carriage driven at high speeds through the streets of Paris and is contemptuously indifferent to the suffering thereby inflicted on the lower classes. One day his carriage cripples a child. Seeing that the child has been seriously hurt, the aristocrat flings several gold coins to the grieving family. The family, to whom the coins represent a fortune, are entirely satisfied, but no one would suppose that the aristocrat has thereby exonerated himself. It's easy to find circumstances of this sort, in which victims may consider themselves compensated even though the perpetrator (or permitter) remains unjustified.

Insisting on an essential rather than a merely accidental connection between the suffering and the compensation will not guarantee justification. If a mother forces her son into months of semistarvation and sensory deprivation in order to impress on him the blessings of ordinary life, he will no doubt find intense pleasure in ordinary experiences thereafter. Here the compensation is essentially connected with the suffering. But even if the pleasure is so intense as to outweigh all the pains of the deprivation, the mother is not thereby justified.

What else is required can be seen in a slight variation on our hostage case. Even if a madman were threatening to cut off five other children's fingers unless you cut off your child's fingers, you would not have a morally sufficient reason to do so. Our claim is based, as before, on considerations of the injustice in the object of the action demanded of you. Rational agent-centered restrictions make that action impermissible. And yet it's not difficult to describe circumstances in which you would have a morally sufficient reason for acting in that way, in which you would be not only not blamed for acting in that way but even praised for it. If your daughter's fingers were caught in machinery in such a way that she would die horribly unless they were amputated at once, and no one but you could perform the action, goodness would require it of you. It seems clear that all that accounts for the difference in the moral status of the act of amputation in these latter circumstances is that it is now the indispensable (or best possible) means of *preventing a greater evil* for the child herself.

Given the constraints raised by considerations of agent-centered restrictions, then, if an agent is to be justified in allowing the suffering of an innocent victim, the agent must (among other conditions) believe (reasonably) that without such suffering greater harm would come to the victim. Analogously, the strictures we have derived from the central thesis of Aquinas's metaethics preclude only such solutions to the problem of evil as fail to show how God's permitting innocent suffering can be the indispensable (or best possible) means of (at least) preventing greater harm to the victim.[80]

80. For a recent attempt at a solution that sets out to avoid that sort of failure, see Stump 1985. McInerny 1976 provides corrections of some misinterpretations of Aquinas's ethical naturalism. We are grateful for comments on earlier drafts of this paper by Richard Creel, James Keller, James Klagge, Scott MacDonald, Alvin Plantinga, Bruce Russell, Nicholas Sturgeon, Richard Swinburne, and Edward Wierenga.

CHAPTER 5

The Transcendentality of
Goodness and the Human Will

Mark D. Jordan

In almost all of Thomas Aquinas's lists of the "transcendental names," mention is made of the good. This is not surprising, since the good figures prominently in the earliest layer of his Latin sources, as well as in the texts of his immediate predecessors. What does surprise is Thomas's description of the transcendental good. Despite the neo-Platonic coloring of many of the "authorities," and despite his liking for neo-Platonic descriptions of the good in other contexts, Thomas's summary description of the transcendental good is explicitly and consistently taken from Aristotle. It describes the good as the end of 'appetite' (*appetitus*).[1]

The repeated description is noteworthy. It suggests that the ordering of the transcendental names as distinct predicates convertible with 'being' is implicated in the arrangement of powers within the soul. Unfortunately, but not coincidentally, Thomas's treatments of the reciprocal causality of intellect and will hit upon at least two *aporiai*, two puzzles that entangle thinking about the good. The first puzzle is connected to a curious doctrine derived from a different, even singular, Peripatetic text. The text is a fragment from the *Eudemian Ethics*, and its doctrine is that the origin of the reciprocal causality lies outside the

1. The translation of *appetitus* as 'appetite' is both incorrigible and unjustifiable. As will become clear, the English term obscures almost entirely the sense of the Latin. But the mistranslation is so firmly established that it seems useless to labor at propagating another. In what follows, the English 'appetite' should be read, cautiously, as a placeholder for the Latin *appetitus*. The meaning of the latter term must be allowed to emerge in the course of the inquiry.

interactions of intellect and will, in God. The second puzzle arises in Thomas's remarks about what seems the possibility for a radical rejection of the highest good by will. Together, the puzzles can seem to deny the efficacy of the good's causality. The good may be present to the human will in every object about it, so the puzzles suggest, but that presence is not sufficient to set the will in motion.

I would like to suggest that the puzzles illuminate the description of the transcendental good in terms of appetite and so cast light on the nature of the good and its place among the transcendentals. My suggestion will be set out in five steps. The first is to recall texts in which the transcendental good is given its Aristotelian description. The second is to explicate the description's use of the notion of appetite (*appetitus*), especially as it applies to the rational power that is the human will. The third and fourth steps are to follow the teaching about will into the puzzles over its causal relation to intellect. I divide these two steps not according to the puzzles, but according to the texts in which they appear. The fifth step, the last, is to see the lessons of the puzzles for the status of the transcendental names.

1. The Good and Appetite

Although no list of "transcendentals" is fixed for Thomas, he does include the good in almost every list he offers.[2] He is also remarkably consistent in describing the good within these lists. In the famous discussion of *De veritate* I.1, the good is described as the agreement of the soul's appetitive power with a being (*ens*).[3] In *De potentia*, which offers the next most continuous discussion, the good figures in a list of four "first beings (*prima entia*)." It is there described as adding to *ens* a relation to appetite.[4] In an earlier text from the *Scriptum* on the *Sentences*,

2. The one exception would seem to be the highly abbreviated allusion in *De substantiis separatis* ch. 11 (Thomas Aquinas 1963, n. 60), "*unam et ens.*" In this and all other Latin quotations, I follow the orthography of the cited edition.

3. *DV* I.1: "*in anima autem est vis cognitiva et appetitiva; convenientiam ergo entis ad appetitum exprimit hoc nomen bonum, unde in principio Ethicorum dicitur quod 'Bonum est quod omnia appetunt'*" (Thomas Aquinas 1970–76, 5.155–59).

4. *DP* IX.7.ad6: "*Oportet autem quod alia tria super ens addant aliquid quod ens non contrahat. . . . Hoc autem esse non potest nisi addant aliquid secundum rationem tantum; hoc autem est vel negatio, . . . vel relatio . . . ; et hoc est vel intellectus, . . . aut appetitus, ad quem importat relationem bonum; nam bonum est quod omnia appetunt, ut dicitur in I Ethic.*" (Thomas Aquinas 1953b, p. 243b). The list of four is also repeated in *DV* XXI.3c : "*Unde istorum nominum transcendentium talis est ordo, si secundum se considerentur, quod post ens est unum, deinde verum post unum, et deinde post verum bonum*" (Thomas Aquinas 1970–76, 598.59–63).

there is no mention of appetite, but the force of the description seems the same. The good is said to add a relation to the end and to have the formulable notion of the final cause.[5]

These descriptions of the transcendental good are confirmed and connected by the discussion in *DV* XXI. The question is entitled "On the Good," and its first three articles are primarily concerned with the relation of good to being and true. It is an important text for the description of the transcendental good. I will comment on two parts of it by selective paraphrase and by collation with related texts from other works.

The first article of *DV* XXI begins by distinguishing ways in which a being can receive additions. It then argues that the good adds to a being so far as the being completes another by serving as its end.

So far then as one being (*ens*) according to its being (*esse*) completes another and consummates it, it has the formulable notion (*ratio*) of an end with respect to what it completes. And so it is that all those who rightly defined the good put in its formulable notion something that belongs to relatedness (*habitudo*) to an end. Hence it is that the Philosopher says in *Ethics* I that 'they best define the good who say that the good is what all desire.'[6]

In the response to the first opposing argument Thomas paraphrases this description as saying that the good "adds on top [of a being] a relatedness to the final cause."[7]

What is more interesting, Thomas translates the Dionysian description of the good into terms set by the Aristotelian. According to Dionysius, the good is what pours itself out. This would seem to imply an action or operation in the good, and that action or operation would seem to be by means of a power in addition to simple being. Thomas

5. *Super Sent.* I, d.8, q.1, a.3c: "*Alia vero quae diximus, scilicet bonum, verum et unum, addunt super ens, non quidem naturam aliquam, sed rationem: . . . verum autem et bonum addunt relationem quamdam: sed bonum relationem ad finem. . . . Si autem considerentur secundum rationem causalitatis, sic bonum est prius; quia bonum habet rationem causae finalis, . . . finis autem est prima causa in ratione causalitatis*" (Thomas Aquinas 1929–56, 1:200).

6. *DV* XXI.1c: "*In quantum autem unum ens secundum esse suum est perfectivum alterius et consummativum, habet rationem finis respectu illius quod ab eo perficitur; et inde est quod omnes recte diffinientes bonum ponunt in ratione eius aliquid quod pertinet ad habitudinem finis: unde Philosophus dicit in I Ethicorum quod 'bonum optime diffiniunt dicentes quod bonum est quod omnia appetunt'*" (Thomas Aquinas 1970–76, 593.198–594.207).

7. *DV* XXI.1.ad1: "*bonum autem superaddat habitudinem causae finalis*" (Thomas Aquinas 1970–76, 594.216–17). Cf. obj.3: "*Sed dicebat quod [bonum] addit respectum ad finem*" (591.17–18); obj.10: "*sed bonum dicit ad determinatum terminum, scilicet ad finem*" (592.62–63); and ad10: "*quamvis bonum dicat aliquam specialem habitudinem, scilicet finis*" (595.299–301).

replies, "When the good is said, according to its formulable notion, to pour itself out, this outpouring is not to be understood as implying the operation of an efficient cause, but according as it implies a relatedness to the final cause. . . . He speaks of the good's pouring out as of the final cause, not the agent cause."[8] The emphasis on the good as final cause could hardly be clearer. Thomas embraces and reconstrues competing descriptions offered by the neo-Platonic traditions according to finality.[9] This should not be taken as a triumph of 'Aristotelianism' over 'Platonism' in Thomas. Such abstractions cannot be applied to the textual evidence and cannot be given coherent meaning outside the texts. Moreover, Thomas everywhere qualifies textual elements drawn from one author or tradition by placing them under principles and schemata drawn from many others. But Thomas's translation of *diffusio* into finality does suggest that his descriptions of the transcendental good will be best understood by beginning with Aristotle's contexts and formulae.

The reiteration of the Aristotelian description is not confined, of course, to the passages on the transcendental good. It is found throughout the corpus in connection with dozens of different topics. Indeed, the description forms one of the most familiar commonplaces that Thomas takes from Aristotle. In many places, as in the passages just reviewed, he attributes it explicitly and precisely to the opening of the *Nicomachean Ethics*. Elsewhere he says, more precisely if less specifically, that it is a teaching of "the philosophers."[10] In the *Ethics*, after all, Aristotle praises the maxim as a teaching of anonymous predecessors. Commenting on the passage, Thomas identifies the predecessors as philosophers.[11]

The distinction for Thomas between Aristotle and Aristotle quoting his predecessors is worth remarking. An authoritative statement by Aristotle is a textual locus subject to interpretation according to authorial intention. Though Thomas's "*intentio*" is rather different from many of the prevailing notions of intention, it does dictate a certain sort of interpretation by context. Now, a maxim reported by Aristotle from the patrimony of philosophic learning is not a textual locus in the same

---

8. *DV* XXI.1.ad4: "*Cum autem dicitur quod bonum sit diffusivum secundum sui rationem, non est intelligenda diffusio secundum quod importat operationem causae efficientis sed secundum quod importat habitudinem causae finalis; . . . dicit autem bonum diffusionem causae finalis et non causae agentis. . . .*" (Thomas Aquinas 1970–76, 594.256–63).

9. For similar translations, see *Super Sent.* I, d.34, q.2, a.1, ad4 and *ST* Ia.5.4.ad2.

10. *SCG* II.47 (para. 2): "*Inest enim omnibus appetitus boni: cum bonum sit quod omnia appetunt, ut philosophi tradunt*" (Thomas Aquinas 1961–67, 2:167b, n. 1237).

11. *In I Ethicorum* lectio 1: "*Et ideo dicit quod philosophi bene enunciaverunt bonum esse id quod omnia appetunt*" (Thomas Aquinas 1969, 5.158–60; Thomas Aquinas 1964, n. 9).

sense. It is what Thomas sometimes calls a "*propositio*," that is, a general truth that is nonetheless subject to several kinds of qualification and delimitation.[12] Thomas quite often constructs his arguments by use of such *propositiones*, just as he often qualifies, reinterprets, or revises them. Taken in itself, the Aristotelian report about the description of the good says very little that is not immediately in need of dialectical clarification.

So it is in the commentary on the *Ethics* that Thomas explains at once what he takes to be the meaning of the inherited philosophic saying. It does not apply only to those beings that have some apprehension of the good. Even inanimate things have appetite for the good, so far as they are moved toward it by divine ordering. "To tend toward the good is to have appetite for the good."[13] This does not mean—at least not yet—that everything tends towards one good. It means, rather, that all tend toward a good. Of course, any good will be such by participation in the highest good. Thus it is also true to say that all things have appetite for the true or highest good, which is God.[14]

The hierarchical relation of lower goods to higher figures importantly in Thomas's study of appetite. But it is just as important, and more urgent when beginning, to see that *appetitus* is not essentially a cognitive power. In things without life and in plants, *appetitus* is observed as what we would variously call properties, tendencies, behaviors, or tropisms. Yet these characteristics are rather the result or consequence of having an unhindered *appetitus*. Thomas speaks of the *appetitus* itself most often as "inclination," but also as "natural desire," "appropriateness" (*convenientia*), "impulse" or "force" (both *impetus*), "being ordered to something" (*ordinatio*), "seeking something," "tending toward something," and "having a natural aptitude for an end."[15] The observation of inclinations or tendencies can be explicated by saying that a thing has a receptivity toward certain objects—has, in

12. See, e.g., *Super Sent.* IV, d.18, q.2, a.5, sol.2, ad1; *DV* II.15.ad1, XXIV.1.ad14; *ST* Ia.77.1.ad6, 87.1.ad3; *DM* VI.ad19.

13. *In I Ethicorum* lectio 1: "*ipsum autem tendere in bonum est appetere bonum*" (Thomas Aquinas 1969, 5.173–74; Thomas Aquinas 1964, n. 11).

14. A good review of the general doctrine is offered by Aertsen 1988a, 356–60, and 337–90 passim. I would demur at Aertsen's thorough reconstruction only over its manner of juxtaposing texts and its overemphasis on *circulatio* as the overriding metaphor of Thomistic metaphysics.

15. See Laporta 1973, pp. 39–56, for a classified survey of passages. Laporta's remains the best attempt at a lexicon of Thomas's terminology for *appetitus*, but it was compiled before the publication of the *Index Thomisticus* and so necessarily covers only a portion of the passages that can now be located.

other words, a capacity for being actualized in a certain way.[16] But the paraphrase in terms of receptivity is incomplete. It does not insist plainly enough that *appetitus* derives directly from a thing's nature and so embodies its teleology. After all, Thomas himself often enough gives 'love' (*amor*) as a synonym for 'appetite.'

The basic terminology is revised, though hardly abandoned, when appetite is to be described in sentient or intellectual creatures. Some indication of this is given in the third article of *DV* XXI, which asks whether the good in its formulable notion is prior to the true. Thomas replies that it is not, because the good is more inclusive notionally than the true and so depends upon it. If the comparison is undertaken as among the things perfected, however, then the good is naturally prior. The perfection or completion of goodness extends to more things than the perfection or completion of truth, and it precedes the true in the temporal order of perfection. As part of this second comparison, Thomas reiterates the Aristotelian description "all things have appetite for the good."[17] Still, the present text has considerably complicated the notion of appetite by introducing the distinction between a capacity for the true and a capacity for the good, that is, between intellect and will.

These two articles from *De veritate* make clear that no sense can be made of the description of the transcendental good without some understanding of appetite in rational creatures and the relative priorities of goods and truths for them. As it happens, of course, both topics receive their least qualified treatment in Thomas's discussions of human beings. The most accomplished of those discussions occurs in the *Summa theologiae*, at the center of which stands a hortatory narration of human action for the best end.

2. The Doctrine of Appetite in the *Summa theologiae*

The analyses of will in Thomas's *Summa* are not produced by introspection, but rather by the mutual correlation of a host of traditional descriptions and explications. Thomas does not attempt to illustrate his distinctions by fresh appeal to direct experience. On the contrary, his illustrations are themselves almost entirely inherited ones. Nor is it clear that Thomas's accounts could be illustrated by introspection, since

16. Laporta 1973, pp. 44–45.
17. *DV* XXI.3c: "*Et ideo omnia appetunt bonum*" (Thomas Aquinas 1970–76, 599.81–82).

they frequently distinguish either acts too swift for dissection (when they are accessible to reflection at all) or notionally distinct aspects of a single act. To read the analyses as something other than what they are—for example, as reports of experienced sequences—would be to suppress what they teach.

The account of will begins in the *prima pars*. Thomas starts there with a list of the soul's powers according to one of the Aristotelian arrangements in *On the Soul*. The five powers are given as the vegetative, the sensitive, the appetitive, the motive, and the intellective.[18] Both the vegetative and the sensitive powers are variously subdivided by Thomas (Ia.78.2–4). Within these further sortings, the will and free judgment appear under the appetitive power (Ia.80.div). The division proceeds from that point by halvings. For beings with mind, appetite is divided into rational or intellective appetite and sensitive appetite or *sensualitas* (Ia.80.2).[19] *Sensualitas* is further divided into the irascible and concupiscible, which will branch out into particular passions further on in the *prima secundae*. Intellectual appetite is divided into will (*voluntas*) and free judgment (*liberum arbitrium*; Ia.83.4).

As was already clear in *DV* XXI, Thomas understands appetite itself as a consequence of the immanent teleology of natural forms: "a certain inclination follows on any form whatever."[20] The immanent teleology may be participated or appropriated at various levels, depending on the reflexivity of the active form. In human beings, in subjects possessed of the freely appropriative capacity of intellect, the natural appetite is participated freely as an appetitive force (*vis*) directed at apprehended objects, toward which it tends so far as they are appropriate to our good.[21]

The distinction between intellective and sensitive appetite is a distinction of hierarchically ordered powers (*potentiae*), with the intellective being the higher (Ia.80.3). Thomas argues this distinction from the passivity of appetite. Any generic difference in what acts on passivities will indicate a difference in kind between passivities. So the difference between what is apprehended by intellect and what by sense makes for a difference between the intellectual and sensitive appetites. One and

---

18. *ST* Ia.78.1; Aristotle, *De anima* I.5. Until otherwise noted, parenthetical references will be to the parts, questions, and articles of the *Summa theologiae*.

19. Compare the trichotomy of natural appetite, sensitive appetite, rational appetite in *ST* Ia.59.1c, 60.1c, IaIIae.26.1c, and elsewhere.

20. *ST* Ia.80.1c: "*quamlibet formam sequitur aliqua inclinatio*" (Thomas Aquinas 1888–1906, 5:282a).

21. *ST* Ia.80.1.ad2: "*conveniens aut bonum*" (Thomas Aquinas 1888–1906, 5:282b).

the same external thing may attract both appetites, but it will do so under different formulable notions or *rationes* (Ia.80.3.ad2).

To say that the will is a rational appetite is to say that it is an appetite responsive to features discerned by reason. Rationality is not an accident inhering in some 'substance' of appetite, nor is appetite a prime matter waiting to be informed. Appetites exist only because they are already specified by forms. But neither is the will an appetite of reason in the sense of an appendage to it. The will is, rather, an appetite of a rational being, of the being that has reason. Because of this, rationality permeates will in the same way that it permeates the other powers of the human soul—passions, sensations, memories. The rationality of will is nowhere more clearly seen than in the special capacity for free judgment.

The distinction between *voluntas* and *liberum arbitrium* as described here is not a distinction between two powers, but rather between two activities of a single power (Ia.83.4). In mind, there is both *intelligere* and *ratiocinari*, both the simple grasp of notions or principles and the discursive drawing of conclusions. So it is in intellectual appetite. To will something is to have a direct appetite for it as end; to choose it is to want it in view of the end, that is, to regard it as *ad finem*.[22] The will is the prior power in the sense that it represents the direct exercise of appetite; free judgment is mediated, calculative. There are many difficulties in describing their relations, but most of them can be postponed beyond this inquiry. All that is needed now is a summary.

The teaching of the *Summa's prima pars* on will and free judgment can be summed up in the following points. First, the created will presented with a vision of the divine essence, which is the highest good, cannot will otherwise than to inhere in it. Second, and absent a vision of that good, the will desires what is apprehended as like it and chooses what seems to lead to it. But, third, the relations of means (*ad finem*) to end (*de fine*) are not known with certainty under the conditions of the present life. Moreover, because everything but the highest good has an admixture of evil, every creature can be apprehended under the aspect of evil. The will thus has considerable latitude in its judgments, including its determinations of where the good itself is most likely to be found among creatures. Fourth, divine influence on judgment is in no way excluded, neither so far as God is the first cause of everything that

---

22. The apparently simple distinction between what is *de fine* and what *ad finem* is much elaborated when Thomas treats of it at the beginning of the *prima secundae*, qq. 1–5. Here I mean no more by it than is meant by the text at hand, which speaks simply.

happens, nor so far as God might strengthen or weaken certain particular motions of the will. What is excluded is that God should exercise a violent or coercive causality on the will. To do so would contradict the nature of the will and so God's own intentions in creating it. Fifth, finally, the analogy between *intellectus/ratio* and *voluntas/liberum arbitrium* suggests that free judgment is always tending to resolve itself back into simple willing, from which it also arises. The discursive calculation of alternative means takes place for the sake of possessing the end to be reached through those means. Appetite is the beginning and end of judgment.

These are the main conclusions to be drawn from the *Summa*'s characterization of rational appetite. Some of them can be taken over immediately for understanding the transcendental good. So, for example, the third point restates a fundamental tenet about the hierarchy of created goods. All created goods are imperfectly good because they are good by participation in various degrees. Freedom of judgment derives not only from the incalculability of means but also from the inadequacy of the offered goods. Again, the fifth point asserts an analogy between intellect and will. This keeps in view the coupling of the true and the good. At the same time, it foreshadows puzzles about the reciprocal causality of intellect and will.

3. Reciprocal Causality in the *Summa theologiae*

When will and judgment are taken up again in the *prima secundae*, Thomas seems more concerned to catalogue the types of act by the will than to repeat basic arguments about it. The catalogue is required in part by the bewildering variety of psychological terminologies Thomas inherits. It is perhaps more deeply motivated by the intention of clarifying the multiple interactions of intellect and will. The summary descriptions of the will combine the elements of rationality and inclination: "the act of the will is nothing other than a certain inclination proceeding from an interior cognizing principle" (IaIIae.6.4). The will can incline only toward good things, not so much in the sense that all existing things are somehow good, but in the sense that the will inclines only to things that are apprehended as good (IaIIae.8.1).

As befits a rational appetite, the will is moved primarily by the intellect (IaIIae.9.1). It is also moved by sensitive appetite, not so much directly as through effects on apprehension. The passions change the character of the whole human being, and so change one's apprehension of what is to be sought and what avoided (IaIIae.9.2). The will also moves itself to want the means to an end, namely, by wanting the end, just as the intellect 'moves' itself to know conclusions by knowing premises (IaIIae.9.3). The will can also be influenced by celestial motions (IaIIae.9.5). More importantly, it is moved by finding its ends in external objects and in God, who is also its origin and constant causal ground (IaIIae.9.4,6). This is by design a fuller and more dynamic picture of the conditions under which the will operates than was given in the *prima*.

In trying to present a fuller picture of motion, the account makes certain puzzles appear. A first puzzle appears in the question, whether the will is moved by some external principle (IaIIae.9.4). A simple answer is that it obviously is, so far as it is an appetite for something external. But a subtler answer is required, since the will also depends on an external principle for its being moved to exercise its power. Whatever is intermittently active must be actualized by something already in act. It is obvious that the will is intermittently active with regard to particular desires. The will begins to want something in particular by wanting an end under which the particular thing falls as means. This requires an act of deliberation (*consilium*), which in turn requires a prior act of will to fix the end about which counsel deliberates. Someone wants to be cured, so she deliberates and decides to find a doctor. But she wants to be cured as a result of deliberation in view of some prior end, and so on. There can be no indefinite regress or else there would be no action. The will's first motion, which begins the alternation of willing and deliberating, must come from outside it.

Thomas seals this conclusion with a reference to *Eudemian Ethics*, which he assumes to be an Aristotelian work. He knows it, in fact, only through an excerpt frequently entitled *Liber de bona fortuna*.[23] The excerpt is first cited by Thomas in *SCG* III.89.[24] It is absent from the related argument in *DV* XXII, as from more distant parallels in the *Scriptum* on the *Sentences*.[25] It is easy to suspect that Thomas first learned of the excerpt between composing *De veritate* and the *Summa contra gentiles*, that is, in 1259 or 1260, according to the received chronology.[26] Once the citation is used in the *Summa contra gentiles*, it reappears regularly in arguments about divine influence on the will,

23. Deman 1928, pp. 38–39.
24. Thomas Aquinas 1961–67, 3:129b, n. 2651.
25. *DV* XXII.12; cf. *Super Sent.* II, d.8, q.1, a.5, ad7.
26. Deman 1928, p. 42.

the relations of will to intellect, and the devil's role in causing sin.[27] In most of these passages, though not that in IaIIae.9, Thomas explicitly names the exterior cause as God, even though the authoritative text is not entirely clear on the point.[28] Before he began to use the passage from the *Eudemian Ethics*, Thomas did treat the question of reciprocal causality between intellect and will. Faced with the objection of infinite regress, he answered in this way: "one does not proceed to infinity; one stops with the natural appetite by which the intellect is inclined to its act."[29] In the exactly parallel question of *ST* Ia, the objection received a different answer:

one need not proceed to infinity, but can stop with the intellect as with the first thing. . . . [T]he principle of taking counsel and of understanding is a certain intellectual principle higher than our intellect, which is God, as Aristotle also says in *Eudemian Ethics* VII; and in this way he shows that one should not proceed to infinity.[30]

Now, the gain from *De veritate* to the first part of the *Summa* is partly a gain in authoritative underpinning for the reply. Instead of falling back on the ill-defined natural appetite of intellect, Thomas can point to God as the ground for deliberation and understanding. But there is more to be garnered from the authority.

The further gain appears in the formulation used by the *prima secundae*. There, in the passage just reviewed, Thomas says: "This however is not to proceed to infinity. So that it is necessary to hold that in the first movement of the will, the will goes forward by the incitement (*ex in-*

---

27. *Quaestiones quodlibetales* I, q.4, a.2 (Thomas Aquinas 1956, p. 8a), probably dating from Easter 1269; *ST* Ia.82.4.ad3 (Thomas Aquinas 1888–1906, 5:304b), dating from 1267–68; IaIIae.68.1c (6:447a), 80.1.obj.3 and ad3 (7:82a, 82b), 109.2.ad1 (7:291b), all dating from 1269–70; *DM* III.3.obj.11 (Thomas Aquinas 1982, 71:71–74), VI.1 (149:407–10), probably dating from 1270, but see below.

28. See Deman 1928, pp. 49–50. The search for an exterior cause here is related not only to Aristotle's regressive arguments for a divine mover, but to the more general Aristotelian doctrine of a "pre-motion" for intermittently causal agents. See Lonergan 1971, pp. 70–71, 99–100.

29. *DV* XXII.12.ad2: "*non est procedere in infinitum; statur enim in appetitu naturali quo inclinatur intellectus in suum actum*" (Thomas Aquinas 1970–76, 642.127–30).

30. *ST* Ia.82.4.ad3: "*non oportet procedere in infinitum, sed statur in intellectu sicut in primo. . . . [P]rincipium consiliandi et intelligendi est aliquod intellectivum principium altius intellectu nostro, quod est Deus, ut etiam Aristoteles dicit in VII Ethicae Eudemicae; et per hunc modum ostendit quod non est procedere in infinitum*" (Thomas Aquinas 1888–1906, 5:304a–b).

stinctu) of some exterior mover, as Aristotle concludes in a certain chapter of the *Eudemian Ethics*."[31]

Here the notion of making a stand in the intellect is set aside. The exterior mover seems to incite the will more directly, not just as a remote ground for deliberation.[32] The turn to God is not just a habitual solution for regress arguments, nor is it an easy inference from an isolated authority. Thomas uses the citation to the putatively Aristotelian text once he finds it because it allows him to preserve the reciprocal causality of will and intellect without having to bring it to a stop in the intellect. But the sense of his remarks will not be clear until the second puzzle appears.

The very next question in the *prima secundae*, on the manner of the will's motion, begins with careful descriptions of 'substance' and of the 'natural,' then reaffirms that "the principle of voluntary motions must be something willed naturally."[33] This is the good in common, and it corresponds to the first principles of demonstration in the speculative order. It is not a bare first principle. It includes, as part of the single natural desire, a will for the good of each power of the willing substance, and so wants the cognition of truth for the intellect, and being and life and other such things for the whole organism.[34] Given this encompassing view of the naturally willed end, it seems quite appropriate to ask in next place whether the will is necessarily attached to its object. In the *prima* the related question elicited the distinction among types of necessity. Here, the question is addressed by the distinction between the exercise and specification in acts of willing (IaIIae.10.2). This terminology, which is peculiar to this part of the *Summa theologiae* and to *DM* VI, was first introduced in IaIIae.9.1 in a distinction between the exercise and the determination of an act.[35] It reappears four

31. *ST* IaIIae.9.4c: "*Hoc autem non est procedere in infinitum. Unde necesse est ponere quod in primum motum voluntatis voluntas prodeat* [some mss. read *procedat*] *ex instinctu alicuius exterioris moventis, ut Aristoteles concludit in quodam capitulo Ethicae Eudemicae*" (Thomas Aquinas 1888–1906, 6:78b).

32. To understand Thomas's sense of *instinctus* is both important and difficult. Further remarks will be found below. For the role of the *Liber de bona fortuna* in determining the sense, see Seckler 1961, pp. 104–14, and Fabro 1988.

33. *ST* IaIIae.10.1: "*principium motuum voluntariorum oportet esse aliquid naturaliter volitum*" (Thomas Aquinas 1888–1906, 6:83a).

34. Cf. *DV* XXII.5 (Thomas Aquinas 1970–76, 624.200–201), where the list is given as part of what is entailed in beatitude.

35. *ST* IaIIae.9.1c: "*Indiget igitur movente quantum ad duo: scilicet quantum ad exercitium vel usum actus; et quantum ad determinationem actus*" (Thomas Aquinas 1888–1906, 6:74a–b). What is new is the term *exercitium*. Thomas asserts in several other places a similar distinction between *usus* and *determinatio*. See, e.g., *In I Ethicorum* lectio 2 (Thomas Aquinas 1964, n. 27).

times later in the same question, then twice in q.10, and then in q.17. There are many other uses in Thomas of the notion of exercise, but outside of these contexts it is not contrasted in this way with determination or specification.

In q.10 of *ST*, Thomas says that there is no necessity with regard to exercise of the will: "Therefore in the first way the will is moved necessarily (*ex necessitate*) by no object, for someone can not think of any object whatever, and so neither will it in act."[36] As regards specification, necessity arises only with regard to the pure example of the power's proper object, that is, the highest good. "So if there be proposed to the will any object that is good universally and according to every consideration, the will will tend to it necessarily, if it wills anything. It cannot will the opposite."[37] For all lesser goods, for all mixed cases, there is no necessity. What is striking in this passage, and what brings forward the second puzzle about the motions of will and intellect, is the apparent allowance of a radical rejection of the act of the will even in the presence of the highest good ("if it wills anything"). Thomas seems to have asserted the opposite in the *Sentences* commentary[38] and in *De veritate*.[39]

This second puzzle arises, like the first, in considering the will's continuous motion. The first puzzle comes from reflecting on the beginning of the motion. The second puzzle comes from reflecting on the possibility that the will might withhold itself from the end of its motion—might check itself, might turn aside. These puzzles are connected directly to the main structural accomplishment of the section on will in the *prima secundae*, which is not just the reconciliation of competing traditional vocabularies, but the interlocking of intellectual and appetitive acts in a continuous and self-perpetuating activity. The issue of continuity is embedded in the very organization of the text. There is no need to go through the whole of it, but some remarks will be helpful in seeing the place of the puzzles within the larger doctrine.

Structurally, the questions on the will in the *prima secundae* resemble a dictionary or, more exactly, a philosophical lexicon in the manner of Aristotle's *Metaphysics* V. A number of terms are introduced, character-

36. *ST* IaIIae.10.2c: "*Primo ergo modo, voluntas a nullo obiecto ex necessitate movetur: potest enim aliquis de quocumque obiecto non cogitare, et per consequens neque actu velle illud*" (Thomas Aquinas 1888–1906, 6:86a).
37. *ST* IaIIae.10.2c: "*si proponatur aliquod obiectum voluntati quod sit universaliter bonum et secundum omnem considerationem, ex necessitate voluntas in illud tendet, si aliquid velit: non enim poterit velle oppositum*" (Thomas Aquinas 1888–1906, 6:86a).
38. *Super Sent.* II, d.25, q.1, a.2 (Thomas Aquinas 1929–56, 2:649).
39. *DV* XXII.5c and ad11 (Thomas Aquinas 1970–76, 624.196–200, 625.313–19).

ized, and then related to the surrounding terms. Yet the order of consideration is not immediately clear. There is a broad division between elicited and commanded acts (qq.8–16 against q.17). The elicited acts are further separated into those having to do with the end and those having to do with means (qq.8–11 against qq.12–16). But the relation of means to ends is then immediately confused by saying that acts having to do with ends had also, when taken loosely, to do with means. Moreover, and without apparent justification, Thomas treats of the acts not in the order in which they occur. "Now counsel precedes election. Therefore we ought first to consider election" (IaIIae.13.div). Again, *usus* is treated in q.16 as the first act of the order of execution, but then *imperium* is introduced in the very next question as preceding *usus* (IaIIae.17.3).

There is, of course, a further complication of sequence, one that is obviously related to the first puzzle. Each of the questions in this section is careful to discuss the various reflexive and reciprocal causalities linking the terms discussed. The will is moved by the intellect, but also by the sensitive appetite (*ex parte obiecti*), by itself, and by external objects—especially God—in several ways (IaIIae.9.1–4). But the will also embraces the particular acts of intellect and moves the intellect to those acts.

The reciprocities embedded in the structure of the questions are also reflected in the analyses of particular powers. Consider what is said of command (*imperium*), which is an act of reason based on a prior act of will. Thomas explains this combination by noting it as a general fact: "acts of the will and of the reason can be done with regard to each other (*supra se invicem possunt ferri*), namely, so far as reason reasons about what is to be willed, and will wills to reason. It happens that the act of the will precedes the act of reason, and conversely."[40] It follows that there are several kinds of acts mixing understanding and willing. In some, the power of a prior act of understanding passes into an act of will, as happens with *usus* and *electio*. In other cases, a certain power of will passes over into an act of reason, as happens with *imperium*. What is just as interesting is that this act of *imperium*, which presupposes and in some sense rests on a prior act of will, embraces within its control a whole range of powers. Thus, *imperium* can control the will, reason, the sensitive appetite, and the actions of exterior members (IaIIae.17.5–7, 9).

---

40. *ST* IaIIae.17.1: "*actus voluntatis et rationis supra se invicem possunt ferri, prout scilicet ratio ratiocinatur de volendo, et voluntas vult ratiocinari; contingit actum voluntatis praeveniri ab actu rationis, et e converso*" (Thomas Aquinas 1888–1906, 6:118a).

It is impossible, then, to regard the linear presentation of acts or partial acts of will in the *prima secundae* as anything but a heuristic device. It is clearly not meant to represent the actual sequence of acts. In the first place, it proceeds, quite properly, backward from proximity to the end, thus narrating in reverse order a part of the chronology. In the second place, the intersecting circles of reflexive and reciprocal causality at work in any actual process of volition render linear representation impossible. It may be possible, for very important moral decisions, to construct a kind of pattern by which the deliberation proceeds from apprehended good, through its being willed, into counsel, and finally onto choice of means (IaIIae.15.3c). But even this much reduced schema is a static and clumsy rendering of actual processes. In fact, and especially with regard to the most important things, the will seems always already to be in motion toward some final end, however obscurely, and the dialectic between choice and deliberation seems to go forward in rapid mutual adjustment.

Precisely because the relations of causal priority are so difficult to put for particular acts caught up in the causal circulation, the puzzles arise at the limits of analysis. They serve as limiting cases in which one hopes to discover basic causes. At the same time, cases at the limit may distort those relations by compressing them. What is needed is more detail. It can be gotten from Question VI in the disputed questions *De malo*.

4. Reciprocal Causality in *De malo*

There has been a long controversy over the dating of *DM* VI that is directly related to Thomas's thinking on the reciprocity of will and intellect. The controversy arises in trying to judge whether the doctrine in the disputed question differs significantly from that in *ST* IaIIae.9–10. There are other chronological considerations of course, such as textual relations to the Parisian condemnations of 1270[41] and the time

---

41. On December 10, 1270, Etienne Tempier, bishop of Paris, condemned a list of thirteen propositions allegedly held or taught by members of the Arts faculty at the university. Of these, two concern the will and seem somewhat like passages in Thomas's earlier works. The bishop condemned the views "that the will of man wills and chooses by necessity" and "that free choice is a passive, not an active power; and that it is necessarily moved by what is desirable." See Denifle and Chatelain 1889, pp. 486–87, doc. 432, items 3 and 9. The suspicion that *DM* VI has something to do with the controversy in and around 1270 is an old one. See Synave 1926, p. [8], n. 1; Lottin 1928 [1960a], pp. 374–75 [=354–55].

of publication by the Parisian stationers.[42] The other considerations are not decisive, and so the controversy swings back again to doctrine. One party to the controversy finds no significant difference of doctrine and so concludes that *De malo* can be earlier than *ST* IaIIae or contemporary with it.[43] The other party finds doctrinal developments large enough to conclude that *DM* VI must have come after the corresponding treatment in the *Summa theologiae*.[44] More complex stories can be told. It may have been, for example, that Thomas took the condemnations of 1270 as an occasion to record changes that had already been taking place in his thinking, even while he chose not to revise the corresponding passages in an elementary work such as the *Summa theologiae*.[45] Once we begin to tell ourselves biographical stories, however, it is difficult to stop—and difficult to prevent them from usurping the sense of the text. The doctrine of any Thomist text must be measured on at least three axes: the axis of the individual work's pedagogical order, including its rhetorical address; the axis of the received authorities and terminologies for any discrete topic; and the axis of the hierarchy of sciences, with their corresponding inhibitions on linguistic confidence. Biographical fictions are likely to conceal all three axes. Even the biographically neutral collation of supposedly parallel passages is likely to ignore the first and third axes. So I set biography aside and urge caution in reading the following collation.

In *DM* VI the announced topic is whether man has "free choice (*libera electio*) of his acts or whether he chooses by necessity."[46] There is much in the question, but what most directly concerns the puzzles about will and intellect begins in the middle of the determination. Thomas there rehearses the distinction, familiar from the *prima secundae* (IaIIae.9.1.ad3), between specification and exercise. Specification is by form, exercise in view of an end. So in the order of specification, the good understood by

42. See the summary remarks by Gils in Thomas Aquinas 1982, pp. 4*–5*.

43. So Lottin 1928 [1960a], p. 375 [355]; Lottin, 1942, p. 258. Lottin 1928 [1960a], pp. 373–75 [353–55], provides an excellent summary of the earlier views on chronology by Mandonnet, Grabmann, Birkenmajer, Synave, and Pelster. Weisheipl considered q. VI an "extra-serial disputation" inserted by anonymous editors after Thomas's death (Weisheipl 1983, p. 364). This view is no longer tenable; see Thomas Aquinas 1982, pp. 4*–5*.

44. So Pesch 1962, pp. 4, 18.

45. Manteau-Bonamy 1979, p. 33. Other questions can be raised about *De malo*'s emphatic condemnation of the view that necessary acts are free because not coerced—a view Thomas seems sometimes to have adopted in earlier texts. See Lonergan 1971, pp. 93–94.

46. *DM* VI: *"liberam electionem suorum actuum aut ex necessitate eligat"* (Thomas Aquinas 1982, 145.1–3). In the section that follows, parenthetical references will refer to the page and line numbers of the Leonine version, as in Thomas Aquinas 1982.

the intellect moves the will. In the order of exercise, the will moves the intellect. To say this differently, the object of intellect is being and the true, first in the genus of formal cause. The object of will is the good, first in the genus of final cause. The objects include each other. The good can be apprehended and so comprised within the true; the true, considered as the end of an intellectual operation, is comprised within the good as a particular good (148–49.326–38).

If we look to the object specifying the act, the motion begins from the intellect (149.341–42). The good that is understood moves the will. If we look to the exercise of the act, however, the beginning or principle of motion is the will. "For the power to which the principal end belongs always moves to act the power to which there belongs what is for the sake of the end. Just so the soldier moves the maker of bits to do work. And in this way the will moves both itself and all other powers [of the soul]."[47] Within the order of exercise, Thomas insists on the complete freedom of the will so far as it is self-moving. But this leads him immediately to recall the problem of infinite regress. The will requires counsel to act; counsel requires a prior will to fix an end for its deliberations. Something external must inaugurate the first act of the will.

Some thinkers try to escape the regress by invoking the celestial sphere. Thomas finds this view impossible. It is far better, he says, to agree with the authority of Aristotle in *De bona fortuna* and to say that the first mover is God, who sets the will in motion according to its nature. "Since [God] moves all things according to the formulable notion of the moveable (*secundum rationem mobilium*), light things upwards and heavy things downwards, so he also moves the will according to its condition, not from necessity but as indeterminately related to many things (*ut indeterminate se habentem ad multa*)."[48] The will begins to want because it is instigated or incited (*instinctum*) by God (149.388–90).

There remains the question of freedom in the order of determination, in treating which Thomas is again more detailed than in the *Summa theologiae*. If some good is proposed to the will that is good in every respect, the will is moved "*ex necessitate.*" But Thomas qualifies this immediately. "I say '*ex necessitate*' so far as the determination of the

47. *DM* VI: "*Nam semper potentia ad quam pertinet finis principalis mouet ad actum potentiam ad quam pertinet id quod est ad finem, sicut militaris mouet frenorum factricem ad operandum. Et hoc modo uoluntas mouet et se ipsam et omnes alias potentias*" (Thomas Aquinas 1982, 149.345–50).

48. *DM* VI: "*Qui cum omnia moueat secundum rationem mobilium, ut leuia sursum et grauia deorsum, etiam uoluntatem mouet secundum eius conditionem, non ex necessitate set ut indeterminate se habentem ad multa*" (Thomas Aquinas 1982, 149.410–15).

act, since it cannot will the opposite, not however as regards the exercise of the act, since someone is able to will not to think now about beatitude, since the particular acts of intellect and will are also his."[49] The same clarification is made in reply to the seventh objection: "the will cannot not will [beatitude], namely so that it wills the opposite; it can, however, not will it in act, since it can, so far as it moves the intellect to its act, avert intellect from thinking about beatitude, and in this respect it does not will even beatitude itself by necessity."[50] With these two passages, we recognize the second puzzle from *ST* IaIIae.

Is there any significant difference between *DM* VI and that part of the *Summa theologiae*? I confess to finding only a difference of clarity. Thomas removes any ambiguity from the *Summa's* phrase, 'if it wills anything,' by connecting a gloss directly to it in *De malo*: if it wills anything, that is, if it does not divert its attention from the range of objects just then under consideration. I should add that I do find differences between both of these texts and Thomas's earlier treatments, including that in *ST* Ia, though I would recall all the cautions about the comparisons of spot to spot when reading complex texts.

This reciprocal causality had been discussed by the *prima* in a brief comparison (Ia.82.4). Generally, the intellect moves the will in the order of finality as the final cause moves the efficient, since the intellect presents the object to will. But, as agent (*per modum agentis*), the will moves the intellect and all the powers of the soul. This is because the will has as its object the common good and end, to which the activity of all particular powers is subject. Thomas immediately adds, in the reply to the first, a summary comparison of will and intellect as powers. Considering both as regards their objects, intellect is prior. Considering intellect as it apprehends the true and the will as a particular power, intellect is still higher, because it understands the will, its acts and objects. But if we consider the will as grasping the universal good and the intellect as a distinct power in the soul, then the will is higher, because its common good embraces the particular good of the intellect

49. *DM* VI: "*Dico autem ex necessitate quantum ad determinationem actus, quia non potest uelle oppositum, non autem quantum ad exercitium actus, quia potest aliquis non uelle tunc cogitare de beatitudine, quia etiam ipsi actus intellectus et uoluntatis particulares sunt*" (Thomas Aquinas 1982, 150.435–40).

50. *DM* VI: "*Quod uoluntas non potest uelle, ita scilicet quod uelit oppositum; potest tamen non uelle actu, quia potest auertere cogitationem beatitudinis in quantum mouet intellectum ad suum actum, et quantum ad hoc nec ipsam beatitudinem ex necessitate uult*" (Thomas Aquinas 1982, 151.548–53).

and its object. It is in this way, Thomas repeats, that the will can move the intellect.

These remarks must seem too simple in comparison with *De malo* and *ST* IaIIae, which is to be expected. The *prima* does not intend to offer a dynamic picture of the relations of will and intellect. It means only to sketch the arrangement of powers at creation, as it were. Whatever doctrinal emphasis Thomas might have put on intellect in the *prima*, the effect was much exaggerated by the static character of its consideration. It is fairer to regard the remarks of the *prima* as incomplete rather than as premature.

If the doctrine of *DM* VI is richer than that of the *prima*, but largely the same as that of the *prima secundae*, we are still left with the two puzzles. It is now possible to give a more precise reading of Thomas's responses to them. The difficulty in the first puzzle is to understand how exactly the chain of willing-and-deliberating starts up. Thomas responds: God must act on the will so that it begins to will, not God explicitly, but something like its own happiness. To will happiness is to will finding happiness through some means. So the will then directs counsel, which produces judgments, and so on. The initial impulse comes not from intellect, however, but from God as external agent. Here one sees confirmed the suggestion already made about the point of the first puzzle. The turn to God, rather than to some ill-defined appetite of intellect, recognizes the separateness of the will under the conditions of the present life. The continuity of volitions and understandings has the continuity of a motet under which runs, as a kind of *cantus firmus*, the will's incited appetite for final happiness.

God's action on the will cannot be reduced to his having created human nature with certain appetites and apprehensions. Thomas makes this clear later in the *secunda pars*, when he invokes the same passage from the *Eudemian Ethics* to address questions about the gifts of the Holy Spirit and the necessity for grace. In the former context, he summarizes the doctrine about the will with an explicit backward reference.

It should be considered that there is in man a twofold moving principle: one interior, which is reason; another exterior, which is God, as was said above; and even the Philosopher says this, in the chapter *De bona fortuna*.[51]

---

51. *ST* IaIIae.68.1: "*Est enim considerandum quod in homine est duplex principium movens; unum quidem interius, quod est ratio; aliud autem exterius, quod est Deus, ut supra dictum est* [as I take it, IaIIae.9.4]; *et etiam Philosophus hoc dicit, in cap. de Bona Fortuna*" (Thomas Aquinas 1888–1906, 7:447a).

And even the Philosopher says, in the chapter *De bona fortuna*, that it does not behoove those who are moved by divine incitement (*per instinctum divinum*) to deliberate according to human reason. They should rather follow [their] inner incitement (*interiorem instinctum*), since they are moved by a better principle than human reason.[52]

The remarks in the article on grace are perhaps more striking. A first objection there asserts that man can will the good without grace because he is master of his own acts and especially of his willing. Thomas replies by tracing out the potential regress from deliberation to prior deliberation. He then says,

And so that this does not proceed to infinity, one should finally come to this, that the free judgment of man is moved by a certain exterior principle which is above the human mind, namely by God, as even the Philosopher proves in the chapter *De bona fortuna*. So that the mind even of a healthy man [that is, man before sin] does not have such mastery over its act that it need not be moved by God.[53]

The teaching is plain. Even in the state of wholeness, the human will must be set in motion by God as by an exterior principle. So Thomas calls the "*instinctus*" of the pseudo-Aristotelian text "divine" and "of the Holy Spirit";[54] he associates it with divine aid (*divinum auxilium*) and grace. It may be indeed that these texts show the almost seamless transition from nature to grace in Thomas's account of human action.[55]

Thomas's insistence on the divine origin of the will's motion must be qualified, however, in view of the second puzzle, about the refusal of the end of willing. In the second set of passages quoted above from *DM* VI, Thomas says quite clearly that the will can refuse to think actually (*actu*) about the highest good. If the will chooses not to think actually about beatitude, it must do so in view of some deliberation and under the aspect of some good. Yet it would seem that nothing could appear as better to deliberation than the completely good. Thomas wants to

52. *ST* IaIIae.68.1: "*Et Philosophus etiam dicit, in cap. de Bona Fortuna, quod his qui moventur per instinctum divinum, non expedit consiliari secundum rationem humanam, sed quod sequantur interiorem instinctum; quia moventur a meliori principio quam sit ratio humana*" (Thomas Aquinas 1888–1906, 7:447b).

53. *ST* IaIIae.109.2.ad1: "*Et cum hoc non procedat in infinitum, oportet quod finaliter deveniatur ad hoc quod liberum arbitrium hominis moveatur ab aliquo exteriori principio quod est supra mentem humanam, scilicet a Deo; ut etiam Philosophus probat in cap. de Bona Fortuna. Unde mens hominis etiam sani non ita habet dominium sui actus quin indigeat moveri a Deo*" (Thomas Aquinas 1888–1906, 7.291b).

54. *ST* IaIIae.68.2: "*Spiritus Sancti instinctus*" (Thomas Aquinas 1888–1906, 7:449a).

55. This is the main assertion in Fabro 1988.

address this objection when he notes that the acts of intellect and will are particulars. The particular act of thinking about beatitude may not possess the same power over the will as the presentation of beatitude itself, and so the will could choose to turn away from thinking about beatitude considered as a particular act.

The will's rejection of the highest good cannot be profitably conceived as raising the counterfactual possibility of defection from beatitude. Beatitude requires the gift of grace in the afterlife; that grace once received, Thomas everywhere teaches, the human will dwells immutably within it. Nor is immutability inconsistent with freedom of choice on Thomas's understanding.[56] On the one hand, the will's rejection of thinking actually about the highest good cannot be seen as a refusal to will altogether. The will cannot will to will nothing. To do so would be to return itself to the time before its first movement. But the will can misdirect or block the taking of counsel, the deliberation that leads to the identification and pursuit of the highest good. The point of insisting on this possibility for rejection is to clarify something in the conditions of the present life. The soul *in via* can always shift attention away from thoughts about the highest good, precisely because the act of thinking about the highest good is itself a particular and imperfect act that can be compared with other particular and imperfect acts. That was implicit in the hierarchy of goods and in the fallibility of human deliberation.

There is more. To insist on the possibility of the will's miscommanding counsel is to insist on the separability of the acts of will from the intellect at the limits of the conditions of the present life. Here the conclusion of the second puzzle rejoins the conclusion of the first. The importance of separability is not to introduce a radically new notion of experienced freedom or to assert a false distinctness in the experience of reciprocity. It is to remind the reader of the deep fragmentation and partiality of our powers for apprehending the true and the good.

5. Reciprocity and Transcendentality

The Thomist doctrine of will has already touched the doctrine of the transcendentals at several points. Thus, freedom of choice was tied directly to the hierarchy of partial goods. Again, the intervention of the

56. See the very interesting distinctions among senses of *diversitas* in *DM* XVI.5c and Oeing-Hanhoff 1956.

topmost member of the hierarchy was required to set the reciprocal actions of will and intellect into motion. But the doctrine of will is connected much more directly to the transcendentals in Thomas's remarks on the order of the true and the good. In the several texts in which he asks about the relative priorities of truth and goodness, Thomas makes the argument by reference to the objects and acts of the powers of intellect and will. In *DV* XXI the relative extensions of appetite and knowledge are used in an argument for the greater universality of goodness.[57] In *ST* Ia, the 'natural' precedence of knowing over willing is an argument for the precedence "unqualifiedly speaking" of the true over the good.[58]

Taken by themselves, such brief discussions of the order of the transcendental names can misrepresent the character of our discoveries about them. The human experience of the good is an experience through intellect and will. It is conditioned by the complex mutual causality of these two, including their liminal separability under the conditions of the present life. The transcendental names are given to things out of the human acts of willing and understanding. However much the names are 'imposed' to signify attributes that transcend human limitations, especially in the highest instances, the names remain conditioned by the limits on human powers. An ordering of the names is a certain view on the interaction of the powers by which we can name. It is not more than a view. It is certainly not a deduction of contents or a description of causal sequences.

Thomas's lists of the transcendental names contain various terms and numbers of terms. This is no sloppiness on his part. It is a reminder of the limits on human discussion of the transcendentals. The plurality of transcendental names is a plurality grounded in the division of human powers according to their objects. Because the reciprocal causality of those powers is ultimately inescapable for the present life, the transcendentals may be ordered and arranged, but never reduced to one. Indeed, different names will quite properly enter and leave the lists depending on the purposes and the powers of inquiry employed. The plurality of the transcendentals remains as a reflection of the refracted and incomplete powers of human engagement with being. This circumstance of inquiry into the transcendentals is well spoken, indeed, in a description of the good as the object of 'appetite,' that is, of a seeking.

57. *DV* XXI.4c.
58. *ST* Ia.16.4c.

CHAPTER 6

Evil and the Transcendentality of Goodness: Suárez's Solution to the Problem of Positive Evils

Jorge J. E. Gracia

The purpose of this paper is fourfold: First, to examine one of the problems that surfaces in the scholastic doctrine of the transcendentality of goodness (henceforth referred to as DTG) when confronted with the notion of evil; second, to present Suárez's solution to that problem; third, to point out two initial difficulties of the solution; and, finally, to uncover a more profound problem that underlies these difficulties and whose solution may serve to identify the course to be followed in a proper understanding of good and evil.

The importance of the topic of the paper should be evident from the attention that issues related to good and evil continue to attract in philosophical circles. Moreover, in recent years, the consciousness of the failure of nonmetaphysical approaches to these issues has again renewed an interest in exploring some of the well-known metaphysical solutions that were proposed in the past. In this context it makes good sense to go back to Francisco Suárez (1548–1617)[1] and see what he had to say about this matter for two reasons: (1) he provides the last and one of the most articulate and comprehensive scholastic discussions of the metaphysics of good and evil before the turn toward epistemology characteristic of modern philosophy sets in, and (2) he explicitly addresses the mentioned issue by suggesting a well-thought-out view that, although founded on previous scholastic tradition, nonetheless offers some elements of originality.

---

1. For information on Suárez's life, see Fichter 1940 and Scorraille 1912–13. For Suárez's works, see Sommervogel 1890–1900.

1. The Issue

DTG was well-known among scholastics, even though the use of the term 'transcendental' in connection with it can be documented only quite late.[2] The roots of DTG, as made clear in other papers included in this collection, go back to the Greeks, but there is ample evidence that it was not until the rise of scholasticism that it became carefully formulated and subjected to independent examination and analysis.[3] In the thirteenth century the phrase "being and goodness are convertible" (*ens et bonum convertuntur*) became standard, although various authors provided different interpretations of it.[4] It should also be clear that the discussion of the transcendentality of goodness was frequently part and parcel of the more comprehensive issue concerning all the transcendental attributes of being, among which the most frequently listed and widely accepted in addition to goodness were unity (*unum*) and truth (*verum*).[5] I shall for present purposes, however, limit the discussion to goodness.

The most widely accepted version of DTG in the later Middle Ages is composed of two main theses:[6]

1. Being and good are convertible in reality.
2. Being and good are not convertible in concept.

Thesis (1) may be unpacked in various ways, but, following some of the most frequently used *formulae* among scholastics, we may render its import in terms of the following two propositions:[7]

---

2. For the history of the term 'transcendental,' see Knittermeyer 1920.
3. The bibliography on the transcendentals is growing steadily. See the Bibliography for this volume.
4. For example, Thomas asks in *De veritate* (ca. 1256–59): "*Utrum ens et bonum convertantur secundum supposita.*" Nicholas Trivet (d. post 1330) asks in *Quodlibet* III: "*Utrum bonum quod respicit ens commune sicut convertibile, sit synonymum.*" And earlier, Albert the Great asked in *Summa de bono* (ca. 1245): "*Utrum bonum cum ente convertatur.*" For lists of questions written on pertinent themes, see Glorieux 1931.
5. There were others as well such as *pulchrum, aliquid, res,* and various disjunctions. Note that I have translated *unum* and *verum* for purely stylistic reasons as 'unity' and 'truth,' although strictly speaking they should be translated as 'one' and 'true.'
6. The *formulae* varied, however, although the meaning was clear. For example, in *ST* Ia.5.1, Thomas states: "*bonum et ens sunt idem secundum rem, sed differunt secundum rationem tantum*" (Thomas Aquinas 1926, vol. 1, p. 29).
7. Suárez refers to many classic texts from Augustine, Boethius, and others that support this analysis. Augustine, for example, writes in q. 24 of *De diversis quaestionibus octoginta tribus* (Augustine 1975, p. 29): "*Omne quod est, in quantum est, bonum est.*" And in *De doctrina christiana* I.32 (Augustine 1981b, p. 27): "*Et caetera quae sunt, nisi ab illo, esse non possunt et in tantum bona sunt, in quantum acceperunt ut sint.*"

1a. Every being, insofar as it is a being, is good.
1b. Every good, insofar as it is good, is a being.

In short, (1) entails that 'being' and 'good' have the same extension, for whatever is a being is good precisely because it is a being, and whatever is good is a being precisely because it is good.

Most upholders of DTG also wished to make clear, however, that the intensional content (*intentio, ratio*) of the terms 'being' and 'good' are not the same. That is the import of (2). 'To be' and 'to be good,' therefore, do not mean the same thing. Intensionally, or "in concept," there are differences between being and goodness.

Now, the issue that I wish to raise in this paper does not have to do with the understanding of these various *formulae*, regardless of the problems that they may pose, or with the meaning of the terms 'good' and 'being,' a widely debated issue in the Middle Ages to which nonetheless I shall have to refer later on. The issue is of a different sort and surfaces when one adds a third thesis, also widely accepted by scholastics, to (1) and (2):

3. Good and evil are opposites.[8]

This claim in turn can be unpacked in the following two *formulae*:

3a. No good, insofar as it is good, is evil.
3b. No evil, insofar as it is evil, is good.

Although (3) was not always accepted by all those who adhered to (1) and (2), most of those who accepted them also subscribed to (3) or to some version of it. For that reason, and in order to simplify subsequent references in this paper to the view we are examining, I shall henceforth consider (3a) and (3b) as parts of DTG.

Now, from (1a) and (3a) we get the following corollary:

4a. No being, insofar as it is a being, is evil.[9]

8. The terms used in the formula differ. Some authors use 'opposites,' whereas others use 'contraries,' but most qualify what they mean in some way. We shall see in the texts that follow that Suárez uses both terms. For their analysis, see *Contrarietas* and *Oppositio* in the glossary to Suárez 1989.
9. Thomas, *ST* Ia.5.3.ad2: "*Nullum ens dicitur malum, inquantum est ens, sed inquantum caret quodam esse*" (Thomas Aquinas 1926, p. 31). Suárez collects many of the classic texts that express (4a) in *Disp.* XI, 1, 3. For references to Suárez, I shall use Suárez 1861. Disputations X and XI, to which most references will be made, appear in vol. 25. For this reference, see p. 356. The translations of the texts into English are taken from Suárez 1989.

And from (1a) and (3b) we get:

4b. No evil, insofar as it is evil, is a being.

The import of (4a) and (4b) is, then, that whatever is a being cannot be evil to the degree that it is a being, and whatever is evil cannot be a being to the extent that it is evil.[10] But herein lies the problem, for (4a) and (4b) seem counterintuitive and open to obvious objections. Suárez himself is aware of those objections and develops with some care the ones he rightly thinks pose the deepest difficulties for DTG.

Suárez considers two paradigmatic counterexamples to DTG in *Disp.* XI, sec.1, para. 4.[11] He introduces them as examples of the two types into which evil is exhaustively divided: the evil of fault (*culpa*) and the evil of penalty (*poena*). The evil of fault occurs when persons knowingly, willingly, and freely do something contrary to their nature or omit doing something prescribed by their nature.[12] The evil of penalty occurs as a consequence of the evil of fault, as a just punishment for it.[13] Suárez introduces the problematic example of the evil of fault in the following way: "an act of vice is evil not only on account of the privation of the opposite virtue. Otherwise prodigality would be as evil as avarice, because both of them prevent the same virtue of liberality; therefore, *an act of vice is evil by reason of its positive entity.*"[14] An act of vice is a

---

10. In keeping with scholastic custom, I shall for present purposes extend the use of the term 'evil' to cover a wide variety of facts that strictly speaking are not regarded as evil in contemporary philosophical circles. Today, the use of the term 'evil' is frequently restricted to (1) moral evils, that is, evils connected to human choice and will, and (2) natural evils, namely, natural disasters and the like. But 'evil' for scholastics has a much broader range of meaning, referring to anything that interferes with the natural development of a thing. Thus they speak of water as being evil for fire because it puts it out, for example. Moral and natural evils are, for scholastics, subcategories of evil more generally conceived. I make this clarification in order to avoid confusing the reader, although the adoption or rejection of the broad scholastic notion of evil makes no difference in the context of the issue discussed in this paper.

11. *Disp.* XI, 1, 4, pp. 356–57.

12. *Disp.* XI, 2, 4–5, pp. 362–63.

13. *Disp.* XI, 2, 4–5, pp. 362–63.

14. *Disp.*, XI, 1, 4, p. 356: "*actus vitii non est malus solum ob privationem virtutis oppositae, alias eamdem malitiam haberet avaritia quam prodigalitas, quia privant eadem virtute liberalitatis; EST ERGO MALUS RATIONE SUAE POSITIVAE ENTITATIS.*" My emphasis. I have translated *actus vitii* as 'act of vice,' following the pattern established by a prior example in the text in which Suárez refers to an act of intemperance. However, it would also be possible, as Scott MacDonald has pointed out to me, to take *actus vitii* to be referring to "the actuality of vice." The latter interpretation squares with the examples of prodigality and avarice that follow in the text and that are themselves vices and not particular acts of vice. This reading, however, does not follow the pattern established by the example of the act of intemperance. So it is not clear which of the two readings Suárez has in mind. It is

conscious, willful, and free act that goes against human nature and/or God's law and, therefore, is evil.[15] Now, the problem that an act of vice poses for supporters of DTG is that such an act is not evil just because it deprives of or prevents the good, which in this case is virtue; it is evil not just in its privative function, but because it is a positive entity. Indeed, an act of vice, just as any other act in which humans engage, falls into the Aristotelian category of action and thus is considered by scholastics, including Suárez, as an accidental being accruing to an individual human substance. But, if an act of vice is a being and, as Suárez points out, "is evil by reason of its positive entity," then DTG must be false, since this consequence contradicts its corollaries (4a) and (4b).

The second counterexample belongs to the category of penalty. Suárez presents it as follows:

pain is an evil of penalty and yet it is something positive. Nor could it be said that pain is evil because it prevents the opposite pleasure; for, although the privation of pleasure may be an evil, nevertheless the existence of pain is a much greater and different kind of evil. Therefore, *evil is not just privation, nor is it something positive only by reason of privation, but it is also itself positive.* Hence, even if we were to suppose that pain did not exclude the contrary pleasure, nevertheless pain itself would be something evil. Therefore, *just as the pleasurable good is positive, so is the evil of sadness or pain positive.*[16]

Pain, according to this text, is evil not just because its experience precludes the experience of pleasure; it is evil apart from any relation it may have to pleasure. Pain is something positive we experience and

---

altogether possible, of course, that Suárez is aware of the ambiguity of the expression *actus vitii* and has both interpretations in mind. At any rate, whether *actus vitii* is interpreted to refer to an act or to the actuality of vice, in either case the positive character of the entity in question is clear. In the first case, for the reasons I shall point out immediately; in the second, because then the reference is to a *habitus*, which is a type of entity found in the Aristotelian categories.

15. Note that there are important differences between an act of vice and a vice. An act of vice is either an act contrary to nature or an act that violates God's commandments, whereas a vice is a habit resulting from repeated acts of vice.

16. *Disp.* XI, 1, 4, pp. 356–57: "DOLOR EST MALUM POENAE, ET TAMEN EST QUID POSITIVUM. *Neque dici poterit dolorem esse malum, quia privat opposita voluptate, nam, licet privatio voluptatis nonnullum malum sit, longe tamen majus, et alterius rationis malum est existentia doloris;* NON ERGO SOLA ILLA PRIVATIO, NEC POSITIVUM TANTUM RATIONE ILLIUS PRIVATIONIS MALUM EST, SED ETIAM IPSUM POSITIVUM. *Unde etiamsi fingamus dolorem contrariam delectationem non excludere, nihilominus ipse dolor esset aliquod malum;* SICUT ERGO BONUM DELECTABILE POSITIVUM EST, ITA MALUM CONTRISTANS, SEU DOLORIFERUM POSITIVUM EST." My emphasis.

cannot be analyzed negatively in terms of the privative or preventive functions it may have with respect to pleasure. Again, as with the case of an act, most scholastics held that pain is something classifiable within one of Aristotle's categories and, therefore, had the status of accidental being. That is one of the reasons why it was taken as a serious counterexample to DTG.

Not content with the example of pain, however, Suárez adds other cases of evils of penalty that could be used to argue against DTG:

> Again, if a sweet thing, for example, is positively agreeable to the taste, likewise a bitter thing is positively disagreeable. Again, error in understanding is a kind of evil of penalty and without doubt is a very different evil from ignorance, which is a kind of privation; therefore, it is a *positive evil by reason of a positive relation to such an object.*[17]

The disagreeable experience of bitterness has some kind of positive entitative status. Likewise, error is more than ignorance, namely, a lack of knowledge; it involves holding the wrong view about something.[18]

Now, defenders of DTG usually adopt one of two strategies when confronted with the counterexamples of pain and certain human acts. The first strategy (A) consists in trying to deal with the counterexamples themselves, showing either (a) that they are evil but not beings or, alternatively, (b) that they are beings but not evil. Following the first alternative (a), some authors have argued, for example, that pain is not a real being but rather a mental phenomenon without objective reality. That is to say, they argue that pain consists only in the way we look at or perceive something, rather than in a reality of some sort. Indeed, they point out, one can with proper training eliminate or at least modify or even ignore one's pain, a clear indication that pain is "all in one's mind," rather than something real.

But, of course, this procedure has not satisfied many philosophers, for the reality of pain seems too evident to those that suffer it to be dismissed summarily as having only mental status. And even if this

17. *Disp.* XI, 1, 4, pp. 356–57: "*Item, si res, verbi gratia, dulcis, est positive conveniens gustui, ita res amara est positive disconveniens. Item error in intellectu est malum quoddam poenae, et sine dubio est longe diversum malum quam ignorantia privationis;* EST ERGO POSITIVUM MALUM RATIONE POSITIVAE HABITUDINIS AD TALE OBJECTUM." My emphasis. Throughout this chapter I have translated the term *convenientia* by 'agreeability' and *disconvenientia* by 'disagreeability.' Douglas Davis and I have discussed the advantages and disadvantages of these and other possible translations in Suárez 1989, pp. 27–28 and 42–43.

18. Error involves holding a false proposition as true. As such, error has entitative status in the mind even if there is no state of affairs in the world that corresponds to that described by the proposition one holds in the mind. Suárez devotes *Disp.* VIII and IX to the discussion of truth and falsity, respectively.

response were deemed unacceptable, the objector can always, and often does, refer to many other counterexamples that are not susceptible to the same sort of treatment.

There have been other supporters of DTG who have therefore adopted (*b*) instead of (*a*) as a way of dealing with the problematic counterexamples: they have accepted that pain and the other counterexamples mentioned are beings, or at least beings of sorts, but have argued that they are not evil. They cite the fact, for example, that pain is a warning of something gone wrong in the human body. If we did not have it, we would not realize that something is wrong, and serious consequences could follow.

But this type of answer is unsatisfactory. It may well be the case that pain is good because it is a warning of bodily malfunction, but whether pain functions as a warning or not, the actual feeling of pain cannot possibly be considered but disagreeable and in certain cases even unbearable. There is no reason why a warning system should be painful. Besides, once the disorder about which pain was a warning has been diagnosed, what further salutary and/or beneficial effect can pain have? Indeed, that pain may be an instrumental good does not entail that it is not also an instrumental evil or even an intrinsic evil. And this kind of rejoinder applies not just to pain, but to most of the other answers given to the counterexamples brought forth to undermine DTG.

For these and similar reasons, some supporters of DTG have adopted a different strategy (B) to deal with these counterexamples. They interpret DTG in such a way as to accommodate these counterexamples without actually trying to reinterpret them so that they may become divested of their being or evil character. These supporters of DTG accept, then, that there are beings that can be evil but argue that they are not evil insofar as they are beings; they are evil for some other reasons. Their strategy is to show that the counterexamples brought against DTG do not actually go against (4a) and (4b) and therefore pose no threat to DTG. This is, indeed, the path that Suárez follows, providing an excellent model of how this strategy works, of its strengths and weaknesses. Let us turn to his view.

2. Suárez's Solution

Suárez's response to the mentioned counterexamples to DTG is to deny neither their status as entities nor their evil character. He is convinced not only that evil acts, pain, the experience of something bitter, and error are evil but that many other positive entities are as well. His procedure is an example of the second strategy described above (B) and consists in introducing a distinction that would accommodate these counterexamples without denying any of the basic tenets of DTG or the positive entitative status and evil character of the counterexamples. The distinction in question, as we shall see, allows him to argue that there are beings that are evil and evils that are beings, but that the first are not evil in virtue of their being, nor are the second beings in virtue of their evilness.

The distinction through which Suárez proposes to accommodate the troublesome counterexamples is that between evil in itself and evil for another.[19] This distinction, however, is part of a much broader and significant view concerning the intensions of 'good' and 'evil' and the ontological reality to which those terms refer. Let me begin with the more specific answer to the problem at hand so that it may be easier to understand the broader implications of Suárez's position.

Suárez's presentation of the distinction between evil in itself and evil for another is as follows:

I. We can divide evil . . . into evil in itself and . . . evil for another. The reason for this is that . . . something can be good in these two ways, and in all the ways in which one of two opposites is said to be, the other can also be said to be. Therefore, what is said to be *evil in itself can be designated evil by privation alone*; and for this reason it is truly said that *evil consists formally in privation alone*.[20]

II. Speaking, however, about what is *evil for another, it can thus be granted that evil*

---

19. There had been other authors before Suárez who had followed a strategy similar to that which Suárez adopts, but the distinctions they had introduced were different from the one used by him. Suárez is well aware of this fact and refers to the distinction between natural and moral evil, attributed to Cajetan, as one such attempt in *Disp*. XI, 1, 6, p. 357. He points out, however, that Cajetan's distinction is actually between "evil without qualification" and "moral evil" rather than between "natural" and "moral evil." But even in those terms Suárez concludes that Cajetan's solution is ineffective, because it fails to take care of the problematic counterexamples. His objections against this distinction are three: (1) the holy Fathers speak primarily of the evil of fault rather than natural evil; (2) if moral evil is positive, it comes from God and therefore it would be good without qualification; and (3) the notions of natural evil and moral evil are the same with respect to disagreeability to nature, for moral evil is contrary to rational natures.

20. *Disp*. XI, 1, 8, p. 358: *"distinguere possumus de malo . . . in se malum et . . . malum alteri; his enim duobus modis . . . posse aliquid esse bonum; quot modis autem dicitur unum oppositorum, potest dici et alterum. Id ergo, quod IN SE MALUM dicitur, A SOLA PRIVATIONE MALUM DE-NOMINARI POTEST; atque hac ratione vere dicitur, MALUM FORMALITER IN SOLA PRIVATIONE POSITUM ESSE."* My emphasis.

consists in something positive and is opposed to good, not privatively, but as a contrary, as pain is opposed to pleasure, vice to virtue and so on.[21]

In (I) Suárez presents the traditional scholastic understanding of evil as privation. According to it, evil is not just any lack. Lacks, such as the absence of wings in a human, are not evil. Evil is the lack of a perfection that something ought to have as dictated by its nature. Thus for a flying type of bird, not to have wings is a privation and consequently evil.[22]

The view of evil presented in (I) does not seem to accommodate the controversial counterexamples to which reference has been made, since privations are nothing positive in reality and the entities in question seem to be something real. But the counterexamples are easily taken care of by the second part of the distinction, presented in (II): evil for another. For in this way what is evil can be something positive and opposed to good. Suárez accepts that there are some beings, like pain, that can be evil even though they are something positive in reality. But he needs to show how this does *not* imply that (4a) and (4b) are false. He shows this by explaining how something positive can be evil for another, which he does in turn by elucidating the intensions of 'evil for another' and 'good for another' in terms of the notions of disagreeability and agreeability, respectively:

this notion of evil [that is, evil for another] is the same as the notion of disagreeability (*disconvenientia*) to something. Therefore, just as good, under the aspect of agreeability (*convenientia*) to another, expresses nothing other than the perfection of one thing, connoting in another [thing] a condition, by reason of which [the other thing] ought to have for itself such perfection, or by reason of which such perfection is congruent with it, so the evil opposed to this good formally and with precision expresses nothing other than the perfection of one thing, connoting in another [thing] a condition, by reason of which [the other thing] has an incompatibility or disagreeability to such a form [that is, perfection]. Therefore, just as that good consists in something positive, so also does the evil opposite to it.[23]

21. *Disp.* XI, 1, 8, p. 358: "*Loquendo autem de eo quod est MALUM ALTERI, SIC CONCEDI POTEST MALUM CONSISTERE IN POSITIVO, et opponi bono non privative, sed contrarie, quomodo dolor opponitur voluptati, vitium virtuti, et sic de aliis.*" My emphasis.

22. Suárez's discussion of privation occurs in *Disp.* LIV. See Suárez 1989, pp. 35–37.

23. *Disp.* XI, 1, 8, p. 358: "*haec autem mali eadem est cum ratione disconvenientis alicui; sicut ergo bonum sub ratione convenientis alteri nihil aliud dicit quam perfectionem unius rei, connotando in alia conditionem aliquam ratione cujus sibi debetur, aut congruit talis perfectio, ita malum huic bono oppositum formaliter ac praecise nihil aliud dicit, praeter perfectionem unius rei, connotando in alia conditionem aliquam, ratione cujus repugnantiam vel disconvenientiam habet cum tali forma; igitur sicut bonum illud in positivo consistit, ita et malum ei oppositum.*"

The conception of evil for another as disagreeability accommodates very nicely the problematic counterexamples. Fault is evil because it is "disagreeable to" the nature of the human being who commits it. Suárez does not waste any time in making the point:

> The answer to the first difficulty . . . is that the evil of fault is an evil which properly pertains to man insofar as he is rational and uses free will, and therefore it is not always said of privation alone, but also of a positive act . . . . This evil, by reason of the act it includes, can be contrarily opposed to a good act or to an act of virtue . . . . Similarly, the very same act is said to be contrary to reason because it lacks the rectitude that it ought to have. Hence, not only is it evil because it excludes from the subject the contrary act or a good habit . . . but because it is itself disagreeable to rational nature.[24]

Likewise pain, a bitter taste, and error are disagreeable to a subject and it is for that reason that they can be considered to be evil. In Suárez's words:

> pain is not in itself evil, for it has its own perfection and whatever degree of such perfection it ought to have for itself. Therefore, pain is something evil [only] insofar as it is disagreeable to man or animal. Hence . . . pain is not evil only causally, that is, because it excludes the opposite pleasure, but also because it is itself disagreeable and inappropriate for an animal. . . . The same answer must be given to the other [counter]examples proposed.[25]

Suárez's solution appears to work well at first glance. The notion of disagreeability seems to explain adequately how some entity can turn out to be evil for some other entity, and likewise the notion of agreeability seems to explain how an entity can be good for another. However, Suárez's use of the notions of disagreeability and agreeability in the understanding of evil for another and good for another have important implications. For evil for another is a type of evil and good for another is a type of good. Suárez must, therefore, explain how

24. *Disp.* XI, 1, 17, p. 360: "*Ad primam ergo difficultatem . . . malum culpae proprie esse malum hominis, ut rationalis est et libero arbitrio utitur; et ideo non semper dici de sola privatione, sed etiam de actu positivo . . . . Hoc malum, ratione actus quem includit, potest contrarie opponi actui bono seu virtutis . . . . Et eodem modo ipsemet actus dicitur contrarius rationi, quia caret debita rectitudine, unde non tantum est malus quia excludit a subjecto contrarium actum, vel habitum bonum . . . sed quia ipsemet est disconveniens rationali naturae.*"

25. *Disp.* XI, 1, 18, p. 361: "*dolorem non esse in se malum, habet enim perfectionem suam et quidquid in latitudine talis perfectionis sibi debitum est; est ergo dolor quid malum tanquam disconveniens homini vel animali. Unde . . . non tantum esse malum causaliter, id est, quia excludit delectationem oppositam, sed etiam quia ipsemet est disconveniens, et disproportionatus animali . . . . Et eodem modo respondendum est ad alia exempla . . . proponuntur.*"

disagreeability is related to evil considered as such and how agreeability is related to good considered as such. This is important, for at stake is not only the consistency of Suárez's view, but also the intensional and ontological analyses of good and evil and ultimately the viability of DTG. Moreover, it is here where some of the problems with Suárez's position surface. I turn to them now.

3. Two Initial Difficulties of Suárez's Position

I restrict myself to pointing out only two difficulties with Suárez's view that may appear rather obvious but that I believe help us uncover a more fundamental problem with the view. There are other difficulties as well, but I do not think they are as interesting philosophically or as useful in uncovering the underlying problem to which I shall refer as the two I wish to discuss. Moreover, the interest that these difficulties have for us is that they indicate certain inconsistencies in Suárez's position which, if avoided, may point the way toward a successful ontological understanding of good and evil.

The difficulties in question have to do with the explanation of the relations (i) between evil considered in itself and disagreeability, and (ii) between good in itself and agreeability. The sources of the difficulties are two theses that Suárez holds:

a. Agreeability extends to all good, including good in itself.
b. Disagreeability extends only to evil for another.

Although Suárez does not always write about good in the same terms, it is clear from a variety of texts, some of which will be cited later, that the fundamental notion he associates with goodness is agreeability, and this not only in the context of good for another but of all good, including good in itself.[26]

On the other hand, the correlative notion of disagreeability applies only to evil for another and not to evil in itself. Evil in itself is to be understood rather as privation, and it is this notion of privation, not the notion of disagreeability, that extends to all evil, including evil for another.[27]

---

26. *Disp.* X, 1, 12, and X, 2, 2 and 4, pp. 332 and 335–36.
27. See *Disp.* XI, 1, 8, p. 358. A couple of these texts have been given in nn. 20 and 39. There are problems with extending the notion of privation, a type of lack, to evil for another, which is supposed to be something real. Davis and I discuss these problems in the Introduction to Suárez 1989, pp. 73ff.

Now, the two fundamental difficulties with Suárez's view to which I wish to refer may be introduced with the following two questions: (1) How can evil in itself not be understood in terms of disagreeability when disagreeability and agreeability, just as evil and good, are correlative notions and agreeability extends to all good, including good in itself? (2) How can the good in itself be understood in terms of the notion of agreeability, when agreeability obviously is a relational notion and what is good in itself is supposed to be good independently of anything else? These two questions help make explicit Suárez's problems, for first, contrary to (a), agreeability does not seem to fit the notion of good in itself, and second, if Suárez wishes to extend the notion of agreeability to all good, he should also extend that of disagreeability to all evil, including, contrary to (b), evil in itself.

A. First Difficulty

The first difficulty has to do with the notion of good, and so we should begin the more detailed discussion of it with the notion of good in general, which might be expressed as follows:

GG: X is good if and only if either X is good in itself or X is good for another.

Now, good for another consists in the agreeability that something has for something else. Thus, we may express this notion as follows:

GA1: X is good for Y if and only if X is agreeable to Y.

This postulate does not seem particularly problematic, except that it tells us little about good. The notion of agreeability needs further unpacking. This is evident when we look at the texts in which Suárez discusses this notion. For example, let us look again at an important passage to which reference was made earlier: "good, under the aspect of agreeability to another, expresses nothing other than the perfection of one thing, connoting in another [thing] a condition, by reason of which [the other thing] ought to have for itself such perfection, or by reason of which such perfection is congruent with it."[28] According to this text and what we may gather from several other passages, agreeability is a relational notion and the terms of this relation are always a

---

28. *Disp.* XI, 1, 8, p. 358. See n. 23 for text. See also *Disp.* X, 1, 12; X, 2, 2; and X, 2, 4; pp. 332 and 335–36.

substance, on the one hand, and a perfection, on the other. By 'substance' Suárez means what Aristotle called a primary substance in the *Categories*, for example, a man, a cat, or a tree.[29] By 'perfection' he means, in the case of agreeability, a form that is agreeable to the substance for which it is considered good. Let us look at three possible situations, ontologically speaking, where we may find agreeability:

Case 1A: In this situation we have two different substances, say A and B, where a form in B, call it b, is agreeable to A. In this case, A, B, and b are all distinct entities in reality in addition to being conceptually distinct. For example, the virtue of liberality (b) of a human being (B) is agreeable to another human being (A), who needs some economic help.

Case 2A: In this situation we have only one substance, say A, where a form in A, call it a, is agreeable to it. In this case A and a are distinct entities in reality in addition to being conceptually distinct. For example, a virtue (a) is agreeable to a human being (A).

Case 3A: In this situation we have one substance, call it A, where a form in A, call it a, may be considered agreeable to it even though it is not really distinct from it. The distinction between A and a is merely conceptual. For example, God's mercy (a) is agreeable to God (A), even though God is not really distinct from his mercy.

In cases 1A, 2A, and 3A we have made explicit the possible ontological structures in which we may find agreeability, but these structures do not by themselves make clear what agreeability is; they only make clear the terms of the relation. One way of elucidating the notion of agreeability is by modifying the understanding of good for another as follows:

GA2: X is good for Y if and only if X is among the features that comprise Y's nature.

I shall provide two examples, both used by Suárez in various contexts, to clarify (GA2). In the first we have two substances, whereas in the second there is only one. Note, however, that in the first example, ice and water, which are not strictly speaking Aristotelian substances, are treated as if they were, but this matter does not affect the analysis.

First example: Let 'X' stand for the coldness of a piece of ice and 'Y' for some water. Suárez would say that the coldness (X) of the piece of ice is good (that is to say, agreeable) for the water (Y) because coldness,

29. *Categories* 5 (2a10–15).

although a feature of the ice, is also a feature included among the features that constitute the nature of water.

Second example: Let 'X' stand for rationality and 'Y' stand for Aristotle. According to (GA2) we can say that rationality (X) is good (that is to say, agreeable) for Aristotle (Y) because rationality is a feature included among the features that constitute the nature of Aristotle, that is, his humanity.

According to (GA2), as illustrated by the two examples mentioned, agreeability is understood as the relation of the features that are considered to be part of a nature to that nature. Note that by 'nature' is meant the set of features that make a thing to be the specific type of thing it is. Thus, Aristotle's nature, as properly expressed by the definition of the species to which he belongs, is a set of features that comprises the features of rationality and animality and whatever else is included and/or implied by them, such as materiality, and so on.

The problem with (GA2) is that it does not cover all the cases Suárez wishes to include within good for another. According to (GA2), only features that are considered to be part of a thing's nature could be good for the thing, although we know, as Suárez did, that there are many things outside a thing's nature that are good for it, such as wealth and pleasure for human beings. In order to capture that dimension of goodness, (GA2) must be further modified to read something like the following:

GA3: X is good for Y if and only if X is included in the set of features that either (a) comprise Y's nature and/or (b) contribute to the fulfillment of Y's nature.

I shall provide two examples to illustrate (GA3). The first example of (GA3) illustrates a situation with two substances, while the second refers to a situation where there is only one.

First example: Let 'X' stand for Alexander's liberality and 'Y' stand for Aristotle. According to (GA3), Alexander's liberality (X) is not included in the set of features that constitute Aristotle's nature but is nonetheless good for Aristotle (Y) because it contributes to the fulfillment of his nature, since it makes it possible for Aristotle to devote time to the exercise of his rational faculties.

Second example: Let 'X' stand for Alexander's virtue and 'Y' stand for Alexander. According to (GA3), the virtue of Alexander (X) is not included in the set of features that constitute his nature but nevertheless is good for him, since it may contribute to the fulfillment of his nature. In accordance with (GA3), then, any feature that is part of a thing's nature and/or contributes to the fulfillment of that nature is a good for the thing. The modifications introduced in (GA3) would seem to take care of most cases in which something is good for another, for it extends the notion of agreeability to situations other than those that involve a relation of the components of a nature to the nature.

(GA3) seems to express pretty well what Suárez has in mind with respect to the notion of good for another, and it does not seem to create immediate problems. But problems do arise when we try to deal with good in itself, for Suárez also wants to understand good in itself in terms of agreeability. Indeed, agreeability is what "good adds to being," namely, what distinguishes the intensions of 'being' and 'good': "Good expresses an agreeability by reason of which a [good] thing is desirable. . . . Hence, it is necessary that *even those things which are said to be good absolutely and according to themselves be so designated.*"[30]
We might express this view as follows:

GI1: *X* is good in itself if and only if *X* is agreeable to *X*.

But (GI1) does not seem to make sense, for the notion of agreeability appears to require two terms, what is agreeable and that to which what is agreeable is agreeable, and (GI1) does not allow for such terms. Indeed, as we saw earlier, Suárez explicitly grants that agreeability requires two terms, a substance and a form. Thus, it is not clear how there can be agreeability if there is only one term. It is case 3A above that poses difficulties, for it makes perfectly good sense to say not only that Alexander's liberality is good for Aristotle because it is agreeable to Aristotle, but also that it is good for Alexander himself insofar as it is agreeable to him, that is, insofar as it makes him a better person by making him more the way he should be as dictated by his nature. But if what we want to say, as Suárez does, is that Alexander himself is good, does it make sense to analyze that goodness in terms of agreeability? How can Alexander be good because he is agreeable to himself? Suárez is well aware of the problem:

30. *Disp.* X, 1, 18, p. 334: "*Bonum vero dicere convenientiam aliquam, ratione cujus habet res, quod appetibilis sit . . . . Unde necesse est,* RES ETIAM ILLAS, QUAE ABSOLUTE ET SECUNDUM SE DICUNTUR BONAE, SIC DENOMINARI." My emphasis. See also *Disp.* X, 1, 18 and X, 2, 4, pp. 334 and 336.

This [agreeability characteristic of goodness] is more clearly evident when the perfection is distinct from the thing itself that is designated good on account of the perfection [Case 2A]. For, when a man is said to be good by reason of virtue, virtue is not formally signified in just any way, but as a certain goodness that includes not only the perfection of virtue, but also the agreeability that virtue has with human nature, connoting a capacity for or propensity to such perfection on the part of the nature itself. *In those things, however, in which there is no distinction between the perfection and the thing that is said to be perfect, this agreeability or connotation seems more difficult to explain* [Case 3A].[31]

Interestingly enough, the only example to which Suárez refers to illustrate this situation is that of God, which I propose to discuss in a moment. From what Suárez tells us in various places, however, it is clear that he did not restrict the notion of good in itself to God. It is also clear, moreover, that what he had in mind was quite different from the example of a virtuous man to which he refers in the passage just cited, for that example illustrates rather how something can be agreeable to something else. Virtue is good for a man because it is agreeable to his nature, and the man is said to be good to the extent he has virtue. In this case we have two ontologically distinct entities, the man (a substance) and his virtue (an accident). But what do we do when the form or perfection is identical with the substance for which it is good? Can we think of a case other than that of God in which a thing would be good in itself and thus agreeable to itself? I believe what Suárez may have in mind might be cases like the following two, although as already stated, he does not provide us with any examples other than that of God:

1. Alexander is good because he has being and to have being is agreeable to him.
2. Alexander is good because he is a substance and to be a substance is agreeable to him.

In each of these cases we have an entity (Alexander) and some kind of a property (being, substantiality) that is agreeable to him, although the property in question is nothing other than the original entity (Alex-

31. *Disp.* X, 1, 18, p. 334: "*Quod clarius patet, quando talis perfectio est distincta ab ipsa re, quae ab illa bona denominatur; nam, quando homo dicitur bonus ratione virtutis, de formali significatur virtus non utcumque, sed ut bonitas quaedam, in quo importatur, non tantum perfectio virtutis, sed etiam convenientia quam habet cum humana natura, connotando ex parte ipsius naturae capacitatem, vel propensionem ad talem perfectionem. IN HIS VERO REBUS, IN QUIBUS NON EST DISTINCTIO INTER PERFECTIONEM ET REM, QUAE PERFECTA DICITUR, DIFFICILIUS VIDETUR EXPLICARI HAEC CONVENIENTIA VEL CONNOTATIO.*" My emphasis. A similar point is made in *Disp.* X, 2, 2, pp. 335–36.

ander). Since, for Suárez, the being and the substance of a thing are not distinct in reality from the thing,[32] the question arises as to how an entity, such as Alexander, can be said to be agreeable to itself (its being and/or substance).[33]

An even more dramatic case of this situation to which Suárez explicitly refers, as already noted, is that of God:

In the most simple substance, which is God, this mode of agreeability, understood to hold between two things distinct in some way in reality, is not properly found. Rather, God is agreeable to himself by the highest identity and simplicity, and his nature is agreeable to his own person and the personality to the nature itself; and this agreeability is in accordance with the nature whereby it is rendered in itself good and perfect, rather than in accordance with that whereby it is said to be agreeable to something.[34]

According to this passage: (1) God is agreeable to himself, (2) God's nature is agreeable to God's person, and (3) God's personality is agreeable to God's nature. But all these agreeabilities are one and the same agreeability of a thing with itself and not the agreeability of a thing with something else, since God, his nature, his person, and his personality are one and the same thing, according to Suárez.

Two explanations of the agreeability of a thing to itself suggest themselves within a Suarecian context. One is explicitly proposed by Suárez; the second may be pieced together on the basis of his overall position. The statement of the first occurs in the following passage:

It must be said, however, that although there may not be a distinction in reality, nevertheless [this relation of agreeability] *is conceived and signified by us* in a way

32. That a thing is not distinct from its substance was generally accepted by scholastics. However, the relation of the being of a thing to the thing and to its components was a matter of dispute. Suárez does not accept any real distinction between a thing and its being, just as he does not subscribe to the Thomistic view that a thing's being is really distinct from its essence. Cf. Owens 1957.

33. I am quite aware of the important distinction between "can be agreeable to itself" and "can be said to be agreeable to itself." The first refers to an ontological fact, the second to the expression of that fact. However, for present purposes, observing the distinction seems neither necessary nor particularly useful.

34. *Disp.* X, 3, 7, pp. 348–49: "*In substantia autem simplicissima, quae est Deus, non reperitus proprie intra ipsam hic modus convenientiae qui intelligitur esse unius rei ad aliam aliquo modo in re distinctam, sed per summam identitatem et simplicitatem est Deus conveniens sibi ipsi et natura eius est conveniens suae personae et personalitas ipsi naturae; sed haec convenientia potius est secundum eam rationem qua redditur in se bona et perfecta, quam secundum eam qua dicitur esse alicui conveniens.*"

similar to [the relation holding between] distinct things, that is, in a way similar to [the relation holding between] a designating form and a designated thing.[35]

Thus, a real distinction between, let us say, the subject of goodness (call it S) and what is good for it (call it g) is not necessary in order for what is good for it (g) to be considered agreeable to the subject (S)—there can be an agreeability between them regardless of their actual identity as long as we are able *to conceive* them separately. Agreeability functions in a way similar to identity, where the separation occurring in the judgment that identifies a thing with itself is purely mental. Accordingly, (GI1) should be read as follows:

GI2: X is good in itself if and only if X is agreeable to Y and Y is identical with X.

So, just as when I say "Cicero is Tully," there is only one thing in reality, which is as it were artificially unfolded into two in the mind, the case is likewise when I say, for example, that Alexander's being or Alexander's substance are agreeable to him. If X can be said to be identical with Y when Y is the same thing as X, then also X can be said to be agreeable to Y when Y is the same thing as X. If Alexander can be said to be identical with the pupil of Aristotle who conquered the ancient world, so can Alexander be said to be agreeable to himself. And the same is the case with God, whose nature, person, and personality, according to Suárez, are all identical with himself.

But Suárez's answer does not seem satisfactory, for there are significant differences between identity and agreeability. They become evident in the fact that the notion of identity is primarily used in sentential contexts where the two terms refer to one and the same thing, that is, in sentences of the sort 'X is identical with Y,' when Y is the same as X. But the notion of agreeability is primarily used in sentential contexts where the two terms do not refer to the same thing, that is, in sentences of the sort 'X is agreeable to Y,' when Y is not the same thing as X.

Whereas in one case we are dealing with a notion in its accepted sense, in the other we are not. Thus, the question arises as to what exactly that nonaccepted sense is, and the burden of proof is on Suárez to indicate the new sense and how it differs from the accepted one.

---

35. *Disp.* X, 3, 7, pp. 348–49: "*dicendum est tamen, quamvis in re non sit distinctio,* A NOBIS TAMEN CONCIPI AC SIGNIFICARI *ad modum distinctorum, id est, per modum formae denominantis et rei denominatae.*" My emphasis.

Unfortunately, Suárez does not provide us with such analysis, leaving us with the problem of explaining how a fundamentally relational notion, which usually applies to situations in which there is a real distinction between the relata, can apply to a situation in which the relata are one and the same thing in reality.

The second solution to Suárez's problem is not explicitly suggested by him as an explanation of how a thing can be agreeable to itself but, as mentioned earlier, may be reconstructed from his overall position and what he says elsewhere. According to this solution, when one is speaking about a thing that is good in itself, the terms of the relation of agreeability should be understood to be the entity that is said to be good, on the one hand, and its nature, on the other. Now, the entity in question is said to be good in itself to the degree that it fulfills the conditions prescribed by its nature. Thus, the entity is said to be agreeable to the degree that it fulfills or has those features that accord with (*conveniens*) the nature. Alexander, then, can be said to be good in himself to the degree that he fulfills or agrees with his nature. Since his nature prescribes the exercise of his reason, among other things, Alexander will be good to the extent that he exercises his reason, and so on. And the same is the case with God: He will be good to the extent that he is what he should be. Of course, for Suárez and other scholastics, God *is* what he should be because, unlike Alexander, he is identical with his nature, and thus this explanation does not apply to him strictly speaking. The way to explain God's goodness in terms of agreeability is only through the first solution suggested—the introduction of a conceptual distinction between relata that are in reality identical. But for Alexander and other nondivine beings, one could argue that this second solution is possible and may be the correct one, for, according to it, the nature of an entity functions as a paradigm of what the entity should be, stipulating its appropriate features. To fulfill that nature, that is, to have those features, is to be agreeable to itself and therefore to be good in itself.

But, we may ask: Have we gained any ground with this move? I do not believe so. We are in fact back where we started; for we still do not know how a thing can be agreeable to itself. Let me explain. A nature can be considered either as identical with the entity of which it is the nature or as distinct from it. If it is identical with the entity, which is the case of God, then we still have to explain how an entity can be agreeable to itself, and so the proposed solution does not help us. But if the nature is distinct from the entity, which may be Alexander's case (although that does not seem to be Suárez's position),[36] then it does not explain how an entity can be *agreeable* to itself, but only how an entity *fulfills* its nature, which seems to be something entirely different. Indeed, even if we were to grant that such fulfillment could be characterized as a kind of agreeability, we would be speaking about the relation between two distinct entities, and that is a different situation from the one required to explain good in itself.

Suárez may be aware of how ineffective this answer is, for he does not try to explain the agreeability of good in itself by referring to natures in the passage where he deals with this issue. Natures may help us in understanding what is good for a thing and also that the nature of a thing and everything prescribed by it is agreeable to the thing, a fact of which Suárez is well aware: "Good [in itself] consists in this, namely, that a thing has the perfection it ought to have and which is agreeable to it."[37] But natures do not help us see how a thing can be agreeable to itself, and that is precisely what Suárez's view of the good in itself would require them to do.

B. Second Difficulty

The second difficulty has to do with evil, and so, just as in the case of good, we should begin our detailed discussion of it with the general notion of evil. Such a notion may be expressed as follows:

EG: X is evil if and only if either X is evil in itself or X is evil for another.

Now, evil for another consists in the disagreeability that something has for something else, so that we may express the notion of evil for another as follows:

EA1: X is evil for Y if and only if X is disagreeable to Y.

This postulate does not seem to be particularly problematic, except that it tells us very little indeed about evil. The notion of disagreeability needs further analysis, as is evident from a text to which we drew

36. For Suárez, the nature is understood either as a concept, which as such has reality only insofar as it is entertained by some mind, or as each and every individual instance of that nature actually existing in the world (e.g., Alexander, Aristotle). But as an individual instance, the nature of Alexander, of course, could not be really distinct from Alexander. See Suárez 1964, pp. 7ff., and 1982, pp. 6–15.

37. *Disp.* XI, 1, 8, p. 358: "*ratio boni in hoc consistat, quod res habeat perfectionem sibi debitam et convenientem.*"

attention already above: "Evil [for another] expresses nothing other than the perfection of one thing, connoting in another [thing] a condition, by reason of which [the other thing] has an incompatibility or disagreeability to such a form [that is, perfection]."[38] According to what we can surmise from this statement and others, disagreeability, like agreeability, is a relational notion and the terms of the relation are always a substance, on the one hand, and a form, on the other. However, the ontological structure of disagreeability turns out to be quite different from that of agreeability. Indeed, Suárez holds that a real distinction between the terms that are disagreeable or incompatible is necessary for there to be disagreeability, something that was not so in the case of agreeability. And this means that only evil for another can be understood in terms of disagreeability; evil in itself consists in privation alone. "A thing is designated evil in itself only from the privation of the perfection that [it ought to have and which is agreeable to it]."[39] There are, then, only two cases in which disagreeability can occur. They parallel cases 1A and 2A of agreeability:

Case 1D: In this situation we have two different substances, say A and B, where a form in B, call it b, is disagreeable to A. In this case A, B, and b are all distinct entities in reality in addition to being conceptually distinct. For example, the cruelty (b) of a human being (B) is disagreeable to some other human being (A).

Case 2D: In this situation we have only one substance, say A, where a form in A, call it a, is disagreeable to it. In this case A and a are distinct entities in reality in addition to being conceptually distinct. For example, a vice (a) is disagreeable to a human being (A).

It is quite understandable why Case 3A of agreeability has no counterpart in the context of disagreeability, for the criterion of what is agreeable or disagreeable to something is provided by the nature of a thing. In the first two cases of agreeability or disagreeability there is no difficulty in seeing how a feature belonging either to the thing itself or to something else can be agreeable or disagreeable, as the case may be, to the thing in question, for the nature of the thing would determine it either way. But it would make no sense to say that something that is not really distinct from a thing and, therefore, is identical with its nature could be disagreeable to it.

38. *Disp.* XI, 1, 8, p. 358. See n. 23 for the text.
39. *Disp.* XI, 1, 8, p. 358: "*ex sola privatione talis perfectionis res in se mala denominetur.*"

All of this seems to make sense, and it becomes even more clear when we try to pin down further what disagreeability entails by modifying (EA1) as follows:

EA2: X is evil for Y if and only if X is not among the features that comprise Y's nature.

I propose two examples to illustrate (EA2). As with the examples of (GA2) given above, in the first there are two substances at work, whereas in the second there is only one. Moreover, in the first example the substances in question, water and fire, are not strictly speaking Aristotelian substances, but they are treated as if they were.

First example: Let 'X' stand for the heat of some fire and 'Y' stand for some water. According to (EA2), the heat of some fire (X) is bad (that is to say, disagreeable) for some water (Y) because the heat is not among the features that constitute the nature of water.

Second example: Let 'X' stand for some pain and 'Y' stand for Alexander. Following (EA2), pain is evil (that is to say, disagreeable) for Alexander because pain is not among the features that constitute Alexander's nature.

But clearly (EA2) is as inadequate in accounting for evil for another as (GA2) was in accounting for good for another, since not to be part of the nature of an entity does not automatically make something bad for it. Honor, for example, is not part of the nature of human beings and yet it is certainly considered a good rather than an evil for them. Therefore, (EA2) must be modified thus:

EA3: X is evil for Y if and only if X is neither (a) included in the set of features that comprise Y's nature nor (b) compatible with those features.

Again, two examples are appropriate to illustrate (EA3). The first example of (EA3) illustrates a situation with two substances; the second refers to a situation where there is only one.

First example: Let 'X' stand for Brutus's act of treachery and 'Y' stand for Caesar. According to (EA3), Brutus's act of treachery (X) is neither among the features that comprise Caesar's nature nor is it compatible with the features of that nature, namely, human nature, since it impedes its fulfillment. But anything that impedes the fulfillment of the nature of something must be considered evil (that is to say, disagreeable) for it, and so Brutus's act of treachery is an evil for Caesar.

Second example: Let 'X' stand for some vice of Caesar's and 'Y' stand for Caesar. Following (EA3), since the vice of Caesar (X) is neither among the set of features that comprise Caesar's nature nor compatible with those features, it must be an evil (that is to say, disagreeable) for him.

Note that in the case of goodness, compatibility was not a sufficient condition of good for another, since something may be compatible with something else and yet be neither good nor bad for it. Lack of hindrance alone could not explain goodness, because it points to a kind of neutrality uncharacteristic of the good. For example, the fact that the president of the United States took a shower this morning is perfectly compatible with my health, but it could hardly be called a good for it. On the other hand, incompatibility is enough to establish evil, for incompatibility involves the kind of obstacle to fulfillment that is precisely characteristic of evil. It should be clear, however, that the incompatibility in question is not the strong sort that would make it impossible for someone to have a vice contrary to his or her nature, for example. The incompatibility we are speaking of is of the sort that allows that possibility but indicates that the evil in question works against the fulfillment of the nature.

All of this seems to make sense; what is not clear is how Suárez can hold that a real distinction between the terms of disagreeability is required in the case of evil and at the same time maintain that such a distinction is not required for agreeability. Suárez seems inconsistent in imposing the requirement of a real distinction for disagreeability and at the same time rejecting such requirement for agreeability. His insistence on this point indicates quite clearly that, as we surmised, it is wrong to escape the first difficulty we saw earlier by understanding agreeability as the relation based on the fulfillment of a nature. For if this were so, Suárez could have explained the disagreeability proper to evil in itself in terms of the unfulfillment of a nature. Yet he does not do so. He explicitly accepts the understanding of evil in itself in terms of the unfulfillment of a nature, but he does not understand that to be a disagreeability. For disagreeability there have to be two distinct terms in reality, according to him.

Of course, we can easily understand the theological motives why Suárez wished to maintain that beings can be agreeable in themselves, while maintaining that they can be evil only in relation to something else. On the one hand, he wanted to preserve the doctrine of the simplicity of God's nature, where his attributes are not really distinct from him and yet both he and his attributes can be said to be good, that is, agreeable. And, on the other hand, he wanted to preserve the traditional scholastic view that evil in itself consists primarily in privation. But, although theologically this may make sense, philosophically it does not look like a viable position for the reasons given.

4. The Underlying Problem

The root of Suárez's difficulties is not theological, however. It is the attempt to reconcile a strongly relational understanding of good and evil in terms of agreeability and disagreeability respectively, on the one hand, with the wish to preserve the notions of good and evil in themselves, on the other. The problem arises from the attempt to place both good for another and good in itself under the single notion of agreeability, for agreeability is a strongly relational notion. What I mean by a strongly relational notion is a notion that expresses a relation in which the relata are distinct entities in reality. For example, fatherhood is a strongly relational notion because it expresses the relation between a father and a daughter (or son), and both the father and the daughter (or son) are distinct entities in reality. By contrast, a weakly relational notion is one that expresses a relation in which the relata are not distinct entities in reality. For example, fulfillment is a weakly relational notion because it expresses the relation between, say, a human being at a certain stage of development and the same human being at a later stage. In this case there is only one human being considered at two different stages of development rather than two simultaneously distinct entities in reality. The relation that ties the two stages of development of the human being, then, is weak. Now, agreeability, like disagreeability, works well when we are dealing with really distinct entities on which the relations are based. But it does not work well when we have only one entity. Suárez understands this point in the case of disagreeability. That is why he does not attempt to explain evil in itself in terms of disagreeability. But he does not follow the same road with agreeability, even though he is aware of the ensuing problems.

Some may wish to object, however, that in fact the notions of *convenientia* and *disconvenientia* are precisely such that they can describe both good and evil for another as well as good and evil in themselves and it is only their understanding suggested here as agreeability and disagreeability, respectively, that causes the problems to which I have referred. One could say, for example, that although a thing cannot be agreeable to itself, it can be *conveniens* to itself in the sense of having what it ought to have or being what it is in its nature to be. Likewise, one could also say that, although a thing cannot be disagreeable to itself, it can be *disconveniens* in the sense of not having what it ought to have or not being what it is in its nature to be.

But this objection is not effective. Indeed, if *convenientia* and *disconvenientia* are interpreted in such a way that they apply to the cases of good and evil in themselves, they cannot be applied to the cases of good and evil for another. For *convenientia* and *disconvenientia* are understood to refer either to strongly relational notions or to weakly relational notions. If they refer to strongly relational notions, then they do not serve to describe good and evil in themselves, where only weakly relational notions could be of use. And if they are understood to refer to weakly relational notions and thus serve to describe good and evil in themselves, then they do not serve to describe good and evil for another, which require a strongly relational analysis.

The underlying problem with Suárez's view in his use of *convenientia* and *disconvenientia* is that he tries to gather under them relations that are very different: the relations of a real thing to another and of a real thing to its nature.

5. Concluding Remarks

Faced with the counterexamples to the theory of evil implied by DTG, Suárez tries to find a solution in an interpretation of good and evil based on the notions of agreeability and disagreeability and on a distinction between good and evil in themselves and good and evil for another. His view proves effective in dealing with the troublesome counterexamples, but it does uncover the difficulties of trying to bring together the strongly relational notions of agreeability and disagreeability with the distinction between good and evil in themselves and good and evil for another.

There are two alternative solutions to the difficulties created by Suárez's attempt to deal with the counterexamples discussed earlier. One is simply to abandon the understanding of all good as agreeability and of evil for another as disagreeability. But if this is done, then one must look for a way to deal with the counterexamples raised by Suárez based on the positive entitative status of some evils.

A second alternative is to stick with the understanding of good as agreeability and evil for another as disagreeability and accept the implications of that position. The most serious one is that beings considered in themselves are neither good (that is, agreeable) nor evil (that is, disagreeable). That they are not evil is something that Suárez gladly accepts, since it is quite concordant with the traditional Christian view on the matter, with the doctrine of evil as privation, and with DTG. What is unacceptable to Suárez is the implication that beings cannot be considered good in themselves. The reasons are obvious. One is theological: God cannot be considered good. The other is philosophical: This view contradicts one of the two fundamental theses of DTG, namely, that being and good are convertible in reality.

Suárez's dilemma illustrates very well the difficulty of a view that presents an overall understanding of good and evil in terms of strongly relational notions while holding on to the basic tenets of DTG. Consistency requires either the abandonment of one of these or their modification. Now, considering the difficulties posed by the counterexamples to DTG and the clear advantages of a strongly relational understanding of good and evil, it would seem that the only wise course to pursue is the abandonment or modification of DTG.[40]

40. I have presented some thoughts in this direction in Gracia 1975 and 1976. I thank John Kronen, Janice Schultz, and particularly Scott MacDonald for their useful suggestions and criticisms.

PART TWO

THE CONCEPT
OF THE GOOD IN
PHILOSOPHICAL THEOLOGY

CHAPTER 7

Aquinas on
Faith and Goodness

Eleonore Stump

1. Introduction

Recent work on the subject of faith has tended to focus on the epistemology of religious belief, considering such issues as whether beliefs held in faith are rational and how they may be justified. Richard Swinburne, for example, has developed an intricate explanation of the relationship between the propositions of faith and the evidence for them.[1] Alvin Plantinga, on the other hand, has maintained that belief in God may be properly basic, that is, that a belief that God exists can be part of the foundation of a rational noetic structure.[2] This sort of work has been useful in drawing attention to significant issues in the epistemology of religion, but these approaches to faith seem to me also to deepen some long-standing perplexities about traditional Christian views of faith.

First, if there is an omniscient and omnipotent God, why would he want human relationships with him to be based on faith? Why wouldn't he make his existence and nature as obvious and uncontroversial to all human beings as the existence of their physical surroundings is?[3] Sec-

---

This paper is a substantially revised version of Stump 1989b, which was published in *The Philosophy in Christianity*, ed. Godfrey Vesey, Royal Institute of Philosophy Lecture Series 23, Supplement to *Philosophy* 1989 (Cambridge: Cambridge University Press, 1989).

1. Swinburne 1981.
2. See, e.g., Plantinga 1983.
3. To answer this sort of question, it is sometimes suggested that if it were indubitable to all of us that God exists, we would be overwhelmed by him, and our capacity to use our

ond, why should having faith be meritorious, as Christian doctrine maintains it is? And why should faith be supposed to make acceptable to God a person whom God would otherwise reject?[4] Finally, why is it that epistemological considerations seem to play so little role in adult conversions? Anecdotal evidence suggests that in many cases conversion to religious belief is not at all the result of the judicious weighing of evidence or a consideration of the requirements of rationality. We might be inclined to account for this state of affairs by supposing there to be some sort of epistemological inadequacy or defect on the part of those being converted. But such a quick and familiar assessment seems blind to an interesting feature of some kinds of conversion stories with which we are all familiar: it is not the case that the person undergoing the conversion weighs epistemological considerations but in an insufficient or confused way; rather, the person undergoing the conversion does not take epistemological considerations into account at all.

These questions suggest that epistemological considerations alone don't do justice to the nature of faith, that more than epistemology is needed to complete the account. Such an additional element in faith was commonly discussed in the works of medieval philosophers and theologians. In this essay I look at Aquinas's account of the nature of faith in order to show something about this other, often unexamined side of faith. At first hearing, Aquinas's account of faith may strike us as implausible and philosophically problematic. I first present his account and then discuss some of the problems it raises. After that I consider the sort of response Aquinas's account provides to the questions concerning faith just raised.

2. Aquinas's Understanding of the Will

Because Aquinas's account of faith assigns an important role to the will, it is helpful to begin with a brief discussion of Aquinas's understanding of the nature of the will. Aquinas's conception of the will is different from the one most of us take for granted. He understands the

---

free will to make significant choices would be undermined. (See, e.g., Swinburne 1979, pp. 211–12.) But this answer can't adequately serve as a defense of Christian views of faith. According to traditional Christian doctrine, angels who stood in the presence of God were nonetheless able to make the significant free choice of rebelling against him.

4. For an interesting answer to these questions, different from the one I pursue in this paper, see Robert Adams 1984. Adams answers the questions I raise here by arguing that some involuntary cognitive failures are nonetheless blameworthy and that sometimes the rightness of beliefs is the feature of them that occasions praise.

will not as the neutral steering capacity of a person's psyche, but as a particular bent or inclination. On his view, the will is an innate hunger, a natural appetite, for goodness. By 'goodness' here, Aquinas means goodness in general and not this or that specific good thing. Determining that this or that *particular* thing (or event or state of affairs) is in fact good is not the business of the will, but rather of the intellect.[5] The intellect presents to the will as good certain things or states of affairs, under certain descriptions. (It is important to emphasize that these representations of the intellect need not be rational or well thought out; they need not even be explicit or conscious. They may be only tacit or implicit, and not in any way conscious, and still count as the reason for a person's willing what she does, if she would refer to those representations in explaining her act of will.) The will wills the things represented as good by the intellect because the will is an appetite for the good and they are apprehended as good. For this reason, the intellect is said to move the will not as an efficient cause moves but as a final cause does, because what is understood as good moves the will as an end.[6]

(This line of approach may strike some people as implausible, perhaps in part because their introspection seems to them to reveal more of a unity than Aquinas's division into intellect and will suggests. Introspection is, of course, a notoriously unreliable guide when it comes to the details of cognitive organization or functioning. That the capacity for semantics and the capacity for syntax are not part of one and the same cognitive capacity is not something readily noticeable on the basis of introspection, for example, and yet that they are not is indicated by the radical difference between Broca's aphasia and Wernicke's aphasia. Having said so much, however, I should also make clear that Aquinas stresses the unity of the agent. Just as neither Broca's area nor Wernicke's area of the brain is sufficient by itself for full functioning as regards language, so neither will nor intellect by itself can function as a person does. Rather, will and intellect are components of a single person, whose functioning as a person is dependent on the joint and

---

5. Those who are uncomfortable with the apparent hypostatization of medieval terminology here may recast the discussion in the more fashionable terms of either programs or modules. For example, talk about the will in this context can be recast in terms of the module responsible for what neuropsychologists sometimes call 'the executive function.' The particular claim of Aquinas's at issue here can then be understood in this way: the module that is responsible for the executive function is organized in such a way as to be activated by the recognition of goodness, but some other module, some component unit of what Aquinas calls intellect, is responsible for processing the recognition of goodness and passing it on to the module that corresponds to what he calls will.

6. See *ST* IaIIae.6.4.ad1; Ia.82.1, 83.1, and 82.4.

interactive functioning of both will and intellect. As long as we are clear on this score and not inclined to identify will and intellect with inner homunculi, we can with equal appropriateness speak of a person's willing something or his will's willing that thing, of a person's understanding or of his intellect's understanding. In this respect we will be in line with current linguistic convention that permits such locutions as 'The hippocampus constructs, stores, and reads cognitive maps.')

On Aquinas's view, the will wills some things by necessity. Because it is a hunger for the good, whatever is good to such an extent and in such a way that a person cannot help but see it as good, the will wills by natural necessity. One's own happiness is of this sort, and so it is not possible for a person to will not to be happy. But even those few things (such as obedience to God's commands, on Aquinas's view) that, independent of circumstances, have a necessary connection to happiness aren't for that reason alone willed necessarily. The willer might not be cognizant of their necessary connection to happiness,[7] or it might be the case that they could be thought of under descriptions (such as unenlightened fundamentalism, in the case of obedience to God's commands) that obscure the connection to happiness. And something of the same sort can be said for the things a person might *mistakenly* suppose to have a necessary connection with her happiness (such as winning a figure-skating competition she has trained many months for). Because these things are in fact not necessary for happiness, they can always be thought of under other descriptions (such as distraction from her long-term goal of becoming a doctor) that sever their connection to happiness. They are therefore not willed necessarily either. Consequently, except for happiness and those things so obviously connected with happiness that their connection is overwhelming and indubitable, the will is not determined to one thing because of its relation to the intellect.

What the intellect determines with respect to goodness is somewhat complicated because the intellect is itself moved by other things. In particular, the will moves the intellect as an efficient cause, by willing it to attend to some things and to neglect others.[8] (The psychological act

---

7. *ST* Ia.82.1 and 2. To those who suppose that cases of suicide are an obvious counterexample to Aquinas's account here, Aquinas might reply that the action of a suicide, and the despair in which it is done, can be explained precisely by assuming that in the view of the suicide, the closest he can get to happiness is the oblivion of death. He chooses the evasion of unhappiness as his nearest approach to happiness.

8. Cf. *ST* IaIIae.17.1. Of course, on Aquinas's theory, the will does so only in case the intellect represents doing so at that time, under some description, as good. Every act of willing is preceded by some apprehension on the part of the intellect, but not every apprehension on the part of the intellect need be preceded by an act of will. (See *ST* Ia.82.4.)

accompanying the common locution 'I don't want to think about it' is an example of what Aquinas has in mind here.) Second, the passions, such as wrath and fear, can influence the intellect, because to a person in the grip of such a passion something may seem good which wouldn't seem good to him if he were calm.[9] The intellect, however, isn't compelled by the passions in any way but can resist them,[10] for example, by being aware of the passion and correcting for its effects on judgment, as one does when one decides to leave a letter written in anger until the next morning rather than mailing it right away.

On Aquinas's views, the will cannot in general be constrained to move in a particular way by something outside the willer, because (with the exception of one's own happiness and divine goodness as seen in the beatific vision) no matter what object is presented to the intellect, it is open to the intellect to consider it under some description that makes it seem not good. So, for example, the further acquisition of money can be considered good under the description *means of sending the children to school* and not good under some other description, such as *wages from an immoral and disgusting job*. On the other hand, it is still possible for the will not to will even things that are clearly and obviously good, because it is always in a person's power not to think of such things and consequently not to will them actually. That is, it is open to the will not to will such things by willing that the intellect not attend to them. (Of course, if the will does so, on Aquinas's account, it is in virtue of some representation on the part of the intellect that doing so is good, at that time, under some description.)

It is apparent, then, that on Aquinas's account of the will, it is part of a complicated feedback system, composed of will, intellect, and the passions, and set in motion by the nature of the will as a hunger for the good.[11]

3. Aquinas's Account of Faith

On Aquinas's view of the relation between intellect and will, intellect clearly has a role to play in all acts of the will. But he also holds that will has a role to play in most, though not all, acts of intellect. That this is so can be seen just from his account of the nature of the will, where he maintains that the will can command the intellect to attend or not to

9. *ST* IaIIae.9.2.
10. Cf. *ST* Ia.81.3 and IaIIae.10.3.
11. I discuss Aquinas's theory of the will and his account of the will's freedom more fully in Stump 1990.

attend to something. But will also enters into acts of intellect in another way, because cognitive assent (that is, acceptance of a proposition or set of propositions) is part of many intellectual acts, and assent of certain sorts pertains to the will.[12]

According to Aquinas, intellectual assent (*assensus*) can be brought about in different ways. Assent to a proposition (about the existence of an entity, the occurrence of an event, or the obtaining of a state of affairs) can be brought about entirely by the object of the intellect (the entity, event, or state of affairs being cognized). Aquinas gives as examples cases in which a person assents to first principles, where the object is known directly, and cases in which a person assents to the conclusions of demonstrations, where the object is known on the basis of other propositions.[13] In either of these sorts of cases, the object of the intellectual act moves the intellect by itself and by itself produces intellectual assent to one thing rather than another. In such cases Aquinas maintains that the object of the intellectual act is sufficient to move the intellect to assent. By this expression he seems to mean that the agent is at that time in an epistemic state in which, as a result of his cognitive relation to the entity, event, or state of affairs being cognized, it is natural and easy for him to assent to a certain proposition and difficult or even psychologically impossible for him not to assent. (A person in this epistemic state might assign a high probability to the proposition he accepts, but he need not. In Trollope's *Barchester Towers* Eleanor Bold considers the following propositions: [1] she will marry Mr. Slope, [2] she will marry Mr. Stanhope, [3] she will marry Mr. Arabin, and [4] she will marry none of the three. Given her introspection, her observations of Arabin, and her background knowledge, she finds it difficult not to believe [3], but, as she herself knows, she is not in a position to assign even a probability of .5 to that proposition.) As an ordinary example of a case in which the object of the intellectual act is sufficient to move the intellect, consider a mother who, whether she wants to do so or not, finds herself assenting to the proposition that the judge dislikes her son's performance in the piano recital because of the way the judge behaves as he listens, his movements and facial expression.

In other cases, however, intellectual assent is obtained in a different way, because the intellect is moved to assent not by its object but by the will, which assents to one proposition rather than another on the basis of considerations sufficient to move the will but not the intellect. Con-

12. See *ST* IIaIIae.2.1; *DV* XIV.1.
13. *ST* IIaIIae.1.4.

siderations are sufficient to move the will when an agent is at that time in a volitional state in which, as a result of his cognitive and conative relation to the entity, event, or state of affairs being cognized, it is natural and easy for him to form a desire or volition for something and difficult or even unthinkable for him not to form it. In such a case there are considerations presented to the intellect, but by themselves they are not sufficient to move the intellect to assent to a proposition. That the intellect does assent in those circumstances is a function of the will's influence. (How exactly the will, the intellect, and the passions [or desires] are related in a case in which the will brings it about that the intellect assents is beyond the scope of this discussion. For present purposes I will suppose that for Aquinas if a person accepts a belief largely in consequence of the will's action either alone or in conjunction with any of the many ways in which desires influence beliefs, that acceptance would count as a case of the will's bringing about intellectual assent.) For example, the mother might believe that the judge takes bribes, and her belief might result not from overwhelming evidence against the judge but from some evidence combined with her dislike of the man, so that the other parents might say of her that she *wants* to think ill of the judge.

It is important to point out that where the object of the intellectual act is sufficient to move the intellect by itself (as distinct from cases in which a person simply has good evidence for a belief), there is no room for will to have a role of this sort in intellectual assent. If the mother's evidence that the judge does not take bribes is overwhelming and un-questionable, then in that epistemic state it will not be possible for her to form the belief that the judge takes bribes, no matter how much she dislikes the judge. Nothing in Aquinas's view about the relations be-tween intellect and will contravenes the common view that we do not in general have direct voluntary control over our beliefs. But in cases where the object of the intellect is *not*-sufficient to move the intellect by itself, then it is possible for will to have an effect on intellectual assent to propositions. In cases of this sort, acts of will enter into the attitudes of believing, forming an opinion, and having faith.[14]

That will can affect intellectual assent in such cases is widely recog-nized, for example, in science, where experimenters frequently must

14. See, e.g., *ST* IIaIIae.5.2; cf. also *DV* XIV.1. Aquinas's example illustrating the role of the will in intellectual acts involves belief based on the testimony of another, as in the case of someone who sees a prophet raise a person from the dead and consequently comes to believe the prophet's prediction about the future. This example, however, doesn't make clear just how the will is supposed to contribute to the act of the intellect.

design their experiments to take account of the fact that, as Aquinas would put it, their wills may bring about intellectual assent largely in consequence of their desire to have results turn out a particular way. (I have in mind, for example, the sort of case double-blind experimental design is meant to exclude.) In cases of this kind Aquinas tends to talk about the will's directing the intellect to assent; we are more likely to explain the situation by focusing on the influence of desires on beliefs. But in spite of the different emphasis, the point is fundamentally the same: in cases where the object of the intellect is not sufficient to move the intellect by itself, that is, where belief is not constrained or compelled by the object of the intellect, it is possible that a person accepts a certain belief largely because of some movement of his will, in consequence of the desires he has in that situation.

The sorts of cases in which will enters into belief that are most likely to occur to us are those in which someone acts badly, as in the example above in which the mother believes the worst of the judge. But it is also possible to think of examples in which a belief based on both will and intellect has something admirable about it. In George Eliot's *Middlemarch*, when Dorothea Casaubon finds her friend and admirer Will Ladislaw in a compromising embrace with the wife of one of his friends, she does not immediately believe the worst of him. Although it is possible (and in the novel is true) that there is an exonerating explanation of Ladislaw's conduct, the evidence available to Dorothea, though not sufficient to determine that Ladislaw's behavior merits disapprobation, is nonetheless powerfully against him. (Another way of putting the same point is to say that although the evidence does not allow Dorothea to assign a probability of 1 to the proposition that Ladislaw is a scoundrel, it does allow her to assign a probability greater than .5.) But because of her commitment to him, Dorothea, in spite of the evidence, cleaves to her view that Ladislaw is not a scoundrel and a traitor to his friend.[15] (Whether Dorothea should be lumped together

15. We might suppose that this is just a case in which Dorothea is weighing evidence, the evidence of what she has seen against the evidence of her knowledge of Ladislaw's character, and coming down on the side of the evidence based on her knowledge of his character. If this were a correct analysis of the case, then it would not constitute an example of will's effecting assent to a belief. But, in fact, I think this analysis isn't true to the phenomena in more than one way. In the first place, Dorothea doesn't deliberate or weigh evidence. Although she reflects on what she has seen, her tendency from the outset is to exonerate Ladislaw. Furthermore, this analysis by itself can't account for Dorothea's standing by Ladislaw. The evidence of the scene she sees is sufficient to outweigh her past experience of him. It is not psychologically possible for her in the immediate aftermath of that scene to think of an innocuous explanation of his conduct, and she is aware of the sad truth that no one, however splendid his character has been, is immune from a moral fall.

with the mother who leapt to the conclusion that the judge took bribes and should be considered irrational in consequence of her commitment to Ladislaw in these circumstances is a separate question that I will not consider here.)

We can spell out this case a little more, using Aquinas's theory of the will, by saying that Dorothea's will brings about her intellectual assent to the exoneration of Ladislaw in consequence of her desire to maintain her personal relationship with him. Dorothea may have had moral reasons for this position; she may have thought that loyalty to friends prohibited adopting a harsh view of them if it could possibly be avoided. Or she may have had more self-interested reasons; if Ladislaw turned out to be a scoundrel, then Dorothea would have lost the good of a relationship with a man who admired her and whose character she could respect. Either way, although her intellect isn't sufficiently moved by its object to determine it to one or another view, her will is; and her belief that Ladislaw is not treacherous to his friend constitutes intellectual assent in which will has a crucial role.

According to Aquinas, will plays a similar role in faith. Considered in its own right, the object of faith is God himself, but since (in this life) our minds cannot comprehend God directly or immediately, the object of faith, considered from the point of view of human knowers, is not God but propositions about him.[16] On Aquinas's view, assent to the propositions of faith lies between knowledge and opinion. (In this paper I will take 'the propositions of faith' broadly to mean all those propositions that are appropriately believed in faith, including those propositions, such as 'God exists,' that in Aquinas's view some persons can know by natural reason and therefore do not need to hold only by faith.) In faith, the intellect assents to propositions believed, as it does in knowledge or opinion, but the assent of faith is not generated by the intellect's being sufficiently moved by its object, as it is in the case of knowledge. Rather, in faith assent is generated by the will, which is moved by the object of faith sufficiently to bring the intellect to assent. In this respect, faith is like opinion, in which will also has a role in the generation of assent. On the other hand, unlike opinion, faith holds to its object with certainty, without any hesitation or hanging back; and in this respect faith is like knowledge.[17] (What Aquinas means by 'certainty' in this connection I will consider in a later section.)

The contribution of will to the intellectual assent in faith occurs in this way. By nature, the will is moved by considerations of goodness.

16. *ST* IIaIIae.1.2.
17. *ST* IIaIIae.1.4, 2.1 and 2.

The ultimate end of the will can be thought of in either of two ways. On the one hand, it is the happiness of the willer; and, on the other hand, it is God, who is himself the true good and thus the perfect happiness of the willer. The propositions of faith, entertained by the intellect, describe the combination of both these ultimate goods, namely, the beatitude of eternal life in union with God, and present it as available to the believer. By themselves, the propositions of faith, together with whatever else is known or believed by the intellect, are not sufficient to move the intellect to assent to the propositions of faith.[18] But the will is drawn to the great good presented in the propositions of faith, and it influences the intellect to assent, in the sort of way familiar to us from science, where the design of experiments is often tailored to rule out just this kind of influence of will on intellect. In the case of faith, on Aquinas's view, will does and should influence the intellect to assent to the propositions of faith. For faith, then, a motion is required both on the part of the intellect and on the part of the will. Furthermore, in consequence of this influence of will on intellect, intellect and will cleave to the propositions of faith with the sort of certainty normally found only in cases of knowledge.[19]

This description of Aquinas's conception of faith, however, doesn't yet distinguish between the faith of committed religious believers and the faith of devils. The devils also believe, and tremble (James 2:19). On traditional Christian doctrine, of course, for some of the propositions of faith, devils have knowledge, and not faith; the proposition that

18. Some propositions of faith, such as the proposition that God is one substance but three persons, might seem to some people sufficient to move the will to *dissent* from them. For considerations of space I leave such propositions of faith and their problems to one side. But for an example of what can be done even in such cases to disarm the claim that some propositions of faith are repugnant to reason, see van Inwagen 1988.

19. Cf. *ST* IIaIIae.4.1; *DV* XIV.1 and 2. In the exposition of Aquinas's account of faith which follows, I leave to one side entirely Aquinas's views of the relation between faith and grace, simply because one cannot work on everything at once. The fact that I do not expound Aquinas's views of grace here should not mislead anyone into thinking that when the will is drawn to goodness in faith, on Aquinas's account we have a natural operation of the will, or one instigated solely by human action. The movement of the will in faith, on Aquinas's view, includes both an act of free will on the believer's part and an infusion of grace on God's part. In this essay I am focusing on the nature of that act of free will and leaving to one side what Aquinas says about its supernatural cause. For discussion of that side of Aquinas's views and a detailed exposition of his theory of faith and grace, see Stump 1989a. In correspondence, William Alston has suggested to me that since on Aquinas's views divine grace brings about faith, one way to explain the justification of beliefs held in faith is to take divine grace as the reliable mechanism responsible for the formation of beliefs held in faith. This is an ingenious and intriguing suggestion, which is not incompatible with but perhaps complementary to the account of the justification of faith defended in this paper.

God exists is a prime example. But for some of the propositions of faith, such as that the man Jesus is the incarnate Son of God, the promised redeemer of the world, or that Christ will come again to establish the kingdom of heaven on earth, the devils must rely on belief rather than knowledge. Nothing in their experience of God or the supernatural realm (at least up to a certain time, such as the time of the harrowing of hell or the second coming) puts them in a position to know that that particular human being is God's chosen means of saving the fallen human race or restoring the earth. With regard to such propositions, on Aquinas's account, the difference between devils and religious believers is not that believers have faith and devils do not, but rather that devils (or any others who are convinced of the truth of Christianity and hate it) do not have what Aquinas calls formed faith, whereas believers do.

The will can move the intellect to assent in two different ways, according to Aquinas. In the case of believers, the will is drawn by God's goodness to move the intellect to assent to the propositions of faith. This way of having the will move the intellect in faith is called 'formed faith' because in it the intellectual assent to the propositions of faith takes its form from the love of God's goodness which animates the will. In the case of the devils, however, the faith they have is unformed by charity and remains perfectly consistent with malice. Even though the devils do not see for themselves the truth of what the church teaches, their will commands the intellect to assent to the teachings of the church, Aquinas says, because they see manifest signs that the doctrine of the church is from God.[20]

This point of Aquinas's is not clear. Why should belief based on evident signs testifying to the truth of what is believed count as a case of will's influencing intellectual assent? Why shouldn't it count instead as a case in which the object of the belief is sufficient by itself to move the intellect? And how does this description of the devils' belief distinguish their sort of faith from the faith of believers? The first part of the answer to these questions comes from noticing that the manifest signs are not direct evidence for the truth of the propositions believed, but rather evidence for the authority of the people and institutions promulgating those propositions (and therefore only indirect evidence for the propositions). The example of unformed faith Aquinas gives in this connection is one where belief in a prophet's prediction arises from seeing that prophet raise a person from the dead. This example sug-

20. ST IIaIIae.5.2.

gests that what Aquinas means by manifest signs inclining the devils to belief is a demonstration of superhuman power that seems attributable only to God. If this is right, then the manifest signs testify to the authority of those promulgating what is believed, and so indirectly to the truth of what is believed, because they indicate that the authority of God supports those who teach the beliefs in question.

(Of course, not every case in which a person holds a belief based on authority is a case in which will enters into the assent to that belief. If a person believes that genes are the unit of inheritance because all reputable biologists say so, it does not seem as if will has a role to play in the formation of his belief. Aquinas's example of a belief based on authority, however, is different. In his example the belief in question is a belief in the truth of a prediction uttered by a person who claims to be a prophet, and assent is given to the belief because the prophet has demonstrated supernatural power. In this sort of case the evidence does not seem sufficient to move the intellect to belief. Even if there were no question about the prophet's power, it would not immediately follow that the prophet's prediction was true. The source of the power might be such as not to guarantee the truth of claims made by the wielder of that power. In this sort of case, then, there is room for the intellect to be moved to assent by the will.)

If we now take seriously Aquinas's claim that what distinguishes diabolical from human belief in God is the *kind* of contribution made by the will to intellectual assent, we will have a clearer understanding of the distinction between formed and unformed faith. In the case of both devils and committed believers, will brings about intellectual assent in virtue of certain strong desires, but in the case of believers the desire in question is a desire directed toward goodness, and in the case of devils it is not. The act of faith on the part of committed believers is formed by charity, or love of God's goodness; and their faith is a virtue, a habit that contributes to perfecting a power or capacity. Since both will and intellect are involved in faith, for faith to be a virtue it has to contribute to perfecting a capacity of the will as well as an intellectual capacity. Now, for Aquinas, the intellect is perfected by the acquisition of truth; and since the propositions of faith are in his view true, the beliefs accepted in faith are perfective of the intellect. In this respect, there is no difference between diabolical and human faith. The act of will on the part of a committed believer, however, takes the form it does because of the charity she has, that is, because of her love of God's goodness. What inclines her will to move her intellect to assent to the propositions of faith, then, is the goodness represented by them. What inclines the will of the devils, on the other hand, is not the goodness of God perceived in the claims of faith, but their perception of God's power—power to be envied, hated, or sought for oneself—allied with those teaching the faith. Power considered just in its own right, however, is not a moral good; and so in being moved by considerations of power alone, the will is moved by an apparent, rather than a real, good. In this way, the devils' act of faith is unformed by charity or love of God's goodness and does not count as a virtue, because it leaves the will unperfected, and the will is one of the two powers involved in the act of faith.[21]

On Aquinas's account of faith, then, the propositions of faith entertained by a believer's intellect are not sufficient to move the intellect to assent; but the will, which is a hunger for goodness, is drawn by them because of the good of eternal life in union with God which the propositions of faith taken together present. Because the will is drawn to this good, it moves the intellect to assent to the propositions of faith; and it moves the intellect in such a way that the consequent intellectual assent has the kind of certainty ordinarily found only in cases of knowledge. It is clear that this account raises many questions; I want to focus on just three of them.[22]

Objection 1

The role Aquinas assigns to the will in faith seems to imply (*a*) an acknowledgment that faith is without epistemic justification and (*b*) a concession of the sorts of charges Freudians often level against faith, namely, that faith is simply another case of wish-fulfillment belief. (*a*) If a believer's intellectual assent to the propositions of faith results primarily from her will's being drawn to the good represented in those

21. *ST* IIaIIae.4.1, 4, 5; 7.1; *DV* XIV.2, 5, and 6.
22. Somewhat different analyses of Aquinas's account of faith are given in the following works: Penelhum 1977; Pojman 1986, esp. pp. 32–40; Potts 1971; Ross 1985 and 1986. My objections to the interpretations of Aquinas in the work of Penelhum and Potts are given in effect in my own analysis above; and the problems they raise for Aquinas's account in my view either are solved or do not arise in the first place on the interpretation of Aquinas presented here. Although there are some superficial differences between my interpretation of Aquinas and that argued for by Ross, my account is in many respects similar to his, and I am indebted to his papers for stimulating my interest in Aquinas's views of faith. Ross insists on rendering '*cognitio*' as 'knowledge' and thus making faith a species of knowledge for Aquinas. In my view, this insistence is more confusing than helpful. Aquinas's criteria for knowledge are much stricter than contemporary standards, which allow as knowledge much that Aquinas would have classified under dialectic rather than demonstration. To render both '*cognitio*' and '*scientia*' as 'knowledge' is to blur what is a distinction for Aquinas and to make his epistemology sound more contemporary than it is.

propositions, there seems to be no reason for supposing that the propositions of faith are *true* or that her belief in them is justified. (*b*) On the other hand, if there is some way of warding off this sort of objection, then it seems as if precisely analogous sorts of reasoning ought to support as true or justified any belief a person wants to be true, such as Cromwell's false but firmly held belief during his last illness that he would be completely restored to health and continue to lead the nation.

Objection 2

Since the certainty of faith seems based at least largely on the action of the will, when the object of faith is not sufficient by itself to move the intellect to assent, why should faith be thought to have any certainty? The certainty of a set of beliefs seems to be or be dependent on some epistemic property of those beliefs. But on Aquinas's account, the certainty of faith stems from the *will's* being moved by the object of faith. Why would he suppose that an act of will is even relevant to the epistemic properties of beliefs?

Objection 3

Aquinas thinks that the way a human believer believes in God is preferable to the way devils believe. But why should he think so? Wouldn't it be better if human intellectual assent were obtained on the basis of considerations that by themselves moved the intellect sufficiently for assent, as in cases of knowledge, or, at least, if assent to beliefs were (like the assent of the devils) based on grounds sufficient to establish the authority of those promulgating the beliefs? There is something apparently inappropriate about obtaining intellectual assent by attracting the will to goodness rather than by moving the intellect, the sort of inappropriateness there is, for example, in using a sewing machine to join two pieces of cloth by gluing the two pieces of cloth together and using the machine as a weight to hold them in place as the glue dries. Aquinas takes God to be the designer and creator of the intellect. Since God is omniscient and omnipotent, he could easily provide the sort of object for the intellect which would enable the intellect to function in the way it was made to do, either by making the propositions of faith so evident that they move the intellect to knowledge, or at least by providing for human beings the sort of evidence that according to Aquinas inclines devils to believe in some propositions of faith on the authority of the church. Why, then, should Aquinas think it is better for belief in the propositions of faith to be generated by the will's inclining to goodness?

4. Aquinas's Account of Goodness

Aquinas's understanding of the nature of goodness provides an important part of the basis on which to reply to these objections, especially to Objection (1a), that faith is unjustified since it is based on the will's hunger for goodness.

The central thesis of Aquinas's metaethics is that the terms 'being' and 'goodness' are the same in reference but different in sense.[23] This claim is likely to strike us as obscure and peculiar, at least in part because we equate being with existence in the actual world, and it is quite clear that goodness is not to be identified with existence in the actual world. But Aquinas's concept of being is much broader than our concept of existence. By 'being,' Aquinas has in mind something like the full actualization of the potentialities a thing has in virtue of belonging to a natural kind; and this is what both 'being' and 'goodness' refer to, though they refer to it under two different descriptions. The expressions 'being' and 'goodness' are thus analogous to the expressions 'morning star' and 'evening star' in referring to the same thing but with different senses.

Aquinas takes the specifying potentiality of human beings to be reason, and he understands the actualization of it to consist in acting in accordance with reason. By converting the specific potentiality of humans into actuality, an agent's actions in accordance with reason increase the extent to which that agent has being as a human person. Because of the connection between being and goodness, such actions consequently also increase the extent to which the agent has goodness as a human person. So human goodness, like any other goodness appropriate to a particular species, is acquired in actualizing the potentiality specific to that species. The actions that contribute to a human agent's moral goodness, then, will be acts of will in accordance with reason.[24] Since, on Aquinas's view, whatever actualizes a thing's specifying potentiality thereby also perfects the nature of the thing, his view about goodness can be summarized by saying that what is good for a

---

23. *ST* Ia.5.1; *DV* XXI.1 and 2. Aquinas's metaethics is discussed in detail in Chapter 4 of this book; see also Aertsen 1988a. For the medieval tradition before Aquinas, see MacDonald 1986.

24. See, e.g., *SCG* III.9.1 (n. 1928); *ST* IaIIae.18.5.

thing is what is natural to it, and what is unnatural to a thing is bad for it. As for human nature, since it is characterized essentially by a capacity for rationality, what is irrational is contrary to human nature and so also not moral.[25] Virtues, on this account, are habits disposing a person to act in accordance with essential human nature; vices are habits disposing a person to irrationality and are therefore discordant with human nature.[26]

Aquinas's attempt to ground a virtue theory of ethics in a metaethical claim relating goodness and being raises many questions and objections; but because I have discussed them elsewhere,[27] I will leave them to one side here and add just one point about the relation of Aquinas's metaethics to his theology. Aquinas takes God to be essentially and uniquely "being itself." Given his metaethical thesis, it is no surprise to discover that Aquinas also takes God to be essentially and uniquely goodness itself. This theological interpretation of Aquinas's thesis regarding being and goodness entails a relationship between God and morality that is an interesting alternative to divine-command theories of morality, which connect theology to morality by making morality a function of God's will or God's commands. Like divine-command theories, the relation between God and morality Aquinas adopts entails that there is a strong connection between God and the standard for morality. The goodness for the sake of which and in accordance with which God wills whatever he wills regarding human morality is identical with the divine nature. But because it is God's very nature and not any arbitrary decision of his that thereby constitutes the standard for morality, only things consonant with God's nature could be morally good. The theological interpretation of the central thesis of Aquinas's ethical theory thus provides the basis for an objective religious morality and avoids the subjectivism that often characterizes divine-command theories.

5. The Relation of Faith to Goodness

On the basis of this sketch of Aquinas's account of goodness and the preceding description of Aquinas's theory of the will, we can consider the objections to Aquinas's views of faith.

25. *SCG* III.7.6 (n. 1915); *ST* IaIIae.71.1.
26. *ST* IaIIae.54.3.
27. Chapter 4 above.

Objection (1) has two parts. Objection (1a) is that the propositions accepted in faith are unjustified, because it is the will's inclining to the good presented in them, rather than the intellect's being sufficiently moved by its object, that is primarily responsible for intellectual assent to those propositions. Objection (1b) is that this way of justifying beliefs held in faith seems to justify wish-fulfillment beliefs in general.

In order for a belief to be justified, there are certain criteria the belief must satisfy. An agent must have acquired it by a reliable method, or it must cohere in the right sorts of ways with his other beliefs, or he must violate no epistemic obligations in holding it, or something else of the sort. In one or another of these ways, depending on the theory we adopt, we suppose that a belief is justified and that a believer may have some reasonable confidence in supposing that what he believes is in fact true.[28] If a belief does not meet such criteria, we regard it as unjustified, or irrational. In general, Aquinas shares such views; he espouses a version of Aristotelian epistemology, and he is often careful to distinguish the epistemological status of the propositions in arguments he is considering. But in the case of faith, epistemological considerations seem not to play a major evaluative role at all for Aquinas. What, then, keeps faith from being unjustified or irrational?

The easiest way to answer this question will be to focus on one particular proposition appropriately held in faith, namely, the proposition that God exists. (Although Aquinas thinks that this proposition can be known to be true by natural reason, he also holds that not all people are in a position to know it by natural reason and that those who are not are justified in holding it on faith.) For different propositions of faith, such as that Christ rose from the dead, different but analogous answers can be given.

To see the answer to the question with regard to the proposition that God exists, we need to consider the connection Aquinas makes between being and goodness. Since 'goodness' and 'being' are the same in reference, where there is being there is also goodness, at least goodness in some respect and to some degree. For that reason, on Aquinas's account, even the worst of human beings, even Satan in fact, is not wholly bad, but has some goodness in some respect. But the relationship between being and goodness also holds the other way around. The pres-

---

28. Nothing in this chapter requires one account of justification rather than another, but of the currently discussed accounts, the one I am inclined to find most plausible is that of William Alston. See, e.g., Alston 1985. On Alston's view, to be justified in believing that p is to believe that p in such a way as to be in a strong position to believe something true.

ence of goodness entails the presence of being. Now, since, as we saw, Aquinas does not take being to be identical to existence in the actual world, this claim does not entail that any good thing we can imagine actually exists. Oedipus in Sophocles' *Oedipus Rex* is basically a good person but may be an entirely fictional character who never existed in reality. The sort of being Oedipus has in that case is just the sort of being appropriate to fictional characters (however exactly we explain that sort of being); Aquinas would not suppose that characters such as Oedipus have existence, even existence of some peculiar or attenuated sort. So in the case of any limited good, however we explain the attribution of being to it, on Aquinas's account the being it has will also be limited and need not include actual existence.

In the case of perfect goodness, on the other hand, things are different. The sort of being entailed by perfect goodness is perfect being, and Aquinas maintains that perfect being not only exists but exists necessarily. At this stage we can simply take this claim about the necessary existence of perfect being as a stipulation on Aquinas's part, although, in fact, the motivation for it is fundamental to his metaphysics.[29] What is important to notice here is that since perfect being is entailed by perfect goodness, if perfect being necessarily exists, then perfect goodness is also necessarily exemplified.

What these reflections on Aquinas's claim about the connection between being and goodness show us is this. If the will hungers for a certain good thing whose goodness falls short of perfect goodness, and if the intellect is moved to assent to the proposition that that thing exists largely because of that hunger on the part of the will, the resulting belief will be unjustified or irrational. This is so because, although it follows from Aquinas's basic metaethical thesis that any particular good thing that is limited in goodness has being of some sort, it does not follow that it actually exists. On the other hand, if the will hungers for goodness that is perfect and unlimited, and if the intellect is moved to

29. For Aquinas, *perfect* being is being that is whole and complete, without defect or limit. But to be entirely whole and without defect, on Aquinas's view, is to be without any unactualized potentiality. Perfect being, then, is altogether actual. Anything that is altogether actual, however, must have its existence included within its essence; otherwise, according to Aquinas, there would be in it the potential for nonexistence. But if perfect being has its existence as part of its essence, if it has no potential for nonexistence, then it is necessarily existent. See, e.g., *ST* Ia.3.4: "*Secundo, [in Deo est idem essentia et esse] quia esse est actualitas omnis formae vel naturae. . . . Oportet igitur quod ipsum esse comparetur ad essentiam quae est aliud ab ipso, sicut actus ad potentiam. Cum igitur in Deo nihil sit potentiale, ut ostensum est supra, sequitur quod non sit aliud in eo essentia quam suum esse. Sua igitur essentia est suum esse.*" Considerations of this sort lie behind his view that perfect being necessarily exists. For a defense of Aquinas's account of divine simplicity, see Stump and Kretzmann 1985.

assent to the proposition that what is hungered for exists or obtains largely because of that hunger on the part of the will, the resulting belief will not similarly be unjustified, for where there is perfect goodness, there is perfect being; and perfect being necessarily exists.

Does Aquinas's clarification of the interrelation of being and goodness constitute an argument for the claim that God exists?[30] It is helpful here to distinguish between what we might call the metaphysical and the epistemological strands of an account of the justification of beliefs. The epistemological strand gives us criteria for determining which beliefs of ours are justified and which are not; for any individual belief, such criteria (at least in theory) enable us to tell whether we are justified in holding that belief. The metaphysical strand, on the other hand, provides an account of the nature of human knowing or of the world and our epistemic relation to it, or something of this sort, which explains the fact that some of our beliefs are justified, but it may do nothing to enable us to differentiate justified from unjustified beliefs in individual cases. Another approach to the same question is to think in terms of levels of justification. We can distinguish between S's being justified in believing p, on the one hand, and S's being justified in believing that S is justified in believing p, on the other. S might be justified in believing p without being in a position to know, or even to believe justifiedly, that she is justified in her belief that p.[31] (As we shall see, Aquinas himself makes a distinction somewhat similar to this one, in distinguishing between the certainty of a belief and the subjective certainty of the believer who holds that belief.)

The explanation of the justification for the propositions of faith provided by Aquinas's account of being and goodness contains only the metaphysical strand, and not the epistemological one as well. It gives reasons for thinking that a believer is justified in believing that God exists, but not for thinking that a believer is in a position to determine that he is so justified. Aquinas's views explain what it is about reality and

30. Since Aquinas identifies perfect being with God, someone might object at this point that if we do not take Aquinas's claim about the necessary existence of perfect being as a stipulation but follow his reasoning from the nature of perfect being to that conclusion, we have an attempt at a proof—a peculiar variation on the ontological argument—of God's existence, so that what Aquinas maintains about perfect goodness can be admitted only by those willing to accept such a proof and its conclusion. But this objection is just confused. The premises of this putative proof are such that they would be accepted only by someone who already accepted the conclusion, so that the putative proof would be blatantly question-begging. Aquinas's reasoning, then, does not constitute a proof for God's existence; it is, rather, a clarification of two standard divine attributes and their interrelations.

31. See, e.g., Alston 1980 (reprinted Alston 1989).

our relation to it which accounts for the justification of this belief held in faith. In ordinary cases, as in the kinds of cases good experimental design is intended to prevent in science, beliefs stemming primarily from the will's moving the intellect to assent to something because of the will's hungering for some good would not have much (if any) justification. Because goodness supervenes on being, limited goods have limited being, on Aquinas's understanding of being; but they may or may not actually exist. Perfect goodness, however, supervenes on perfect being; and, according to Aquinas, perfect being necessarily exists. If the will moves the intellect to assent to the existence of a thing on the basis of the will's hungering for the good of that thing, and if the good of that thing is not some limited good but perfect goodness, then in that case, on Aquinas's account, the resulting belief in the existence of that thing will have a great deal of justification. What is *perfectly* good not only is something that exists but in fact something that exists necessarily, since it supervenes on perfect being, which exists necessarily. Given this metaphysical theory, that is, given the supposition that goodness and being have the characteristics this theory ascribes to them, a believer S is justified in believing the claim he holds on faith.

But, of course, to say this is not to say that we are in a position to determine that we are justified in this belief. We might not have a good argument for (or we might not even accept) some or all of the metaphysical theory in question here; or we might accept it but not believe that any goodness or any being is perfect, so that the will's hungering for the good represented by the propositions of faith is just another instance of the will's hungering for a limited good, which may or may not exist. And Aquinas's account gives us no certain procedure for deciding whether a good that the will hungers for is a perfect or a limited good. For these reasons, Aquinas's account constitutes only the metaphysical and not the epistemological strand of a theory of justification for the belief held in faith. His account tells us what justifies this belief, namely, the nature of God, but not how we can *determine* with any high degree of probability *that* it is justified. And for these reasons, although his account constitutes an argument that a believer S is justified in believing the propositions held in faith, it does not give us an argument that S is justified in believing that he is justified in believing the propositions held in faith.

Although I have focused here on the belief that God exists (and will continue to emphasize that belief in what follows), it is not too hard to see how to extend this account to deal with other beliefs of faith. They might be acquired and justified in a manner similar to the belief that

God exists. Consider, for example, the belief that Christ rose from the dead. We would have to add some considerations either of other metaphysical attributes of God and their relation to the divine goodness or of the perfectly good will of God, and these additional considerations will be the basis of a metaphysical (but not epistemological) strand of a theory of justification for this belief. On the other hand, other beliefs of faith, such as the belief in "one catholic and apostolic church," might be acquired or justified derivatively from a belief justified in the first way.[32]

As I have developed the reply to Objection (1a), that on Aquinas's account beliefs held in faith are unjustified, it has implicit within it also a reply against Objection (1b), that Aquinas's account of faith warrants wish-fulfillment beliefs in general. In wish-fulfillment beliefs, such as the belief of a lazy, untalented student that he has done well on the exam he did not study for, the will moves the intellect to assent to the truth of a proposition asserting the existence of some good because of the will's desire for that good. But since for Aquinas limited goods may fail to exist, nothing in the will's hungering for limited goodness constitutes a reason for supposing that such a proposition is true; and so the belief that results from this process is unjustified. But since what the will hungers for in the case of faith is perfect goodness, there is not the same disconnection between the good hungered for and the existence of that good in the case of faith as there is in the case of wish-fulfillment. For this reason, the beliefs held in faith are not in the same camp as wish-fulfillment beliefs.

32. I am grateful to William Alston for helping me work through this point. As a rough example of the way in which the account of faith presented here could be extended to other beliefs of faith, consider an unreflective, historically uninformed undergraduate S who reads the Acts of John for the first time and rejects it, although he accepts the Gospel of John as authoritative for Christianity, because he unreflectively rejects as not good the character presented as the Apostle John in the Acts. S believes on faith that (p) the Gospel of John is authoritative but the Acts is not. His belief, however, is not an example of a case in which the object of the intellect is sufficient to move the intellect; rather, his belief results at least in part from some influence of the will, based on his dislike of the character presented as the apostle in the Acts and his desire not to admit such a character into his list of religious heroes. For the sake of the example, let it also be the case that his reaction is appropriate, that the character presented as the Apostle John in the Acts is not worthy of moral praise. Then the existence of a perfectly good, necessarily existent God, all of whose decrees and interactions with human beings are also perfectly good, is what justifies S's belief that p. It does not follow, however, that S is justified in believing that he is justified in believing p. These suggestions for extending the account defended in this paper are, of course, very sketchy; filling them out would require a great deal more detailed work.

But there is perhaps one other thing to say about the objection that Aquinas's account of faith warrants wish-fulfillment beliefs. Besides the worry about the epistemological status of wish-fulfillment beliefs, we are inclined to find such beliefs objectionable because we think allowing will to guide intellect as it does in the case of wish-fulfillment beliefs is bound to lead to frustration or disappointment on the believer's part (or, as in the case of Cromwell, on the part of one's friends or followers). Without taking anything at all away from such commonsensical objections to wish-fulfillment beliefs, I want to point out that on Aquinas's account of the will there is another side to the story. According to Aquinas, a person necessarily wills her own happiness, and happiness is the ultimate end for the will; but a person's true happiness consists in her uniting with God. Therefore, the hunger of the will is not stilled until the willer is either in union with God or on the road to union with God, with the other desires of the will in harmony with that final goal. As Augustine puts it, addressing God, "Our hearts are restless till they rest in thee." But in that case, following the lead of the will, though frustrating or otherwise inadequate and deficient in the short run, is not an obstacle to human flourishing in the long run, if the process of following the will's hunger is carried on to its natural conclusion. If a person doesn't give up prematurely and settle for something ultimately unsatisfactory (as she may be inclined to do by desires preferring her own immediate pleasure or power to greater goods), following the desires of her heart, on this account, does end not only in her flourishing but also in the fulfillment of her heart's desire.

These replies to Objection (1) may serve only to exacerbate the worry embodied in Objection (2), that nothing in Aquinas's theory can account for the certainty he ascribes to those who have faith. As I argued above, Aquinas's account of the will as a hunger for the good and his conception of goodness and being provide the metaphysical strand of a theory of justification of belief but not the epistemological strand. They explain what it is about the world which, on Aquinas's view, makes the belief that God exists justified, but they don't put us in a position to determine with any great degree of probability that that belief is in fact so justified. What, then, allows Aquinas to say that believers have certainty with regard to the propositions of faith?

In fact, Aquinas concedes the main point of this objection. In a distinction analogous to the one I draw above between the metaphysical and the epistemological strands of the justification of belief, or between levels of justification, Aquinas says we can think of certainty in two different ways: either in terms of the cause of the certainty of the propositions' truth or as a characteristic of the person believing those propositions. The cause of the certainty of the propositions of faith is something altogether necessary, namely, God himself. Considered with regard to the cause of the certainty of the propositions' truth, then, faith is at least as certain as any other true beliefs entertained by human reason. That is, given God's nature and will, the propositions of faith are as certain as any propositions can be. On the other hand, however, if we consider the certainty of faith with regard to the person who believes, then the certainty of faith is considerably less than the certainty of many things about which human beings have knowledge, because some or all the propositions of faith are beyond reason for any human being.[33] The certainty of faith, then, is a certainty based on the cause of the certainty of the propositions' truth and not a certainty that is a characteristic of believers.

Aquinas's position here may strike us as lame or defeated. He begins with the bold claim that the *propositions* of faith have the same sort of certainty as mathematical propositions known to be true, and he ends with the disappointingly weak claim that, even so, *believers* can't be anything like as certain about the propositions of faith as mathematicians can be about mathematical truths. What exactly is this distinction of Aquinas's with regard to certainty? And does it undermine what is generally seen as a key characteristic of faith, namely, the deep confidence of believers in the truth of the propositions believed?[34]

One way to understand Aquinas's distinction with regard to certainty is to recast it in terms of levels of justification. So understood, Aquinas's concern is to differentiate between a person's justification in believing the propositions of faith and her justification in believing that she is justified in believing the propositions of faith. From the fact that a person S is justified in a belief p, for example, that there is a tree in front of her, it does not follow that she is justified in believing that she is justified in believing p. A child, for example, might hold p and be entirely justified in doing so without even having (much less being

---

33. *ST* IIaIIae.4.8.
34. As everyone must recognize, a believer's adherence to the propositions of faith has a manifold basis, which includes religious experience, participation in a religious community such as a church, and so on. I certainly do not intend to ignore the importance of such elements in forming or sustaining adherence to faith. But what is of concern to me here is just that part of the explanation of a believer's adherence to the propositions of faith which is provided by Aquinas's account of goodness and being and his theory of the nature of the will, and so I will say nothing here about religious experience or Christian community. For an account of the importance of religious experience in forming and sustaining belief in God, see Alston forthcoming.

justified in having) the belief that he was justified in believing *p*. Aquinas's view is that as regards the cause of the certainty of the propositions of faith, they are as certain as any propositions, but that as regards their certainty with regard to the person who believes them, their certainty is less than other propositions known. Perhaps what he has in mind is that a person *S* who believes the propositions of faith is as justified in holding those beliefs as it is possible for him to be, because the "cause of the certainty" of the propositions of faith is God himself. But it does not follow that *S* is justified to the same degree in believing that he is justified in believing the propositions of faith, so that with respect to this level of justification the believer is more justified as regards, for instance, mathematical truths he knows than as regards the propositions of faith.

Though this approach may help in understanding Aquinas's distinction, it only exacerbates the worry about his position because, on the face of it, it seems as if it is the higher-order level of justification that must play a role in the assurance of religious believers. Does Aquinas's point about the certainty of faith leave him unable to account for the confidence believers have in the truth of the propositions believed in faith? If Aquinas thought that believers' confidence consisted in simple cognitive certainty, then the answer to this question might be affirmative. But his view is more complicated, in part because of the crucial role of will in faith. On Aquinas's view, we can explain the assurance and confidence of believers in two ways, based either on intellect or on will. As regards intellect, a believer might not be in a position to know, or even to have a great deal of justification in the belief, that his belief in the propositions of faith is justified. But if he thinks of the propositions of faith as Aquinas does, as based on the necessary nature and perfectly good decrees of God, then he is in a position to believe justifiedly that if his belief in the propositions of faith is justified at all, it is justified with the maximal justification possible for human beliefs. On the other hand, as regards the will, although a believer may not know, or even have a great deal of justification in the belief, that his belief in the propositions of faith is justified, he is in a position to know that if the propositions of faith are true, then his happiness can be achieved and the deepest desires of his heart can be fulfilled only by adherence to the propositions of faith. So while a person will not hold the propositions of faith with the sort of simple cognitive certainty he holds mathematical truths he knows, if he assents to the propositions of faith at all, on Aquinas's view he will hold them with the greatest possible commitment. This way of interpreting Aquinas's position, then, helps to explain his claim that although in the case of faith the object of the intellect isn't sufficient to move the intellect by itself, it nonetheless inclines the will to move the intellect to the sort of unwavering assent given in cases of knowledge.

These replies to Objections (1) and (2) seem only to sharpen the point of Objection (3). Why would Aquinas think that the will's moving the intellect to assent to the propositions of faith is the way such assent ought to be obtained? He clearly supposes that for human persons in this life basing assent to the propositions of faith on the will in virtue of a desire for God's goodness is in general preferable to the way intellectual assent is obtained in the case of knowledge, when the object known is sufficient by itself to move the intellect, or to the way intellectual assent is produced in the case of the devils who, he thinks, see God's power working in those promulgating the faith and accept some of the propositions of the faith because of their concern with power. An omniscient, omnipotent God could make the propositions of faith so manifest that intellectual assent would be generated without any intervention on the part of the will. And we might be inclined to join Bertrand Russell in charging God with having provided "not enough evidence." But Aquinas is so far from supposing that God ought to have provided sufficient evidence that he plainly takes it to be an important feature of faith that the object of intellect in the case of faith is not enough by itself to move the intellect, that, instead, the intellect has to be moved by the will, which is drawn to the good represented in the propositions of faith.

To understand why Aquinas takes this position, it is important to see what he thinks the point of faith is. Both intellect and will have a role in faith, but we tend to assume unreflectively, as Russell clearly did, that the first and most important effect the acquisition of faith produces in the believer is a change in intellectual states. Consequently, we might suppose, the *immediate* point of faith is some alteration of the intellect.[35] If we think of the efficacy of faith in this way, it is certainly understandable that we should feel some perplexity. Why would an omniscient, omnipotent God, himself the creator of the intellect, arrange things in such a way that certain crucial states of intellect must be brought about by means that bypass the natural functioning of the intellect? Aquinas, however, sees the role of faith differently, and in his position there is the solution of this difficulty. On Aquinas's view, the most important immediate point of faith is not its influence on the intellect, but its

35. The *ultimate* point of faith is, of course, salvation.

operation on the will. Of course, given the kind of connection Aquinas postulates between intellect and will, it is plain that whatever has an effect on the will first operates on the intellect (in the way I have described in section 2 above). But, on Aquinas's view, the purpose of the changes in intellect brought about in the acquisition of faith has to do with the consequent and corresponding changes in the will.

On traditional Christian doctrine, which Aquinas accepts, all human beings are marred by original sin. Original sin entails, among other things, that a post-fall person tends to will what he ought not to will, that he tends to will his own immediate pleasure and power over greater goods, and that this inborn tendency of will results sooner or later in sinful actions, with consequent moral deterioration. In such a state a person cannot be united with God in heaven but is rather destined to be left to himself in hell. God in his goodness, however, has provided salvation from this state, which is available for all, although not all avail themselves of it. The story of how this salvation is brought about has two parts, one the doctrine of the atonement, which is outside the scope of this paper, and the other the doctrine of justification by faith.[36] Justification is the process by which the inborn defect of the will is corrected and in which God brings a person from a state of sin to a state of justice. In faith the will desires the goodness of God, which is what the propositions of faith taken together show the will. This desire for God's goodness naturally carries with it a repugnance for what is incompatible with God's goodness, and so for one's own sins. When a believer has such a love of God's goodness and hatred of her own sins, then God can carry on the work of fixing the bent will of the believer without violating her free will and turning her into a sort of robot. In loving God's goodness and hating her own sins, the believer in effect wants to have a will that wills what is good; and so by working to cure her will of its evil, God is giving her the sort of will she herself wants to have.[37] Without the believer's act of will in faith, however, God could not act on her will to fix it without violating the very nature of the will he was trying to make whole. Since it is also a central part of Christian doctrine that the believer cannot fix the defect in her will herself,[38] it is clear that on traditional Christian views the act of will in faith is essential to salvation.

36. I discuss the doctrine of the atonement in Stump 1988a, and I consider justification by faith in more detail in Stump 1989a.
37. For elaboration of this point, see Stump 1988b.
38. For some explanation and argument in support of this view, see Stump 1989a.

But if the act of will in faith has the importance it does in the scheme of salvation, then since on Aquinas's theory the will is moved by the intellect's representing certain things as good, the point of Objection 3 seems only sharpened. In view of all that has just been said, a proponent of this objection might hold, isn't it clear that a good God ought to make the propositions of faith manifest to everyone, either by making the object of the intellect sufficient by itself to move the intellect or by making the authority of those promulgating those propositions evident, so that everyone would naturally form the act of will requisite for salvation?

On Aquinas's account of the way faith works, a believer's will is drawn by the goodness represented in the propositions of faith, although her intellect is not sufficiently moved by its object to assent to the propositions of faith. That is, the goodness of God is made manifest through the propositions of faith (for instance, in the claims that Christ suffered and died for the salvation of all people), but the truth of those propositions is not. Suppose now, however, that a person were to see manifestly and evidently either the truth of the propositions of faith or the authority of those promulgating such propositions. Then what such a person would know is that there exists an entity of unlimited power, the ruler of the universe, who draws human beings into union with himself through the redemptive power of the incarnate Christ. If such a person were then to ally herself with God, it might be because of an attraction to God's goodness, or it might also be because of a desire to be on the side of power.

Since, on the doctrine of original sin, human beings are already marred by a tendency to prefer their own power to greater goods, a tendency that faith is precisely designed to cure, there is consequently a great danger in allowing the things asserted in the propositions of faith to be overwhelmingly obvious. There would be a danger in trying to attract overweight people to Weight Watchers meetings by promising to begin the meetings with a lavish banquet; but it would be a limited danger, because one could plan more ascetic meetings for later. Eventually, then, one could decouple the excessive desire for food and the desire for the good of temperance represented by Weight Watchers meetings, so that the former desire would be diminished and the latter enhanced. But in the case of God, if it once becomes overwhelmingly obvious that an omniscient, omnipotent, perfectly good God exists and has a redemptive plan of the sort presented in the propositions of faith, then it also becomes overwhelmingly obvious that endless power is necessarily coexemplified with perfect goodness and that human beings can be on the side of power in allying themselves with goodness.[39] In that case, however, it ceases to be possible to decouple the desire for power and the desire for goodness, so that the former is diminished and the latter is enhanced. What these sketchy considerations suggest is that the failure to provide sufficient evidence for all the propositions of faith and the requirement that intellectual assent be produced by the will's attraction to goodness not only are no embarrassment for Aquinas's account of faith but in fact constitute an important means of furthering the purpose he takes faith to have, namely, the moral regeneration of post-fall human beings.

6. Conclusion

There is, then, another way of thinking about faith, which sees the main and immediate purpose of faith in its role in the moral life of the believer, rather than in its influence on the intellect. On this way of thinking about faith, the justification for faith is different from that for most other sorts of belief, because it is grounded not primarily in some relation of the intellect to its object, but rather in the will's relation to its object, where the nature of the will is understood as Aquinas takes it. Aquinas's understanding of faith does not enable us to *know* what is believed in faith (in his sense of knowledge), but it can nonetheless explain how what is believed in faith is maximally justified. Furthermore, this approach to faith has the advantage of explaining why an omniscient, omnipotent, perfectly good God would let the epistemic

39. Someone might object that anyone who believes God to be both omnipotent and perfectly good will also believe that in allying himself with perfect goodness he is putting himself on the side of power and that therefore it is not possible to decouple the desire for goodness from the desire for power in the case of believers. The objector's premise seems to me fundamentally correct, but the conclusion he seeks to draw from it doesn't follow. Someone who believes in an omnipotent, perfectly good God will believe that in following goodness he is also associating himself with power. But as long as it is not overwhelmingly obvious to a believer that there is a being who is both omnipotent and perfectly good, it will not be overwhelmingly obvious that in following what seems to him good he is allying himself with power. For example, in the case of someone such as Mother Teresa, although it is clear that she has dedicated herself to goodness, it is not equally obvious, to believers observing her and even (one supposes) to her herself, that she is on the side of power. In such a case it is possible for the desire for goodness and the desire for power to pull a person in different directions, in spite of her belief in an omnipotent, perfectly good God; and so it is possible to decouple the desire for goodness from a desire for power when it is not overwhelmingly obvious that there is an omnipotent, perfectly good God. For a sensitive and penetrating portrayal of this point, see the representation of the temptations of Christ in Milton's *Paradise Regained*. I am grateful to Steve Maitzen for calling my attention to this objection.

relation of human beings to himself rest on faith, rather than knowledge, and why a person's having faith should be thought to be meritorious in any way, because it holds faith to be the beginning of a moral reform of the will, of a kind that simple knowledge of the propositions of faith by itself could not bring about. And, finally, this way of thinking about faith accounts for the common conviction that epistemological considerations play little role in initiating most conversions. On Aquinas's account of faith, what is happening in such cases (or, at any rate, in the case of true conversions) is not that the intellect is weighing and judging epistemological considerations but that the will is drawn to a love of God's goodness and in consequence moves the intellect to assent to the propositions of faith.

It is important to say explicitly and emphatically that nothing in this position of Aquinas's denies reason a role in the life of faith. In a tradition going back at least as far as Augustine, Aquinas takes *understanding* the propositions of faith to be the outcome of a process for which faith is a necessary condition. Having once acquired faith in the way spelled out here, the believer is then in a position to reflect philosophically on the propositions of faith, to engage in the enterprise of natural or philosophical theology.[40] But on Aquinas's view it would be a mistake to suppose that faith is *acquired* by such an exercise of reason. Although reason may clear away some intellectual obstacles that bar the believer's way to faith, assent to the propositions of faith is initially produced by the will's hungering for God's goodness and moving the intellect in consequence. And the point of this proceeding on the part of the intellect and will is not a peculiar acquisition of certain states of intellect but the moral regeneration of a post-fall human being from his tendency to prefer his own power and pleasure to greater goods.

With this understanding of faith, then, it is possible to see a solution to some long-standing puzzles about faith and to integrate the justification for faith with general Christian views about the role of faith in the scheme of salvation.[41]

40. For a discussion of the role of reason in the life of faith and a consideration of the different states of acquiring faith and reflecting on it, see Kretzmann forthcoming.

41. I am indebted to Norman Kretzmann, Scott MacDonald, Steven Maitzen, and Alvin Plantinga for comments or suggestions, and I am particularly grateful to William Alston for his many helpful comments on earlier drafts of this paper.

CHAPTER 8

A General Problem of Creation:
Why Would God Create Anything at All?

Norman Kretzmann

1. Introduction

Judaism, Christianity, and Islam agree that God is the absolutely perfect being who created the world. There's something puzzling about that description. Why would an absolutely perfect being create anything at all?

The general explanation of creation being asked for in that question must lie along either one of two divergent lines. The starting points of those two lines can be represented in two rudimentary answers to the question: one, "Because it is a consequence of his nature"—the beginning of a necessitarian line—and the other, "Because he freely chooses to do so"—the libertarian line of explanation. Explanations lying along the necessitarian line will try to show that an absolutely perfect being is essentially productive. And so the necessitarian line entails that there cannot be a state of affairs consisting of an absolutely perfect being's existing all by itself. On the other hand, libertarian explanations deny that God is essentially productive and insist that God could have been absolutely perfect without being a creator. Such libertarian explanations may or may not go on to try to say why God freely chooses to create.

Much of my understanding of this issue stems from medieval Christian philosophers. They generally adopted libertarian explanations of creation, at least partly because they had interpreted the data of Scripture as requiring that sort of account (in, for example, Psalms

134/135:6, James 1:18, and Revelation 4:11).[1] But, of course, Scripture wasn't the only constraint on their explanations. There was also Christian theology with all its inherent Greek philosophy, some of which plainly had a tendency to produce explanations that lay along the necessitarian line. These were exemplified most flagrantly in the neo-Platonist emanationism that had been taken over by medieval Islamic philosophers, and their writings were well known to thirteenth- and fourteenth-century Christian theologians. This apparent difference between the biblical data and the philosophy in Christianity is one important source of tension in medieval Christian explanations of creation.

I want to begin uncovering the explanations and the tension in them by raising some simple questions about creation as Augustine raised them.[2]

2. Creation and Volition

In the beginning God created the heaven and the earth. Why? In one of his treatises on Genesis, Augustine says, "Anyone who asks 'Why did God make heaven and earth?' should be given this answer: 'Because he willed it.'"[3] That answer isn't quite as empty as it sounds. Part of Augustine's purpose in giving the answer "Because he willed it" is to bring out the special significance of the ex nihilo aspect of creation as he sees it: "For when it is said that God produced [the world] out of nothing (ex nihilo), all that's meant is that there wasn't anything *from* which he might have produced [it]; and yet he did produce [it], [simply] *because he willed*."[4] The obvious significance of the ex nihilo doctrine is the denial of any independently pre-existing stuff out of which God made the world, but Augustine is extending the scope of the doctrine beyond

1. Psalms 134/135:6: "All things whatsoever that he willed he made, in heaven and in earth, in the seas and all deep places." James 1:18: "Of his own will begat he us. . . ." Revelation 4:11: "thou hast created all things, and for thy pleasure they are and were created."

2. My discussion of Augustine was substantially complete in 1986, when I presented an earlier version of this article as a lecture in an NEH Summer Institute on the philosophy of religion. Teske 1988 contains a good discussion of material precisely relevant to issues I discuss here, including some material not cited here. It should be consulted by anyone interested in further research into Augustine's position on these issues. I am grateful to Scott MacDonald for calling my attention to Teske's article.

3. *De Genesi contra Manichaeos* I.ii.4 (*PL* 34.175).

4. *Ad Orosium* i.3 (*PL* 42.671).

matter to motive. If creation is out of nothing, then the volition to create not only uses nothing but also derives from nothing. The fullest possible explanation for creation ex nihilo appears to be the volition of the omnipotent creator.

Still, Augustine's empty-sounding answer is bound to prompt most people to ask a second question, as he realizes. "Anyone who [then] asks *why* God *willed* to make the world is looking for a cause of God's will. But every cause has an effect (*efficiens est*), and everything that has an effect is greater than what is effected [by it]. But nothing is greater than God's will."[5] "God's will," he says in another place, "is the cause of heaven and earth and is therefore greater than heaven and earth. Now anyone who asks 'Why did God *will* to make heaven and earth?' is looking for something greater than God's will; but he cannot find anything greater than that."[6]

Those two passages together strongly suggest that Augustine's position on explaining creation is not simply libertarian but voluntarist, denying the possibility of any meaningful search for a general explanation of creation beyond "God *willed* it." But there are two features of those passages that leave the voluntarism looking half-baked. In the first place, there is no good reason why Augustine's cause-greater-than-effect principle couldn't be weakened to a more plausible cause-at-least-as-great-as-effect principle. On that weaker, more plausible principle, everything he says would be compatible with a case in which something as great as God's will played a causal role in God's volition to create. And there are promising candidates for that causal role among other aspects of God's own nature (and of course only among them). An explanation of God's volition to create as caused by some other aspect of his nature is theoretically possible, and it would leave this apparent voluntarism compatible with the necessitarian line of explanation, as we'll see.

In the second place, Augustine's voluntarism here seems to stem from his view that the only explanation that could count as an answer to "Why did he will it?" would be an explanation in terms of the kind of causation involved in creation itself, as if the question were "What is related to God's will as his will is related to creation?" God's will is the external agent cause of creation. But no necessitarian explanation that might derive from or be compatible with Christian theology could have any tendency to lead to an account in which God's will is causally deter-

5. *De diversis quaestionibus LXXXIII* q. 28 (PL 40.18).
6. *De Genesi contra Manichaeos* I.ii.4 (PL 34.175).

mined by an external agency. The only threat Augustine is protecting God's autonomy from is an unimaginable threat. And in taking that overly protective stance he appears to be blocking a kind of further inquiry that would ordinarily be the most appropriate basis for asking "Why?" about any act of any will—an inquiry into the internal sources of it, the reason, motive, or purpose of the volition. Sources altogether internal to an agent who is, as God is, altogether invulnerable to passions pose no threat to the agent's autonomy.

3. Motivation for the Volition to Create

But there is a simpler and even more convincing sort of reason for not taking Augustine's voluntarism in these passages at face value. In many of his other discussions of creation, perhaps most, Augustine himself neither sounds like a voluntarist nor allows voluntarism to block his own attempt to explain God's volition. In commenting on Psalms 134/135:6, "All things whatsoever that he willed, he made" (*omnia quaecumque voluit, fecit*), Augustine begins by observing that God was "not compelled" to make anything, that "the cause of all the things he made is his will." Then he contrasts God's case with ours in this respect: "You make a house because if you didn't, you'd be without shelter; need (*necessitas*) compels you to make a house, not free will," and similarly as regards your clothing and food—"All these you make because of need. God made [whatever he made] because of goodness; he needed nothing that he made. And that's why [it says] 'all things whatsoever that he *willed*, he made.'"[7] In the light of what we've already seen Augustine saying, it's no surprise to find him here implying still more clearly that God's volition to create is an instance of *free* will; nor is it surprising to see God described as self-sufficient. As Augustine puts it elsewhere, "Where there is no needfulness (*indigentia*), there is no need (*necessitas*); where there is no lack (*defectus*), no needfulness. But there is no lack in God; therefore, no need."[8] What is surprising about the passage contrasting human making with divine making is that (human) actions willingly performed for good reasons are denied inclusion under "free will." After all, no one is absolutely necessitated even in the getting of food, shelter, and clothing. The contrast Augustine points out is not really between unfree and free actions but rather between

7. *Ennarationes in Psalmos* CXXXIV.10 (*PL* 37.1745).
8. *De diversis quaestionibus LXXXIII* q. 22 (*PL* 40.16).

actions performed out of self-interest and actions performed out of "goodness." And that contrast leaves us with a further question. We expect goodness to be ascribed to God, but just how is God's goodness supposed to constitute his motive or reason for doing what he has no need to do? As regards human actions, if we say that one was performed out of self-interest and the other out of goodness, we might very well mean that the second action was altruistic. But altruism is not the aspect of goodness Augustine points to as an explanation of God's act of creation.

His primary basis for associating creation with goodness is pretty clearly in the Genesis story itself, where the basis explicitly provided is an observation not about the nature of the creator but about the nature of the creation. In Genesis the same thing is said specifically six times about the work of the six days, "God saw that it was *good*,"[9] and then more emphatically regarding the whole: "God saw every thing that he had made, and, behold, it was *very good*."[10] From these appraisals it appears to follow that the production of good was God's intention, and in general the motivation for an agent whose intention is the production of good is the agent's goodness. Augustine generously develops this sort of explanation of God's volition in another of his discussions of Genesis 1: "'God saw that it was good'—What meaning can be assigned to those words that appear everywhere [in this chapter] other than approval of a finished product skilfully wrought, that is, wrought with the skill that is the wisdom of God? But God wasn't previously so ignorant that he could only discover that his work was good when it was complete. Far from it! Nothing he created would have been created if he hadn't known it very well beforehand. Therefore, when he sees that a thing is good—a thing he wouldn't have made at all if he hadn't seen it was good before he made it—he is teaching us, not learning for himself, that it is good. . . . And in fact there were three main points concerning the work of creation that had to be reported to us and that it was right for us to know: *who* made it, *how*, and *why*. So what Scripture says is: 'God said "Let there be light"; and there was light. And God saw that the light was good.' So if we ask '*Who* made it?', the answer is 'It was God.' If we ask '*How*?', the answer is 'God said "Let it be"; and it was.' If we ask '*Why*?', the answer is 'Because it is *good*.' Nor is there any originator more excellent than God, any skill more effective than God's word,

9. Genesis 1:4, 10, 12, 18, 21, 25. There is no specific appraisal of the work of the second day; vv. 10 and 12 both concern the work of the third day.
10. Genesis 1:31.

any purpose better than that something good should be created by a good God."[11]

When Augustine does open the door to explanations of creation, he opens it wide. But for all its detail, that passage gives us next to nothing by way of an answer to Augustine's second question. Why does God will to create the world? Because he is good and knows it to be good. Augustine says he's shown God's purpose in creating, but we're left wanting to know *why* a perfectly good God would create any world, even one he knows to be very good. What could be the *point* of it? Augustine plausibly treats the goodness God finds in the newly created world as aesthetic rather than moral, and Revelation 4:11 suggests that God created for his own pleasure. But such an explanation seems incompatible with the concept of an absolutely perfect being (who cannot want entertainment) besides being rife with new problems of its own.

That third general question, about the point of creation, may not have been asked (or answered) by Augustine, but it certainly did exercise later medieval philosophers. The first suggestion of the kind of answer to it the medievals took most seriously is found not in Genesis, but in Plato's creation story. But before moving explicitly to the Greek side of the Christian heritage, I want to suggest that we have already seen both the biblical and the metaphysical sides, the Jewish and the Greek sides of this heritage in Augustine's treatments of creation. In his voluntarist mood, his insistence on God's absolute self-sufficiency and on the primacy and absolute independence of God's volition represents one prominent (libertarian) strain in Greek thought, whereas his expansive, informal account of the who, how, and why of creation is biblical with hardly a trace of philosophy in it.

4. Plato's Explanation of Creation

The basis for an answer to our third question and the classical starting point for necessitarian explanations of creation is this passage in Plato's *Timaeus*: "Let us now give *the reason why* the maker made becoming, and the universe. He was *good*, and in him that is good no envy ever arises regarding anything. Being devoid of envy, he wanted everything to be *like himself*, as far as possible. . . . God desired that everything should be *good* and nothing evil, as far as possible. . . . For him who is

---

11. *De civitate Dei* XI.21. See Teske 1988, p. 247, for more texts to this effect.

most good *it neither was nor is permissible* to do anything other than what is most beautiful."[12]

The stories of creation in Genesis and the *Timaeus* are enough alike that Augustine wondered whether Plato had not plagiarized his from Moses.[13] But there are at least four noticeable relevant differences between them. In the first place, Plato's world maker, the Demi-urge, is not omnipotent and is not creating the world out of nothing, but is merely shaping and ordering matter that is already in existence. That is what gives Plato's denial of envy in him its point,[14] and that is why it would be impossible in this context even to attempt a radical voluntarism in which the existence of the world has no explanation beyond the maker's volition. Second, in the *Timaeus* the primary, explicit ascription of goodness is to the maker, not to the world he makes—although that world is described in the end as "most beautiful." Third, we are offered the beginning of an account of the point of creation: the production of something as much like the good creator as created things can be. Finally, although the *Timaeus* passage explains the origin of the world in terms of an agent's action, it also includes a strong suggestion that that action is a consequence of the agent's nature. The suggestion is that the making of the world, or at least the character of the world that gets made, is *not* a result of the maker's free choice: "For him who is most good it neither was nor is *permissible* to do *anything other* than what is most beautiful."

Whatever Plato himself may have intended by this, the later Platonists, who influenced medieval thought far more than Plato did directly, strengthened this line of explanation, arguing (as we'll see) that it is part of the essence of goodness to give rise to being and goodness—in other words, that the existence of a world is an inevitable consequence of God's perfect goodness rather than the result of a freely chosen action of his. Medieval Christian philosophers were deeply influenced and sometimes attracted by that part of their Greek heritage even when they were convinced that it had to be repudiated. Thomas Aquinas's accounts of creation strike me as providing a paradigm of that sort of tension in Christian thought.

---

12. *Timaeus* 29E–30B.

13. *De civitate Dei* XI.21.

14. Teske 1988, pp. 249 and 251–53, provides several striking passages in which Augustine in his accounts of creation is careful to deny that the creator could be envious. Plato's denial of envy in the Demi-urge seems connected with the world maker's intention to produce something as much *like* himself as possible. Augustine's denial of envy in God is connected with God's permitting anything besides himself to exist *at all*.

5. Libertarian and Necessitarian Strains in Aquinas

Is God free to choose whether or not to create? Aquinas's official answer to that question is an emphatic, unqualified yes: "one must hold, without any doubt, that God produced creatures in existence by a free choice of his will, without any natural necessity."[15] But I believe that his conceptions of God, goodness, creation, and choice entail a negative reply.[16] It seems to me that he resolutely adopted the libertarian line but was drawn to and sometimes even expressed a necessitarian line. I think that the necessitarian and libertarian strains in Aquinas's account of creation might be reconciled, but I don't think he reconciled them. And so I see no way of avoiding the inconsistency (or, at least, ambivalence) in Aquinas's account as it stands.

I begin with the libertarian position, the one Aquinas explicitly adopts. It is part of his concept of God that God has freedom of choice.[17] But God's volition is not entirely characterized by free choice, since "God *necessarily* wills his own being and his own goodness, and he *cannot* will the contrary."[18] In keeping with Aquinas's understanding of divine simplicity, God's goodness, like everything else properly ascribable to God himself, is simply God himself conceived of by us in a particular way. Conceived of as goodness, God himself is recognized by Aquinas as the universal, unique, ultimate *final* cause: "the ultimate end is God himself, since he is the highest good."[19] In willing his own goodness, therefore, God is willing the one universal natural end, regarding which no choice is possible. And so Aquinas recognizes that some aspects of God's activity can be both necessitated and volitional although, of course, not both necessitated and freely chosen.

Nevertheless, even God's willing his nature (and existence) is not, according to Aquinas, incompatible with every sort of freedom: "in respect of its principal object, which is its own goodness, the divine will does have necessity—not, of course, the necessity of constraint, but the necessity of natural order, which is not incompatible with freedom."[20] That this freedom compatible with the necessity of natural order is not freedom of choice is clear from Aquinas's restricted assignment of

---

15. *DP* III.15c. The question is "whether things proceeded from God by a necessity of nature or by a choice of will."
16. I have argued this in Kretzmann 1983b.
17. See, e.g., *SCG* I.88: "QUOD IN DEO EST LIBERUM ARBITRIUM."
18. *SCG* I.80 (n. 676).
19. *SCG* I.74 (n. 636).
20. *DV* XXIII.4c.

choice to only one aspect of the action of God's will: "since God wills himself as the end but other things as things that are for the end, it follows that in respect of himself he has *only* volition, but in respect of other things he has *selection*. Selection, however, is always accomplished by means of free choice. Free choice, therefore, is suited to God."[21] And the term 'free choice,' he makes clear, "is used in respect of things one wills *not* necessarily, but of one's own accord."[22]

So Aquinas appears to be an incompatibilist regarding freedom of choice, but he recognizes another kind of freedom in volition that is compatible with the necessity of natural order—*willingness*, it might be called. This state of willing freely although necessarily is not hard to exemplify in ordinary circumstances. A human being is susceptible to emotions necessarily, essentially. But if his positive attitude toward this susceptibility is just what it would have been if he had freely chosen an inner life characterized by emotions from among available relevant possibilities and had found that it measured up to his expectations, then he wills susceptibility to emotions freely though necessarily. I call that state "willingness" because it seems more natural to describe such a person as being willingly susceptible to emotions than as willing that susceptibility. In God's case, then, willingness, not freedom of choice, characterizes the divine will "in respect of its principal object, which is its own goodness."

Since God's freedom of choice is essentially connected with his willing of things other than himself, it is, on this view, associated solely with creation in some way or other. Ascribing *any* free choice to God conceived of as eternal, simple, and purely actual, is obviously not easy, even when its objects are restricted to things other than God. Of course, Aquinas recognizes that difficulty, taking up and rejecting many putative reasons for asserting that God wills *everything* he wills under the necessity of natural order.[23] But one obstacle in the way of exempting creation from the necessity of natural order was, I think, never dealt with satisfactorily by Aquinas.[24] This obstacle is located in the divine attribute of goodness, which we have already seen presented (by Plato and by Augustine) as essentially associated with creation.

---

21. *SCG* I.88 (n. 732).
22. *SCG* I.88 (n. 730).
23. See, e.g., *DV* XXIII.4; XXIV.3.
24. See, e.g., his rejoinders to objections 1, 5, 12, and 14 in *DP* III.15. (Obj. 12 is in n. 27 below, his rejoinder to it in n. 28 below; obj. 1 and his rejoinder are in n. 29 below, obj. 14 and his rejoinder in n. 30 below.)

The essence of goodness is an aspect of the essence of God, who is, Aquinas says, "goodness itself, not merely good."[25] The particular locus of the obstacle in goodness is its essential self-diffusiveness, brought out in a neo-Platonist principle Aquinas often appeals to, sometimes attributing it to Dionysius: *Goodness is by its very nature diffusive of itself and (thereby) of being.*[26] I think this Dionysian Principle, the root of which can be discerned in the *Timaeus* passage, expresses an important truth about goodness, most obviously about the goodness of agents, which is the only kind at issue here. (There is no obvious inconsistency in the notion of knowledge that is unexpressed, never shared by the agent who possesses it even if he is omnipotent, but there is inconsistency in the notion of goodness that is unmanifested, never shared, even though united with omnipotence.)[27] The use Aquinas makes of the Dionysian Principle on many occasions suggests that he, too, considers it to be important and true, at least most of the time.[28] But, of course, the principle also looks as if it must give rise to a necessitarian line of explanation of creation, one in which creation would be a natural consequence of God's nature in its perfect goodness,[29] or in which God's goodness would be understood to cause his

25. *SCG* I.38 (n. 310).

26. "Dionysius," or pseudo-Dionysius, is the otherwise unidentified author of four Christian neo-Platonist treatises and ten letters dating from the sixth century. These works had special authority during the Middle Ages, when they were thought to have been written by the Athenian Dionysius mentioned in Acts 17:34 as having been converted by Saint Paul's sermon on Mars Hill. On the history of this principle see esp. Peghaire 1932; also Kremer 1965.

27. This point is brought out well in *DP* III.15. obj.12: "In II Timothy 2:13 it says 'God remains faithful and cannot deny himself.' But since he himself is his goodness, he would deny himself if he denied his goodness. And he would deny his goodness if he did not diffuse it by sharing it, for that is a *proprium* of goodness." (See n. 28 below for Aquinas's rejoinder.)

28. See the list in Peghaire 1932, p. 19*, nn. 45 and 46, and scattered references in subsequent notes in his article. Aquinas's rejoinder to the objection quoted in n. 27 above contains one of his rare rejections of the Dionysian Principle: "If God were to deny his goodness in such a way as to do something contrary to his goodness, or something in which his goodness was not expressed, it would follow, *per impossibile*, that he would deny himself. But that would not follow even if he did not share his goodness at all, for it would be no loss at all to goodness if it were not shared."

29. See, e.g., *DP* III.15.obj.1: "Dionysius says [*De divinis nominibus* IV], 'Just as our sun, neither reasoning nor choosing, but by its very being illuminates with its light all things willing to share it, so the divine goodness by its essence sheds its rays of goodness proportionally for all existing things.' But the sun, illuminating without choice and reason, does this by a necessity of nature. Therefore, God also produces creatures by a necessity of nature in sharing his goodness." Aquinas's rejoinder: "Dionysius's simile must be understood as having to do with the *universality* of the diffusion; for the sun pours its

volition to create, somewhat as our nature causes our volition for happiness.[30] And the fact that the volition to create, like the volition for happiness, is governed by the necessity of natural order would in no way militate against its being done with the freedom of willingness, even though not with the freedom of choice.[31]

Aquinas, as we've seen, is explicitly opposed to such a line of explanation. Nevertheless, he sometimes writes in a way that indicates that he does see God's creating as an instance of the natural self-diffusion of goodness, as in this passage, where he is discussing not creation itself but God's goodness: "The communication [or sharing] of being and goodness proceeds from goodness. This is indeed evident both from the nature of the good and from its definition. . . . But that diffusion is suited to God, since he is the cause of being for other things."[32] If that diffusion is no more than "*suited* to God" (*competit Deo*), it sounds as if God could conceivably not be characterized by it, or as if he could turn it on or off, in which case the essential diffusiveness of goodness would pose no threat to God's having a free choice whether or not to create. But it seems Aquinas has no right to the convenient weakness of "suited to," the same expression he sometimes uses in associating free choice

---

rays onto all bodies, not distinguishing one from another, and so does the divine goodness. But [the simile] is not understood as having to do with a privation of will." If the objection had focused exclusively on the absence of *choice*, Aquinas would not have been able to characterize it as suggesting a privation of *will* in God's sharing of goodness.

30. See, e.g., *DP* III.15.obj.14: "Everyone who wills wills his ultimate end of necessity, as a human being of necessity wills to be happy. But the ultimate end of the divine will is the sharing of his goodness, for he produces creatures in order to share his goodness. Therefore, God wills this of necessity, and so of necessity he produces." Aquinas's rejoinder: "The ultimate end is not the sharing of goodness, but rather the divine goodness itself; it is out of love for it that God wills to share it. For he does not act because of his goodness as if desiring what he does not have, but as if wanting to share what he has, because he acts not out of desire for the end, but out of love for the end."

31. In *DP* XV.3, Aquinas's reply is made up of four arguments intended to support his very strong libertarian thesis, which insists that creation proceeds from "a free choice of his will . . . with no natural necessity." But the first, third, and fourth arguments conclude only that creation proceeds from will rather than from nature. As we have seen, Aquinas clearly distinguishes between volition and free choice, and so showing that creation proceeds from will is not yet to show that it proceeds from free choice. Furthermore, by his own lights, the dichotomy between will and nature (or natural necessity) invoked in these conclusions is a false dichotomy; some of what God wills he wills with "the necessity of natural order." The conclusion of the second argument does mention choice: "The fact that he established a creature in this [or that] determinate degree [of inequality] was a consequence of a choice of will, not of natural necessity." This conclusion concerns not creation generally, however, but the creation of some universe in particular, and, as we will see, there are good reasons for supposing that free choice can operate as regards *what* to create even if not as regards *whether* to create. (Cf. the article cited in n. 16 above and the immediately following essay in this volume.)

32. *SCG* I.37 (n. 307).

with God.[33] God is perfect goodness itself, and goodness is *essentially*—from its nature and from its definition—diffusive of itself and being. Doesn't it follow that the volition to create is a consequence of God's nature?

As more pointed evidence that it does, consider this passage in which Aquinas *is* discussing God's willing the existence of things other than himself, and notice in it the echoes of the *Timaeus*: "every agent, to the extent to which it is in act and perfect, produces something like itself. Thus this, too, pertains to the nature of the will, that the good which anyone has he communicates to others as much as possible. And it pertains above all to the divine will, from which every perfection is derived in virtue of a kind of likeness."[34]

If perfect goodness is an aspect of God's essence, and self-diffusiveness is essential to goodness, it looks as if creation has got to be an inevitable consequence of God's nature—unless the diffusion of goodness can somehow be completely accounted for within the divine nature. The passages we have just been considering, like almost all those in which Aquinas is relying on the Dionysian Principle, speak of the communication of the divine goodness to other things. But in the earliest of his three big theological works (and only there, as far as I know) he presents the following intriguing argument for the plurality of the divine Persons in the triune God: "As Dionysius says, . . . the good is communicative of itself. But God is good in the highest degree; therefore, God will communicate himself in the highest degree. But he does not communicate himself in the highest degree in creatures, because they do not receive *all* his goodness. Therefore, there must be a *perfect* communication, resulting in his communicating all his goodness [with] another. But that cannot be in a diversity of essence; therefore, there must be more than one distinct [Person] in the unity of the divine essence."[35] I think this Trinitarian application of the principle deserves further consideration in its own right, but it cannot by itself dispel the principle's tendency to initiate a necessitarian account of creation. For even if the Son's being begotten by the Father and the Holy Spirit's proceeding from the Father and the Son can be considered an essential intrinsic diffusion of goodness and being, in the Christian theology to which Aquinas subscribes it is the *triune* God that is characterized as "goodness itself, not merely good."[36] And so even when the plurality of

33. See, e.g., *SCG* I.88 (n. 732), quoted on p. 216 above.
34. *ST* Ia.19.2c.
35. *Super Sent.* I, d. 2, q. 1, a. 4, s.c.
36. *SCG* I.38 (n. 310); see p. 217 above. In at least one place, in a work written after

the divine Persons has been explained on this basis, the essential self-diffusiveness of goodness as an aspect of the essence of the triune God remains in force, calling for *extrinsic, volitional* diffusion, or creation. Although God's will is the total cause of creation, in bringing it about that something besides God exists, his will, it seems, does not freely choose but acts, willingly, in a way necessitated by the natural order, the relevant aspect of which in this case is the diffusiveness of goodness and being that is essential to goodness itself, God's own essence.

Aquinas's principal strategy for avoiding that necessitarian, Platonist, perhaps heretical outcome[37] is to rely on his own novel interpretation of the Dionysian Principle, an interpretation that strikes me as counterintuitive. He proposes that the diffusiveness essential to goodness be understood *not* as "the operation of *efficient* causation" but as having *solely* "the status of *final* causation."[38] This attempt to introvert the principle has nothing to recommend it as an interpretation. For one thing, drawing of the sort essential to final causation is *contrary* to diffusing. Of course, goodness has an attractive as well as a productive side, but the principle is an expression of the *productive* side of goodness, as Aquinas's predecessors unanimously recognized.[39] It seems wrong-headed to propose reading it as expressing *exclusively* the *attractive* side of goodness. More important, Aquinas's final-causation-only proposal leaves him with no explanation at all of God's willing the existence of other things. The diffusiveness of goodness conceived of as final causation can't be extended to the drawing of anything other

---

Summa contra gentiles and around the time he was beginning *Summa theologiae* (1265–67), Aquinas himself makes this identification very emphatically: "That which is per se one itself, which is God, unknown and supersubstantial (i.e., above every substance), and which is the good itself (i.e., the very essence of goodness), and which is itself that which is (i.e., per se being itself)—namely, the triune unity itself, in which, I maintain, there are no degrees, all three being at once and equally God, and *at once and equally the good itself* (the Son is no 'shadow of goodness,' as Origen and Arius said)—that, I say, we can neither speak nor think of, considered as it is in itself. For in this present life we cannot see the very essence of God, which is unity in trinity" (*In librum beati Dionysii De divinis nominibus expositio,* c. 1, l. iii, n. 81).

37. At least nineteenth-century Catholic orthodoxy is clearly opposed to this outcome: "If anyone should not confess that the world and all the things contained in it, both spiritual and material, are produced ex nihilo by God as regards their entire substance, or should say that God did not create by a volition free from every necessity but created as necessarily as he necessarily loves himself, or should deny that the world was established for the glory of God, let him be anathema" (First Vatican Council [1870], sessio III, canones "de deo rerum omnium creatore" 5; Denzinger 1976, n. 3025). I do not know of any earlier pronouncement as explicit as this, but William Anglin called my attention to the condemnation of Abelard at the Council of Sens for maintaining that God could not do otherwise than he does (Denzinger 1976, n. 726).

38. *DV* XXI.1.ad4.

39. See Peghaire 1932, pp. 6*, 9*, 12*, 15*, and 17*.

than God himself toward it unless there *is* something else. But in the case in which God, perfect goodness, exists alone, why *would* God will to cause anything else to begin to exist?

Is Aquinas headed toward voluntarism regarding creation, then? That way out might seem firmly closed to him by his own emphatic repudiation of what he calls "the *error* of certain people who said that all things depend on the simple divine volition, without any reason."[40] But there are crucial passages in which it becomes clear that he perceives that sort of voluntarism to be mistaken mainly in its universality, in its claiming that "*all* things depend on the simple divine volition, without any reason." On one occasion when Aquinas considers the question "whether any cause can be assigned to divine volition," he answers that "in *no* way does God's volition have a cause." But he has to deal with the objection that "if God's volition has no cause, it follows that all the things that are made depend on his simple volition and have no other cause, which is absurd." His rejoinder to this objection certainly does sound like voluntarism regarding creation: "Since God wills effects to occur on account of causes, any effects that presuppose some other effect do not depend on God's volition alone, but on something else [as well]. But the *first* effects depend on the divine volition *alone*."[41] And yet it is an ambivalent voluntarism, as can be seen from an earlier passage in the same Question: "Since God wills things other than himself only *because* of the end which is his own goodness, as was said, it does not follow that anything *else* moves his will *except* his own goodness."[42]

Despite the occasional flashes of voluntarism in Aquinas's discussions of creation, I think he is committed to providing some explanation of God's volition to create. But he is aware of the difficulty of doing so in view of the apparently closed system constituted by God as perfect will drawn to God as perfect goodness. His libertarian explanation of the volition to create begins with claims that look like the beginning of the necessitarian line: "in willing himself God also wills other things,"[43] and "God wills himself and other things in one act of will."[44] Aquinas recognizes that someone could well infer from statements of this sort that God therefore wills all other things necessarily, as he wills himself; but Aquinas rejects that inference on the grounds of God's self-sufficiency: "since the divine goodness can be without other things and, indeed,

40. *SCG* II.24 (n. 1008).
41. *ST* Ia.19.5.ad3.
42. *ST* Ia.19.2.ad2.
43. *SCG* I.75 (n. 639).
44. *SCG* I.76 (n. 647).

nothing is added to it by means of other things, there is in him no necessity to will other things in virtue of the fact that he wills his own goodness."[45]

No matter how much detail I added to this account of Aquinas's position, it would in the end still be dominated by these two opposing forces: Platonist self-diffusiveness and Aristotelian self-sufficiency.[46] The rift in Aquinas's account of creation seems to be the widening of a crack in his characterization of God, a crack that runs not between the Jewish and the Greek elements in Christian theology, but between two main strands within Greek philosophy itself. The tension between necessitarian and libertarian explanations of creation in Aquinas is a tension between aspects of Platonism and Aristotelianism, respectively. He seems to me to have deliberately committed himself to the Aristotelian side despite his marked tendency to think along the Platonist line, as in this argument for God's willing things other than himself: "To the extent to which something has the perfection of a power, its causality is extended to more things and over a wider range. . . . But the causality of an end consists in the fact that other things are desired because of it. Therefore, the more perfect and the more willed an end is, the more the will of the one willing the end is extended to more things by reason of that end. But the divine essence is most perfect in the essential nature of goodness and of end. *Therefore*, it will diffuse its causality as much as possible to many things, so that many things will be willed *because* of it—and especially by *God*, who wills it [the divine essence] perfectly in respect of all its power."[47]

But nowhere else have I seen him weave the Platonist and Aristotelian strands together so neatly as in this passage: "Speaking absolutely, he [God] of course does not will them [things other than himself] necessarily . . . because his goodness has *no need* of things that stand in an ordered relationship to it, and the manifestation of it can be appropriately accomplished in various ways.[48] *And so there remains for him a*

45. *SCG* I.81 (n. 683).
46. As presented, e.g., in *Metaphysics* XII.9 (1074b15–34).
47. *SCG* I.75 (n. 644).
48. My translation here follows the Leonine edition (Thomas Aquinas 1970–76): "*bonitas eius his quae ad ipsam ordinantur non indiget, et eius manifestatio convenienter pluribus modis fieri potest.*" The version of this passage in the Marietti edition (Thomas Aquinas 1931) is even more in line with my own interpretation, supporting the translation "*except as a* manifestation of it, *which* can be appropriately accomplished in various ways" (*bonitas eius his quae ad ipsam ordinantur, non indiget nisi ad manifestationem, quae convenienter pluribus modis fieri potest*). The Busa edition (Thomas Aquinas 1980c) presents precisely the same reading as the Marietti, a reading not even included in the Leonine's critical apparatus. I am grateful to Peter van Veldhuizen for first calling my attention to the discrepancy between the Leonine and Marietti editions.

free judgment for willing this one or that one, just as in our own case."[49] As I read this passage, it comes very close to saying what I think Aquinas *should* say about God's need to create something: that goodness does require things other than itself as a manifestation of itself, that God therefore necessarily though altogether willingly wills the being of something other than himself, and that the free choice involved in creation is confined to the selection of which possibilities to actualize for the purpose of manifestation. But even if we can occasionally find Aquinas thinking Platonist thoughts, he interrupts them often enough with Aristotelian pronouncements, such as "the divine goodness is complete in itself, even if *no* creature were to exist,"[50] or "It is *not* necessary, if God wills that his own goodness be, that he will that other things be produced by him."[51]

I once suggested a way of getting rid of the inconsistency or ambivalence in Aquinas's account of creation, along the following lines.[52] Aquinas's "necessity of natural order, which is not incompatible with freedom," could simply be extended to cover God's willing the existence of something or other besides himself. We could then agree with Aquinas that "God cannot will that he not be good and, consequently, that he not be understanding or powerful or any of those things which the essential nature of his goodness includes,"[53] granting as well that this necessity of willing is not incompatible with one sort of freedom, the sort I called "willingness."[54] But I would then want to go on to urge, in accordance with the Dionysian Principle, that God's bringing into existence something other than himself is among "those things which the essential nature of his goodness includes." Although it couldn't be said on the basis of this revision that God is *free to choose* whether or not to create, it could consistently be said that God *freely, although necessarily, wills* the existence of something besides himself.

6. Goodness, Trinity, and Creation in Bonaventure

I still think that suggestion is on the right track. But since making it I have looked at Bonaventure's answer to the question why God created anything at all. Bonaventure's answer strikes me as extending and en-

49. *DV* XXIV.3c.
50. *DV* XXIII.4c.
51. *SCG* II.28 (n. 1054).
52. See Kretzmann 1983b.
53. *DV* XXIII.4c.
54. See p. 216 above.

riching the line of thought I took in attempting to repair Aquinas's account.[55]

Bonaventure was born a few years earlier than Aquinas, but the two of them were colleagues and almost exact contemporaries; both were appointed to chairs of theology in the University of Paris on the same day in 1256, and both died in 1274. In their explanations of creation they used virtually the same elements and principles, but their results were quite different in ways that seem to reflect a difference in their intellectual backgrounds, which has at least a little to do with the fact that Aquinas was a Dominican and Bonaventure a Franciscan. The inconsistency or ambivalence in Aquinas's account stems, I've been saying, from his decided commitment to Aristotelian self-sufficiency in his conception of God combined with his hesitant appreciation of the insight and explanatory power of the Dionysian Principle, or Platonist self-diffusion as a basic characterization of God. Bonaventure managed to unify those ingredients, I think, partly because he was, like many other Franciscans, an Augustinian Platonist whose attitude toward Aristotelianism was never warmer than guarded tolerance. I don't have any evidence that Bonaventure's explanations of creation were written with Aquinas's in mind, but at least some of them could have been, and they often read as if they were. Whatever the historical relationship between the two may have been, I present Bonaventure's views in the light of our discussion of Aquinas, and so I'm not much concerned with preserving the order in which Bonaventure developed or presented his position.

I begin with sketchy remarks about being and goodness.[56] We've already seen being and goodness linked together in the Dionysian Principle: Goodness is essentially diffusive of itself and (thereby) of being. The basic ancient and medieval thesis connecting being and goodness, fully subscribed to by Aquinas, can be conveniently expressed, to begin with, as the claim that the two terms 'being' and 'goodness' are alike in their reference but different in their senses—that they are like the terms 'evening star' and 'morning star' in referring to one and the same entity despite their different senses. Bonaventure wholeheartedly adopts this analysis and insightfully identifies the single referent of 'being' and 'goodness' as God himself, distinguishing their two senses in terms of the dominant Old and New Testament conceptions of God: "The one mode [of contemplating the invisible and eternal things of

---

55. For much relevant, helpful information, see Keane 1975.
56. For more detail, see Eleonore Stump and Norman Kretzmann, "Being and Goodness" (Chapter 4 in this volume).

God] looks primarily and essentially to God's *being*, and says that God's foremost name is 'He Who *Is*.' The other mode looks to God's *goodness*, and says that his foremost name is this very *'Goodness.'* The first approach looks more to the Old Testament, which stresses *the unity of the divine essence*, for it was said to Moses: 'I Am Who Am.'[57] The second approach looks to the New Testament, which reveals *the plurality of [the divine] Persons* . . . Christ, our Teacher, . . . attributes to God the name 'Goodness' as belonging to him essentially and exclusively, for he says: *'No one is good but only God.'*"[58] There's no mystery about why Bonaventure would associate God's Old Testament name with divine unity, or the plurality of the divine Persons with the New Testament, but how, exactly, is the name "Goodness" supposed to reveal the plurality? Since the New Testament was seen as the completion and interpretation of the Old, in Bonaventure's view the concept of being has to be completed and understood in terms of goodness. And since he fully accepts the Dionysian Principle, he can be said to begin with what he takes to be the New Testament conception of God as essentially *dynamic* in his self-diffusiveness. Bonaventure thus naturally employs the Dionysian Principle as his primary explanatory device in accounting for God's nature or activity. Thus the account of the plurality of the divine Persons in terms of the essential diffusiveness of goodness, which, as we saw, Aquinas considered only peripherally, early in his career, becomes the centerpiece of Bonaventure's mature account: "Good is said to be self-diffusive; therefore, the highest good is that which diffuses itself the most. Now, diffusion cannot stand as the highest unless it is intrinsic yet active, substantial yet personal, essential yet voluntary, necessary yet free, perfect yet unceasing." I am interrupting the passage here to point out that the first adjective in each pairing is more readily associated with static self-sufficiency, or the *being* side of the being-goodness relationship, whereas the second adjective brings out dynamic self-diffusion, or the *goodness* side. *Static*: intrinsic, substantial, essential, necessary, perfect; *dynamic*: active, personal, voluntary, free, unceasing. "Thus, in the supreme good, there must be from all eternity an actual and consubstantial producing, the producing of a hypostasis as noble as the One who produces by way of both generation and spiration. So, there is produced an Eternal Principle, who is an eternal Co-producer. And thus, there is the producing of one Beloved and one Co-beloved, of one Engendered and one Spirated. So,

57. Exodus 3:14.
58. Mark 10:18 and Luke 18:19. *IMD* V.2.

in all, there are the Father, the Son, and the Holy Spirit. Otherwise, this good would not be supreme, since it would not be *supremely* self-diffusive."[59]

In Bonaventure's system the full diffusion of goodness constitutive of the triune nature of God is a necessary concomitant of perfect goodness, divine Fatherhood being characterized as *fontalis plenitudo*, the full, unstinting flowing of a spring.[60] This feature of Bonaventure's dynamic conception of God seems to have been directly repudiated by Aquinas in a characterization of divine Fatherhood that could hardly contrast more sharply with Bonaventure's. After affirming that "innascibility," signified by the name "unbegotten," is proper to God the Father, Aquinas deals with some attempts to give positive content to these negative terms: "Some people say that innascibility . . . considered as a property of the Father is not spoken of only negatively, but that either it means that the Father is from no one and is the source of others, or it means universal authority, or even *fontalis plenitudo*. But that is evidently not true. . . . Primary and simple things are designated by negations, as when we say that a point is that which has no part."[61] In this later, presumably more representative, treatment of divine Fatherhood by Aquinas it is hard to see even the basis for the plurality of Persons, let alone a source of creation.

Bonaventure's contrasting treatment of the Trinity as the primary, supreme instance of self-diffusiveness takes it to be simply the indispensable first stage of the diffusion of goodness that proceeds into creation. "Because [God] is most perfect, he is of the highest goodness; *because* he is of the highest goodness, he wills to produce *many* things and to communicate himself."[62] And this volition, as we've already seen Bonaventure noting, is "essential yet voluntary, necessary yet free."[63] "In God the essential nature of productive diffusion occurs in this way: his being is supremely good; therefore, it supremely diffuses itself."[64]

The supreme diffusion, as we've seen, is the generation and spiration resulting in the plurality of the divine Persons. The diffusion that is creation is immeasurably feebler in its effect, but in its cause it is the divinely willed manifold manifestation of the full being and goodness of the triune God. In keeping with the motive of divine manifestation, the creature of the first day is light, the paradigmatic material repre-

59. *IMD* VI.2.
60. *In Sent.* I, d. 27, p. 1, a. un., q. 2.
61. *ST* Ia.33.4.ad1.
62. *In Sent.* II, d. 1, p. 2, a. 1, q. 1.
63. P. 225 above.
64. *CH* XI.11.

sentation of self-diffusing being, as had been pointed out by Robert Grosseteste, who was second only to Augustine as the philosophical teacher of the Franciscans, including Bonaventure: "Light of itself diffuses itself in every direction, so that a sphere of light as great as you please is engendered instantaneously from a point of light."[65] As for the immeasurable disparity between the divine Persons and creatures, "diffusion is utterly final (*ultimata*) in that the [perfectly good, omnipotent] producer gives everything he *can* give. But a creature cannot receive everything that God can give. And so, just as a point adds nothing to a line—nor do a million points—a creature's goodness adds nothing to the creator's goodness."[66] "The temporal diffusion [of goodness] in a creature is only like a center or a point in respect of the immensity of the eternal goodness. That is why a diffusion greater than creation can be conceived of, the one in which the diffusing [goodness] does communicate its whole substance and nature to another. Therefore, there would not be a highest good if it could lack that diffusiveness really or conceptually."[67]

I've been providing evidence of Bonaventure's reliance on the *efficient* causality inherent in goodness, as expressed in the Dionysian Principle. Aquinas, at least in his most systematic pronouncements, relied instead on the Aristotelian conception of the good as the universal object of desire, the ultimate *final* cause. But Bonaventure also recognized and relied on the Aristotelian conception, in keeping with the altogether sensible neo-Platonist tradition, which included *both* these aspects, the Platonic and the Aristotelian, the productive and the attractive, in its account of the essence of goodness.[68] As Bonaventure puts it, "The reason why causality is attributed to the will is that the *essence (ratio) of causing, both efficient and final, is goodness.* For the good is said to be diffusive, *and* the good is that for the sake of which all things [are and act]. But an efficient cause does not actually produce an effect except for the sake of an end. Therefore, that which expresses the conjoining of an efficient source with an end explains the actual occurrence of causing. But volition is the act in accordance with which a good is turned toward (*reflectitur supra*) a good, or goodness. Therefore, it is volition that unites an efficient cause with an end. . . . And that is why we attribute causality to God under the aspect of will."[69]

65. *De luce seu de inchoatione formarum*; Robert Grosseteste 1912, 51.11–13.
66. *CH* XI.11.
67. *IMD* VI.2. For further discussion of Bonaventure on the Trinity, see Kretzmann 1989a and 1989b.
68. See, e.g., Dionysius, *De divinis nominibus* I.5, IV.4.
69. *In Sent.* I, d. 45, a. 2, q. 1, resp.; cf. ad 2.

7. Conclusion

Aquinas, like Bonaventure and most other medieval theologians, saw the structure and the history of the world as a cosmic cycle willed by God, the manifold manifestation of his goodness in the procession of creatures from him and the return of creatures to him. Given that world view and the concept of God as perfect goodness personified, could there be an explanatory mechanism more apt than the neo-Platonist dual-aspect conception of goodness, suggesting the circulation of all created good from the heart of goodness and back again? Bonaventure took full advantage of this dual-aspect conception. Aquinas, who knew it well and sometimes tried it out, in the end left it to one side, leaving himself with a one-sided orthodox Aristotelian conception that seems to have given him more trouble than help.[70]

70. I am grateful to William Haines, Scott MacDonald, William Mann, and, especially, Eleonore Stump for very helpful comments on earlier drafts of this paper.

CHAPTER 9

A Particular Problem of Creation:
Why Would God Create This World?

Norman Kretzmann

1. Introduction

What is the status of this world among all possible worlds? Is it the best of them? If it isn't, then why would an absolutely perfect being create it? If it is, then the best possible world involves a great deal of evil; so why would an absolutely perfect being create it? These reasons for asking why God would create this world constitute half of the particular problem of creation I want to address. I call this first half the status problem, and I deal with it before introducing the second half.

Both halves of the particular problem of creation are related to the traditional problem of evil, which I am not going to discuss here in its standard form. But the particular problem of creation is introductory to the problem of evil, and one reason it's worth considering is that a solution to the particular problem of creation can be expected to point to a certain sort of solution to the problem of evil.

Before beginning with the status problem itself, I want to say a little about the connection between the particular problem of creation and the general problem I discuss in the immediately preceding essay. The question I raise there is why God, the absolutely perfect being, would create anything at all; and at one point (near the end of Section 5) I summarize my own position by saying that God's goodness requires things other than itself as a manifestation of itself, that God therefore necessarily (though freely) wills the creation of something or other, and that the free choice involved in creation is confined to the selection of which possibilities to actualize for the purpose of manifesting goodness.

I put it that way in part because I am there dealing primarily with Aquinas's account of creation, according to which God freely chooses not only *what* to create but also *whether* to create. So, although I disagree with Aquinas's claim that God is free to choose whether to create, I'm inclined to agree with him about God's being free to choose what to create.

A passage I quote from Aquinas in the preceding chapter clearly states his claim that God is free to choose what to create—and states it together with a treatment of the general problem of creation I find easy to accept—so I use that passage again, this time to set the stage for an investigation of the particular problem: "Speaking absolutely, he [God] of course does not will them [things other than himself] necessarily (as was shown in the preceding Question), because his goodness has no need of things that stand in an ordered relationship to it, *and the manifestation of it can be accomplished in various ways.* And so there remains for him *a free judgment for willing this one or that one,* just as in our own case."[1] In that last phrase, "just as in our own case," Aquinas is saying that God's choice of what to create in order to achieve the end of manifesting his goodness is like our choice among various courses of action leading in different ways to our naturally necessitated end. Since I take God's manifesting his goodness in creating to be a naturally necessitated end but Aquinas does not, his analogy between God's case and ours strikes me as suiting my position on the problems of creation better than it suits Aquinas's own official position.

2. The Status Problem

The Standard Position

I tend to agree with Aquinas that God has free choice regarding what to create, but I believe that most philosophers who have considered this issue have come down on the other side of it. The standard philosophical position seems to be that since God is omniscient, omnipotent, and perfectly good, he must create the best of all possible worlds if he creates anything at all; he is, therefore, *not* free to choose what to create. Probably the earliest version of the standard position appears in the passage from Plato's *Timaeus* I cite in the preceding chapter: "God desired that *everything* should be *good* and *nothing evil, as far as possible.*

---

1. *DV* XXIV.3c. Cf. "A General Problem of Creation" (Chapter 8 in this volume), n. 48.

For him who is most good it neither was nor is *permissible* to do anything other than what is *most* beautiful."[2]

Even Aquinas sometimes says things suggesting that he is on his way to the standard position, as in these discussions of the reason for distinctions and gradations among creatures: "Every agent tends to introduce its own likeness into its effect in the respect in which the effect can receive it, [and] an agent does this the more perfectly to the extent to which it is a more perfect agent, . . . but God is the most perfect agent. It belonged to God, therefore, to introduce his own likeness in created things most perfectly, to the extent to which it is suited to a created nature. But . . . since the cause transcends the effect, that which is simple and one in the cause is found as composite and multiple in the effect. . . . Therefore, there had to be multiplicity and variety in created things so that God's perfect likeness would be found in them in accordance with their mode [of being]."[3] Again, "there had to be various gradations among creatures in order for there to be in creatures a perfect representation of God."[4]

What these passages appear to show is that Aquinas takes the degree of perfection in the created world to be, not surprisingly, the degree of its resemblance to perfect goodness, the degree of its success as a manifold manifestation of God's nature. Because the uncreated, simple, eternal nature of God, who is being itself, is radically unlike the modes of being available to created, composite, temporal things, the resemblance of creature to creator must be imprecise. But, because of God's status as the most perfect agent, spelled out in the passages I just quoted, it looks as if the resemblance must also be as *nearly* precise as *possible*. In other words, it looks so far as if Aquinas's God does have to create the best of all possible worlds.

Parts and Order

But that conclusion is ruled out once we see the whole extent of Aquinas's treatment of the status problem, because in his treatment there is no room for a concept as simple, or simpleminded, as the familiar notion of the best of all possible worlds. Aquinas analyzes any world, or universe (as he more often says), into two kinds of ingredients: its *parts* (or simply "things") and the *order* of its parts. He recog-

2. *Timaeus* 29E–30B.
3. *SCG* II.45 (n. 1220).
4. *SCG* II.45 (n. 1222).

nizes two sorts of order: the *arrangement* of the parts relative to one another and their *directedness* toward their end, but these two sorts of order can usually be treated together simply as *order*.[5] The parts and the order of a universe are variable in different ways. As a result of these different sorts of variability for parts and for order, even though God's nature entails that any universe God might create would have to be the best possible universe in respect of its *order*, *no* universe *could* be the best possible universe in respect of its *parts*.

For a first look at this crucial difference between order and parts (or things), consider the following passage: "In virtue of *the most appropriate order* bestowed on these things by God, in whom the good of the universe is founded, the universe—supposing these things [to be in it]—cannot be better. If any one of these *things* were better, the proportion of the *order* would be destroyed, just as the tunefulness of a harp would be destroyed if one string were stretched more than it had to be. Nevertheless, God could make *other* things, or *add* others to these things after they were made, and in that case [or in either of those cases] that universe would be *better*."[6]

Aquinas is claiming that the order of the actual world (or of *any* world God might have actualized) is the best possible. In respect of its order, "the universe . . . cannot be better." But that doesn't mean, except in the broadest terms, that there is a single, best possible cosmic order regardless of parts. In respect of its order the universe cannot be better "supposing *these* things [to be in it]." Suppose that, for starters, we picture a world the parts of which are just A, B, and C, "the most appropriate order" for which is alphabetical, let's suppose. Part of what would make alphabetical order the best possible order for that world is just the nature of those parts; it is the best possible order *for them*. So although this or that part—C, let's say—could have been better considered in itself, occurring as super-C, if *it* had been better in that way while the other parts remained as they are, then in the resultant world of A, B, and super-C "the *proportion* of the order would be destroyed." The ABsuper-C world would not be created by God. Still, God could create a whole set of *better* parts super-A, super-B, super-C (such that super-A and super-B were improvements of the same sort as super-C and proportioned to super-C), in which case he would create an intensively better version of the ABC world. Or he could create *more* parts—

---

5. I think that by 'parts' or 'things' in this context, Aquinas typically means species rather than individuals, and I proceed on that basis even though I ordinarily just use his very broad terms 'parts' or 'things.'

6. *ST* Ia.25.6.ad3.

A, B, C, D, and E—in which case he would create an additively better version of the ABC world. Or he could create altogether *different* parts X, Y, Z, each of which is intensively better than its counterpart in the ABC world, in which case he would create a different world, intensively better than the ABC world.[7]

Once more, this time taking a perhaps more readily extendible model of parts and order, the fact that the two parts of the sentence "Chris runs" are perfectly all right themselves and could not be better ordered misleads no one into thinking that there could not be a better literary production. The actual world as Aquinas sees it is, we might say, like "Chris runs" in being an optimally ordered set of parts good of their kinds, but a set of parts that are in themselves less good in some respects than those in other (unactualized) sets, or a set less rich in parts than other (unactualized) sets. There is even scriptural backing for this view of the actual world in Aquinas's reading of the culminating divine appraisal of creation: "That is why it says in Genesis 1:31 'God saw *all* the things that he had made, and they were *very* good' although of the things taken one by one he had said that they were *good*. The things taken one by one were of course good in their natures, but all the things taken together were '*very* good' because of the *order* of the universe, which is the final and finest actualization (*perfectio*) involving the things."[8] So the fact that the actual world is the best of all possible worlds *involving these parts* should not mislead anyone into thinking of it as the best of *all* possible worlds.

Additive and Intensive Improvements

In his most detailed analysis of the status problem Aquinas tries to show all the respects in which it is possible and all the respects in which it is impossible for God to make a world better than this one or to make this world better than it is.[9] Although some of these improvements are concerned with variability of *parts*, the whole analysis is organized around considerations of the possibility of improvement in *order*. I can introduce this analysis most efficiently in the form of an outline.

Cosmic order
    (1) The order *among the parts* (Arrangement)
        (1.1) Considered as regards the ordered *parts*

---

7. The distinctions between a better world and a better version of the actual world, and between intensive and additive improvements, are Aquinas's own, as we'll see.
8. *SCG* II.45 (n. 1228).
9. *Super Sent.* I, d. 44, q. 1, a. 2.

   (1.11) *Additive* improvement: POSSIBLE[10]
   (1.12) *Intensive* improvement
     (1.121) *Partial*: IMPOSSIBLE[11]
     (1.122) *Total*
       (1.1221) In terms of *essential* goodness: POSSIBLE[12]
       (1.1222) In terms of *accidental* goodness: POSSIBLE[13]
  (1.2) Considered as regards the *order* of the parts
   (1.21) *Additive* improvement: IMPOSSIBLE[14]
   (1.22) *Intensive* improvement
     (1.221) In the order associated with *essential* goodness: IMPOSSIBLE[15]
     (1.222) In the order associated with *accidental* goodness: POSSIBLE[16]
(2) The order *directed toward an end* (Directedness)
  (2.1) Considered as regards *the end*
   (2.11) Improvement: IMPOSSIBLE[17]
  (2.2) Considered as regards *the order*
   (2.21) Improvement: POSSIBLE[18]

Aquinas develops this analysis in replying to the question "whether God could make a better universe,"[19] and one of the issues is whether improvements of certain sorts would result in this world's becoming better than it is or in its being replaced with a better world. The analysis is intended to show that in respect of "improvements" (1.121), (1.21), (1.221), and (2.11), this world is as good as possible. In respect of improvements (1.11), (1.1222), (1.222), and (2.21), however, God could make this world better; in respect of (1.1221), God could make a better world.[20] A closer look at a few of these improvements, possible and

 10. E.g., *ABC* + *DE*, where the result is neither merely an improved version of the *ABC* world nor an altogether different, better world.
 11. E.g., *AB*super-*C*, destructive of the *ABC* world's order.
 12. E.g., *XYZ*, where $X > A$, $Y > B$, $Z > C$, and the result is a world different from and better than the *ABC* world.
 13. E.g., super-*A*super-*B*super-*C*, where the result is a better version of the *ABC* world.
 14. Because additive improvement in this respect presupposes initially unordered parts, impossible in any world created by God.
 15. Because such an improvement in order presupposes different parts.
 16. E.g., a thing's getting better at achieving its natural end, where the result is a better version of the world affected in this way.
 17. Because it presupposes an ultimate goal better than God, the absolutely perfect being.
 18. E.g., a thing's getting better at achieving its natural end, where the result is a better version of the world affected in this way, just as in (1.222).
 19. *Super Sent.* I, d. 44, q. 1, a. 2.
 20. There is a sense in which God could also make a better world in respect of (1.221), but only in making a better world in respect of (1.1221). And it seems to me possible, and possibly important, to recognize (1.222) and (2.21) as respects in which this world could *become* better.

impossible, will clarify Aquinas's position and contribute to this investigation of the status problem.

An *additive* improvement of the arrangement in respect of the parts (1.11) is possible "by the addition of more parts in such a way that many other species would be created and the many grades of goodness there can be would be increased; for between even the highest creature and God there is an infinite gap. And in this way God could have made or could make a better universe. But that universe would be related to this one as whole to part, and so it would be neither entirely the same nor entirely different."[21]

As for *intensive* improvement of the world's arrangement in respect of parts, we've already seen why a *partial* improvement of this sort (1.121) cannot be accomplished without a worsening of the world. *Total* intensive improvement in terms of *essential* goodness (1.1221) is "possible for God, who can establish infinitely many other [intensively better] species, although in that case there would not be the same parts or, consequently, the same universe." The other sort of total intensive improvement (1.1222) *would* count as bettering the actual world—for example, making every thing a better instance of what it is.

An *additive* improvement of the world's arrangement in respect of the order itself (1.21) would have to be an extension of order to some unordered parts, but "if no addition is made to the *parts* of the universe," this sort of improvement is impossible because "in the universe there is nothing that has not been ordered." So in this respect the actual world is as good as any world could be.

Intensive improvement of the actual world's arrangement insofar as it has to do with *accidental* goodness (1.222) takes place whenever any part gets better at being the sort of thing it essentially is, "since the order is better to the extent to which anything [in it] expands to a greater good," thereby better fulfilling its role in the world's arrangement—for instance, human beings behaving more rationally. In at least some such cases, it seems, the world *becomes* better as distinct from being *made* better by God. But there could be no corresponding improvement having to do with *essential* goodness (1.221)—that is, better *sorts* of things—"unless there were different parts and a different universe."

As for (2) in the outline, since the *directedness* of the actual world, like that of any world that might have been created by God, is an orientation toward God himself, there can be no improvement of this order as regards the end itself (2.11), since "nothing can be better than God"—another respect in which this world is as good as any world could be.

21. All the quotations in this portion of the article are from *Super Sent.* I, d. 44, q. 1, a. 2.

This is the broad sense of 'order' in which there *is* a single, best cosmic order regardless of parts. Given the absolute perfection of that unique, universal, ultimate end, however, and the high degree of disorientation within at least the essentially rational part of the actual world, "the order toward the end *could* be improved [(2.21)] insofar as the [accidental] goodness of the parts of the universe and their ordered relationship to one another [—their arrangement—] increased, because the more closely they associated themselves with the end, the more a greater likeness of God's goodness would result—which is the purpose of all things."

So Aquinas's analysis of evaluative differences among possible worlds reveals four respects in which God could make this world better (two of which are also respects in which it could just become better, with God's help), one respect in which God could make a different, better world, and four respects in which this world is as good as possible.

God's Choice of a World That Is Not the Best

There are obviously many difficulties and intriguing suggestions in this analysis, but I have to leave most of them unexamined now. What I do want to call attention to in connection with the status problem is the conclusion that seems to emerge regarding Aquinas's position at this stage of our investigation—on the basis of (1.11) or (1.122), for instance—the conclusion that *omniscient, omnipotent, perfectly good God chooses to create a world that is not the best of all possible worlds.* That claim certainly looks incoherent. Given his conception of God, the only way Aquinas can dispel the appearance of incoherence is to maintain that for God to choose to create this world is *not* for him to choose less than the best. And in the context established by this first worrisome conclusion, the only way he can maintain *that* is to deny that there is a best possible world. But such a denial is just what his analysis develops in detail, I think.

In Aquinas's system no possible world is empty, since God exists necessarily—that is, in every possible world. If the position I take on the general problem of creation is justified, it is also the case that no possible world contains God alone—that is, the absolutely-perfect-being-and-nothing-else state of affairs is impossible. Then, since nothing besides God is absolutely perfect, no possible world is absolutely perfect. But it does not follow that emptier is better where worlds are concerned, since, as the analysis shows—for example, in the discussion of (2.21)—the degree of perfection in a world depends on the degree to which God's goodness is manifested in it, the degree to which it represents God. The optimal ordering of its parts, whatever they may be, is one respect in which a world can represent God in the highest degree possible (for those parts), but since "between even the highest creature and God there is an infinite gap," there cannot be an optimal *set* of parts. I think Aquinas would agree that the nature of the creator entails that whatever world he chooses to actualize is optimally *ordered*, considering the essential aspects of the order itself, as in (1.21) and (2.11). An improved version of the actual world, or even a different world better than the actual world, would be just like the actual state of the actual world as regards the essentials of its necessarily optimal order. And so the possible improvements relevant to the status problem all have to do with parts rather than with order as such.

But if we focus on (1.11) as presenting a paradigm of that sort of possible improvement—an additive improvement to the order among the parts considered as regards the ordered parts—we can see that the series of possible worlds stemming from it is ranked with respect to the richness of their sets of parts in an infinite series. This means that omniscient, omnipotent God can no more choose the additively optimal *set* of parts than he can pick out the largest fraction between zero and one. God's inability to create a world than which no better world is possible is just another, hitherto neglected, aspect of the logical character of omnipotence. The complaint that God is not omnipotent because he can't make the best of all possible worlds—if anyone were tempted to make such a complaint—would be even less intriguing than the old complaint that God is not omnipotent because he can't make a rock so big that he can't lift it. It would be on a par with a complaint that God is not omnipotent because he can't make a rock so big that he can't make a bigger rock.

If the relevant possible additive improvements consist in increasing multiplicity or complexity—having more parts or more gradations of goodness among parts—then it does seem that such improvements are illimitable simply on the basis of arithmetical considerations. In creating, God undertakes to represent simple, eternal, perfect goodness in a composite, temporal, necessarily imperfect medium. It's like undertaking to represent a geometer's straight line (which is continuous, infinite, and invisible) by nothing but penciled dots. An *accurate* representation can be effected by means of only two dots, even though that would be as *imprecise* as an accurate visible representation of a line could be. Preserving the perfection of the *order* of the elements would require that any additional representational dots occur in positions that preserve the representation of the line's one-dimensional straightness, and the addition of dots to the representation in that way could, I think, be said to improve the dotty representation, to enhance its capacity for conveying the nature of the continuous, straight, one-dimensional thing to be represented. But, of course, there can't be a theoretically *best* representation of that sort.

God's Choice of a World Less Good Than One He Could Choose

Even if on grounds of this sort everyone agreed that it is absurd to complain that God did not create the best of all possible worlds, since there is no such thing, it remains true on this account of the status problem that God could have created a world better in certain respects than this one, that *omniscient, omnipotent, perfectly good God chooses to create a world less good than another he could create.* But if God could do better, how can he be perfectly good?

In "A General Problem of Creation" (Chapter 8) I argue that it is impossible that a perfectly good God do nothing at all extrinsic to himself. And according to my attempted explanation here of Aquinas's claim that God could create a world better than this one, it is also impossible that God create something than which he could not create something better. My conclusion in the preceding essay and my explanation in this one taken together entail that perfectly good (omniscient, omnipotent) God must create a world less good (in respect of the richness of its set of parts, for example) than one he could create.

Still, if that's what is to be said in response to the status problem, it might occur to someone to think that if the best of all possible beings cannot avoid choosing something less good than he could choose, then no being is or can be perfectly good. Perhaps "perfectly good" is just the expression of a confusion, like "perfectly long." Like Aquinas, I think that the logical truth that God's actions conform to the principle of noncontradiction entails no limit on his power.[22] And if it would be a violation of the principle of noncontradiction for God to create a world better than any other world he could create, then a fortiori that logical truth which does not diminish his power also leaves his *goodness* undiminished. God's being that than which nothing better can be conceived of cannot entail his producing a world than which none better can be conceived of. No matter which possible world he actualizes, there must be infinitely many possible worlds better than the actual world in some respect or other.

---

22. *SCG* II.25: "QUALITER OMNIPOTENS DICATUR QUAEDAM NON POSSE."

The Creator's Predicament

All the same, these observations also seem to make the creator's choice of what to create much more a quandary or predicament than it might otherwise seem to be—a predicament Aquinas portrays in a word when he observes that "it is suited to the highest good to make what is *better*."[23] I conclude my discussion of the status problem by trying to dispel or at least to mitigate this impression of a predicament for the creator.

I've been saying that there could not be a theoretically best dotty representation of a geometrical line. But even though any such representation must fall infinitely short of the thing to be represented, once a certain level of precision has been reached, no representation would be *practically* better, better *as a representation*, even though there would still be infinitely many theoretically better representations possible. Changing the analogy slightly, a photostat that could not be a more precise representation of a typewritten page except in ways that lie below the threshold of perceptibility is *practically* although not theoretically a perfect photostat—considered as the sort of thing a photostat is intended to be, a representation. Suppose, then, that the actual world considered as a representation of God is as good as possible in the sense that any world better than this one in terms of improved precision of representation would be no better at all in its capacity to represent God to any possible created percipient. That is, suppose that the limitations essential to created intelligence are such that the actual world is as good a representation of God as there could be for created intelligences. Then it would be irrational for God to choose to create any world theoretically better than this one, and to act irrationally is not only out of the question for God, it is also incompatible with any full-fledged instance of free choice.

God's Reason for Choosing This World

But even if genuine free choice must be rational choice, and even if I have made a hypothetical case for the rationality of God's choice of a world theoretically less good than another he could have chosen, have I made that case in such a way as to leave no options—establishing the rationality at the expense of the choice? Not if there is more than one world that is as good as possible considered as a representation—which

---

23. *SCG* II.45 (n. 1223). It is worth noting that in the Anderson translation of Book II this sentence—"*Summo autem bono competit facere quod melius est*"—is translated as 'Now, it befits the supreme good to make what is *best*' (emphasis added).

seems quite plausible, given the radical differences between God and the medium of representation.

But a question emerges at this point. What could be a sufficient reason for the creator's choice of this world rather than another that does the representing job equally well—that is to say, supremely well? Free choice can be reconciled with a sufficient reason for choosing one of the options, but nothing that could count as a full-fledged instance of choice could take place in the absence of a reason to choose. Suppose that Aleph and Alpha are worlds that would be equally (supremely) good as representations. In that case there is a sufficient reason for God's choosing to create *either* Aleph *or* Alpha. And if, as seems reasonable, we think of a world as a maximal set of compossible things, it is impossible to create *both* Aleph and Alpha. But a reason sufficient for choosing *either* Aleph *or* Alpha is a reason sufficient for choosing one of them. So it seems to me that God's having a genuine choice regarding what to create is a defensible possibility.

What is the status of this world? It is not the best of all possible worlds, but neither is any other. Still, it seems it must be as good a representation of God's goodness as there can be. And that is why God would create it, or one that is equally good as a representation.

3. The Freedom Problem

Jeopardizing Creation

The status problem is the first half of the problem of creation I'm calling particular: Why would God create *this* world? Expressed in that way, the particular problem of creation has the ring of the problem of evil. But because Aquinas's treatment of the status problem includes his denial that there is a best possible world, our investigation of the status problem has stayed further away from the traditional problem of evil than it would have done if we'd been dealing with the claim that this world is the best of all possible worlds. The status problem in the form in which we've been dealing with it could have been raised about this world even if our world contained nothing that we ordinarily recognize as moral or natural evil. But the second half of my particular problem of creation wouldn't be seen as problematic at all if there were no moral evil.

Medieval theologians and philosophers considered moral evil to be the basic evil, the one in which to find the explanation of the occurrence of psycho-physical pain, natural disasters, and all the other varieties of evil. For purposes of this investigation I will follow their lead, at least to the extent of focusing exclusively on moral evil. In the Christian doctrine those thinkers were explaining and elaborating, the origin of every sort of disruption or deterioration of the pristine goodness of creation—that is, the origin of all evil—lay in created will. The first, fundamentally disordering acts of moral evil stemming from created will are acts of *anti*creation, freely chosen disruptions of what had been perfectly ordered.

Important as the disordering of creation is, especially for all who live in it, that external consequence of moral evil is less important for problems of creation than is its internal source. Why did moral evil occur in a perfectly ordered world? How *could* moral evil occur in a perfectly ordered world? Aquinas's short answer to such questions points to *irrationality* as the root of the explanation. Irrationality is not a defect of intellect, the *cognitive* faculty of reason, but is, instead, perversity in the *will*, the *appetitive* rational faculty, which to some extent directs the intellect's attention. Will is no less essential than intellect to rationality; to make a rational creature is to make a creature with a will. A perfectly ordered created will would not have misdirected its associated intellect, causing it to overlook the unreason in disobeying its creator's command, or causing it to find some apparent good in what it would otherwise have recognized as evil. And newly created wills, like all other newly created things, were indeed perfectly ordered. But to make a creature with a will is to make a creature that is essentially self-ordering or free to some considerable extent, and no being of that sort can be entirely preserved in perfect order by an outside agent or reordered from outside as long as it remains the sort of being it is—rational, hence volitional, hence self-ordering or free. Having made a world one of whose parts was a rational creature, not even omnipotent God could guarantee that world's freedom from irrationality. And, the story goes, the irrationality came, insinuating anticreation into a world that had been *very* good. And so, of course, we have the problem of freedom: Why would omniscient, omnipotent, perfectly good God jeopardize the pristine goodness of creation by choosing to make a world with a free creature as one of its parts?[24]

24. In dealing with the status problem, I follow Aquinas's analysis and solution quite closely because it's the best I know of. My approach to the freedom problem has much less to do with Aquinas directly. What strikes me as the most promising approach to a solution is not one I've found Aquinas taking, although he is in possession of most of its ingredients. I think it will become clear that my divergence from him on this score is linked to my disagreement with his handling of the general problem of creation.

Representation and Understanding

We've seen Aquinas claiming, in more than one way, that a "likeness of God's goodness . . . is the purpose of all things."[25] Likeness is one basis of natural representation, and the point of creating, I've been saying (following Aquinas following Plato), is representation—God's manifold manifestation of his simple, eternal, perfect goodness. But representation is minimally a three-place relationship. The movement of a prehistoric glacier is represented by grooves in the rock, but only if they're seen and understood; so, too, "the heavens declare the glory of God and the firmament showeth his handiwork" only if they're seen and understood. Anyone maintaining that creation is a representation of God's goodness must be prepared to say for *whom*. Now, the representation that creation is can't be for *God's* contemplation: omniscient goodness needs no looking glass. If creation is representation, as I've been saying it is, the observer-understander that constitutes a necessary condition for the occurrence of representation must be a part of the created world—a further narrowing of the range of God's choice of what to create. In short, any created world that could fill the bill that's been drawn up in the preceding chapter and this one would have to include created understanding.

The only understanding we're sure there is in the world is human. Human understanding is part of the cognitive faculty of reason, which is essentially connected with the appetitive faculty of reason, which is will, which is essentially free. This line would have a chance of turning into a short, decisive argument for the necessity of freedom in the world if human understanding were the only possible created understanding. But nobody believes that there can't be created understanding other than human, least of all the medieval theologians I've been drawing on, who thought that angels are another part of creation that can understand. Angelic understanding is associated with will and freedom, too, and of course the doctrine is that angelic freedom is the condition out of which the aboriginal anticreation erupted. So expanding the range of created understanding to include the angelic along with the human just turns up another instance of requisite comprehension coupled with risky will.

But suppose we set aside the doctrinal data on angels and eschew all speculation about extraterrestrials, asking instead whether there is an essential connection between cognition and volition. Obviously volition

25. *Super Sent.* I, d. 44, q. 1, a. 2; pp. 233–38 above.

entails cognition, but must any creature that has cognition have volition, too? I'm inclined to think so, but I neither can nor need to argue for such a claim now. All I need at this point is what I think I'm already entitled to: if creation is representation, then creation requires created cognition. And I will not now take cognition to entail volition and (thereby) freedom.

I am, however, taking human cognition as my only instance of created cognition—again, without now relying on an essential connection between cognition and volition even in human nature in particular. And so it may also be worth noting that the use I'm making here of human cognition has nothing to do with the *representational* role assigned particularly to human nature in Christian doctrine. Since humanity is singled out as being created in the image of God, it must be what's distinctive about human beings that's particularly representative of God, and that's their rational nature, their intellect and will. And since the image-of-God status entails will, and will entails freedom, it's easy to see a short but not very satisfying solution to the freedom problem developing along that line. But for my present purpose what is important about human rational nature has nothing to do with its image-of-God status, nothing to do with its particular contribution to the manifold manifestation. All that matters now is its cognitive faculty's indispensable contribution of an observer-understander of creation,[26] which is the complex representation of God's simple goodness.

Establishing the need for created cognition in a representational creation gives us a start on a solution to the freedom problem. But in order to get that start, I've been making use of a simplified concept of God's manifold manifestation, one that derived naturally from our discussion of the status problem, but one that also allows creation to seem more like a 3-D movie than the outpouring of God as perfect goodness. My arguing for the necessity of created cognition on the receiving end of the communication of goodness has been correspondingly simplified. In moving away from those expedient simplifications now, I won't have to retract anything I've just been arguing for; I mean only to enrich it, largely by drawing on material already developed in

26. It is important to notice that I am here speaking of human rational nature quite generally. The human observer-understander I am concerned with is the human species considered diachronically throughout its existence, past, present, and future—not merely the species at its present state of developing its capacities to observe and understand the world. My supposition (p. 239 above) that "the limitations essential to created intelligence are such that the actual world is as good a representation of God as there could be for created intelligences" depends on distinguishing between essential limitations and those that are merely characteristic of a particular stage of development.

these two articles. When I've done so, I think it will be clear that what God's actual world requires among its parts is a creature that isn't merely an observer-understander but also a person; and personhood entails freedom.

Personhood and Freedom

The enriching process I now embark on to fill out my sketch of a solution to the freedom problem requires me to stick my neck out even further, making broad generalizations and bold assertions without much more than hints of argumentation. I begin by doing things of that sort with regard to the concept of a person.

A state as complex as personhood in a temporal mode of existence—our sort of personhood—has as its determining characteristics not just actual conditions such as an inner life but, more importantly, inclinations, dispositions, potentialities. (I use 'potentialities' as the generic term.) The specifying potentialities of personhood can all be subsumed under the heading of personal relationships, I think. Such preconditions of personhood as intellect and will are necessary conditions of entering into personal relationships and needn't be separately stipulated. A being, human or otherwise, is a person if and only if, and to the extent (in range and depth) to which, it enters into personal relationships. The existence of persons requires the reality of personal relationships, and vice versa. I don't have a definition of personal relationship, but I think that for my purpose a readily recognized paradigm will do, and loving is the clearest and most appropriate choice.

It should be clear at once that being loved by a person is not a sufficient condition of having entered into a personal relationship. To the extent to which an active/passive distinction applies to a personal relationship, only taking the active role (or one of the active roles) counts as entering into the relationship.

The last claim I need to make in this brief foray into the nature of personhood is crucial, but it also strikes me as obviously true. I put it forward for now as an appeal to philosophical intuition. Fully actualized personal relationships (and therefore personhood) are impossible without freedom on both sides of the relationship. There can be no full-fledged love if either the loving person or the loved person isn't free; love can be neither automatic nor coerced. There can't be programmed persons or artificial personhood. Personhood entails freedom.

My purpose in making these claims about personhood will emerge very soon.

Productive Goodness and Love

In my attempt to resolve the general problem of creation I talk about a dual-aspect account of goodness, one that gives equal importance to both the productive and the attractive sides of goodness, especially in connection with understanding God conceived of as perfect goodness. I also make a good deal of use of the Dionysian Principle: Goodness is essentially diffusive of itself and (thereby) of being. I use it as an expression of the productive side of goodness, limiting our consideration of goodness in this context to the goodness of agents. Now, Dionysius himself insightfully identifies this aspect of goodness as love. As far as I know, Aquinas doesn't explicitly or wholeheartedly endorse that identification. But his own conception of love accommodates the identification quite well, as we'll see, and on at least one of the occasions on which he seems attracted by the Dionysian explanation of creation he writes as if he's also attracted by the identification of productive goodness as love: "Here I say *the divine love* [quoting Dionysius] '*did not permit him to remain in himself*, without offspring'—that is, without the production of creatures. Instead, love 'moved him to activity' in accord with the best possible mode of activity, insofar as he produced all things in being. *For the fact that he willed to diffuse and to communicate his goodness to others as far as that was possible—that is, by way of likeness—and that his goodness did not remain in himself alone but flowed out to other things, was an outgrowth of the love associated with his goodness.*"[27]

On this view, to say, as Christianity says, that God is love is to present God's essence under a conceptual aspect that can also be recognized as the aspect of God's goodness in which it diffuses itself and being in the act of creation: God is productive goodness. Creation, then, is the aspect of the act of divine love to which only the intra-Trinitarian loving relationships are logically prior.

But might the outpouring of productive goodness or divine love be *entirely* contained within the loving union of the divine Persons? Peter Geach thinks so: "Love is just what God is, and is eternally; before the mountains were brought forth or ever the Earth and the world were made; *independently of any creatures made or yet to be made.* . . . The wisest of the Greek and Roman pagan thinkers divined that God is endowed with an eternal and blessed life independently of the world; for Christians God's eternal life is a life of love, but this truth does not annul or make trivial the truth discovered by the pagans. . . . The contrary doctrine, that God needs created persons to love or else is not a loving God,

27. *In librum beati Dionysii De divinis nominibus expositio* c. 4, l. ix (n. 409).

can have crept in among Christians only through ignorance or neglect or misunderstanding of the doctrine of the Trinity. . . . the Divine Life of the three Persons is nothing else than their eternal mutual love. . . . God is love because, and *only* because, the Three Persons eternally love each other."[28] In that last quoted sentence Geach transforms "God is love," the transcendent comfort of Christians for 2,000 years, into a Dear-John letter from the triune God to every one of those unsuspecting loving creatures. I really can't believe that more than the merest handful of Christians have ever understood "God is love" as Geach says it must be understood. Still, Geach's treatment of this issue is reminiscent of Aquinas's (as distinct from Bonaventure's), and I think it leaves Geach, like Aquinas, with no way of explaining creation. But, as far as I can see, "the Divine Life of the three Persons" can be characterized as "nothing else than their eternal mutual love" *without* in any way blocking the Dionysian explanation of creation in terms of that same personal relationship. In creation it is *the triune God*, presumably in the Person of the Father, the Son, or the Holy Spirit, who is the loving person, while the loved persons are created, not divine, and hence capable, as the divine Persons are not, of rejecting as well as of participating in God's love. In fact, the Dionysian explanation of creation seems particularly well suited to a God whose inner life, so to speak, is describable as eternal love. And if it is God as love who is manifested in creation, then creation must include created persons, who must be free.

A Dual-Aspect Account of Love

What features of productive goodness are illuminated by identifying it as love? My answer grows out of what I first learned in reading Aquinas, but I'm not now vouching for its faithfulness to the details of his account. And, again, I am sketching the answer in sweeping lines, ignoring for now all the details and difficulties in order to present the concepts I need, and concentrating on full-fledged or ideal love as if it were the only sort worth considering, although the account I am offering easily accommodates perverse or stunted love as well.

Of course, love has its place among human passions, and everybody knows some of love's emotions. But there can be full-fledged loving that is full-fledged action as distinct from passion, and none of the various emotions associated with human love seems essential to all kinds of love even among human beings. In any case, neither passion nor emotion can be associated with God's love, which is at issue now.

28. Geach 1977, pp. 70–71, 71–72, 75, 80; emphasis added.

Full-fledged love, as I've been saying, is a relationship between persons. Love of truth, of music, of home, even love of oneself is not full-fledged love; it is called love by an extension of the term, or it involves illusion. The genus of this personal relationship is desire, and the desire that is full-fledged loving has two equally important objects: the well-being of the loved person and union with the loved person. Sexual union is the sort likely to spring to mind first, but almost everybody knows there are many other respects in which persons can be united, from family life and companionship to the beatific vision, which has some special importance for this final stage of my investigation.

But can any personal relationship whose genus is desire involve omnipotent God as one of the related persons? How can any desire constitute an eternal state of an omnipotent will? In two ways. First, "desire" need not indicate unfulfilled wanting, as it perhaps most often does; it can indicate also the wanting or willing of what one fully possesses, which in the case of divine love would be especially pertinent to the eternal mutual love of the divine Persons. But, in the second place, even omnipotent God can have a desire that is unfulfilled if it is a desire for something that can only be freely given by another person.[29] Even an omnipotent person cannot ensure by fiat even the well-being of another person, much less union with that person. So it seems to me that both aspects of loving are attributable to God without significant revisions of the ordinary senses of the terms involved.

Attractive Goodness and Love

For the sake of handy reference I call the desire for the loved person's well-being *benevolent* loving, and the desire for union with the

29. The metaphysical symbiosis entailed by personhood may seem to make God dependent on beings other than himself. The first thing to notice in this connection is that God's absolute independence could not rule out logical dependence. E.g., being omniscient depends logically on knowing that 2 + 2 = 4, and so God considered as omniscient is logically dependent on knowing that 2 + 2 = 4. God considered as a person is likewise logically dependent on the existence of other persons. But the claim at issue here is that God's nature entails a loving relationship with other persons, and that not even omnipotent God can guarantee another person's love for him. This sort of dependence cannot be explained as merely logical. Still, God's nature as a person would be fulfilled in his fully loving others; his love for other persons could not be in any way dependent on their love for him. (Even among imperfect persons, x's love for y would be recognized as weak or defective if it depended on y's loving x.) What must depend on other persons' love for God is what might be described as the best outcome of the loving relationship. The best outcome, union with God, is not independent of a creature's free choices; but a created person's union with God is not an aspect of God's nature. God's love for other persons, which of course is an aspect of his nature, is in no way dependent on any will other than God's.

loved person *univolent* loving. Then it seems to me that everything we've seen so far suggests that the love with which productive goodness is identified is *benevolent* loving, that creation is to be seen as a demonstration of God's willing not just the being but also the well-being of creatures and particularly of persons, the creatures with whom a full-fledged loving relationship is theoretically possible.

But *univolent* loving also has an essential role to play in the understanding of divine goodness. Near the end of the preceding chapter I say that "Aquinas, like Bonaventure and most other medieval theologians, saw the structure and the history of the world as a cosmic cycle willed by God, the manifold manifestation of his goodness in the procession of creatures from him and the return of creatures to him. Given that world view and the concept of God as perfect goodness personified, could there be an explanatory mechanism more apt than the neo-Platonist dual-aspect conception of goodness, suggesting the circulation of all created good from the heart of goodness and back again?" It's the *return* to God which involves the attractive more than the productive side of goodness, but also univolent more than benevolent loving, especially on the side of the created person. It's also the return to God which requires created volition, rational *appetite*, more than created cognition; and rational appetite entails freedom. Although the personal relationship between God and created persons cannot begin without God's first loving them, it cannot culminate as God wills without their loving him.

It isn't hard to see how the attractive side of God's goodness and God's univolent love for created persons are involved in the return to God, nor is it hard to see the involvement of created persons' univolent love for God, desire for union with God, in that process. But can created persons enter into a *full-fledged* loving of God as I've been analyzing loving here? What sense can be made of a creature's *benevolent* love for God? Could anyone manage to have a genuine desire for God's well-being, for the well-being of omniscient, omnipotent, perfectly good God?

I can think of only one sort of way in which such a desire could make sense, and it, too, is essentially associated with the return to God. The success of the return to God cannot be altogether achieved simply by God's willing it. God *would have* all to be saved, but some aren't.

Of course, the culmination of the upward curve in the cosmic cycle is not merely *God's* well-being, but it can hardly come as a surprise to learn that what's good for God is good for creatures, and in any case it's generally true that a loving person perceives the well-being of the loved person as a contribution to his or her own well-being. So it seems to me that a created person's desire for God's well-being precisely in respect of creation's return to God is by no means absurd. And it has even occurred to me that at least the second and third petitions of the Lord's Prayer might be read as attempts to teach created persons to love God in just that way.

Why would omniscient, omnipotent, perfectly good God jeopardize the pristine goodness of creation by choosing to make a world with a free creature as one of its parts? Because no world whose goodness was not jeopardized in that way could serve as a representation of productive goodness, God's loving, and of attractive goodness, God's inviting of love.[30]

---

30. Thomas Hardy's "New Year's Eve" (1906) illuminates a position than which none more opposed to mine could be conceived of:

> "I have finished another year," said God,
>   "In grey, green, white, and brown;
> I have strewn the leaf upon the sod,
> Sealed up the worm within the clod,
>   And let the last sun down."
>
> "And what's the good of it?" I said,
>   "What reasons made you call
> From formless void this earth we tread,
> When nine-and-ninety can be read
>   Why nought should be at all?
>
> "Yea, Sire; why shaped you us, 'who in
>   This tabernacle groan'—
> If ever a joy be found herein,
> Such joy no man had wished to win
>   If he had ever known!"
>
> Then he: "My labours—logicless—
>   You may explain; not I:
> Sense-sealed I have wrought, without a guess
> That I evolved a Consciousness
>   To ask for reasons why.
>
> "Strange that ephemeral creatures who
>   By my own ordering are,
> Should see the shortness of my view,
> Use ethic tests I never knew,
>   Or made provision for!"
>
> He sank to raptness as of yore,
>   And opening New Year's Day
> Wove it by rote as theretofore,
> And went on working evermore
>   In his unweeting way.

From *The Complete Poems of Thomas Hardy*, ed. James Gibson (New York: Macmillan, 1978). I am grateful to William Haines, Scott MacDonald, William Mann, and, especially, Eleonore Stump for very helpful comments on earlier drafts of this paper.

CHAPTER 10

The Best of
All Possible Worlds

William E. Mann

Genesis 1:31 says that the world God created was very good. What is it for the world to be good? Why did God choose to create this particular world over all the other possible worlds he might have created?[1] Concern for questions of this kind can be traced back to Plato's *Timaeus*. The latter question is one of the leitmotifs of Arthur O. Lovejoy's classic study *The Great Chain of Being*. But the question, when coupled with plausible intuitions about God's nature, is the source of a dilemma. If God's nature includes being maximally free, all-powerful, and completely sovereign over all aspects of creation, then it would seem that he could have created just any world or refrained from creating altogether. However, if God's nature also includes being perfectly good and all-loving, then it would seem that there are many worlds that he could not have created; in fact, it would seem that he could create only a maximally good world. And so it would seem that God cannot simultaneously be maximally free and perfectly good.

The task of this chapter is to see whether and to what extent these two intuitions about God's creative choice can be made consistent. I begin by examining two extreme views in the history of philosophy about God's creative choice, views that will serve to dramatize the issues but that exact too high a price from our intuitions. I develop these two views in a chronological order spanning roughly four and a half centuries. It is not necessary to my case that the chronological order also be

1. If one prefers, one can phrase the second question as "Why did God choose to create the actual world the way it is?" I use the notion of possible worlds as a heuristic device in this essay without taking a stance on their ontological status.

causal. It is sufficient that it be dialectical. I then search for an inhabitable middle ground. The reconnoitering consists of an examination of presuppositions about the comparative values of possible worlds and of presuppositions about God's nature.

1. Three Grades of Voluntaristic Involvement

The bishop of Paris's condemnation in 1277 of 219 propositions in philosophy, theology, and science provides us with a convenient place to begin our exploration. There are two strands of thought contained in the condemnation that abetted the development of an extreme version of voluntarism at the hands of fourteenth-century Franciscan philosophers. One of the strands can be followed by beginning with proposition 34: "that the first cause cannot make many worlds" (Denifle and Chatelain 1889, p. 545). The intent of condemning this proposition was to deny the necessity of the Aristotelian doctrine that our world order—the totality of things bounded by the spherical circumference of the fixed stars—is unique. It may be true that our world is unique, but if so, that truth is not necessary: it lay within God's unlimited power to create more than one world. To modern ears it sounds as though proposition 34 could be the denial of one or more of these positive theses about God's powers:

(1) God can make many worlds successively in time.
(2) God can make many contemporaneous worlds in different spatial locations.
(3) There are at least two possible worlds such that God can make *both* of them to be actual.

Contemporary philosophers, familiar with possible-worlds semantics for modal logic, would insist that thesis (3) is categorically different from theses (1) and (2). They would claim that when understood properly, the notion of an actual world entails both that *any* possible world might have been actual and that *no more than one* possible world can be actual.[2] As Leibniz would put it more than four centuries later, "I call *World* the whole succession and the whole collection of all existent things, so that it [can] not be said that several worlds could exist in different times and different places" (Leibniz 1875–1890, vol. 6, p. 107). Thus even if the only constraint on God's powers is the inability to

---

2. If I understand him correctly, not even David Lewis takes himself to be denying these claims. See Lewis 1986, pp. 97–104.

bring about contradictions—and that surely was the message conveyed by the Condemnation of 1277—these philosophers would insist that (3) cannot be true.

But it seems that whatever analysis of 'possible world' (perhaps, for example, *a maximally consistent set of propositions, all of which are true*) that is alleged to make thesis (3) a logical impossibility will also make theses (1) and (2) logically impossible. Conversely, whatever analysis of 'possible world' that makes theses (1) and (2) logically possible (for example, *the totality of things bounded by a spherical circumference of fixed stars*) will also make thesis (3) logically possible. On these issues medievals and moderns may thus disagree more on the correct analysis of 'possible world' (and 'actual world') than on what is true about the actual world and other possible worlds.[3] Modern commentators have noted that the Condemnation of 1277, while attempting to stifle the contamination of Christian dogma by Aristotelian physics, ironically had the effect of encouraging non-Aristotelian physical speculation, since the denial of crucial aspects of Aristotelian physics seemed to entail no contradictions.[4] It is enough for our present purposes to note that proposition 34, if it did not encourage speculation about other possible worlds in the post-Leibnizian sense of the term, did encourage speculation about other "actual" worlds, whose inhabitants, histories, and physics might differ from those of our world.

The second strand can be teased out of the condemnation of proposition 163: "that the will necessarily pursues what is firmly believed by reason [*quod firmiter creditum est a ratione*], and that it cannot abstain from that which reason dictates. Moreover, this necessity is not compulsion, but the nature of the will" (Denifle and Chatelain 1889, p. 552). It is significant that this proposition does not confine itself to *human* wills. It would have been hard for a reader to miss the point that one of the consequences of the condemnation of proposition 163 is that God's will does not necessarily follow his reason; it can abstain from what his reason dictates.

When combined, the two strands yield the following version of the *potentia Dei absoluta*. God's *power* is unlimited. God can do anything whatsoever that does not involve a contradiction. In particular, he is not constrained by merely *physical* necessity. He has the power to create any

3. Moderns have disagreed with other moderns about this. See the criticism of David Lewis's views in Stalnaker 1976.

4. See Blumenberg 1983, pp. 160–63; Dick 1982, pp. 28–43; Dijksterhuis 1961, pp. 161–63, 173–74; Funkenstein 1986, pp. 57–63; Grant 1971, pp. 27–29; Grant 1974, pp. 45–50; and Grant 1982, pp. 537–39.

metaphysically possible world. God's *will* is similarly unlimited. It is emphatically not necessitated by God's reason. The Condemnation of 1277 had the effect of giving pride of place to two of the traditional divine attributes, omnipotence and freedom. Just as the preeminence of God's omnipotence came to play an important role in metaphysics, determining what is, what might be, what must be, so the preeminence of God's will became important in value theory, determining ultimate ends, good and bad, right and wrong.

Theological voluntarism is any general thesis to the effect that relative to some domain, God's will is determinative. A specific version of theological voluntarism undergirds divine command theories of moral obligation: God's enjoining (forbidding) an action is what makes the action right (wrong). It is easy to confuse this version with another version of theological voluntarism that holds that God's will determines what is good and what is bad. If intrinsic goodness is supposed to be goodness independent of *all* attitudes, then this second variety of theological voluntarism denies that anything is intrinsically good, for God's approving attitude is always necessary in order for something to be good. Parallel remarks hold for intrinsic badness: a thing is bad or evil just because God disapproves of it.

Under the influence, perhaps, of the Condemnation of 1277, Franciscan thinkers during the first half of the fourteenth century put forward the ingredients of an extreme version of theological voluntarism.[5] I identify two stages of Franciscan voluntarism, the second more extreme than the first. I then look briefly at a third, even more extreme, stage, due not to the Franciscans but rather to Descartes.

Lovejoy called attention to a passage from *De Rerum Principio*, which he guardedly attributed to John Duns Scotus but which is now ascribed to Vital du Four. "Every creature has an accidental relation to the goodness of God, because nothing is added to his goodness from them, just as a point adds nothing to a line."[6] The passage is embedded in a section in which du Four argues against the idea that God wills what he wills out of necessity: the opinion du Four is especially concerned to excoriate is the opinion, attributed to Avicenna, that God's will neces-

---

5. Franciscan activities in the direction of voluntarism had begun before the condemnation and may indeed have shaped some of the elements of it. See Korolec 1982 for further details and references.

6. Du Four 1891, p. 307; see Lovejoy 1936, p. 156. All translations are mine unless otherwise indicated. I include, as an appendix to this essay, a translation of the section of *De Rerum Principio* in which the passage appears.

sarily wills whatever God's knowledge perceives to be a better course of action.

One can interpret du Four's remark in such a way that it allows that some creatures have intrinsic value, even that some creatures are intrinsically more valuable than others, but simply denies that the existence of any of them can add to God's goodness. This interpretation would stress that God's goodness is perfect and infinite, thus that the addition of any amount of created goodness cannot increase his goodness. In fact, one can maintain further that the addition of any amount of created goodness cannot increase the aggregate amount of goodness in existence, since God's goodness alone provides an infinite amount of goodness in existence. Such an interpretation is consistent with everything else du Four says. Moreover, medieval philosophers of du Four's time were sufficiently well versed in the logical peculiarities of the concept of infinity to make, appreciate, and dispute such observations.[7] But these observations might have been made equally well by means of an analogy that compared finite line segments to an infinitely long line: the addition of them to it would increase neither its length nor, so to speak, the amount of length in existence.[8] What is the point of the *point* in du Four's analogy? Serious consideration of that analogy suggests a voluntaristic interpretation of du Four's remark.

Points cannot add to the length of a line because by their nature points have no length to add. Creatures, on analogy, cannot contribute to the stock of goodness in existence, not only because that stock has infinite value before their arrival on the scene, but also because by their nature creatures have no goodness to contribute. It is a mistake, on this interpretation, to think of any possible world that God might have created as being by its nature better or worse than any other. All possible worlds—or at least all the parts of all possible worlds whose existence depends on being created—are by their nature equally valueless. Unlike points, however, which cannot (logically) acquire length, creatures can acquire goodness. They acquire goodness only through the activity of God's will. The analogy is thus not perfect. That points have no length "by their nature" is a way of saying that a point's having length is *against* its nature. That creatures are not good "by their nature" is a way of saying not that goodness is against their natures but rather that there is nothing in their natures that *entails* that they are

---

7. See Murdoch 1982, pp. 564–91.
8. Not everyone would have assented to this. See the discussion of the "paradox of unequal infinities" in Murdoch 1982, pp. 569–71.

good. With the possible exception of God, nothing is good by its nature. Goodness is not an intrinsic property of (created) things, nor does it supervene necessarily on a thing's intrinsic properties. Goodness is an extrinsic, relational property of things, founded solely in God's will.

The view portrayed in this interpretation owes us an account of Genesis 1:31: "And God saw every thing that he had made, and, behold, it was very good." A curious feature about this passage is its *not-quite* paratactic structure. It could be recast as two independent units related only by topic—"God saw every thing that he had made; it was very good"—except for the presence of 'behold.' The view we are considering can exploit this feature. God's seeing that the created world is very good cannot merely be a matter of his taking notice of a feature of creation that exists independently of his attitudes, shaping those attitudes. It is rather that God's seeing that creation is very good just is his approving it, and his approving it is what constitutes its goodness, what makes it good. 'Behold' functions here to signify the indissoluble relationship between the performative act of God's seeing that the world is very good and the intrinsic result of that act, namely, that what is seen to be good has its goodness constituted by that very act of seeing.

This interpretation of du Four's text claims that the actual world, like every other possible world, has no natural, intrinsic goodness in itself, and that what we would normally think of as intrinsic goodness in the actual world is goodness conferred by God's approving activity. Although it is not strictly dictated by du Four's text, I shall for the sake of convenience call the view expressed in this interpretation "du Four's view."

Du Four's view is clearly a robust specimen of theological voluntarism. Its chief source of attractiveness is the same intuition that motivates divine command ethical theories. If God is genuinely sovereign over creation, then his sovereignty ought not to be merely executive and judicial, but also legislative. If his functions were confined to creating and judging according to values over which he had no say, then he would not be sovereign over those values. Although he might by his activities be an impressive *conduit* of value, he would not be the *font* of value. One positive feature of du Four's view is that it depicts God as the source of goodness in the most straightforward way imaginable.

On du Four's view, God's will does not operate by acknowledging the good-making intrinsic properties of things; his will establishes what properties *count* as good-making. Analogous remarks apply to badness or evil. God could have created a world whose inhabitants are incapable of scientific discovery, aesthetic appreciation, and moral sentiment, who

are exquisitely sensitive to the pain to which they are perpetually subjected, and who rise above that pain solely to inflict torture on helpless
animals. Had God declared that world to be good, ipso facto it would
have been good. Had he "seen" that the actual world, the world he did
create, was very rotten, it would have been very rotten. Any world God
picks can have any dimension of value he declares it to have, just in
virtue of his act of declaration.[9] The pursuit of wisdom is a good thing,
but it might have been replaced by the practice of sadism. Charity is a
virtue, but in some possible worlds hardness of heart is the *summum
bonum*.

Some voluntarists flinch at these consequences; du Four might be
one of them. Immediately before the passage about points and lines, du
Four says that "since the will of God is not moved per se except to an
adequate good, which is his goodness, it is not moved necessarily to
what it wills, except for all those divine and solely intrinsic qualities that
are essentially connected to his goodness" (*De Rerum Principio*; Du Four
1891, p. 307). God does will some things of necessity, including his own
goodness. One might then try to argue that God's necessarily willing his
goodness precludes him from willing as good those things that are
incompatible with his goodness. If hardness of heart in creatures is
incompatible with God's goodness, then there could be no possible
world in which God's will determines hardness of heart as a good.

This maneuver collapses, however, if God's being essentially good
places no constraints whatsoever on what he might will to be good and
will to be bad with respect to creatures. William of Ockham appears to
have held this second, more extreme version of voluntarism. One of
Ockham's more salient doctrines is a *separability thesis*. Surely if anything
is an unconditional, intrinsic evil for a theist, it is hatred of God. Yet
according to Ockham,

God can cause any independent thing (*omne absolutum*) without [causing] anything else that is not identical to that independent thing. But the act of hating

---

9. It might seem that on du Four's view, counterfactual comparisons of value cannot
be made. Suppose one claims that the world would have been better had Hitler never
been born. A plausible analysis of counterfactuals in terms of possible worlds might
maintain that (most of?) those worlds identical in history to the actual world up to the
time at which Hitler was born and in which Hitler is not born have better subsequent
histories than the actual world. But if nonactual possible worlds have no value at all, how
can such comparisons be made? A defender of du Four's view can maintain that by
holding as fixed the good-making characteristics of the actual world, we can apply them
to assessments we make of other possible worlds. What we must not forget is that those
good-making characteristics are entirely the product of God's will.

God, insofar as it is an independent thing in itself, is not identical to the deformity and wickedness of the act. Therefore God can cause whatever is independent in the act of hating or rejecting God, [while] not causing any deformity or wickedness in the act. (Ockham 1981, p. 342)

Ockham believes that the badness of any created thing is always distinct from and accidental to the thing itself. The same holds true of creaturely goodness: in a passage immediately following, Ockham says that the goodness of love of God is separable from the love. This part of Ockham's view, although provocatively illustrated, does not go beyond du Four's view. But Ockham also holds a particularly strong version of the thesis that God is essentially good: "The divine wisdom is the same as the divine essence in all the ways in which the divine essence is the same as the divine essence; so also for divine goodness and justice. Nor does any distinction exist there within the nature of the thing, or even nonidentity" (Ockham 1970, p. 17). Divine goodness and divine justice are not *parts* of the divine essence: they *are* the divine essence.[10] God's essence is to be perfectly good, which is the same essence as to be perfectly just.

Because he holds both the separability thesis and the thesis that God's essence is to be perfectly good, Ockham must think that God's being perfectly good has no necessary consequences concerning goodness in the created world. There is nothing overtly contradictory about Ockham's position, but it leaves unexplained how God's perfect goodness makes any difference to the goodness of the created world. Because God's will determines what counts as created goodness and because God's perfect goodness places no constraints on what he could have willed for creatures, Ockham's position assigns God's perfect goodness to a kind of explanatory limbo.

Perhaps it is worse than that. Consider Ockham's case of creaturely hatred of God. The separability thesis implies that it could have been good. Ockham's voluntarism entails that hatred of God is good if and only if God wills it so. In the idiom of possible worlds, there is a world, w, in which God wills that creaturely hatred of him is good. However, according to Ockham, God is essentially and perfectly good, or perfectly good in all possible worlds. Thus in w a perfectly good God wills that hatred of him is good. Consider now the following claims. (A) If

10. For a discussion of this and related issues concerning Ockham's version of God's simplicity, see Marilyn McCord Adams 1987, vol. 2, ch. 21.

hatred of God is good, then one ought to hate God. (B) If God is perfectly good, then God is the proper object of love. (C) If God is the proper object of love, then one ought to love God. (D) There is no possible world in which a perfectly good God confronts his creatures with a fundamental moral dilemma not of their own making. If (A) is true, then the creatures in *w* ought to hate God. If (B) and (C) are true, then the creatures in *w* ought to love God. Thus the creatures in *w* are confronted with a fundamental moral dilemma not of their own making, contrary to (D). The set of claims (A)–(D) is thus inconsistent with the separability thesis and the thesis that God's essence is to be perfectly good.

An Ockhamite can avoid the inconsistency by denying the necessity of any of claims (A)–(D). A conservative deployment of that strategy would be to maintain that one or more of the claims is an impostor. A less conservative deployment would be to deny that there are any necessary truths or—what is not the same—to assert that even if there are necessary truths, God's omnipotence is such that he can alter them. Neither du Four nor Ockham regarded this as a possibility. A third version of voluntarism, then, the *ne plus ultra* of voluntarism, is to claim that God's power extends even over the realm of necessity. Descartes is notorious for having asserted this thesis. In his reply to the sixth set of objections to his *Meditations* he explicitly embraces theological voluntarism with regard to both goodness and necessity.

As for freedom of will, it is in God in a way far different from [the way it is] in us. For it is repugnant to the will of God not to have been indifferent from eternity to all that has taken place or ever will take place, because nothing good or true, or nothing that is to be believed or done or omitted can be imagined, for which the idea will have been in the divine intellect before God's will decides that it be of that kind as a result. Nor do I speak here of priority of time; it is not even prior in order, or nature, or the processes of reason (*ratione ratiocinata*), as they say—namely, such that that idea of good impelled God to choose one thing over another. Certainly, to give an example, he did not thus will to create the world in time because he saw it to be better thus than if he created from eternity; nor did he will the three angles of a triangle to be equal to two right angles because he knew it could not be made in another way, etc. On the contrary, because he willed to create the world in time, it is thus better so than if he had created from eternity, and because he willed the three angles of a triangle necessarily to be equal to two right angles, therefore now this is true and cannot be made in another way; and so on for the rest. (Descartes 1904, pp. 431–32)

2. Rationalism, *ou l'optimisme*

Whether he knew about the fourteenth-century Franciscans or not, Leibniz did know about Cartesian voluntarism. The following passage from Leibniz's *Discourse on Metaphysics* gives some of his reasons for rejecting it.[11]

I am far removed from the sentiments of those who maintain that there are no principles of goodness and perfection in the nature of things, or in the ideas that God has of them; and that the works of God are good only for the formal reason that God has made them. For if this were so, God, knowing that he is the author of them, would not have to regard them afterwards and find them good, as Holy Scripture testifies. . . . In saying that things are not good through any principle of goodness, but solely through the will of God, one destroys, without thinking of it, it seems to me, all the love of God and all his glory. For why praise him for what he has done if he would be equally praiseworthy in doing everything to the contrary? Or where will his justice and his wisdom thus be, if there remains only a certain despotic power, if the will takes the place of reason, and if, according to the definition of tyrants, that which pleases the most powerful is by that very fact just? Besides, it seems that every will presupposes some reason for willing and that this reason is naturally anterior to the will. This is why I find, moreover, this expression of some other philosophers utterly strange, who say that the eternal truths of metaphysics and geometry—and as a consequence, also the principles of goodness, justice, and perfection—are only the effects of the will of God. Instead, it seems to me that they are the consequences of his understanding, which does not depend on his will, any more than his essence [does]. (Leibniz 1875–1890, vol. 4, pp. 427–28 [sec. 2])

According to Leibniz, God surveyed all the infinitely many possible worlds and chose to create the actual world because it was the best. When God looked out over the possible worlds, what exactly did he see? Why did he choose the best?

Near the end of the essays on theodicy Leibniz presents a lengthy epitome of Lorenzo Valla's dialogue, *De libero arbitrio*.[12] Leibniz applauds Valla's attempt to show that God's *foreknowledge* of free, sinful actions is compatible with their being free and sinful. He is less happy,

11. For further discussion of Descartes's voluntarism, see Leibniz, *Essais de Théodicée*, paras. 180–86; Leibniz 1875–1890, vol. 6, pp. 221–28.
12. A translation of this work can be found in Cassirer, Kristeller, and Randall 1948, pp. 155–82.

however, with what he perceives to be agnosticism on Valla's part about whether God's *will* to create sinful persons is compatible with their being solely responsible for their sins. Leibniz adopts the artifice of writing a continuation of Valla's dialogue in order to show that such agnosticism is ill founded. The continuation recapitulates many of Leibniz's characteristic doctrines, including the claims that to create a person different in any respect from the way that person is would be not to create *that* person, but some counterpart, and that the existence of certain sinful actions is an essential component of the world's being the best world possible. The continuation gives us a strikingly vivid picture of how Leibniz conceived the possible worlds to be ordered in terms of value. The Goddess Pallas guides Theodorus, a high priest, through the realm of possible worlds:

The apartments [each "apartment" corresponds to a possible world] arose in a pyramid; they became ever more beautiful as one ascended towards the apex, and they represented more beautiful worlds. One arrived at last in the supreme ["apartment"] that completed the pyramid, and which was the most beautiful of all; for the pyramid had a beginning, but one did not see the end; it had an apex, but no base; it went on increasing to infinity. It is because (as the Goddess explained) among an infinity of possible worlds there is the best of all; otherwise God would not have decided to create any of them. But there is not any of them which does not have yet less perfect [worlds] beneath it: that is why the pyramid descends forever to infinity. (*Essais de Théodicée*, paragraph 416; Leibniz 1875–1890, vol. 6, p. 364)

The imagery of a "great chain of being" might have suggested that the possible worlds are arranged on a scale of betterness like the links on a chain. We might have supposed, to put it more formally, that the better-than relation displays *connectivity* in the realm of all possible worlds,[13] that is, for any two possible worlds, w and u, either w is better than u or u is better than w. Leibniz's choice of a pyramid, however, suggests a different picture.

We may distinguish the semantic properties of the better-than relation from its substantive conditions. The semantic properties are just those properties that would be assigned to the relation on any reasonable interpretation of it. With respect to any domain, but relativized to the realm of possible worlds, the semantic properties include:

13. There are familiar Cantorian worries about the notion of the realm or set of all possible worlds. No harm will come to us in this essay if we indulge ourselves in the supposition that the notion makes sense.

Irreflexivity: No possible world is better than itself.
Asymmetry: For any possible worlds, *w* and *u*, if *w* is better than *u*, then *u* is not better than *w*.
Transitivity: For any possible worlds, *w*, *u*, and *v*, if *w* is better than *u* and *u* is better than *v*, then *w* is better than *v*.

The substantive conditions of the better-than relation are those conditions Leibniz imposes on it with respect to the realm of possible worlds, and which give rise to his vision of an infinitely descending pyramid of possible worlds:

Seriality: Every possible world is better than some other possible worlds.

Seriality is that feature in virtue of which the pyramid has no base.

Maximality: Some possible world is better than every other possible world.

Maximality plus Asymmetry entail that *only* one world is better than every other possible world. For suppose that there are *two* worlds, *w* and *u*, such that *w* is better than every other possible world and *u* is better than every other possible world. Then *w* would be better than *u* and *u* would be better than *w*. But that contradicts Asymmetry. So Maximality, eked out with Asymmetry, is that feature in virtue of which the pyramid has a genuine apex, not merely a highest plateau.

Comparability: For any possible worlds, *w* and *u*, either *w* is better than *u* or *u* is better than *w* or *w* and *u* are equal in value.

Comparability differs from connectivity in that the former but not the latter allows two or more possible worlds to be equal in value, thus allowing a chain structure to become a pyramid structure.

The imagery of a pyramid accommodates comparability for a reason that Leibniz could fully appreciate.[14] Consider any locus of points within a pyramid such that each point is the same distance from the apex as every other point in that locus. There will be infinitely many such loci in a pyramid, each one of which will be composed of infinitely many points.[15] If the pyramid is Leibniz's pyramid of possible worlds, any

14. One of Leibniz's favorite illustrations of the law of continuity is the rotation of a plane through a cone, thus generating the conic sections. See Leibniz 1875–1890, vol. 3, pp. 51–52; vol. 4, pp. 375–76.
15. "The infinity of possibles, however great it be, is not greater than that of the wisdom of God, who knows all the possibles. One can even say that if this wisdom does

such locus will be a family of possible worlds, each world of which is no closer to and no further from the apex, the best possible world. It is natural to think, then, that in Leibniz's pyramid of possible worlds, each member of such a family is no better (no closer to the best possible world) and no worse (no further from the best possible world) than any of its confreres. Under these circumstances it is natural to suppose that all the worlds in the family are equal in value.

It is Leibniz's contention that God's choice to create the best possible world was not made accidentally. God created the best world because he knew that it was best. But how exactly is his knowing connected to his choosing? Could he have chosen another, suboptimal world? Was his choice necessitated?

Leibniz thinks it important to distinguish between metaphysical necessity and moral necessity. God's selecting the best possible world was not metaphysically necessitated because there were other possible worlds that might have existed, insofar as nothing internal to them disqualified them from existing.[16] God's selecting the best possible world was morally necessitated, yet to act with moral necessity is to act from a reason or motive that "inclines without necessitating."[17] This notion has understandably troubled some of Leibniz's critics.[18] I think that the best way to make it intelligible, if it can be made intelligible, is along the following lines.

---

not surpass the possibles extensively—since the objects of the understanding could not go beyond the possible, which in a sense is only [the] intelligible—it surpasses them intensively, because of the infinitely infinite combinations that it makes of them, as well as the thoughts it has of them. The wisdom of God, not content to embrace all the possibles, penetrates them, compares them, weighs them one against the other, in order to rate the degrees of perfection or of imperfection, the strong and the weak, the good and the bad. It goes even beyond the finite combinations; it makes an infinity of infinites of them, that is to say, an infinity of possible orders of the universe, each of which contains an infinity of creatures. And by this means the divine wisdom distributes all the possibles that it had already envisaged separately into so many universal systems that it compares again between them. And the result of all these comparisons and reflections is the choice of the best from among all these possible systems, which wisdom makes in order to satisfy goodness fully; this is precisely the plan of the actual universe. And all these operations of the divine understanding, although they have among themselves an order and a natural priority, always occur together, without their having among themselves a temporal priority" (*Essais de Théodicée*, para. 225; Leibniz 1875–1890, vol. 6, p. 252).

16. The "internal" contents of (a concept corresponding to) a possible world exclude facts about its comparative status with respect to other worlds. See in this connection Adams 1982, pp. 246–48.

17. The major texts are in *Essais de Théodicée*, paras. 45, 201 (Leibniz 1875–1890, vol. 6, pp. 127–28, 236–37); *Abregé de la Controverse reduite à des Argumens en forme*, obj. 8 (ibid., vol. 6, pp. 385–87); and Leibniz's fifth paper to Clarke, paras. 7–10, 76 (ibid., vol. 7, pp. 390–91, 409).

18. See, e.g., Lovejoy 1936, pp. 173–74.

Suppose that you are confronted with a situation of choice in which you know that you can either make one deserving person happy or just as easily make each of two deserving people as happy as the one would have been. The morally necessary thing to do in such a situation is to make the two people happy instead of just the one. The notion of moral necessity is a deontic notion, not in the sense of specifying what your duties or obligations are to other people—you may have no relevant duties or obligations to the people in question—but rather in the sense of specifying what is required of you if you are to behave as a fully rational agent. You can choose to make just the one person happy, but so to choose, in the imagined circumstances, is to choose in a rationally suboptimal way. To the extent to which you are guided by the ideal of a fully rational agent, you are inclined but not necessitated to make rationally optimal choices. The more closely your life emulates that of a fully rational agent, the more ingrained this inclination will be, and the more unthinkable you will find it that *you*, constituted as you are, could choose in any other way.

God's nature is to be supremely knowledgeable, powerful, and good; for Leibniz the medley of these traditional attributes entails that God is a supreme rational optimizer. God's selecting the best possible world, then, was morally necessitated, not because he was duty-bound to create it, but because it is unthinkable that a being with his nature, a being beyond moral reproach, would do less than the best. "For as a lesser evil is a kind of good, a lesser good is likewise a kind of evil if it places an obstacle to a greater good: and there would be something to reprove in the actions of God if there had been a way of doing better."[19]

What is most troublesome about this approach is that moral necessity qua unthinkability seems to get promoted to logical necessity in the case of God. If God's choosing optimally flows from his nature, then, even though he was not duty-bound, he cannot have chosen suboptimally *without ceasing to be God*, which is impossible. Yet Leibniz regards God's choice of the best possible world as free; in fact, it is the expression of a perfectly free will. Leibniz's conception of freedom falls into a family, some of whose other prominent members include the opinions of Plato, Saint Anselm, Kant, and Hegel. The family resemblance resides in the notion that to act freely is to act rationally, with the corollary that insofar as an action is not validated by reason, it is unfree.[20] Leibniz's conception is that perfect freedom would be manifested in a being

---

19. *Essais de Théodicée*, para. 8; Leibniz 1875–1890, vol. 6, p. 107. See also *Discourse on Metaphysics*, sec. 3 (ibid., vol. 4, pp. 428–29).
20. I have discussed this notion of freedom somewhat more fully in Mann 1988.

whose will is subservient to a rational faculty that in itself is cognitively perfect, ignorant about nothing and subject to no mistakes. Such freedom is approximated by the good angels and the souls in bliss and achieved by God, even though it is characteristic of all these beings that they are less and less able to choose anything but the optimal outcome. It is a distinctive but disturbing consequence of this general conception of freedom that in the case of God, at least, an action can be both necessitated and free.

It is not hard to find criticisms of Leibnizian optimism. Voltaire made the character of Pangloss in *Candide* look foolish by having him continually aver, in the teeth of all sorts of moral evil, that all is for the best in the best of all possible worlds. And even if, as Alexander Pope maintained, all partial evil is universal good, it is not clear that theists need or want to enlist Leibniz's aid.[21] Leibniz has some defenses against these and other objections. It will deepen our understanding of his views if we examine some of the contentious areas.

The idea that some possible worlds are equal in value might seem to run contrary to two other features of Leibniz's philosophy, his Principle of Continuity and his denial of situations of rational equipoise.

When Leibniz discusses the Principle of Continuity, he typically illustrates it with examples that involve a linear ordering along a single dimension of change. For example, as one moves the second focus of an ellipse farther and farther away from the first focus, one generates a family of elongated ellipses, subsequent members of which come closer than any given difference to a parabola. It is a presupposition of this sort of example that no two ellipses could occupy the same position in the sequence of ellipses. When Leibniz applies the Principle of Continuity to hierarchies in nature, they form the same kind of linear ordering.

I think, therefore, that I have good reason for believing that all the different classes of being, whose union forms the universe, exist in the ideas of God (who has distinct knowledge of their essential gradations) only as so many ordinates of a single curve, where the totality of these ordinates does not allow the insertion of any others because that would indicate disorder and imperfection. Men are connected with the animals, these with the plants, and these again with the fossils, which will be connected in their turn with bodies that the senses and the imagination represent to us as perfectly dead and shapeless. Now, since the Principle of Continuity requires that, as the essential determinations of one being approach those of another, so all the properties of the former must gradually approach those of the latter, it is necessary that all the orders of

21. See Adams 1972.

natural beings form a single chain in which the different classes, like links, connect so closely the one to the other that it is impossible for the senses and the imagination to fix the precise point where any one begins or ends; all the species which border on or which occupy, so to speak, the regions of inflection and retrogression (of the curve) have to be equivocal and endowed with characters which belong to the neighboring species equally.[22]

One might have expected, then, that the possible worlds would also be "only so many ordinates of a single curve."

It is important to distinguish between what is essential to Leibniz's Principle of Continuity and what is solely an artifact of his illustrations of it. As a principle of change, the Principle of Continuity maintains that all changes are smooth, *legato*, continuous: as Leibniz puts it on several occasions, there are no leaps in nature. As a principle of order, it maintains that phenomena that admit of degrees of intensity have continua that are *dense*, that is, between any two instances of the phenomenon in question, there is a third instance, intermediate in intensity. Applied thus to the realm of possible worlds, the Principle of Continuity gives us this:

Continuity: For any possible worlds, w and u, if w is better than u, then there is a world, v, such that w is better than v and v is better than u.

The pyramid imagery that Leibniz invokes at the end of the essays on theodicy is compatible with this conception of continuity, since this conception does not rule out the possibility of there being two or more worlds of equal value. Continuity in itself does not impose a strict linear hierarchy on a degreed phenomenon. The illusion that it does is encouraged by the use of examples—the locus of points constituting a line, or the conic sections generated by the rotation of a plane through a cone—in which the linear hierarchy is induced by properties of the example independent of its continuity.

However, the supposition that there are two or more worlds of equal value seems to run afoul of Leibniz's repeated denial of the possibility of "indifference of equipoise," that is, his denial of genuine cases of choice in which there is no reason to choose one alternative over the other. If there were two worlds equal in value, then God would have no

22. Translation in Mates 1986, p. 147. The original text is printed in Guhrauer 1846, vol. 2, p. 32, which I have not been able to consult. A translation of a longer excerpt containing the text is contained in Leibniz 1896, pp. 712–14. See also Lovejoy 1936, pp. 144–45; and, for what appears to be the same text in a different context, Leibniz 1951, pp. 184–88.

reason to create the one over the other. Under those circumstances, he would create neither world.[23] "A perfect indifference is a chimerical or incomplete supposition," Leibniz says at one point, taking it to be ruled out by the Principle of Sufficient Reason.[24] Any alleged case of choice in a situation of equipoise is always incompletely understood or incompletely specified: there is always a reason or cause that tips the balance in favor of one alternative, even though the reason or cause be unknown to us.[25] There cannot be cases like Buridan's ass, who, situated equidistant between two bales of hay, dies of starvation. For if the universe were divided by a plane bisecting the ass, the two half-universes would not be exactly the same (*sic!*).[26] In reply to Samuel Clarke's assertion that God could make two cubes of matter perfectly equal and alike, and then arbitrarily assign them to different spatial locations, Leibniz says:

The resolutions of God are never abstract and imperfect, as if God decreed first to create the two cubes, and then decreed separately where to put them. Men, limited as they are, are capable of proceeding thus: they resolve upon some thing, and then they find themselves perplexed about the means, about the ways, about the places, about the circumstances. God never takes a resolution about the ends without taking [a resolution] at the same time about the means and all the circumstances. And I have even shown, in the *Theodicy*, that properly speaking, there is only a single decree for the universe in its entirety, through which he has resolved to admit it from possibility to existence. Thus God will not choose a cube without choosing its place at the same time, and he will never choose between indiscernibles.[27]

It is possible to save the letter of Leibniz's views if not the spirit. The pyramid imagery implies that there are possible worlds that are equal in value. God would have no reason to choose one over the other. However, all the worlds that are equal in value to some other worlds are *suboptimal*. Even if God had no reason to choose among the members of a family of equal rank, the question of his choosing under those circumstances is made nugatory by the fact that for any of these subopti-

23. "When two incompatible things are equally good, and both in themselves and in their combination with other things, the one has no advantage over the other, God will not produce either of them" (Leibniz's fourth paper to Clarke, para. 19; Leibniz 1875–1890, vol. 7, p. 374).

24. Leibniz 1875–1890, vol. 2, pp. 56–57.

25. *Essais de Théodicée*, paras. 35, 46; Leibniz 1875–1890, vol. 6, pp. 122–23, 128.

26. *Essais de Théodicée*, para. 49; Leibniz 1875–1890, vol. 6, pp. 129–30.

27. Leibniz's fifth paper to Clarke, para. 66; Leibniz 1875–1890, vol. 7, p. 407. The reference to the *Essais de Théodicée* appears to be to vol. 6, pp. 147–48 (para. 84).

mal worlds, there is a better world that could be chosen. What is important to Leibniz's vision is that the best possible world is unique: there is no room at the apex for two or more worlds.

Why should we think that the Maximality condition could be true, that is, that it could be the case that there is a best possible world?[28] Might it not be that for any world whatsoever, there is a greater, ad infinitum? At times Leibniz espouses what seems to be a hard-line response. If there were no best possible world, God would not have had sufficient reason to create anything, and so he would not have created anything. But he did create something; therefore, what he created is the best.[29]

The ingredients are in place, however, for a more positive answer. Leibniz claims that 'the best possible world' is unlike 'the perfect creature.'[30] The former but not the latter has an *intrinsic maximum*. A phenomenon that admits of degrees has an intrinsic maximum if and only if the phenomenon has some degree that *cannot* be surpassed. Given Kripke-like views about the necessary connection between heat and molecular motion, it follows that coldness has an intrinsic maximum— the complete absence of molecular motion—but (as far as I know) heat does not. What seems to be crucial in the identification of cases of intrinsic maxima is that there be some way of specifying the maximum other than saying 'the degree such that no greater degree is possible.' In the first section of the *Discourse on Metaphysics* Leibniz asserts, in effect, without providing such a specification, that omniscience and omnipotence are the intrinsic maxima, respectively, of the degreed phenomena of knowledgeability and power.[31]

I conjecture that Leibniz may have thought that there is an intrinsic maximum to the better-than relation among possible worlds because he thought that the best possible world is the maximal expression of two dimensions. It is "the simplest in hypotheses and the richest in phenomena."[32] If this is what Leibniz had in mind, then it is incumbent on him to do two things. He must give grounds for believing that simplicity of hypotheses and richness of phenomena are themselves no-

28. See in this connection Norman Kretzmann's "A Particular Problem of Creation: Why Would God Create This World?" (Chapter 9 in this volume).

29. *Essais de Théodicée*, paras. 8, 195–96, 226; Leibniz 1875–1890, vol. 6, pp. 107, 232–33, 252–53. See Blumenfeld 1975.

30. *Essais de Théodicée*, para. 195; Leibniz 1875–1890, vol. 6, p. 232.

31. Leibniz 1875–1890, vol. 4, p. 427. See Mann 1975 for a defense of the claim that the divine attributes have intrinsic maxima.

32. *Discourse on Metaphysics*, sec. 6; Leibniz 1875–1890, vol. 4, p. 431. See also *Principes de la Nature et de la Grace, fondés en raison*, para. 10; ibid., vol. 6, p. 603.

tions that have intrinsic maxima, and that they can be maximized simultaneously, that is, that the maximization of one does not entail the diminishment of the other. Leibniz attempts to address the latter issue,[33] but, to the best of my knowledge, not the former.

I have tried to convey a sympathetic picture of Leibniz's views because I think that some criticisms of them miss the mark. As any shrewd voluntarist would tell you, the real problems lie deeper.

3. Incommensurability and Simplicity

Voluntarists would object to two central features of Leibniz's picture. To say that possible worlds have *any* value ranking—let alone a *complete* one—prior to and independent of God's choice is to reject the claim that God's will is utterly sovereign over the realm of value. And to say that God's choice is determined by his knowing which world is optimal is just to say that his will is *determined*; the attempt to subsume freedom under rational optimality cannot blink that fact. Leibniz depicts God as a big spender in the bazaar of possible worlds. The availability and the prices of the merchandise are beyond his control, and his purchasing behavior is distressingly predictable.

Put that way, of course, Leibniz's picture is not very attractive. But then neither was the portrait of the willful tyrant offered by the voluntarists. So the choice between voluntarist and rationalist can seem to be Hobson's choice.

Where the fourteenth-century Franciscans see a desert landscape of equally valueless possible worlds in the absence of God's will, Leibniz discerns a pyramid structured by the Seriality, Maximality, and Comparability conditions on the better-than relation. We need not accept either alternative. I wish to sketch one among many other accounts that might be given. Against the voluntarists, the account maintains that there are necessary substantive conditions on the better-than relation as it applies to possible worlds. Against Leibniz, it denies one of the substantive conditions he favors, namely, Comparability. Recall that Comparability is the thesis that for any two possible worlds, either the one is better than the other or vice versa or the two are equal in value. Comparability may seem to be more secure than either Seriality or Maximality, but it is important to see what happens if one denies it. Comparability is false if there are pairs of worlds such that the better-than

---

33. See *Essais de Théodicée*, para. 208; Leibniz 1875–1890, vol. 6, p. 241.

relation does not order them: neither is the one better than the other nor are they equal in value. Let us call such worlds *incommensurable*. So Comparability is false if there are incommensurable possible worlds.[34]

It would be more plausible to believe that some possible worlds are incommensurable if it is plausible to believe that the actual world is, so to speak, incommensurable with itself, that is, if there are incommensurable values in the actual world. The adage about apples and oranges can be construed as an expression of such a belief, but a deflationary interpretation of the adage would have it that our predicament is merely epistemological: it is just very hard to make the right value discriminations between apples and oranges. I want to consider another kind of example, one that will tell in favor, I hope, of genuine incommensurability over epistemological uncertainty.

Suppose that Teresa is torn between two callings. She is a very talented soprano whose voice could enrich the operatic world. She also believes that the dying poor have a claim on all her energies. She perceives that she is not able to pursue both callings; she can follow one wholeheartedly only to the detriment of the other. She could pursue the operatic career and dedicate her earnings to a hospice, but that in itself would be to decide in favor of the one calling over the other. She could decide to follow the operatic career until she is fifty and then devote the remainder of her life to the dying poor. So to decide, however, will only compound the problem that may trouble Teresa the most. Which calling should she follow, the operatic career, the vocation of caring for the dying poor, or the mixed sequential life?

It redounds to Teresa's credit that she should anguish about the decision. I suggest that it misdiagnoses and oversimplifies her plight to describe it as induced by lack of knowledge about which kind of life is really better. There is something fantastic to the claim that following the operatic career is better than living the life of caring for the dying poor, or even the more modest claim that *Teresa's* following an operatic career is better than her caring for the dying poor. But there is something equally fantastic about the reverse ranking, or the claim that the two callings are exactly equal in value. The fantasy resides not so much in one's pretending to know what one does not know as it does in one's thinking that there is a correct answer to the question "Which life is the best life to live?" or even to the question "Which life is the best life for Teresa to live?" To deny the appropriateness of the question is not to

34. A fortiori, incommensurability among possible worlds will falsify connectivity, the stronger condition that orders possible worlds in a chain rather than a pyramid.

deny that Teresa can make mistakes about the decision. She may believe wrongly that she will have the courage and perseverance to live out whichever life she chooses, or she may believe mistakenly that she will be unhappy and regretful no matter which choice she makes.

One can dig in one's heels and say that there really is a correct answer. Many consequentialists and deontologists will join forces on this point. Some will claim that all apparent incommensurabilities dissolve in the universal solvent of the Principle of Utility. Others will appeal to a detailed schedule of rank-ordered duties that they allege to discover attached to the Categorical Imperative. And there are still others. I cannot prove that they are wrong, but I am not thereby obliged to agree with them. Nor in denying what they assert am I thereby committed to holding that there is never a correct answer in related cases. I think that there is a correct answer to the choice between a life of caring for the dying poor and a life singlemindedly devoted to becoming a champion crossword puzzle solver.

Consider now two possible worlds. We may suppose that they are identical in their histories up to the time at which Teresa makes her decision. In one of them—call it the Opera World—she decides to pursue the operatic career, and she becomes one of the outstanding sopranos of her generation. In the other—the Hospice World—she decides to care for the dying poor; her life sets an inspirational example. Suppose that the two worlds are as similar in their subsequent histories as they can be, consistent with Teresa's different choices. (There are other possible worlds corresponding to other scenarios.) Must it be the case that one of them is better than the other or that they are equal in value?

I want to suggest that it is plausible to think that the Opera World and the Hospice World are incommensurable with each other. Perhaps the most tempting alternative to incommensurability, given the similarity of the two worlds, would be to say that they are equal in value. But that alternative is implausible. For to say that they are equal in value is to ignore or deny the anguish and the momentousness attached to Teresa's decision. Moreover, consider a third possible world, the Opera-Plus-*Tosca* World, which is maximally like the Opera World except that in the Opera-Plus-*Tosca* World, Teresa gives one more performance of *Tosca* than she gives in the Opera World. It seems clear that ceteris paribus, the Opera-Plus-*Tosca* World is better than (and thus commensurable with) the Opera World. If the Opera World and the Hospice World were equal in value, then it would follow that the Opera-Plus-*Tosca* World is better than the Hospice World. But that seems absurd: imagine someone saying "If only Teresa had given one more performance, she would have vindicated her choice of career." A natural inclination is to say in reply that no number of additional performances would make a difference, not because the performances are worthless, but rather because the value they have is categorically different from the value realized in caring for the dying poor.[35]

Instead of desert landscapes or pyramids, think of possible worlds as falling into clusters. *Within* each cluster Comparability holds; each world is either better than or worse than or equal in value to every other world in the cluster. (This kind of comparability within a cluster is compatible with the individual worlds' having *internal* incommensurable values.) So, for example, the Opera World and the Opera-Plus-*Tosca* World are within the same cluster. *Between* any two clusters Comparability does not hold. The Opera World and the Hospice World are in two such clusters. Not even an omniscient being can rank two worlds from two different clusters, for there is nothing on which to base the ranking.[36]

The idea that possible worlds fall into partitioned clusters is not apt to win Leibniz's assent. As we have seen, the Principle of Sufficient Reason is already haunted by the specter of possible worlds in rational equipoise, whose exorcism comes about through their being suboptimal. The denial of Comparability poses an even greater threat. For let us suppose that either the Opera World or the Hospice World (it makes no difference which) is the actual world. The actual world, according to Leibniz, is the best of all possible worlds. We would expect the actual world to be better than all other possible worlds. But if the actual world is the Opera World, then it is *not* better than the Hospice World, not because it is tied with the Hospice World, but because the better-than relation is not defined between the two worlds. (Parallel remarks hold in the case in which the actual world is the Hospice World.) At the most, the actual world could only be the best possible world in the cluster of worlds to which it belongs. It might be that the Opera World and the Hospice World are optimal members of their respective clusters, but if

35. For further discussion of incommensurability, see "The Fragmentation of Value" in Nagel 1979, pp. 128–41; Griffin 1986, pp. 75–92; and Raz 1986, pp. 321–66.

36. Possible-worlds semantics for modal logic distinguishes several modal systems by means of the formal properties of the *world-accessibility* relation. For example, in a system as strong as S5 the world-accessibility relation is reflexive, symmetric, and transitive. Even so, the relation is not connected in S5. There could be partitioned equivalence classes of possible worlds. Within each such class every world would be accessible to every other world, but between any two such classes the world-accessibility relation would not hold. See Hughes and Cresswell 1968, p. 67, n. 39; and Forbes 1985, pp. 14–15.

they are incommensurable, what reason could God have for choosing to create the one over the other? It would have to be either on rational grounds other than betterness or on no grounds at all. The latter alternative would horrify Leibniz. So would the former, since Leibniz ties the notion of betterness so closely to the notion of rationality of choice. But *pace* Leibniz, sometimes the rational thing to do is choose randomly, especially in cases of equipoise or incommensurability.[37]

Consider the following argument on behalf of Leibniz. It is possible for A to be commensurable with B and with C even though B and C are incommensurable with each other. Apples and oranges may be mutually incommensurable, but they are both better than (and thus commensurable with) persimmons. Possible worlds might fall into partitioned clusters, but the best of all possible worlds would be a world better than (and thus commensurable with) every other world in every cluster. The best possible world is, after all, the world richest in phenomena. What better sign of its richness than that it be so full of so many goods that it is a candidate—in fact, a winner—in every cluster of worlds of incommensurable goods?

It follows on this argument that neither the Opera World nor the Hospice World can be the best of all possible worlds, since they are incommensurable with each other whereas the best possible world must be commensurable with every other world. The consequence of this observation, suitably generalized, is that if anyone is ever confronted with a choice between incompatible and incommensurable alternatives, then the world is not the best possible. Since Leibniz is committed to the view that this world is the best possible, it follows that no one is ever confronted with a choice between alternatives that are both incompatible and incommensurable. People like Teresa are often confronted with incompatible alternatives. In every such case, then, the alternatives must be commensurable. Thus the Opera World and the Hospice World are commensurable after all. In short, the argument works only by smuggling Comparability back in. Incommensurability is the bane of Leibniz's ideal of God as the great, rational optimizer.

The picture of possible worlds forming clusters is no more pleasing to voluntarists than it is to Leibniz. A thesis about the incommensurability of some possible worlds is quite different from the voluntaristic thesis that possible worlds are valueless apart from God's will. Moreover, given the ways in which the identities of possible worlds are fixed, it seems clear that if the Opera-Plus-*Tosca* World is better than the

37. See Mann 1988.

Opera World, it is necessarily better, and that if the Opera World and the Hospice World are incommensurable, then they are necessarily incommensurable. If these are necessary truths, then it seems that not even God could have altered them. Ockhamite voluntarists would object to these claims by denying that there are any necessary truths about values. Cartesian voluntarists could allow for the existence of such necessary truths and insist that nevertheless God could have altered them.

There is a third alternative that attempts to capture what is tempting about voluntarism and its rival, objectivism, regarding the status of necessary truths. It maintains that there are necessary truths, including necessary truths about values, that God could not have altered them, but that even so, God's will is causally responsible for them. A being can be causally responsible for something that that being could not have avoided. But in such a case, one might protest, the being does not act freely. So it is natural to assume that the third alternative avoids Ockhamite and Cartesian voluntarism only by denying complete freedom to God, thus curtailing God's sovereignty. On the other hand, objectivists will suspect that if God's will is responsible for the necessary truths, then they are not genuinely necessary. Both assumptions, I suggest, are premature.

In insisting on the primacy of God's will, voluntarists portray God's will as primordial, conditioned by nothing, having no content necessary to it, capable of flailing out in any direction it chooses, setting up all the rules, including, according to Descartes, the rules of logic. In contrast, Leibniz's depiction of God's creative choice depends on a will that is constrained by the dictates of divine reason, which in turn is constrained by the structure of the possible worlds. In both cases, God's will and God's reason or understanding are conceived of as separate faculties or modules of the divine mind. The disagreement then centers on which faculty takes precedence over the other. We have seen that the effect of proposition 163 in the Condemnation of 1277 was to issue a license to voluntarists.

It is hard to resist the speculation that the condemnation of proposition 163 was directed against Saint Thomas Aquinas,[38] although Aquinas's discussion of the relation between human intellect and will is more complex than the doctrine condemned in proposition 163.[39] In applying itself to will versus intellect in general, however, proposition 163 obliterates a distinction that is crucial to Aquinas's thought. Divine in-

38. See Wippel 1977, pp. 192–93, n. 54.
39. See *ST* Ia.82.3–4; Thomas Aquinas 1980b, p. 305.

tellect and will are related very differently from the way in which human intellect and will are related.

In us, in whom power and essence are distinct from will and intellect, and intellect in turn distinct from wisdom, and will distinct from justice, something can be in [our] power that cannot be in a just will or in a wise intellect. But in God power, essence, will, intellect, wisdom, and justice are the same. Whence nothing can be in the divine power that cannot be in his just will and in his wise intellect.[40]

Humans are constituted in such a way that their wills are distinct from their intellects, but in God, will and intellect are identical. Aquinas relies here on the doctrine of God's *simplicity*, which maintains that God has no parts or components of any kind. The doctrine makes for tough metaphysical sledding.[41] But if, as I think, it is a defensible doctrine, then it has a striking application in the present context. From Aquinas's point of view, asking the question "Which takes priority, God's will or God's intellect?" is like asking the question "Which is larger, 2 + 2 or 4?" 'The will of God' and 'the intellect of God' do not refer to two separate faculties in God. They are rather two ways of referring to the same divine activity, picking out, from our point of view, two aspects of that activity. If we wish to stress the sovereign, independent, creative aspect of God's activity, then it is appropriate to describe it as his willing or commanding. If we wish to point to the wisdom of God's activity, then it is appropriate to refer to it as his knowing or directing.[42]

Voluntarists and rationalists are thus engaged in a debate that presupposes something that Aquinas would deny. The divine activity that constitutes the creation of this world is an expression of a perfectly sovereign will and a perfectly wise intellect or—what amounts to the same thing—a perfectly sovereign intellect and a perfectly wise will. Aquinas's appeal to simplicity, in addition to sidestepping the deadlock between voluntarist and rationalist, also helps to make sense of the third alternative concerning the relation between God and the necessary truths. God cannot have willed (or have known) otherwise than that 2 + 2 = 4: that is entailed by the fact that '2 + 2 = 4' is necessary. But that '2 + 2 = 4' is itself necessary depends on God's willing (or knowing) it to be necessary. '2 + 2 = 4' has no status independently of God's willing (or knowing) activity and does not impose any external

---

40. *ST* Ia.25.5.ad1; Thomas Aquinas 1980b, p. 226.
41. For further discussion of it, see Mann 1982, Morris 1985a, and Mann 1986.
42. *ST* Ia.25.5.ad1; Thomas Aquinas 1980b, p. 226.

constraint on that activity. '2 + 2 = 4' is part of the expressive content of a perfectly wise will, as are all the other necessary truths. The fact that God cannot have willed (or have known) otherwise than that 2 + 2 = 4 poses no threat to his freedom. On the doctrine of divine simplicity, the activity by which God wills (or knows) that 2 + 2 = 4 is identical with God's nature or essence. Thus his not willing (or knowing) that 2 + 2 = 4 would be tantamount to his not willing (or knowing) himself as a perfectly sovereign, omniscient being. *Pace* the Cartesians, not even God can do that. Why not? Not because of some constraint from a realm of implacable necessary truths outside the will (or knowledge) of God, but rather simply because God is his willing (or knowing) himself, which is his willing (or knowing) his nature and all its entailments.

Cartesian voluntarists seek to exalt the sovereignty of God by claiming either that there are no necessary truths to bind him or that there are no *necessarily* necessary truths.[43] One cannot show that their view is contradictory, for any such attempt will rely on principles of inference and modality that Cartesians will insist beg the question. One can show, however, in Oscar Wilde fashion, that the Cartesian view is not naughty but *boring*. Suppose one says that if their view is true, then there is something that God cannot do, namely, institute a realm of necessary truths (or necessarily necessary truths; no harm is done if we ignore this variation from now on). The best he can do is determine a realm of contingent truths. Cartesians will respond that it is not that God *cannot* institute necessary truths; it is just that he *does* not. Now the ennui begins to set in. Consider the claim that God does not institute any necessary truths: is the claim itself necessarily true or contingently true? If it is necessarily true, then, contrary to what the Cartesians advertised, there is at least one necessary truth; moreover, one that says of itself that it was not instituted by God. Is the claim then contingently true? If it is, then God could have instituted necessary truths: to deny this would be to revert to the position that the claim in question is, after all, necessarily true. So the Cartesian position is that God chose to create a world in which there are no necessary truths instead of a world in which there are necessary truths. If we ask the question why, we will be told, I presume, that God had no reason or that if he did, we do not know what it is. We might ask the question why it *seems* to us that there are necessary truths, hinting along the way that God is, on this Cartesian account, guilty of deception. Wily Cartesians have the resources to

43. This distinction is not merely verbal. See Mann 1989 and the references cited therein for further discussion of it. The distinction makes no difference to my present argument.

answer this question. And in a pinch there is always a final trump card that they can play. They can claim that it may be that the actual world has no necessary truths and has all sorts of necessary truths at the same time, citing with approval Emerson's bon mot that a foolish consistency is the hobgoblin of little minds. The important point is that although Cartesians can say all this and more—What, by their lights, could they be *debarred* from saying?—we are not obligated to believe them, especially since we have an account of God's sovereignty vis-à-vis the necessary truths that does not lead to Cartesian excess.

If the ability to institute genuinely necessary truths is a part of God's sovereignty, then we should not be surprised to find that there are necessary truths about goodness, badness, and betterness. That happiness is good, that hatred of God is bad, and that some values are incommensurable with others are surely all candidates. If God is simple, and if there are possible worlds that are necessarily incommensurable, that fact will necessarily be known and willed by God. Voluntarists will be mistaken in assuming that God's will has priority over his intellect and that God could have willed just any constellation of values to be good. Leibniz will be mistaken in assuming that God's intellect has priority over his will, that there must be a best of all possible worlds, and that we live in it. Genesis 1:31 says that the world God created was very good, not that it is the best.[44]

[Appendix]

[Vital du Four, *Quaestionum de rerum principio*, Question 4, article 1, section 3, translated from the text in Du Four 1891, p. 307:]

God does not act from the necessity of will, as Avicenna says: that is, [in such a way] that knowledge comprehends a better way of producing, but the right and perfect will, with at least the necessity of immutability, always adheres to reason and knowledge; and through that the will of God immutably wills to produce things according to the better way that his knowledge perceives.

On the contrary, whenever the will or another power is moved per se toward some formal object, having a necessary relation (*habitudinem*) to that thing, then it is moved necessarily toward those things that have an

44. I thank Scott MacDonald and Derk Pereboom for comments on an earlier version of this essay. Support for research was provided by a University of Vermont Summer Research Fellowship for 1988 and a National Endowment for the Humanities Fellowship for College Teachers and Independent Scholars for 1988–89, hereby gratefully acknowledged.

essential relation to that object, and it is not moved necessarily toward those things that have an accidental relation (*ordinem*) to that object. For example, our intellect, perceiving the natural truth of certain first principles, naturally perceives the conclusions that are necessarily drawn from them, but not those that have an accidental relation, or [are related] contingently, to those principles.

This is evident in men who are able to sense (*in viribus sensitivis*), since [the senses] naturally perceive those things that are essentially connected to the proper objects at the same time as [they perceive] the objects. So touch, in sensing what is warm, at the same time perceives what is lukewarm. But they do not perceive at the same time what is accidentally connected; so if what is warm is white or sweet, they do not perceive those.

Wherefore since the will of God is not moved per se except to an adequate good, which is his goodness, it is not moved necessarily to what it wills, except for all those divine and solely intrinsic qualities that are essentially connected to his goodness. But every creature has an accidental relation to the goodness of God, because nothing is added to his goodness from them, just as a point adds nothing to a line. Thus with no necessity does he will something extrinsic. He does nothing except insofar as he wills and just as he wills; thus he makes or produces nothing extrinsic of necessity.

CHAPTER 11

Metaphysical Dependence, Independence, and Perfection

Thomas V. Morris

1. Introduction

There seem to be numerous ways to conceive of God, many different starting points and procedures for exploring the nature of divinity, even for traditional monotheists who stand within the circle of Jewish or Christian faith. Two such avenues of theological reflection have risen to a sort of prominence among contemporary philosophers of religion. We might say that one concentrates on being, whereas the other focuses on goodness. What we can refer to as "creation theology" takes as its starting point and touchstone for conceptual elucidation the idea of God as creator of the world, ultimate cause of such beings as there are in this universe. The alternative procedure now commonly known as "perfect-being theology" centers on the conception of God as the greatest possible, or maximally perfect, being, an individual who has the greatest possible array of properties it is intrinsically good to have. Historically associated with these two approaches to thinking about God are, respectively, cosmological and design arguments, on the one hand, and ontological arguments, on the other.

In recent years perfect-being theology has come to attain something of an ascendancy in the practice of many philosophical theologians, although it has not been much discussed in theory as a discrete conceptual approach, preferable in principle to its rivals.[1]

---

1. This is discussed in the introduction to Morris 1987a.

The relative popularity of perfect-being theology nowadays can seem a bit puzzling to an onlooker, and to many who prefer the practice of creation theology. To see why, we need to contrast a bit more these two conceptual approaches.

A great many contemporary philosophers who are attempting to delve more deeply into the idea of God are themselves religious believers, Jews or Christians. And as such, it would seem that they would have a preferential regard for any theological method that is clearly revelational, drawing upon the religious scriptures accepted as revelational by their own religious communities. And practically all of these philosophers are people who have high regard for modern, scientific methods of thought. On both these scores, it can seem as if creation theology is preferable to perfect-being theology. For the procedure of creation theology is to start with the idea of God as creator of the world. And if it is asked why this particular idea should be the source and control for our articulation of a detailed conception of deity, the answer can be quite straightforward: This is the most prominent and most fundamental idea of the biblical revelation, from the opening lines of the Book of Genesis and throughout all the rest. The idea of God as our creator is arguably the central religious idea in Christianity and Judaism. And the deepest religious thought concerning God as savior of the world seems to presuppose this conviction of creaturely dependence. So the core of creation theology seems to have the most impeccable of revelational credentials.

Moreover, it can be employed in a way that looks closely akin to well-known procedures of scientific inference. Creation theology can be explanatory in thrust. That is to say, the basic idea of God as creator can be derived from revelation, or as the metaphysical correlate of a Schleiermachian sort of religious experience, but it is most often developed, explicated, and enlarged in an explanatory vein. All those properties are attributed to God that are deemed necessary for his existence and creative activity to be able to provide an explanation for why there is a physical universe at all, and for why it has many of the most basic features we find it to have. And this, of course, seems to be just the sort of basic procedure of explanatory postulation so common in the theoretical sciences.

Perfect-being theology, on the other hand, seems to begin and to proceed very differently. It can appear to be both nonrevelational and nonscientific, the worst sort of purely speculative enterprise. For it begins with a single idea that is not to be found fully formed in any religious scripture, and it further develops by a method that can seem utterly subjective. The idea, of course, is the claim that God, as the greatest possible, or maximally perfect, being exemplifies an unsurpassable array of great-making properties, or perfections, properties intrinsically good to have, properties that enhance the valuational and metaphysical stature of their bearer. From this one highly abstract idea, perfect-being theology moves toward a more detailed conception of divinity by means of value intuitions and logic. In order to develop the root idea of maximal perfection, the perfect-being theologian must consult his own intuitions about what properties are intrinsically good to exemplify, about what arrays of such properties are possibly exemplified, and about which such arrays are better or greater than others. The final conception is generated primarily by value intuitions and is regulated largely by considerations of logical consistency. But whence comes that root idea of God as a greatest possible being? And is such a procedure of development reliable?

The questions that can be raised about perfect-being theology are many. But it has become increasingly evident in recent years that objections to this direction of theological reflection can be answered, and furthermore that this procedure has many grounds on which it can recommend itself.[2] It can be viewed as perfectly consonant with the main thrust of biblical revelation, a helpful interpretive guide for reading that revelation, and as an idea whose implicit biblical rooting is only enhanced by its intrinsic intuitive appeal. The intuitions that undergird it can be viewed as a form of general revelation necessary for the reception and understanding of any special revelation. It can be used to integrate other theological approaches and can be drawn upon to solve apparent problems of logical consistency in traditional theological claims. Yet, it is still held suspect by many. In this essay I hope to move toward eliminating two possible sources of resistance to it as the overall best method for basic theistic conceptual explication. I first indicate a way in which it need not be thought to be a rival of creation theology after all, and I attempt to block one implication widely thought to follow from perfect-being theology, a metaphysical view embraced by a few philosophers but, rightly I suspect, renounced by more. If I can come anywhere close to accomplishing these two tasks, I will have made some small progress toward overcoming some very common worries about perfect-being theology, and I will have been able to display some

2. This is argued in Morris 1984a and 1987b, and in Schlesinger 1988.

important theological views about metaphysical dependence, independence, and perfection.

2. Creation and the Proof of Perfection

Perfect-being theologians are wont to claim that their view of God as "that than which no greater can be conceived" is the pinnacle of traditional theism. It is thought by most to be the loftiest realization of ultimate truth ever vouchsafed to human minds. But it has been considered by many other philosophers standing in the tradition of Hume to be nothing more than the ultimate expression of the most obsequious human proclivity for fatuous flattery and appeasement.

Many theists themselves are sometimes ambivalent about the concept of divine perfection. Is the ascription of perfection to God in the last analysis anything more than, in McTaggart's memorable phrase, "a piece of theological etiquette"? Is it a super-added bit of what Matthew Arnold called "over-belief"? Or, on the contrary, can it be seen as a natural capstone to independent, metaphysically serious theistic convictions, an idea in which the theistic metaphysical vision actually culminates?

I think it can be shown that a number of traditionally held, serious, and important theistic metaphysical beliefs together entail that God is a greatest, even *the* single greatest, possible being, beliefs that severally can be independently plausible to theists who may otherwise feel uncertain about the explicit claim of maximal perfection for God. In particular, these are beliefs typically endemic to creation theology. So if the derivation I have in mind is successful, a new logical link will be forged between these two otherwise apparently rival approaches to the concept of God.

We'll now proceed by examining a simple deductive argument whose premises will be the metaphysical claims that can be independently plausible to theists of a traditional bent, especially those inclined toward creation theology, and whose conclusion will be the claim of perfection for God. Each premise is briefly commented upon.

(1) There is a singular font of all existence, a being who, necessarily, would be the ultimate cause of anything else that might exist.

This first premise expresses the core of the theistic vision of reality as rooted in and dependent upon a singular creative source. This is the vision motivating creation theology and captures its central idea. It is intended to entail the necessity of the divine being's existence as well as that being's responsibility for the possibility of any other being's existence.

(2) There are objective values to things (objects are greater or lesser in overall value as determined by the properties they have).

The theist's universe is one in which there are values that are objective, and in which things have intrinsic as well as extrinsic value. Intrinsic value can be thought of here as something like greatness in metaphysical status or stature. The commitment expressed in this second premise is a belief that in neo-Platonist times had all the luster of the self-evident, but that independently of that context has had significant intuitive appeal for great numbers of theists. From the perspective of a text central to the creation theologian, God looked upon his creation, and "God saw that it was good" (Genesis 1:10, 12, 18, 21, 25, 31). It should be pointed out, however, that the truth of (2) here need not be taken necessarily to entail that *all* things have intrinsic value, only that at least some things have such objective value. And, as in the case of many such metaphysical propositions, (2) is meant to be taken as a necessary truth, a feature that will be rendered explicit in the next premise:

(3) Necessarily, everything that has intrinsic value is value commensurable with its ultimate cause.

This of course goes well beyond the mere claim that things have objective value. Whether rooted in the common assumption that, at least at some level, like begets like, or in some deeper metaphysical intuition sometimes expressed in an imitation model of property exemplification tied in with the vision expressed by (1), this premise is a proposition strongly endorsed by many theists upon reflection. In order to be able to appreciate the plausibility it has had for many theists, it is important to realize that (3) does not entail the more controversial thesis that all things, or even all things with intrinsic value, are value commensurable with all other such things.[3]

(4) Necessarily, no effect exceeds its ultimate cause in metaphysical stature or value.

3. The lack of such an entailment is argued in Morris 1984a.

(4) introduces explicitly the equivalence between value and metaphysical stature or status. This is intended to function as an illuminating redescription of intrinsic value in this context.[4] The substance of the premise is an attempt to capture in a metaphysical principle of unrestricted generality the sort of insight behind the well-known, homely adage that "no stream rises higher than its source." This is, of course, akin to principles commonly endorsed in medieval times that no effect can have more reality than its cause (a kinship that becomes evident with the eighth premise of this argument).

(5) The value or metaphysical stature that the ultimate source of all existence has, it necessarily has.

The purpose of this premise in the argument, a proposition that, again, many theists would endorse upon reflection but that alone entails nothing concerning the degree of God's greatness, is merely to block a process-theology conception of divine perfection, a perspective not consonant with traditional theism. According to the process theologian (like, for example, Charles Hartshorne), God's being the greatest possible being consists in his being unsurpassable in greatness by any other being, but also in his continually increasing in greatness. God, on that view, is surpassable, but only by himself. Changes in divine greatness are ruled out by (5), and so the process conception is ruled out by (5). Now, it is true that something weaker than (5) would suffice to rule out the process-theology conception of deity. It would be enough for this purpose to claim that the value that the ultimate source of all existence has it cannot have begun to have and cannot cease to have.[5] But I think that any arguments that might be produced to motivate and defend this weaker claim could be incorporated into an argument for the stronger claim as well, which thus better, or more fully, articulates the relevant theoretical and intuitive considerations operative at this point.

(6) God is the ultimate source of all existence.

The function of (6) is merely to explicitly identify God as the being spoken of in (1), the controlling identification of creation theology. God is the First Cause, the font of all else. And once this identification is made, it follows that

---

4. On this, see Morris 1987b.
5. In modal categories I have explicated elsewhere, it has its value with the modality of strong immutability. See Morris 1984b.

(7) God is a greatest possible being.

For by (2) there are things in existence with intrinsic value that, by (1) and (6), are caused to exist by God. From (3) they are value commensurable with God, and from (4) we get that none of them is greater than God. Likewise, consider the possibility of some object's existing that does not as a matter of fact now exist. If it were to exist, either it would have intrinsic value or it would not. If it did not have intrinsic value, it could not be greater than God in intrinsic value. If it did have intrinsic value, then by (1), (3), and (6) it would be both dependent on and commensurable with God, but by (4) it thus could not be greater than God. And by adding (5), we have it that the intrinsic value, the metaphysical greatness, that God as a matter of fact has could not possibly be surpassed by any being, himself included. Thus we have it that, in a fully traditional sense, God is a greatest possible being.

But most theists who stand in the tradition of perfect-being theology have wanted to claim a bit more, that God is not only *a* greatest possible being, but that he is, in addition, *the* (single) greatest possible being, necessarily unequalled as well as unsurpassable. One way we could get this extra claim would be to employ a well-known ancient philosophical notion and articulate the traditional metaphysical claim that

(8) Necessarily, value is a function of plenitude of being,

and to join this with the proposition akin to (4) that

(9) Necessarily, no effect equals its ultimate cause in plenitude of being,

from which, together with previous premises, it will follow that

(10) God is the greatest possible being.

It is in such a way as this that the central claim of maximal perfection for God can be deductively derived from metaphysical premises that severally can have a plausibility, intuitive or otherwise, for traditional theists, independently of whether they have previously made explicit judgments about (7) or (10).

Premises (1)–(6), along with (8) and (9), display components of a theistic world view whose theological capstone is (10). It is in this sense, and only this sense, that the displayed propositions, along with their connections, add up to a proof. The sort of argument we have as a result is not guaranteed to prove anything to anyone. Indeed, many theists who endorse (7) or (10) might find one or more premises of the argument a good bit more dubious than either conclusion they are taken to support. Obviously, however, there is a legitimate conceptual and metaphysical function that the giving of such a proof can accomplish. It can serve to explicate logical connections between distinct theses that serve to partially constitute a metaphysical view, and it can display important relations holding between a particular, questioned claim and other supporting claims that need not, and indeed may not, themselves be objects of the same query. In this case, I think that the construction of such an argument clearly can serve to display tight connections between the claim of perfection for God and other beliefs traditionally endemic to a theistic world view centering on the idea of creation. Insofar as these other claims are serious pieces of metaphysics and not mere gestures of theological etiquette, the claim of perfection can deductively claim these credentials and inherit its proper place in this category of serious theistic philosophy. And insofar as the logical links displayed here do hold, we can conclude that perfect-being theology, rather than existing as a completely rival alternative to creation theology, can be seen to be deductively connected with it. If the heuristic procedures contained in perfect-being theology help us to proceed beyond the bounds established by the revelational and explanatory moorings of creation theology, I think it both can and should be looked upon by the creation theologian with favor.

3. Perfection, Independence, and Simplicity

Many perfect-being theologians present their focal idea as one having significant theoretical virtue. It is often said to be an especially simple and powerful idea that can serve to order and unify a great deal that is said about God. In his recent book *New Perspectives on Old-Time Religions* George Schlesinger has for example claimed that there are "two basically different views concerning the nature of Divine attributes." He goes on to explain:

One way of looking at characteristics like omnipotence, omniscience, omnibenevolence, omnipresence, immutability, immateriality, and so on, is to see them as independent, unique properties exemplified by God. The alternative is to think of them as tightly interconnected, each one of them being merely a different aspect of one and the same primary property, namely, absolute perfection.[6]

There is a unity and simplicity about perfect-being theology that is theoretically attractive. But some perfect-being theologians have claimed that perfection entails a kind of austere metaphysical simplicity that seems to go far beyond that unity discerned by Schlesinger, the kind formulated in the somewhat obscure medieval doctrine of divine simplicity. This is the general thesis that within the being of God there is absolutely no composition or ontological complexity such as is to be found in created objects.

According to the idea of divine simplicity, as it has been defended in recent years, God is without spatial parts, temporal parts, and the sort of metaphysical complexity that would be involved in his exemplifying properties ontologically distinct from himself. Thus, when it is said that God is omnipotent and that he is omniscient, for example, the simplicity theorist holds that what is meant is not that there are these properties distinct from God which he exemplifies, but rather that God himself is identical with omnipotence, that he is metaphysically indistinct from omniscience, and so on.[7]

Those who endorse divine simplicity typically see it as following from the idea of God as a perfect being.[8] Yet, not all perfect-being theologians agree that perfection entails or in any way requires this extreme sort of metaphysical simplicity. In fact, the issue over divine simplicity may mark the single greatest division among those who attempt to work within the parameters of perfect-being theology. As such, it is an issue of considerable importance for contemporary philosophical theology.

I think that it is important for us to examine one central facet of this issue, the prominent claim of representative simplicity theorists that perfection entails or in some way requires simplicity through considerations of aseity, or the ontological independence that characterizes God. It is this often repeated claim that will now be my focus. First, because it is the main link alleged to hold between perfection and the doctrine of divine simplicity. Second, because the ontological independence of God is an important consideration for any theist who endorses the idea of God as absolute creator of all else. If we can block the claim

6. Schlesinger 1988, p. 5.
7. Variants of the doctrine of divine simplicity are examined in Morris 1985a.
8. See, e.g., Stump and Kretzmann 1985, and Mann 1983.

that perfection entails, by way of aseity, the most extreme form of divine simplicity, we can eliminate one pervasive contemporary worry about perfect-being theology on the part of many philosophers and theologians who either claim not to understand this form of alleged simplicity, or find it so bizarre as to render incredible any theological view entailing it.

In a recent article William E. Mann has said of the doctrine of divine simplicity (DDS):

> The DDS . . . is motivated by the consideration that God is a perfect being, and that qua perfect, he must be independent from all other things for his being the being he is. . . . If God himself were composite, then he would be dependent upon his components for his being what he is, whereas they would not be dependent upon him for being what they are.[9]

It seems clear from the context within which these claims appear that Mann intends these considerations to preclude God's having spatial or physical parts, temporal parts, and in addition the sort of ontological complexity that would ensue from his exemplifying numerically distinct properties. It seems to be Mann's contention that it is aseity, or the sort of ontological independence required by perfection, that rules out God's having any of these sorts of composition or complexity. The argument turns upon the identification of aseity as a great-making property or ingredient of perfection, a fairly uncontroversial judgment among perfect-being theologians, and on the claim that any of these forms of composition or complexity would involve an asymmetrical dependence relation incompatible with divine aseity.

The doctrine of divine simplicity meant to be supported in this way can be thought of, as indicated, in terms of three component theses, which for convenience we can label 'spatial simplicity,' 'temporal simplicity,' and 'property simplicity.' Let us postpone for a moment the examination of Mann's claims as applied to spatial composition and temporal composition, and focus first on what is the most hotly controversial, the most unusual, and the most distinctive component of the doctrine of divine simplicity, the thesis of property simplicity. If divinity, or God's nature, is thought of as encompassing numerous, ontologically distinct properties such as omnipotence, omniscience, and aseity, then God's dependence on, for example, the property of omniscience is apparently supposed to follow from some such consideration

9. Mann 1983, p. 268.

as its being the case that if God did not have that property, it would follow that he would not be what he is (namely, omniscient), or, assuming as perfect-being theologians typically do that he is essentially omniscient, if omniscience did not exist or were not exemplified, God would not exist.

But consider the following: if God has the property of omniscience essentially, and he necessarily exists, as perfect-being theologians also standardly hold, then omniscience itself has essentially the property of being exemplified by God. If God did not exist, the property of being exemplified by God would not be exemplified and, arguably, would not itself exist, and since this is by supposition an essential property of the property of omniscience, then omniscience would not be what it essentially is, which is to say that the property of omniscience would not itself exist. If such a form of *per impossibile* reasoning gives us any sort of dependence of God on omniscience, it seems equally well to give us a similar dependence of omniscience on God, contrary to what Mann thinks.[10] The argument was that if God were composite in the somewhat unusual sense relevant to, and precluded by, property simplicity, a dependence relation would obtain with God on the receiving end only, and that this would be inconsistent with his perfect ontological independence. But the supporting form of reasoning we have examined fails to establish a solely one-way dependence relation. If God is composite or complex in virtue of having properties and he thus in some sense depends on his properties, they, too, seem to depend in at least the same sense on him.

But is any such dependence of a sort that would impugn or be incompatible with the sort of ontological independence almost any perfect-being theologian would want to ascribe to God? Mann may think that anything that can be called dependence is incompatible with divine aseity. But I think not. From God's having a property, it need not be thought to follow that he is in any unacceptable way ontologically dependent on that property. All that we have seen is apparently that between God and any metaphysically distinct property exemplified by him, a mutual logical dependency will exist, which consists in nothing more than the mutuality of the necessity of the relata on each side of the relation. Nothing clearly follows from God's merely having properties, and having properties essentially, which need be taken to impugn

10. Of course, this argument, which derives from Morris 1987b, takes there to be such a property as the property of being exemplified by God, an assumption that Mann could reject. But as we shall come to see, a dependence of the property of omniscience on God can be derived from perfect-being theology without any such assumption.

the ontological independence rightly expected of divine perfection. So, contrary to the view of simplicity theorists such as Mann, the thesis of property simplicity does not seem to be required by perfect-being theology, by way of considerations of independence.

4. Simplicity, Composition, and Dependence

Does any of the three components of the doctrine of divine simplicity follow from the conception of God as a perfect being, by way of a connection between composition and dependence? We can make an initial attempt to answer this question simply and straightforwardly by directing our attention first to the component thesis that has been the least controversial among theists of a traditional bent, the thesis of spatial simplicity.

The thesis of spatial simplicity is just the claim that God does not have spatial, or physical, parts. The doctrine of divine simplicity can be fairly plausible at this point, as many theists have claimed that God is incorporeal, regardless of their views on the idea of divine simplicity as a whole. But our question here is whether spatial simplicity can be argued plausibly to follow from perfect-being theology by way of considerations of divine independence. Consider, then, the claim that spatial composition involves an asymmetrical dependence of the whole on its parts.

With certain sorts of spatially composite wholes, the existence of such a dependence relation is altogether obvious. Take, for example, the case of an ordinary clock. A clock depends on its parts in a sense in which they do not depend on it: From the fact that all, or even any, of the parts of the clock are broken, it will follow that the clock is broken, but from the fact that the clock is broken it will not follow that all of the parts of the clock are broken. The parts severally have an integrity not dependent on the integrity of the clock, but the clock does not have this lack of dependence on its parts. Under such conditions it does seem quite clear that we have a substantive asymmetrical dependence relation of some sort connected with composition.

It will be useful to display precisely the conditions under which we have found spatial composition in the case of a clock to involve a dependence of the whole on its parts, and to do so in the form of a conjunctive proposition whose truth entails the obtaining of the dependence relation:

S (1) If all the spatial parts of a clock were to be damaged or destroyed, it
would follow that the clock would be damaged or destroyed, but
(2) it is not the case that if the clock were to be damaged or destroyed, it
would follow that all its spatial parts would be damaged or destroyed.

And of course the conditions displayed by S could be generalized to
give us conditions under which, and presumably, under which alone,
any spatially composite whole will depend asymmetrically on its parts.
If an S-type proposition holds true of every spatially composite whole,
then, assuming divine aseity to preclude God's standing on the dependent end of any such asymmetrical relation, it seems to follow that God
is not a spatially composite whole. That is to say, the thesis of divine
spatial simplicity does appear to have support from perfect-being theology, through considerations of divine independence.

Let us then turn our attention to the apparently analogous notion of
temporal simplicity, the idea that God is without any temporal parts
whatsoever. We need to ask whether temporal composition always involves an asymmetrical dependence of the whole on its parts incompatible with the sort of independence ascribed to God by perfection considerations, and thus whether perfect-being theology entails temporal
simplicity by this route.

What is a temporal part? Do all temporal objects have temporal
parts? If so, is this a necessary truth? Is a temporal part an extensionless
temporal point, and thus without duration or "temporal spread"? Or is
it, rather, a duration of some positive magnitude? These are difficult
questions, but for our purposes we can think of temporal parts as being
time slices of objects, slices of any size, so to speak, from extensionless
instants to lengthy durations not exceeding in length the careers of the
objects whose parts they are. Although there could be serious metaphysical controversy over the precise ontological status of temporal
parts, let us simply grant here for the sake of argument that all temporal objects have temporal parts, and that this is a necessary truth
about temporality.

Granting all this, we may now go on to ask whether, as in the case of
spatial composition, we find that temporal wholes appear to depend
asymmetrically on their temporal parts. Let us return to our example
of an ordinary clock. A clock is a temporal as well as a physical, spatially
extended object. We can focus our question by asking whether a clock
stands in the sort of asymmetrical dependence relation to its temporal
parts that it stands in to its spatial parts.

To arrive at an answer, we can construct a proposition isomorphic with S, laying out parallel dependence conditions for the case of temporal composition:

T (1) If all the temporal parts of a clock were to fail to exist, it would follow that the clock would fail to exist, but
(2) it is not the case that if the clock were to fail to exist, it would follow that all its temporal parts would fail to exist.

The problem with T is that, of course, it is false. T(1) is true, but the second conjunct, T(2), is false. If a particular clock never were to have existed, no temporal parts of it would have existed either. That just follows from the ontology of the relation between any temporal object and its temporal parts. What T(2) says to be false is true, and so T as a whole is false. Temporal wholes just do not stand in an asymmetrical dependence relation to their temporal parts. Although it is true that the best way to prevent a temporal whole's existing through a time is to prevent one of its parts from existing at that time, it is also true that the best way to prevent a temporal part of an object from existing at a time is to prevent that object from existing at that time. This is symmetry at its best.

We thus do not find the same ground for claiming temporal simplicity to be required by perfection as we found in the case of spatial simplicity. Contrary to what Mann seems to think, it does not look as if there is a simple entailment connection between temporal simplicity and perfection through a consideration of divine aseity.

But let us look again for a moment at property simplicity. This component of the doctrine of divine simplicity lays it down that God does not exemplify properties ontologically distinct from himself. The aseity motivation for property simplicity is the claim that if God did stand in this sort of relation, there is an analogous and somewhat extended sense in which he would be a composite whole standing in an asymmetric dependence relation on his parts, in this case, his properties. The assumption here is that the metaphysics of property exemplification is analogous in one important respect to the metaphysics of spatial composition: that it involves a one-way ontological dependence relation, the sort of relation that would be incompatible with divine aseity.

To test this assumption, we can once again return to our example of a clock, a clear case of an object that exemplifies properties distinct from itself, and we can again construct a proposition isomorphic with S, this time laying out parallel dependence conditions for the metaphysics of property exemplification:

P (1) If all the properties of a clock were to fail to be exemplified, it would follow that the clock would fail to exist, but
(2) it is not the case that if the clock were to fail to exist, it would follow that all its properties would fail to be exemplified.

The most salient feature of P is that it seems quite clearly to be true. Even apart from the standard semantics of counterfactuals with impossible antecedents, P(1) is true. And surely P(2) is as well. Despite the possible failure of the round clock on the wall ever to exist, it is obviously the case that a great many of its properties could still be exemplified—the property of being round, and the property of hanging on the wall, for example. What P(2) says is not the case is not the case, and so P as a whole is true. The clock depends on its properties in a way in which its properties do not depend on it.

As in the case of proposition S, the conditions displayed by P could be generalized to give us conditions under which, and under which alone, any object exemplifying properties distinct from itself will depend asymmetrically on those properties. If a P-type proposition holds true of every object exemplifying properties distinct from itself, then, assuming divine aseity to preclude God's standing on the dependent end of any such asymmetrical relation, it seems to follow that God is not an object exemplifying properties distinct from himself. That is to say, the doctrine of divine property simplicity does appear to have support from perfect-being theology, through considerations of divine independence.

But this seems to create a problem, for it appears clearly to contradict the rebuttal to Mann I have offered earlier. There I concluded that it does not follow from God's having properties that he stands in an asymmetrical dependence relation on those properties. A generalization of P, however, would indicate otherwise. And worse yet, if a P-type proposition can launch a successful defense of property simplicity from aseity considerations, it will not be the case merely that Mann is *mostly* right in his claim that divine independence requires divine simplicity— he will be *completely* right: It will not just be the case that aseity requires spatial and property simplicity but not (because of the falsehood of T) temporal simplicity; aseity will secure all three forms of simplicity, and thus the doctrine as a whole. For if property simplicity is true, so is temporal simplicity, regardless of the inability of any T-type proposition to capture or display that truth. If God exemplifies no properties distinct from himself, then he exemplifies no temporal properties. But it is a necessary truth that an object with no temporal properties has no temporal parts—it is not a temporal object at all. So if because of composition and dependence considerations divine aseity requires spatial and property simplicity, through the latter it requires temporal simplicity as well. If this argument works, it vindicates Mann's claim that perfection requires the doctrine of divine simplicity through requiring divine ontological independence. So, what are we to make of this?

In his *Monologion* Anselm wrote in defense of divine simplicity that[11]

everything composite needs for its existence the parts of which it is composed; and what it is it owes to its parts. For through them it is whatever it is; whereas what they are they are not through it; and so it is not at all supreme. Hence, if the Supreme Nature were composed of many goods, then what holds true of everything composite would also have to hold true of it.

I want to suggest that Mann, following Anselm, has assumed an ontological egalitarianism that no perfect-being theologian should accept, especially insofar as he endorses a central idea emphasized by creation theologians. It is in general not the case that whatever is true of created objects is true of God; likewise, it is not the case that whatever is true of composition and complexity in the case of created objects must be true of any composition and complexity in the case of the creator as well. At least, this is what I want to argue.

Consider the God-transform of P:

GP (1) If all the properties of God were to fail to be exemplified, it would follow that God would fail to exist, but
(2) it is not the case that if God were to fail to exist, it would follow that all God's properties would fail to be exemplified.

I submit that from the perspective of any enlightened perfect-being theology, or for that matter, from the perspective of any ontologically thoroughgoing theism—any theism according to which God is necessarily the creator of anything that might exist distinct from himself—GP is different from P in an interesting and important way: It is false.

The perfect-being theologian can grant the truth of GP(1), whether from considerations about the standard semantics of counterfactuals

11. Anselm 1974, pp. 26–27.

with impossible antecedents or, preferably I think, from considerations about the intrinsic metaphysical content of the conditional. But it seems clear to me that a plausible perfect-being theology, or any thoroughly theistic metaphysic that sees God as necessarily the font of all existence, will decisively reject GP(2) as false. What GP(2) says not to be the case clearly is the case from any such perspective, and not merely because we have once again a counterfactual with an impossible antecedent. On the most exalted conception of deity, the conception with which we are working here, if God were, *per impossibile*, to fail to exist, nothing else would exist either: nothing would exist to exemplify any of those properties that would have been God's, and, moreover, none of those properties themselves would exist to be exemplified.[12] If it is objected that this is an impossible consequence, it can be pointed out that from the theological perspective being assumed, so is the consequent of GP(1). Both conditionals, however, can be evaluated independently of the consideration of the metaphysical impossibility of their antecedents and consequents—they can be assessed with respect to the metaphysical propriety of the connection in each case between antecedent and consequent, on the basis of the intrinsic conceptual or metaphysical content of the conditional. From such a point of view GP (1) comes out true but GP(2) comes out false, rendering GP as a whole false.

In any ontology in which everything distinct from God depends on him for its existence, composition and complexity relations into which God enters will be importantly different from composition and complexity relations holding among created objects. Asymmetrical ontological dependence relations obtaining among the latter will not hold in the same way among the former. It is only through failing to see some of the most important metaphysical implications of a thoroughly theistic ontology, an ontology with God as the source of all existence distinct from himself, that such a perfect-being theologian as Anselm could assume that whatever holds true of composition and complexity in the creaturely realm would also hold true of composition and complexity on the side of God. If there is any substantive sense in which God depends on his properties, it will also be true that his properties depend, and depend in a deeper ontological sense, on him.[13] Thus, God will never be on the receiving end only, so to speak, of an ontological dependence relation.

12. The ontological commitments underlying this claim are explicated in Morris and Menzel 1986.
13. This sort of view is defended in Morris and Menzel 1986, and obliquely in Morris 1985b.

If the doctrine of property simplicity cannot after all derive support from perfect-being theology by way of aseity considerations, then a derivation of temporal simplicity by this route is also blocked. But what of spatial simplicity? Its derivation from aseity by way of the generalization of an S-type condition seemed in good order. But consider directly the application of this sort of condition to God. Supposing God to be a spatially composite whole, we get:

GS (1) If all the spatial parts of God were to be damaged or destroyed, it would follow that God would be damaged or destroyed, but
(2) it is not the case that if God were to be damaged or destroyed, it would follow that all God's spatial parts would be damaged or destroyed.

GS looks both bizarre and difficult to assess if we are attempting, as in the case of GP, to bring to bear on this assessment the relevant metaphysical features of a thoroughly theistic ontology. Perhaps it could be argued that GS seems to be just as strong a candidate for truth as our original S, its bizarreness aside, and that this just shows that spatial composition in the case of deity is incompatible with the dependence relations to be found in a thoroughgoing theism. In this case, spatial simplicity would follow from divine aseity.

But consider the following: In the case of the clock, S is true just in case another proposition S* is true:

S* (1) If all the spatial parts of a clock were to have failed to exist, it would follow that the clock would have failed to exist, but
(2) it is not the case that if the clock were to have failed to exist, it would follow that all its spatial parts would have failed to exist.

And likewise, we should expect GS to be true only if the analogous proposition GS* is true:

GS* (1) If all the spatial parts of God were to have failed to exist, it would follow that God would have failed to exist, but
(2) it is not the case that if God were to have failed to exist, it would follow that all God's spatial parts would have failed to exist.

But it seems that GS* can be ruled out in much the same way that GP was ruled out. If God is absolute creator of everything distinct from himself (everything neither identical with, nor partially and essentially composing, him), then the nonexistence of God would entail the nonexistence of all spatial objects whatsoever, which is an entailment denied by GS*(2), rendering this conjunct of GS*, and thus the whole conjunctive proposition of which it is a part, false. But if, as in the case of S and S*, GS is true only if GS* is, we must conclude from the falsity of GS* that GS is false as well, despite any possible appearances to the contrary. And if both GS* and GS are false, then we do not after all have here any grounds for thinking that spatial composition in the case of God would involve any substantive asymmetrical dependence relation incompatible with divine aseity, and thus for thinking that the thesis of spatial simplicity is required in this way by perfect-being theology.

I do not want to give the impression that I think matters are altogether pellucid concerning the relation between the thesis of spatial simplicity and the claim of aseity for God. All that I would want here to insist upon is that from the perspective of the distinctively exalted conception of deity captured by perfect-being theology, we have not clearly seen any convincing reason to think that aseity entails any of the three component theses of the doctrine of divine simplicity. And we thus have seen no good reason to think that perfection requires simplicity in this way.

But perhaps other arguments could be forged to link simplicity to perfection by means of different mediating considerations. Some perfect-being theologians, for example, have reasoned that all physical objects suffer from defects or imperfections such as corruptibility and contingency, and thus that it follows from this that God, an altogether perfect being, is not a physical object, that he is incorporeal. And from the doctrine of divine incorporeality, it will follow directly that God is not a spatially composite whole.[14] Likewise, it could be argued that temporal simplicity follows from perfection by means of considerations of potentiality and actuality. Some perfect-being theologians, such as Aquinas, have claimed that in God there are no unactualized potentialities, and that this denial is motivated by a consideration of divine perfection. The argument would then move from the claim that being either temporally located or temporally extended necessarily involves having unactualized potentialities to the conclusion that God cannot be a temporal individual, and thus that the thesis of temporal simplicity is required by perfection. For the thesis of property simplicity, however, I see no other, even remotely plausible arguments from perfection.

Whatever one makes of the plausibility of these other possible links between perfection, on the one hand, and the theses of spatial and

14. For such arguments, see Wainwright 1974.

temporal simplicity, on the other, I think we can agree that the doctrine of divine simplicity as a whole is not clearly motivated from the side of perfect-being theology by aseity, by any other single consideration, or by any obvious set of considerations equally acceptable to perfect-being theologians. And if I am right about this, one major worry about perfect-being theology often expressed by contemporary philosophers can be dismissed.

5. Conclusion

The arguments of this essay have attempted to display unsuspected connections between perfect-being theology and the sort of creation theology that focuses on the notion of God as that being independent of the world on whom everything in the world is dependent. I have also sought to dispel the claim that certain other connections do hold between perfection, dependence, and independence, such as to incorporate the traditional doctrine of divine simplicity within the bounds of perfect-being theology. If my results hold, then perhaps the procedure of perfect-being theology as the main avenue for conceptually explicating the idea of divinity will have been made a bit more attractive to those who otherwise might resist it. The best philosophical theology may yet be one that both explains being with an eye on creation and navigates its conceptual way by the coordinates of goodness, absolutely perfect goodness.

Boethius's *De hebdomadibus*

*(How Can Substances Be Good in Virtue of the Fact That
They Have Being When They Are Not Substantial Goods?)*
Translated by Scott MacDonald

[Prologue]

Y'ou ask that I should set out and explain a little more clearly the
obscurity of that question from our hebdomads which concerns the
way in which substances are good in virtue of the fact that they have
being when they are not substantial goods.[1] <5> And you say that this
should be done because the method of writings of this sort is not known
to all. Now I myself am your witness how eagerly you have embraced
these things before. But I contemplate the hebdomads on my own for
myself and keep my thoughts in my memory rather than share them
with any of those who, out of perversity and impudence, permit nothing to be composed without jest and laughter. <11> Therefore, do not
object to the obscurities associated with brevity which, since they are a
faithful guardian of a secret, have the advantage of speaking only with
those who are worthy. For that reason I have put forward first terms
and rules on the basis of which I will work out all the things that follow,
as is usually done in mathematics (and other disciplines also).

5

10

15

[The Axioms]

[I.] <18> A conception belonging to the common understanding is a
statement that anyone approves once it has been heard. There are two

---

1. The Latin texts are Boethius 1978a and Peiper 1871. The line numbers from Rand's
text are given in angle brackets in the text of the translation. In preparing this translation, I have consulted the translations of Stewart, Rand, and Tester in Boethius 1978a,
Boethius 1981, and de Rijk's suggestions for translating the axioms in de Rijk 1987.

20 types of these. One type is common in the sense that it belongs to all men—e.g., if you propose: "If you take away equals from two equals, what remain are equals," no one who understands it denies it. The other type belongs only to the learned, even though it comes from such conceptions as belong to the common understanding—e.g., "Things

25 which are incorporeal are not in a place," and others that the learned but not the uneducated acknowledge.

[II.] <28> Being and that which is are different. For being itself does not exist yet, but that which is exists and is established when it has taken on the form of being.

30 [III.] <31> That which is can participate in something, but being itself participates in no way in anything. For participation comes about when something already exists; but something exists when it has assumed being.

[IV.] <35> That which is can have something besides what it itself is;

35 but being itself has nothing besides itself mixed into it.

[V.] <38> Being something *merely* and being something *in virtue of the fact that it has being* are different. For an accident is signified in the former case, a substance in the latter.

[VI.] <41> Everything that participates in being so that it exists

40 participates in something else so that it is something.[2] Hence, that which is participates in being so that it exists; but it exists so that it might participate in anything else whatever.

[VII.] <45> Every simple has its being and that which is as one.

[VIII]. <47> For every composite, being and it itself are different.

45 [IX.] <49> Every difference is discord, but likeness is to be sought. And what seeks another is itself shown to be naturally the same sort as that very thing which it seeks.

These things that we have set down to begin with, therefore, are enough. A careful interpreter of the reasoning will fit each one to its

50 arguments.

[The Question]

<56> Now the question is of this sort. Things which exist are good. For the common view of the learned holds that everything which exists tends toward good. But everything tends toward its like. Therefore, the

2. I follow de Rijk's reading (1987), omitting the *est*, with the best manuscripts, and emending *alio uero* to *aliquo*.

things which tend toward good are themselves good. <6o> But we   55
have to ask how they are good, by participation or by substance?

If by participation, they are in no way good in themselves. For what is
white by participation is not white in itself in virtue of the fact that it
itself has being. And the same applies to other qualities. <65> Therefore, if they are good by participation, they are in no way good in   60
themselves. Therefore, they do not tend toward good. But that was
granted. Therefore, they are not good by participation but by
substance.

Now for those things the substance of which is good, what they are
are good.[3] But that which they are they have from [their] being. <71>   65
Therefore, their being is good; and therefore, the being itself of all
things is good. But if [their] being is good, those things which exist are
good in virtue of the fact that they have being, and, for them, being is
the same as being good. Therefore, they are substantial goods because
they do not participate in goodness.   70

<75> But if being itself is good in their case, there is no doubt that
since they are substantial goods, they are like the first good. And hence,
they will be this good itself, for nothing is like it besides it itself. It
follows from this that all things which exist are God, which is an im-
pious claim. Therefore, they are not substantial goods, and hence   75
being is not good in their case. Therefore, they are not good in virtue
of the fact that they have being. But neither do they participate in
goodness, for then they would in no way tend toward good. Therefore,
they are in no way good.

[The Solution]   80

<86> A solution of the following sort can be offered to this question.
There are many things that, although they cannot be separated in
actuality, nevertheless are separated in the mind and in thought. For

---

3. The awkward English in this sentence reflects what seems to me to be Boethius's use
of painstakingly precise Latin terminology. The Latin text of the short argument in
which this claim occurs is: "*Quorum vero substantia bona est,* ID QUOD SUNT BONA SUNT; *id
quod sunt autem habent ex eo quod est esse. Esse igitur ipsorum bonum est.*" The emphasized
clause is the cause of the awkward English. Boethius's understanding of the expression *id
quod sunt* in this passage seems to me to be the following. He takes *id quod est* to signify the
essence of a thing ('that which it is' or 'what it is'—notice that this use of *id quod est* is
different from its use in the Axioms). Since many things share one essence, Boethius uses
id quod sunt ('that which they are,' 'what they are'). But there are many such essences, and
Boethius wants to claim that all of these are good; hence the last plural verb: *bona sunt.*

85 example, although no one separates a triangle (or other [geometric figures]) from the underlying matter in actuality, nevertheless, distinguishing it in the mind, one examines the triangle itself and its essential character apart from matter. Therefore, let us remove from our mind for a little while the presence of the first good. (That it does exist is, of course, certain on the basis of the view of the learned and the un-

90 learned and can be known from the religions of barbarian races.) <95> Therefore, having removed this for a little while, let us suppose that all things which are good exist. And let us consider how those things could be good if they had not flowed down from the first good.

From this point of view I observe that, in their case, that they are

95 good and what they are are different. For let one and the same good substance be supposed to be white, heavy, and round. Then that substance itself, its roundness, its color, and its goodness would all be different, for if these items were the same as the substance itself, heaviness would be the same as color, [color] as good, and good as heaviness.

100 <105> But nature does not allow this. Therefore, in their case, being and being something would be different; and then they would indeed be good but they would not have [their] being itself as good. Therefore, if they did exist in any way, then they would not be from the good and they would be good and they would not be the same as good; but, for

105 them, being and being good would be different.

But if they were nothing else at all except good, neither heavy nor colored nor extended in spatial dimension nor were there any quality in them excepting only that they were good, then it would seem that they are not [merely] things but the source of things. <115> Nor

110 would "they" seem [so], but rather "it" would seem [so], for there is one and only one thing of this sort that is only good and nothing else.

But because they are not simple they cannot exist at all unless that thing which is only good willed that they exist. Therefore, they are said to be good because their being flowed from the will of the good. For the

115 first good, because it is, is good in virtue of the fact that it is.[4] But a second good, because it flowed from that whose being itself is good, is itself also good. <124> But the being itself of all things flowed from that which is the first good and which is such that it is properly said to be good in virtue of the fact that it is. Therefore, their being itself is

120 good, for it is then in it [—that is to say, the first good].

4. In this sentence I translate the phrase *in eo quod est* with 'in virtue of the fact that it is' rather than the usual 'in virtue of the fact that it has being' because Boethius is talking here about the first good, which is simple and therefore cannot be said to *have* properties.

In this the question has been resolved. For although they are good in virtue of the fact that they have being, nevertheless they are not like the first good. For it is not just in any way whatever in which things have being that their being itself is good, but because the being itself of things cannot exist unless it has flowed down from the first being, i.e., the good. Therefore, [their] being itself is good and it is not like that from which it has being. <134> For [the first good] is good in virtue of the fact that it is in whatever way it is, for it is not anything other than good. But [a second good] could perhaps be good but it could not be good in virtue of the fact that it has being unless it were from [the first good]. For then it would perhaps participate in good; but they could not have being itself, which they would not have from the good, as good. Therefore, when the first good is removed from them in the mind and in thought, these things could not be good in virtue of the fact that they have being, even though they could be good. And since they could not exist in actuality unless that which truly is good had produced them, their being is good, and that which flowed from the substantial good is not like it. <146> And if they had not flowed from it, they could not be good in virtue of the fact that they have being, even though they could be good—this is because they would be both other than the good and not from the good, while that thing is itself the first good and is being itself and the good itself and being good itself.

[Objections and Replies]

And will it not also be necessary that white things are white in virtue of the fact that they have being, since those things that are white have flowed from the will of God so that they are white? Not at all. For being and being white are different in their case because of the fact that he who produced them so that they exist is indeed good but not white.[5] <155> Therefore, it followed from the will of the good that they are good in virtue of the fact that they have being. But it did not follow from the will of what is not white that the essential character such that a thing is white in virtue of the fact that it has being belongs to it; for they have not flowed down from the will of the white. And so, because he who willed those things to be white was not white, they are white *merely*. But because he who willed those things to be good was good, they are good *in virtue of the fact that they have being*.

125

130

135

140

145

150

155

---

5. I follow de Rijk (1987) in reading an *eis* in the first clause.

Therefore, according to this reasoning, must not all things be just since he is just who willed them to exist? No indeed. <165> For being good has to do with essence, but being just with an act. In him, however,

160   being is the same as acting, and therefore being good is the same as being just. But, for us, being is not the same as acting, for we are not simple. For us, therefore, being good is not the same as being just; but, for us, all [and only] the things in virtue of which we have being are the same.[6] Therefore, all things are good [but] not also just.

165   Further, good is of course general, but just is specific, and a species does not descend into all [the members of its genus]. Therefore, some things are just, some another [species of good], [but] all things are good.

---

6. The phrase I have translated 'in virtue of which we have being' is *in eo quod sumus*. Except for the fact that the verb is in the first person plural, it is the same phrase as the phrase that I have translated consistently throughout as 'in virtue of the fact that it has being (they have being)' [*in eo quod est (sunt)*]. Maintaining consistency in the present passage would lose the sense.

Bibliography

Adams, Marilyn McCord. 1987. *William Ockham*. 2 vols. Notre Dame: University of Notre Dame Press.

Adams, Robert Merrihew. 1972. "Must God Create the Best?" *The Philosophical Review* 81:317–32. Rpt. in Robert M. Adams 1987. Pp. 51–64.

———. 1982. "Leibniz's Theories of Contingency." In *Leibniz: Critical and Interpretive Essays*, ed. Michael Hooker. Minneapolis: University of Minnesota Press.

———. 1984. "The Virtue of Faith." *Faith and Philosophy* 1:3–15. Rpt. in Robert M. Adams 1987. Pp. 9–24.

———. 1987. *The Virtue of Faith and Other Essays in Philosophical Theology*. Oxford: Oxford University Press.

Aertsen, Jan A. 1985. "The Convertibility of Being and Good in St. Thomas Aquinas." *The New Scholasticism* 59:449–70.

———. 1988a. *Nature and Creature: Thomas Aquinas's Way of Thought*. Leiden: Brill.

———. 1988b. "Die Transzendentalienlehre bei Thomas von Aquin in ihren historischen Hintergruenden und philosophischen Motiven." In *Thomas von Aquin (Miscellanea Mediaevalia*, vol. 19), ed. A. Zimmermann. Berlin: de Gruyter. Pp. 82–102.

Alan de Lille. 1953. *Quoniam homines*. Ed. P. Glorieux. "La Somme *Quoniam homines* d'Alain de Lille." *Archives d'histoire doctrinale et littéraire du moyen âge* 28:113–364.

Albert the Great. 1890–99. *Opera omnia*. Ed. Augustus Borgnet. Paris: Vivès.

———. 1893. *Commentarii in libros Sententiarum*. In Albert 1890–99, vol. 25.

———. 1951–. *Opera omnia*. Ed. B. Geyer et al. Munster: Aschendorff.

———. 1951. *Summa de bono*. Ed. Heinricus Kuehle. In Albert 1951–, vol. 28.

———. 1960. *Metaphysica* (I–V). Ed. B. Geyer. In Albert 1951–, vol. 16, pt. 1.

———. 1972. *Super Dionysium de divinis nominibus*. Ed. Paulus Simon. In Albert 1951–, vol. 37, pt. 1.

———. 1978. *Summa theologiae*. Ed. Dionysius Siedler, Wilhelmo Kuebel, and Henrico Georgio Vogels. In Albert 1951–, vol. 34, pt. 1.

Alexander of Hales. 1924. *Summa theologica*, Book I. Editiones Collegii S. Bonaventurae ad Aquas Claras. Rome: Grottaferrata.

Alston, William P. 1980. "Level Confusions in Epistemology." In *Studies in Epistemology* (*Midwest Studies in Philosophy*, vol. 5), ed. Peter A. French, Theodore E. Uehling, Jr., and Howard K. Wettstein. Assoc. ed. Robert Feleppa. Minneapolis: University of Minnesota Press. Pp. 135–50.

———. 1985. "Concepts of Epistemic Justification." *The Monist* 68:57–89.

———. 1989. *Epistemic Justification: Essays in the Theory of Knowledge*. Ithaca, N.Y.: Cornell University Press.

———. forthcoming. *Perceiving God*.

Anselm. 1974. *Anselm of Canterbury*. Ed. and trans. Jasper Hopkins and Herbert Richardson. New York: Edwin Mellen Press.

Augustine. 1865. *Ennarationes in Psalmos*. *Patrologiae Latinae Cursus Completus*, vol. 37. Paris: Migne.

———. 1877. *De moribus Manichaeorum*. *Patrologiae Latinae Cursus Completus*, vol. 32. Paris: Migne.

———. 1886. *Ad Orosium*. *Patrologiae Latinae Cursus Completus*, vol. 42. Paris: Migne.

———. 1887a. *De diversis quaestionibus octoginta tribus*. *Patrologiae Latinae Cursus Completus*, vol. 40. Paris: Migne.

———. 1887b. *De Genesi contra Manichaeos*. *Patrologiae Latinae Cursus Completus*, vol. 34. Paris: Migne.

———. 1892. *De natura boni*. Ed. Iosephus Zycha. *Corpus Scriptorum Ecclesiasticorum Latinorum*, vol. 25, pt. 2. Leipzig: Feytag.

———. 1955a. *De civitate Dei*. Ed. B. Dombart and A. Kalb (revision of the fourth Teubner edition). *Corpus Christianorum Series Latina*, vols. 47–48. Turnhout: Brepols.

———. 1955b. *The De natura boni of Saint Augustine*. Trans. A. Anthony Moon. Washington D.C.: Catholic University of America Press.

———. 1956. *De libero arbitrio*. Ed. W. M. Green. *Corpus Scriptorum Ecclesiasticorum Latinorum*, vol. 74. Vienna: Tempsky.

———. 1961. *Confessions*. Trans. R. S. Pine-Coffin. New York: Viking Penguin.

———. 1963. *The Trinity*. Trans. Stephen McKenna. *Fathers of the Catholic Church*, vol. 45. Washington, D.C.: Catholic University of America Press.

———. 1966. *The Catholic and Manichaean Ways of Life*. Trans. Donald A. Gallagher and Idella J. Gallagher. *The Fathers of the Catholic Church*, vol. 56. Washington, D.C.: Catholic University of America Press.

———. 1968. *De Trinitate*. Ed. W. J. Mountain. *Corpus Christianorum Series Latina*, vol. 50. Turnhout: Brepols.

———. 1972. *The City of God.* Trans. Henry Bettenson. Harmondsworth, U.K.: Pelican Books.

———. 1975. *De diversis quaestionibus octoginta tribus.* Ed. A. Mutzenbecker. *Corpus Christianorum Series Latina,* vol. 46a. Turnhout: Brepols.

———. 1981a. *Confessiones.* Ed. L. Verheijen (based on the edition of M. Skutella; Leipzig: Teubner, 1934). *Corpus Christianorum Series Latina,* vol. 27. Turnhout: Brepols.

———. 1981b. *De doctrina christiana.* Ed. W. M. Green. *Corpus Scriptorum Ecclesiasticorum Latinorum,* vol. 80. Vienna: Tempsky.

Beaty, Michael, ed. 1990. *Christian Theism and the Problems of Philosophy.* Notre Dame: University of Notre Dame Press.

Blumenberg, Hans. 1983. *The Legitimacy of the Modern Age.* Trans. Robert M. Wallace. Cambridge, Mass.: MIT Press.

Blumenfeld, David. 1975. "Is the Best Possible World Possible?" *The Philosophical Review* 84:163–77.

Boethius. 1860. *In Topica Ciceronis Commentariorum libri sex. Patrologiae Latinae Cursus Completus,* vol. 64. Paris: Migne.

———. 1871. *Anicii Manlii Severini Boetii Philosophiae Consolationis Atque Opuscula Sacra.* Ed. Rudolph Peiper. Leipzig: Teubner.

———. 1978a. *The Theological Tractates and the Consolation of Philosophy: Text and Translations.* Ed. and trans. H. F. Stewart, E. K. Rand, and S. J. Tester. Cambridge, Mass.: Harvard University Press.

———. 1978b. *Contra Eutychen et Nestorium.* In Boethius 1978a.

———. 1978c. *De Trinitate.* In Boethius 1978a.

———. 1978d. *Quomodo substantiae in eo quod sint bonae sint cum non sint substantialia bona (De hebdomadibus).* In Boethius 1978a.

———. 1981. "How Are Substances Good Insofar as They Exist, Since They Are Not Substantial Goods? (*De hebdomadibus*)" (Preliminary draft). Trans. Paul Vincent Spade. Translation Clearing House, Department of Philosophy, Oklahoma State University.

———. 1988. *In Ciceronis Topica.* Trans. Eleonore Stump. Ithaca, N.Y.: Cornell University Press.

Bonaventure. 1882–. *Opera Omnia.* Editiones Collegii S. Bonaventurae. Ad Claras Aquas: Quaracchi.

———. 1882–89. *Commentarium in Sententias.* In Bonaventure 1882–, vols. 1–4.

———. 1891a. *Collationes in Hexaemeron.* In Bonaventure 1882–, vol. 5.

———. 1891b. *Itinerarium mentis in Deum.* In Bonaventure 1882–, vol. 5.

Brady, Ignatius. 1953. "Two Sources of the Summa de homine of Saint Albert the Great," *Recherches de théologie ancienne et médiévale* 20:222–71.

Cajetan (Thomas de Vio Cardinalis Cajetan). 1952. *Scripta Philosophica: De Nominum Analogia et De Conceptu Entis.* Ed. Zammit and Hering. Rome: Institutum Angelicum.

Campbell, John, and Robert Pargetter. 1986. "Goodness and Fragility." *American Philosophical Quarterly* 23:155–65.

Cassirer, Ernst, Paul Oskar Kristeller, and John Herman Randall, Jr., eds. 1948. *The Renaissance Philosophy of Man*. Chicago: University of Chicago Press.

Chenu, Marie-Dominique. 1974. *Introduction à l'étude de saint Thomas d'Aquin*. 3d ed. Paris: Vrin.

Clarembald of Arras. 1965. *Commentary on De hebdomadibus*. Ed. Nikolaus M. Haering. In *Life and Works of Clarembald of Arras*. Toronto: Pontifical Institute of Mediaeval Studies.

Davis, Douglas. 1986. "Is Evil a Relation?" Ph.D diss., State University of New York, Buffalo.

———. 1987. "The Privation Account of Evil: H. J. McCloskey and Francisco Suárez." In *The Metaphysics of Substance*, ed. Daniel O. Dahlstrom. Washington, D.C.: American Catholic Philosophical Association.

Deman, Th. 1928. "Le 'Liber de bona fortuna' dans la théologie de S. Thomas d'Aquin." *Revue des sciences philosophiques et théologiques* 17:38–58.

Denifle, Henricus, and Aemilio Chatelain eds. 1889. *Chartularium Universitatis Parisiensis*, vol. 1. Paris: Delalain.

Denzinger, H. J. D. 1976. *Enchiridion Symbolorum*. Fribourg: Herder.

Descartes, René. 1904. *Meditationes de Prima Philosophia*. Ed. Charles Adam and Paul Tannery. In *Oeuvres de Descartes*, vol. 7. Paris: Léopold Cerf.

Dick, Steven J. 1982. *Plurality of Worlds*. Cambridge: Cambridge University Press.

Dijksterhuis, E. J. 1961. *The Mechanization of the World Picture*. Trans. C. Dikshoorn. Oxford: Oxford University Press. Rpt. 1986, Princeton, N.J.: Princeton University Press.

(pseudo-)Dionysius. 1889. *De divinis nominibus*. Patrologiae Graecae Cursus Completus, vol. 3. Paris: Migne.

———. 1987. *Pseudo-Dionysius: The Complete Works*. Trans. Colim Luibheid and Paul Rorem. New York: Paulist Press.

Dod, Bernard G. 1982. "Aristoteles Latinus." In Kretzmann et al. 1982. Pp. 45–79.

Donagan, Alan. 1982. "Aquinas on Human Action." In Kretzmann et al. 1982. Pp. 642–54.

Du Four, Vital. 1891. *De Rerum Principio. Joannis Duns Scoti . . . Opera Omnia*, vol. 4. Paris: Vivès.

Duhem, Pierre. 1917. *Le système du monde*, vol. 5. Paris: Hermann.

Fabro, Cornelio. 1960. *Partecipazione e causalità*. Turin: Società editrice internazionale.

———. 1963. *La nozione metafisica di partecipazione*. 3d rev. ed. Turin. Società editrice internazionale.

———. 1988. "Le 'Liber de bona fortuna' et l''Éthique a Eudème' d'Aristote et la dialectique de la divine Providence chez Saint Thomas." *Revue thomiste* 88:556–72.

Fichter, J. H. 1940. *Man of Spain.* New York: Macmillan.

Foot, Philippa. 1978. "The Problem of Abortion and the Doctrine of Double Effect." In *Virtues and Vices.* Berkeley: University of California Press. Pp. 19–32.

———. 1983. "Utilitarianism and the Virtues." *Proceedings and Addresses of the American Philosophical Association* 57:273–83. Revised 1985.

Forbes, Graeme. 1985. *The Metaphysics of Modality.* Oxford: Clarendon Press.

Funkenstein, Amos. 1986. *Theology and the Scientific Imagination from the Middle Ages to the Seventeenth Century.* Princeton, N.J.: Princeton University Press.

Geach, Peter. 1977. *The Virtues.* Cambridge: Cambridge University Press.

Geiger, L.-B. 1942. *La participation dans la philosophie de S. Thomas d'Aquin.* Paris: Vrin.

Gilbert of Poitiers. 1966. *The Commentaries on Boethius by Gilbert of Poitiers.* Ed. Nikolaus M. Haering. Toronto: Pontifical Institute of Mediaeval Studies.

Glorieux, P. 1933–34. *Répertoire des maîtres en théologie de Paris au XIIIe siècle.* 2 vols. Paris: Vrin.

Gracia, Jorge J. E. 1973. "The Convertibility of *unum* and *ens* According to Guido Terrena." *Franciscan Studies* 33:143–70.

———. 1975. "The Meaning of Desirable." *Philosophy and Phenomenological Research* 35:398–401.

———. 1976. "The Ontological Status of Value." *The Modern Schoolman* 53:393–97.

Grant, Edward. 1971. *Physical Science in the Middle Ages.* New York: John Wiley & Sons.

———, ed. 1974. *A Source Book in Medieval Science.* Cambridge, Mass.: Harvard University Press.

———. 1982. "The Effect of the Condemnation of 1277." In Kretzmann et al. 1982. Pp. 537–39.

Griffin, James. 1986. *Well-Being.* Oxford: Clarendon Press.

Guhrauer, G. E. 1846. *Gottfried Wilhelm Freiherr von Leibniz: Eine Biographie.* 2 vols. Breslau. Rpt. 1966, Hildesheim: Georg Olms.

Hadot, Pierre. 1970. "Forma essendi: Interprétation philologique et interprétation philosophique d'une formule de Boèce." *Les études classiques* 38:143–56.

———. 1973. "La distinction de l'être et de l'étant dans le De hebdomadibus de Boèce." In *Die Metaphysik im Mittelalter* (*Miscellanea Mediaevalia*, vol. 2), ed. A. Zimmermann. Berlin: de Gruyter. Pp. 147–53.

Hartman, Robert S. 1962. "For the Best Account of the Difference, If Any, between 'The Good is a Non-natural Quality' and 'The Good is a Transcendental.'" *Review of Metaphysics* 16:149–55.

Henninger, Mark G. 1987. "Aquinas on the Ontological Status of Relations." *Journal of the History of Philosophy* 25:491–515.

———. 1989. *Relations: Medieval Theories, 1250–1325.* Oxford: Oxford University Press.

Hessen, Johannes. 1958. "Omne ens est bonum: Kritische Untersuchung eines alten Axioms." *Archiv fuer Philosophie* 8:317–29.

Hoenes, Michael. 1968. *Ens et Bonum Convertuntur: Eine Deutung des scholastischen Axioms unter besonderer Beruecksichtigung der Metaphysik und der Ethik des hl. Thomas von Aquin.* Bamberg: Rodenbusch.

Honnefelder, L. 1987. "Der zweite Anfang der Metaphysik. Voraussetzungen, Ansaetze und Folgen der Wiederbegruendung der Metaphysik im 13./14. Jahrhundert." In *Philosophie im Mittelalter,* ed. J. P. Beckmann et al. Hamburg: Meiner.

Hughes, G. E., and M. J. Cresswell. 1968. *An Introduction to Modal Logic.* London: Methuen.

Irwin, T. H. 1980. "The Metaphysical and Psychological Basis of Aristotle's Ethics." In Rorty 1980. Pp. 35–53.

Keane, Kevin P. 1975. "Why Creation? Bonaventure and Thomas Aquinas on God as Creative Good." *Downside Review* 93:100–121.

Kenny, Anthony, and Jan Pinborg. 1982. "Medieval Philosophical Literature." In Kretzmann et al. 1982. Pp. 11–42.

Kim, Jaegwon. 1984. "Concepts of Supervenience." *Philosophy and Phenomenological Research* 45:153–77.

Knittermeyer, H. 1920. *Der Terminus transszendental in seiner historischen Entwickelung bis zu Kant.* Marburg: J. Hamel.

Korolec, J. B. 1982. "Free Will and Free Choice." In Kretzmann et al. 1982. Pp. 629–41.

Kosman, L. A. 1980. "Being Properly Affected: Virtues and Feelings in Aristotle's Ethics." In Rorty 1980. Pp. 103–116.

Kremer, Klaus. 1965. "Das 'Warum' der Schoepfung: 'quia bonus' vel/et 'quia voluit'? Ein Beitrag zum Verhaeltnis von Neuplatonismus und Christentum an Hand des Prinzips 'bonum est diffusivum sui'." In *Parusia: Studien zur Philosophie Platons und zur Problemgeschichte des Platonismus,* Festgabe fuer Johannes Hirschberger, ed. Kurt Flasch. Frankfurt am Main: Minerva. Pp. 241–54.

Kretzmann, Norman. 1983a. "Abraham, Isaac, and Euthyphro: God and the Basis of Morality." In Stump et al. 1983. Pp. 27–50.

———. 1983b. "Goodness, Knowledge, and Indeterminacy in the Philosophy of Thomas Aquinas." *Journal of Philosophy* 80:631–49.

———. 1988. "*Lex Iniusta Non Est Lex*: Laws on Trial in Aquinas's Court of Conscience." *American Journal of Jurisprudence* 33:99–122.

———. 1989a. "Reason in Mystery." In *The Philosophy in Christianity,* ed. Godfrey Vesey. Cambridge: Cambridge University Press. Pp. 15–40.

———. 1989b. "Trinity and Transcendentals." In *Trinity, Incarnation, and Atonement,* ed. Ronald Feenstra and Cornelius Plantinga. Notre Dame: University of Notre Dame Press. Pp. 79–109.

———. forthcoming. "Evidence against Anti-evidentialism."

Kretzmann, Norman, Anthony Kenny, and Jan Pinborg, eds. 1982. *The Cambridge History of Later Medieval Philosophy.* Cambridge: Cambridge University Press.

Kuehle, Heinrich. 1930. "Die Lehre Alberts des Grossen von den Transzendentalien." In *Philosophia Perennis: Festgabe Josef Geyser,* ed. Fritz-Joachim von Rintelen. Regensburg: Josef Habbel. 1:129–47.

Kuhn, Helmut. 1962. *Das Sein und das Gute.* Munich: Koesel-Verlag.

Laporta, Jorge. 1973. "Pour trouver le sens exact des termes: Appetitus naturalis, desiderium naturale, amor naturalis, etc. chez Thomas d'Aquin." *Archives d'histoire doctrinale et littéraire au moyen âge* 40:37–95.

Leibni[t]z, Gottfried Wilhelm. 1875–1890. *Die philosophischen Schriften.* 7 vols. Ed. C. I. Gerhardt. Berlin: Weidmann. Rpt. 1965, Hildesheim: Georg Olms.

———. 1896. *New Essays concerning Human Understanding.* Trans. Alfred Gideon Langley. New York: Macmillan.

———. 1951. *Leibniz: Selections.* Ed. Philip P. Wiener. New York: Charles Scribner's Sons.

Lewis, David. 1986. *On the Plurality of Worlds.* Oxford: Basil Blackwell.

Lohr, C. H. 1982. "The Medieval Interpretation of Aristotle." In Kretzmann et al. 1982. Pp. 80–98.

Lonergan, Bernard J. F. 1971. *Grace and Freedom: Operative Grace in the Thought of Thomas Aquinas.* Ed. J. Patout Burns. London: Darton, Longman & Todd, and New York: Herder and Herder.

Lottin, Odon. 1928. "La date de la question disputée 'De malo' de saint Thomas d'Aquin." *Revue d'histoire ecclésiastique* 24:373–88. Revised version in Lottin 1960a. Pp. 353–72.

———. 1942. "Libre arbitre et liberté depuis saint Anselme jusqu'à la fin du XIIIe siècle." In *Psychologie et morale aux XIIe et XIIIe siècles,* vol. 1. Gembloux: Duculot. Pp. 11–389.

———. 1960a. *Psychologie et moral aux XIIe et XIIIe siècles,* vol. 6. Gembloux: Duculot.

———. 1960b. "L'Influence littéraire du Chancelier Philippe." In Lottin 1960a. Pp. 149–69.

Louden, Robert B. 1984. "On Some Vices of Virtue Ethics." *American Philosophical Quarterly* 21:227–36.

Loux, Michael. 1973. "Aristotle on Transcendentals." *Phronesis* 18:225–39.

Lovejoy, Arthur O. 1936. *The Great Chain of Being.* Cambridge, Mass.: Harvard University Press.

Luscombe, D. E. 1982. "Natural Morality and Natural Law." In Kretzmann et al. 1982. Pp. 705–19

MacDonald, Scott. 1986. "The Metaphysics of Goodness in Medieval Philosophy before Aquinas." Ph.D. diss., Cornell University.

———. 1988. "Boethius's Claim That All Substances Are Good." *Archiv fuer Geschichte der Philosophie* 70:245–79.

_____. 1989a. "Aristotle and the Homonymy of the Good." *Archiv fuer Geschichte der Philosophie* 71:150–74.

_____. 1989b. "Augustine's Christian-Platonist Account of Goodness." *New Scholasticism* 63: 485–509.

_____. 1990. "Egoistic Rationalism: Aquinas's Basis for Christian Morality." In Beaty 1990.

_____. forthcoming(a). "Later Medieval Ethics." In *Encyclopedia of Ethics*, ed. Lawrence C. Becker. New York: Garland Publishing.

_____. forthcoming(b). *The Metaphysics of Goodness: The Early-Thirteenth-Century Contributions of William of Auxerre, Philip the Chancellor, and Albert the Great.*

McInerny, Ralph. 1961. *The Logic of Analogy.* The Hague: Nijhoff.

_____. 1968. *Studies in Analogy.* The Hague: Nijhoff.

_____. 1976. "Naturalism and Thomistic Ethics." *The Thomist* 40:222–42.

_____. 1990. *Boethius and Aquinas.* Washington, D.C.: Catholic University of America Press.

Mann, William E. 1975. "The Divine Attributes." *American Philosophical Quarterly* 12:151–59.

_____. 1982. "Divine Simplicity." *Religious Studies* 18:451–71.

_____. 1983. "Simplicity and Immutability in God." *International Philosophical Quarterly* 23:267–276. Rpt. in Morris 1987a. Pp. 253–67.

_____. 1986. "Simplicity and Properties: A Reply to Morris." *Religious Studies* 22:343–53.

_____. 1988. "God's Freedom, Human Freedom, and God's Responsibility for Sin." In Morris 1988a. Pp. 182–210.

_____. 1989. "Modality, Morality, and God." *Noûs* 23:83–99.

Manteau-Bonamy, H. M. 1979. "La liberté de l'homme selon Thomas d'Aquin (La datation de la Q. Disp. DE MALO)." *Archives d'histoire doctrinale et littéraire du moyen âge* 54:7–34.

Mates, Benson. 1986. *The Philosophy of Leibniz.* New York: Oxford University Press.

Morris, Thomas V. 1984a. "The God of Abraham, Isaac and Anselm." *Faith and Philosophy* 1:177–87.

_____. 1984b. "Properties, Modalities, and God." *Philosophical Review* 93:35–55.

_____. 1985a. "On God and Mann: A View of Divine Simplicity." *Religious Studies* 21:299–318.

_____. 1985b. "Necessary Beings." *Mind* 94:263–92.

_____, ed. 1987a. *The Concept of God.* Oxford: Oxford University Press.

_____. 1987b. "Perfect Being Theology." *Noûs* 21:19–30.

_____, ed. 1988a. *Divine and Human Action: Essays in the Metaphysics of Theism.* Ithaca, N.Y.: Cornell University Press.

_____, ed. 1988b. *Philosophy and the Christian Faith.* Notre Dame: University of Notre Dame Press.

Morris, Thomas V., and Christopher Menzel. 1986. "Absolute Creation." *American Philosophical Quarterly* 23:353–62.

Murdoch, John E. 1982. "Infinity and Continuity." In Kretzmann et al. 1982. Pp. 564–92.

Nagel, Thomas. 1979. *Mortal Questions*. Cambridge: Cambridge University Press.

Ockham, William. 1970. *Scriptum in Librum Primum Sententiarum Ordinatio: Distinctiones II–III*. Ed. Stephanus (Stephen) Brown. In *Guillelmi de Ockham Opera Theologica*, vol. 2. St. Bonaventure, N.Y.: St. Bonaventure University.

———. 1981. *Quaestiones in Librum Secundum Sententiarum (Reportatio)*. Ed. Gedeon Gál and Rega Wood. In *Guillelmi de Ockham Opera Theologica*, vol. 5. St. Bonaventure, N.Y.: St. Bonaventure University.

Oeing-Hanhoff, Ludger. 1956. "Zur thomistischen Freiheitslehre." *Scholastik* 31:161–81.

Owens, Joseph. 1957. "The Number of Terms in the Suarezian Discussion on Essence and Being." *Modern Schoolman* 34:147–91.

Peghaire, Julien. 1932. "L'axiome 'Bonum est diffusivum sui' dans le néoplatonisme et le thomisme." *Revue de l'Université d'Ottawa*, special section, vol. 1. Pp. 5*–30*.

Pence, Gregory E. 1984. "Recent Work on Virtues." *American Philosophical Quarterly* 21:281–97.

Penelhum, Terence. 1977. "The Analysis of Faith in St. Thomas Aquinas." *Religious Studies* 13:133–51.

Pesch, Otto M. 1962. "Philosophie und Theologie der Freiheit bei Thomas von Aquin in quaest. disp. 6 De malo." *Muenchener theologische Zeitschrift* 13:1–25.

Peter Lombard. 1971–81. *Sententiae in IV libris distinctae*. Editiones Collegii S. Bonaventurae ad Claras Aquas. Rome: Grottaferrata.

Philip the Chancellor. 1985. *Philippi Cancellarii Parisiensis Summa de bono*. Ed. Nicolaus Wicki. Bern: Francke.

Plantinga, Alvin. 1974. *The Nature of Necessity*. Oxford: Oxford University Press.

———. 1983. "Reason and Belief in God." In Plantinga and Wolterstorff 1983. Pp. 16–93.

Plantinga, Alvin, and Nicholas Wolterstorff, eds. 1983. *Faith and Rationality: Reason and Belief in God*. Notre Dame: University of Notre Dame Press.

Pojman, Louis. 1986. *Religious Belief and the Will*. London: Routledge and Kegan Paul.

Potts, Timothy. 1971. "Aquinas on Belief and Faith." In *Inquiries in Medieval Philosophy: A Collection in Honor of Francis P. Clarke*, ed. James F. Ross. Westport, Conn.: Greenwood. Pp. 3–22.

Pouillon, D. H. 1939. "Le premier Traité des Propriétés transcendentales: La *Summa de bono* du Chancelier Philippe." *Revue néoscolastique de philosophie* 42:40–77.

Quinn, Philip. 1978. *Divine Commands and Moral Requirements*. Oxford: Clarendon Press.

Raz, Joseph. 1986. *The Morality of Freedom*. Oxford: Clarendon Press.

Remigius of Auxerre. 1906. *Johannes Scottus*. Ed. E.K. Rand. *Quellen und Untersuchungen*, vol. 1, no. 3. Munich: C. H. Beck.

Rijk, L. M. de. 1987. "On Boethius' Notion of Being: A Chapter in Boethian Semantics." In *Meaning and Inference in Medieval Philosophy: Studies in Memory of Jan Pinborg*, ed. Norman Kretzmann. Dordrecht: Kluwer.

Robert Grosseteste. 1912. *De luce seu de inchoatione formarum*. Ed. L. Baur. *Beitraege zur Geschichte der Philosophie des Mittelalters* 9:51–59.

Roland-Gosselin, M.-D. 1948. *Le 'De ente et essentia' de s. Thomas d'Aquin*. *Bibliothèque Thomiste*, vol. 8. Paris: Vrin.

Rorty, Amelie O., ed. 1980. *Essays on Aristotle's Ethics*. Berkeley: University of California Press.

Ross, James F. 1985. "Aquinas on Belief and Knowledge." In *Essays Honoring Allan B. Wolter*, ed. Girard Etzkorn. St. Bonaventure, N.Y.: Franciscan Institute. Pp. 245–69.

——. 1986. "Believing for Profit." In *The Ethics of Belief Debate*, ed. Gerald D. McCarthy. Atlanta, Ga.: Scholars Press. Pp. 221–35.

Scheffler, Samuel. 1982. *The Rejection of Consequentialism*. Oxford: Clarendon Press.

——. 1985. "Agent-Centred Restrictions, Rationality, and Virtues." *Mind* 94:409–419.

Schlesinger, George. 1988. *New Perspectives on Old-Time Religion*. Oxford: Oxford University Press.

Schneider, Johannes. 1967. *Das Gute und die Liebe nach der Lehre Albert des Grossen*. Munich: Schoeningh.

Schrimpf, Gangolf. 1966. *Die Axiomenschrift des Boethius (De hebdomadibus) als philosophisches Lehrbuch des Mittelalters*. Leiden: Brill.

Schulemann, Guenther. 1929. *Die Lehre von den Transzendentalien in der scholastischen Philosophie*. Leipzig: F. Meiner.

Scorraille, J. de. 1912–13. *François Suárez de la Compagnie de Jésus*. 2 vols. Paris: Léthielleux.

Seckler, Max. 1961. *Instinkt und Glaubenswille nach Thomas von Aquin*. Mainz: Matthias-Gruenewald.

Shoemaker, Sydney. 1980. "Causality and Properties." In *Time and Cause*, ed. Peter van Inwagen. Dordrecht: Reidel. Pp. 109–135. Rpt. in Sydney Shoemaker, *Identity, Cause, and Mind*. Cambridge: Cambridge University Press, 1984. Pp. 206–233.

Simpson, Peter. 1987. *Goodness and Nature*. Dordrecht: Nijhoff.

Sommervogel, C. 1890–1900. *Bibliothèque de la Compagnie de Jésus*. Paris: Picard.

Stalnaker, Robert. 1976. "Possible Worlds." *Noûs* 10:65–75.

Stump, Donald V., James A. Arieti, Lloyd Gerson, and Eleonore Stump, eds. 1983. *Hamartia: The Concept of Error in the Western Tradition*. New York: Edwin Mellen Press.

Stump, Eleonore. 1983. "Hamartia in Christian Belief: Boethius on the Trinity." In Stump et al. 1983. Pp. 131–48.

———. 1985. "The Problem of Evil." *Faith and Philosophy* 2:392–423.

———. 1988a. "Atonement According to Aquinas." In Morris 1988b. Pp. 61–91.

———. 1988b. "Sanctification, Hardening of the Heart, and Frankfurt's Concept of Free Will." *Journal of Philosophy* 85:395–420.

———. 1989a. "Atonement and Justification." In *Trinity, Incarnation, and Atonement: Philosophical and Theological Essays*, ed. Ronald Feenstra and Cornelius Plantinga. Notre Dame: University of Notre Dame Press. Pp. 178–209.

———. 1989b. "Faith and Goodness." In *The Philosophy in Christianity*, ed. Godfrey Vesey. Cambridge: Cambridge University Press. Pp. 167–92.

———. 1990. "Intellect, Will, and the Principle of Alternate Possibilities." In Beaty 1990.

Stump, Eleonore, and Norman Kretzmann. 1985. "Absolute Simplicity." *Faith and Philosophy* 2:353–82.

Suárez, Francisco. 1861. *Disputationes metaphysicae*. Ed. C. Berton. *Opera omnia*, vols. 25 and 26. Paris: Vivès.

———. 1964. *Francis Suárez: On Formal and Universal Unity (Disputationes metaphysicae VI)*. Trans. James F. Ross. Milwaukee: Marquette University Press.

———. 1982. *Suárez on Individuation (Disputationes metaphysicae V)*. Trans. Jorge J. E. Gracia. Milwaukee: Marquette University Press.

———. 1989. *The Metaphysics of Good and Evil according to Suárez: Disputations X and XI*. Trans. Jorge J. E. Gracia and Douglas Davis. Analytica Series. Munich and Vienna: Philosophia Verlag.

Swinburne, Richard. 1979. *The Existence of God*. Oxford: Clarendon Press.

———. 1981. *Faith and Reason*. Oxford: Clarendon Press.

Synave, Paul. 1926. Review in *Bulletin thomiste* 3:8.

Teske, Roland J. 1988. "The Motive for Creation according to Saint Augustine." *The Modern Schoolman* 65:245–53.

Thierry of Chartres. 1971. *Commentaries on Boethius by Thierry of Chartres and His School*. Ed. Nikolaus M. Haering. Toronto: Pontifical Institute of Mediaeval Studies.

Thomas Aquinas. 1882–. *S. Thomae Aquinatis Doctoris Angelici. Opera Omnia. Iussu impensaque Leonis XIII, P.M. edita* (Leonine edition). Rome: Vatican Polyglot Press.

———. 1882. *Commentaria in Aristotelis Peri Hermeneias et Posteriorum Analyticorum*. In Thomas Aquinas 1882–, vol. 1.

———. 1888–1906. *Summa theologiae*. In Thomas Aquinas 1882–, vols. 4–12.

———. 1918–30. *Summa contra gentiles*. In Thomas Aquinas 1882–, vols. 13–15.

———. 1926. *Summa theologica*. Ed. De Rubeis, Billuart et al. 4 vols. Turin: Marietti.

———. 1929–56. *Scriptum super Sententias*. Ed. P. Mandonnet and M. F. Moos. Paris: Léthielleux.

———. 1931. *Quaestiones disputatae: De veritate*. Ed. P. Bazzi et al. Turin: Marietti.

———. 1948. *Le 'De ente et essentia' de s. Thomas d'Aquin*. Ed. M.-D. Roland-Gosselin, O.P. *Bibliothèque Thomiste*, vol. 8. Paris: Vrin.

———. 1950. *In librum beati Dionysii De divinis nominibus expositio*. Ed. C. Pera. Turin: Marietti.

———. 1953a. *Questiones disputatae*. Ed. R. M. Spiazzi et al. 9th rev. ed., 2 vols. Turin: Marietti.

———. 1953b. *Quaestiones disputatae de potentia*. In Thomas Aquinas 1953a.

———. 1954a. *Opuscula theologica*. Ed. R. A. Verardo, R. M. Spiazzi, and M. Calcaterra. 2 vols. Turin: Marietti.

———. 1954b. *Expositio super Boetium De trinitate et De hebdomadibus*. In Thomas Aquinas 1954a.

———. 1954c. *In octo libros Physicorum Aristotelis expositio*. Ed. M. Maggiolo. Turin: Marietti.

———. 1955. *Expositio super librum Boetii De Trinitate*. Ed. B. Decker. *Studien und Texte zur Geistesgeschichte des Mittelalters*, vol. 4. Leiden: Brill. Rpt. with corrections, 1959.

———. 1956. *Quaestiones quodlibetales*. Ed. R. M. Spiazzi. 9th rev. ed. Turin: Marietti.

———. 1961–67. *Liber de veritate catholicae fidei contra errores infidelium*. Ed. P. Marc. 3 vols. Turin: Marietti.

———. 1963. *Treatise on Separate Substances (Tractatus de substantiis separatis)*. Ed. and trans. F. J. Lescoe. West Hartford, Conn.: Saint Joseph College.

———. 1964. *In decem libros Ethicorum Aristotelis ad Nicomachum expositio*. Ed. R. M. Spiazzi. Turin: Marietti.

———. 1969. *In decem libros Ethicorum Aristotelis ad Nicomachum expositio*. In Thomas Aquinas 1882–, vol. 47.

———. 1970–76. *Queastiones disputatae de veritate*. In Thomas Aquinas 1882–, vol. 22.

———. 1976. *De ente et essentia*. In Thomas Aquinas 1882–, vol. 43.

———. 1980a. *S. Thomae Aquinatis Opera Omnia*. Ed. Robert Busa. Stuttgart-Bad Cannstatt: Frommann-Holzboog.

———. 1980b. *Summa theologiae*. In Thomas Aquinas 1980a, vol. 2.

———. 1980c. *Quaestiones disputatae de veritate*. In Thomas Aquinas 1980a, vol. 3.

———. 1982. *Quaestiones disputatae de malo*. In Thomas Aquinas 1882–, vol. 23.

van Inwagen, Peter. 1988. "And Yet They Are Not Three Gods But One God." In Morris 1988b. Pp. 241–78.

Vanni Rovighi, Sofia. 1972. *L'anthropolgoia filosofica di san Tommaso d'Aquino*. Milan: Vita e pensiero.

Wainwright, William J. 1974. "God's Body." *Journal of the American Academy of Religion* 42:470–81.

Weber, Edouard-Henri. 1974. *Dialogue et dissensions entre saint Bonaventure et saint Thomas d'Aquin à Paris (1252–1273)*. Paris: Vrin.

Weisheipl, James A., ed. 1980a. *Albertus Magnus and the Sciences*. Toronto: Pontifical Institute of Mediaeval Studies.

———. 1980b. "Life and Works of St. Albert the Great." In Weisheipl 1980a. Pp. 13–51.

——. 1983. *Friar Thomas D'Aquino*. Washington, D.C.: Catholic University of America Press.

William of Auxerre. 1980–87. *Summa aurea*. Ed. Jean Ribaillier. Editiones Collegii S. Bonaventurae ad Claras Aquas. Rome: Grottaferrata.

Wippel, John F. 1977. "The Condemnations of 1270 and 1277 at Paris." *Journal of Medieval and Renaissance Studies* 7:169–201.

Wohlman, Avital. 1988. *Thomas d'Aquin et Maimonide*. Paris: Cerf.

Wolter, A. B. 1946. *The Transcendentals and Their Function in the Metaphysics of Duns Scotus*. Washington, D.C.: Catholic University of America Press.

Zemach, Eddy M. 1968. "The Transcendentals." In *Further Studies in Philosophy*, ed. Ora Segal. Jerusalem: Magnes Press. Pp. 138–62.

Index